Hidden Champions of the Twenty-First Century

Hermann Simon

Hidden Champions of the Twenty-First Century

Success Strategies of Unknown World Market Leaders

 Springer

Hermann Simon
Simon-Kucher & Partners
Haydnstr. 36
53115 Bonn
Germany
hermann.simon@simon-kucher.com

ISBN 978-0-387-98146-8   e-ISBN 978-0-387-98147-5
DOI 10.1007/978-0-387-98147-5
Springer Dordrecht Heidelberg London New York

Library of Congress Control Number: 2009928014

Printed on acid-free paper

Springer is part of Springer Science+Business Media (www.springer.com)

Acknowledgments

This book would not have been possible without the responsiveness and cooperation of thousands of companies, managers, and employees of the hidden champions throughout the world. Their information and data were collected in countless interviews, workshops, consulting projects, presentations, and surveys. I would like to thank all interview partners as well as my colleagues in the worldwide offices of Simon-Kucher & Partners who assisted in research, analysis, and interpretation.

Ingo Lier and Doro Hayer managed the documentation and information flow professionally. Jennifer Hoehr, Gunnar Market and Brie Casazza polished up the text. Astrid Blume and Kerstin Schoene in our research department helped me make the hidden champions a little less "hidden" by incessantly digging out data and relevant information. Elizabeth Doyle-Aseritis did an excellent job as copy editor. I would like to thank them all for their outstanding commitment and their perseverance—truly hidden champions' virtues.

I am indebted to the team at Springer in New York, and particularly to Nicholas Philipson and Daniel Valen, who provided most valuable advice and pushed the project through.

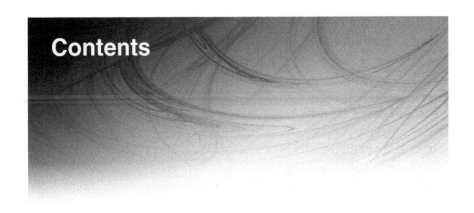

Contents

Chapter 12: The Lessons of the Hidden Champions 351

Introduction

How I Discovered the Hidden Champions

The original idea of researching the strategies of unknown world market leaders originated in 1986. Back then, I met Professor Theodore Levitt, the famous marketing guru who taught at the Harvard Business School. Three years earlier, in 1983, Professor Levitt had popularized the term "globalization" in a groundbreaking article in the *Harvard Business Review*.[1] During our meeting, we started a discussion about export success. Why are some countries particularly dominant in exports? Why do others fail? Two years later, when I was a visiting professor at the Harvard Business School, the topic came up again. Some 20 years later, we could continue our discussion in practically the same form. Ted Levitt passed away in 2006. I dedicate this book to him.

As was true in the past, the strong export performance of countries like Germany, Switzerland or Sweden is not due to large corporations. Large, internationally active firms with significant exports exist in all highly developed industrial countries. In my discussion with Professor Levitt, we speculated that the cause of the continuing export success of the German-language and Scandinavian countries could be traced to small and midsize companies. Countries such as the USA, France or Japan that have distinctly fewer such companies or are not as active internationally do not perform as well in exports. I gradually discovered that countless midsize companies are world leaders in their markets. The contention that these market leaders spearhead globalization has not changed in the last decade. If anything, their role in the globalization process has become even more crucial.

I have presented and discussed this topic across all five continents. In doing so, I discovered that there were hidden world market leaders everywhere. I found them in America, Brazil, Japan, South Africa, Korea, New Zealand, and in many other countries. With respect to culture, strategy and leadership, it became clear that there are striking similarities among these companies. Nevertheless, the majority of this company breed could still be found in the German-Scandinavian countries. I estimate that 80% of all midsize world market leaders come from this region. At the end of the 1980s, I coined the term "hidden champions" for these unusual companies. In 1992, an article in the *Harvard Business Review* received significant attention.[2] The wordplay with such seemingly contradictory terms as "hidden" and "champion" contributed to the mystique. "Hidden champions" has since become a commonly used term around the world. A search of the term "hidden champions" on google.com produces 70,200 hits as of August 27, 2008. The first book on the topic has been published in 17 countries.[3] "Hidden champions" even made the cover story of *Business-Week* magazine (see Fig. I.1).

The way in which the hidden champions concept has been received has changed over the course of time. The strategies and leadership methods were initially viewed by some as strange, exotic or outdated. Some observers considered hidden champions to be extremely specialized and

Fig. I.1 Hidden champions in international publications

fanatically dedicated small-town tinkers working in a tiny niche, with virtually no chance of long-term survival in the age of large corporations, diversification and globalization. Others thought that such midsize enterprises were condemned to remain small, become technologically obsolete and ultimately succumb to the lack of risk diversification—the flipside of their narrow focus. In addition, their management methods were frequently considered archaic, patriarchal, authoritarian, and increasingly out of touch with a modern workforce. No doubt such assessments are true in a few cases. Yet the world and the ways of the twenty-first century hidden champions have developed completely contrary to these skeptics' expectations. This book reveals the spectacular successes of the hidden champions at the beginning of the twenty-first century.

More than ever, I am convinced that consistently superb management and strategies are more likely to be found among the hidden champions than in large corporations. Yet management research, teaching, and literature persist in focusing on large, well-known companies. General Motors was the star of the 1950s; IBM stole the limelight in the 1970s. Both were seen as models of excellent business management. Today, the stars are companies such as Microsoft and Nokia or Internet firms like eBay and Google. Without a doubt these enterprises are very successful. But the glory of General Motors and IBM has faded with time, just as Microsoft and the other star companies of our day may look considerably less glamorous when viewed from the perspective of 2035. Also, what can the average business observer really learn from stars of the century such as Nokia and Google, companies as unique in their respective disciplines as Albert Einstein or Tiger Woods? Fundamentally "normal" companies like the hidden champions, which have reached leading positions in their markets with specific strategies, are far more suitable role models and instructive examples. Small and midsize enterprises across the world can learn a lot more from these little-known market leaders than from the highly visible large corporations.

One aspect I would like to point out to the reader is that the huge amount of facts and data offered in this book is predominantly based on material supplied by the companies themselves. It was impossible to individually check the data and assumptions of hundreds of companies in often highly fragmented markets, and I cannot guarantee the accuracy of all company statements and data.

Notes

1   See Theodore Levitt, "The Globalization of Markets," *Harvard Business Review*, May–June 1983, pp. 92–102. The term "globalization" first came into existence in 1944; in 1981 it started to become commonly used. Only after Levitt's article was the term widely used in the business mainstream.

2   See Hermann Simon, "Lessons from Germany's Midsize Giants," *Harvard Business Review*, March–April 1992, pp. 115–123.

3   Hermann Simon, *Hidden Champions: Lessons from 500 of the World's Best Unknown Companies*, Boston: Harvard Business School Press 1996.

Chapter 1
The Mystique of the Hidden Champions

Large corporations are the subject of close and constant scrutiny by academic researchers, analysts, shareholders, and journalists. Hidden champions, on the other hand, remain a virtually unexplored source of knowledge. Scattered across the globe, thousands of these highly successful companies are concealed behind a curtain of inconspicuousness, invisibility and, in some cases, deliberate secrecy. This applies to the products these companies make, how they beat the competition or—even more difficult to research—how they are managed internally. Even their names are known to only a handful of experts, consultants, journalists, and researchers.

This secretiveness contrasts starkly with the dominant positions the hidden champions enjoy in their markets. Many of them have global market shares of over 50%, and some even hold shares in their relevant markets of 70%–90%. On average, they are more than twice the size of their strongest competitors. Only a few large multinationals achieve comparable market positions. Far from lagging behind in the globalization process, the hidden champions are the vanguard of globalization. In the course of the past decade, they have grown and strengthened their competitiveness at a dramatic rate. Among the impressive characteristics of these small and midsize companies is their enduring, sustainable approach towards global excellence.

Few management researchers examine such long-term success strategies without being influenced by the fads of the day. Perhaps the most notable is the American researcher Jim Collins, who, tellingly, works as a freelance academic rather than at one of the major-league universities. In his book *Good to Great*, he describes findings that in many cases agree with mine.[1] To take one example from Collins: the lower the executives' public profile, the more successful their companies are long term. Could there be a better argument in favor of the hidden champions remaining hidden?

H. Simon, *Hidden Champions of the Twenty-First Century*,
DOI 10.1007/978-0-387-98147-5_1, © Hermann Simon 2009

Who Are They? A Selection of Hidden Champions Around the World

So who are these hidden champions of the twenty-first century? Although their products constantly surround us, most are completely unknown to us. To illustrate their diversity, we will begin by taking a brief look at a selection of hidden champions from various countries. This random selection offers an initial impression of the type, market position, and typical characteristics of these companies.

Baader

In Iceland, qualified mechanics are known as "Baader men" because they were trained on Baader systems. With a global market share of 80%, Baader is the world's leading supplier of fish processing systems.

McIlhenny

McIlhenny was founded in 1896 and has only one production site in the world, Avery Island in Louisiana, US. From there, McIlhenny's main product "began its journey to set the culinary world on fire." Today, the product (a.k.a. Tabasco) is sold in more than 160 countries. "It is the most famous, most preferred pepper sauce in the world."

3B Scientific

Did you encounter a model skeleton last time you took a first-aid course? It was probably produced by 3B Scientific, the global market leader in anatomical teaching aids.

International SOS

This Singapore-based company is the world leader in international emergency rescue services. In September 2006, International SOS organized the first direct medical emergency flight from China to Taiwan in more than half a century.

Höganäs and Hoeganaes Corporation

These two namesakes are the world's leading suppliers of powder metallurgy. They have a common origin but are independent today. Höganäs from Sweden is the "world's leading supplier of metal powder technology" whereas Hoeganaes Corporation, based in Cinnaminson, New Jersey, US, ranks number one globally in "ferrous and ferrite powders."

Tetra

Do your children have a fish tank? If so, you may know TetraMin, the most popular food for ornamental fish. Tetra is the world market leader in aquarium and pond supplies, and its market share is 3.6 times higher than that of its closest competitor.

Bobcat

Would you have guessed that Bobcat, a company from Gwinner, North Dakota, US, is the "world leader in compact industrial, construction, and agri-business equipment." With 3,300 employees, this little-known firm is also the biggest employer in North Dakota.

Gallagher

New Zealand has 3.3 million people and 70 million sheep, the ideal location when it comes to innovations for fencing in sheep and cattle. This environment produced Gallagher, the global market leader for electric fences.

Saes Getters

Until I ran into this world market leader from Italy, I was unaware that a getter is a chemically reactive material that helps to retain a vacuum. Saes has an 85% share in the world market for barium getters and generates 98% of its revenues outside its Italian home market.

Hamamatsu Photonics

"Photon is our Business" is the slogan of Hamamatsu Photonics, a world leader in light sources for technical and medical applications. With net sales of more than $800 million[2] and 3,600 employees, it is one of the midsize star firms in Japan.

Arnold & Richter, Sachtler

While in Tokyo recently, a colleague and I ran into a professional camera team out filming. The initial assumption that the camera team involved two hidden champions from Germany in action right in the heart of Tokyo was confirmed: the cameraman was, of course, using an ARRI camera and a Sachtler tripod. Both of these companies are global market leaders, and their products have won several technical Oscars.

Petzl

In spite of its German-sounding name, Petzl is a French hidden champion. Initially producing caving and safety equipment, Petzl is currently "the leading innovator in the vertical world." "Vertical world" comprises vertical sports such as rock-climbing, mountaineering or cave exploration, as well as professional applications such as work at heights or difficult access rescue operations. The company is the world leader in harnesses, rope-blocking snap links, front lamps, and similar products.

Lantal

Lantal is an abbreviation for Langenthal in Bern, Switzerland. This small town is home to the global leader in customized cabin interiors for passenger aircraft. Lantal's global market share is 60%, and its customers include more than 300 airlines, including Boeing and Airbus. Singapore Airlines' Raffles Class or Lufthansa's First and Business Classes are designed by Lantal.

Tandberg and Polycom

The market for video conferencing systems is just taking off. With a global market share of 40%, the market leader Tandberg comes from an unlikely place, Norway. Its closest competitor is Polycom from the US. Sony is about 100 times larger in revenues, but these small specialists beat the giant in video conferencing technology.

W.E.T. and Webasto

Heated car seats are a blessing when it's cold in winter. The probability is more than 50% that the heating technology in your car comes from W.E.T. Automotive Systems, as W.E.T. is the world market leader. And if you need a remote-controlled heater for your car, the global number one leader in this field is Webasto.

De La Rue

Where does money come from? From De La Rue: this UK-firm is the largest printer and maker of security paper, and it produces the banknotes for more than 150 countries.

Belfor

Belfor is the global market leader in the removal of fire and water damages. With revenues of more than $800 million and about 3,200 employees, Belfor is more than twice the size of its strongest competitor and is the only company that can offer these services around the world.

Ulvac

Ulvac from Japan accounts for a 96% global market share in LCD panel coating equipment and a 70% share in plasma display coating equipment. Ulvac's core competency is vacuum technology, and the application in various fields generates about $2 billion in revenues.

Orica

This Australian firm is the global leader in explosives for mines and quarries. Orica offers its innovative and comprehensive blasting services in more than 50 countries.

CEAG

There are hundreds of millions of cell phones in the world today, and a quarter of them are charged by devices from CEAG. Headquartered in Germany with 270 employees, this world market leader employs more than 18,000 people in China and has a daily production output of one million charging devices.

Gartner

Skyscrapers are becoming increasingly common, but who builds the facades? In many cases it is Gartner, the undisputed number one in the world for jobs of this kind. As buildings reach higher and higher into the sky, each new record-breaker creates a sensation—some time ago Taipei 101 was the world's tallest building with 101 stories. Gartner storm-tested the facade elements for Taipei 101 with an aircraft jet engine. The skyscraper was later put to a real-life test by an earthquake measuring 6.8 on the Richter scale; the facade survived unscathed. Gartner is also supplying the facade of Burj Dubai, the new record-holder as the tallest building in the world.

Zimmer, DePuy, Biomet, and Stryker

Warsaw, Indiana, has a population of only 12,145 and is called the "ortho-pedic capital of the world." This little town hosts three world lead-ers in orthopedic products (implants), i.e., replacements for hips, knees, and other joints. Zimmer, DePuy, and Biomet are all based in Warsaw, and a fourth global contender, Stryker, is not far away in Kalamazoo, Michigan, US.

Technogym

Would you have guessed that the world's number two in fitness equip-ment comes from an Italian village by the Adriatic Sea called Gambet-tola? Because of its outstanding innovation and new designs, Technogym was selected as the exclusive supplier of fitness equipment to the Bei-jing Olympics in 2008. Founder Nerio Alessandri, a fitness enthusias, has vowed to overtake Life Fitness, the current US-based world market leader, in the next three years.

Gerriets

Gerriets produces theater curtains and stage equipment. As the world's only manufacturer of large stage curtains, it has a 100% market share in this segment. Whether you visit the Metropolitan Opera in New York, the Scala in Milan, or the Opera Bastille in Paris, the curtains are from Gerriets.

Embraer

You are familiar with Boeing and Airbus, the makers of big aircraft. But Embraer? This company from Brazil is the world's number one in regional jets and has recently outmaneuvered Canada's Bombardier, currently number two. However, a new contender is already lurking in the shadows, Russia's Sukhoi.

O.C. Tanner

Recognizing the contributions of others in a tangible form is as old as civilization itself. So when Obert C. Tanner started his "recognition" business in the basement of his mother's home in Salt Lake City over 80 years ago, he couldn't claim he had invented a whole new type of product. But he did pioneer a whole new kind of business focused on helping companies appreciate people who do great work. The company that O.C. Tanner founded—and which still bears his name—has since grown into the world market leader in employee recognition programs, with over $400 million in annual revenues, healthy operating profits, and no debt.

Klais

Organs made by Klais are known the world over. The instruments crafted by this globally operating company can be heard in the Cologne Cathedral and Philharmonic Hall, the National Theater in Beijing, the Kyoto Concert Hall in Japan, in Caracas, London, Brisbane, Manila (a bamboo organ), and in the Petronas Twin Towers in Kuala Lumpur. You might find it hard to believe that Klais has a total workforce of only 65 people. Globalism is not a question of company size, but of spirit.

Electro-Nite

With a global market share of 60%, Electro-Nite from Belgium is not only the global number one in sensors for the steel industry, but the market leader in every one of the more than 60 countries where it operates.

Sappi

Sappi stands for South African Pulp and Paper Industries. Sappi is the world's leader both in coated fine paper and in dissolvable pulp. With 16,000 employees, Sappi manufactures in 45 locations throughout the world.

Essel Propack

Would you expect that your toothpaste tube is made by a company from India? Essel Propack, based in Mumbai, has a global market share of 33% and is the dominant force in laminated tubes for toothpaste and similar substances. It runs 23 plants all over the world, from Russia to Venezuela to the Philippines.

Plansee

Plansee in Reutte, Austria, is the world's leading manufacturer of high-performance materials made with refractory metals and composites. It is a shining example of a true high-tech company.

Dickson Constant

If you have a soft blind over your balcony, the odds are it's a Dickson Constant from France. This company is the world market leader in technical textiles used for blinds, truck sheeting, inflatable advertising objects, and special protective clothing. Dickson manufactures 25 million square meters per year, sells in over 100 countries, and has an export quota of 70%.

Molex

Founded by the Krehbiel family in 1938, Chicago-based Molex has grown to become the number two global supplier of electronic, electrical and fiber optic interconnect solutions, switches, and application tooling. Molex remains focused on the automotive, data, telecom, consumer electronics, industrial and medical market segments where they are number one and two. Molex has sustained a compound annual growth rate of 12% over the last 21 years, more than double the market rate for its industry and has revenues of $3.4 billion.

Jungbunzlauer

When you're drinking Coca-Cola, the name Jungbunzlauer is unlikely to be the first thing that springs to mind. But this Austrian-Swiss global leader supplies the citric acid for every Coca-Cola produced and sold.

Nivarox and Universo

You have probably never heard of Nivarox, but there's a very high chance that this dwarf from Switzerland manufactured the regulating mechanism inside your wristwatch. The company has a global market share of 90%. And have you ever thought about who makes the tiny wristwatch hands? Here, the market leader is Universo.

SGS

SGS is the world leader for product auditing and certification, with annual revenues of $3.6 billion.[3] Due to globalization and an increasing need for quality assurance, SGS is growing rapidly.

Brainlab

Brainlab offers surgeons an instrument-positioning system that works like the navigation system in your car. This fast-growing company is helping surgeons to more precisely plan and carry out surgical operations. With about 3,000 systems installed worldwide, Brainlab accounts for 60% of the global market today.

Delo

Unnoticed by consumers, adhesives from Delo have become indispensable in many areas ranging from airbag sensors to chips in bankcards and passports. The adhesives are also found in half of all cell phones worldwide, especially in the most advanced models. In new technologies such as smartcards, Delo is a leading global player. Its adhesives can be found in 80% of all chip cards produced.

Enercon

Enercon is one of the major names in the field of wind turbines. Although it has only been in existence since 1984, it is the clear technological leader in wind power generation, with annual revenues exceeding $4 billion and a workforce of 10,000. Enercon owns more than 40% of all patents worldwide for wind power generation.

Omicron

Founded in 1984, this global market leader in scanning probe and tunnel-grid microscopes enables nanotechnology companies to actually observe their own products.

Beluga

If you want to move two 368-ton harbor cranes from Antwerp, Holland, to San Juan, Puerto Rico, Beluga Shipping is on hand to help you. Established as recently as 1995, this service company currently has 40 heavy-lift vessels. It is among the world market leaders in heavy-duty shipping.

Nissha

"Let's Nissha it," is the unofficial slogan of this company from Kyoto, Japan's historic capital. Nissha is the world leader for small touch panels with a global market share of 80%. Its only competitor is the German company Kurz.

Amorim

Amorim from Portugal is the world leader in cork products and cork flooring. This company produces three billion cork stoppers per year. It benefits from the natural resources in its home country (Portugal boasts 80 million cork oaks), but reaches out into the whole world.

Jamba

Jamba is the world's number one for cell phone ring tones. In January 2007, Peter Chernin, the president of News Corp, called Jamba "our most interesting acquisition in the mobile space."[4] His reasoning was that there are one billion televisions and one billion Internet connections in the world today — but almost three billion cell phones.

Netjets

Netjets pioneered the fractional ownership concept for private jets. This firm manages more aircraft than all other fractional aircraft companies combined, and its 700 jets take off 370,000 times annually.

EOS

EOS is the world's leading provider of laser sintering. This process enables the production of three-dimensional physical objects from computer data.

Did you recognize the names of any of these companies? Probably not. And they are all world market leaders. We could go on almost indefinitely with similar descriptions of hidden champions. Hidden champions serve every segment of industrial goods, consumables, and services.

The Veil of Secrecy

Why have these outstanding companies, all of which occupy leading positions in their markets worldwide, remained hidden? There are many reasons, but the most obvious is that a large number of the products offered by hidden champions go unnoticed by consumers. Many of these companies operate in the "hinterland" of the value chain, supplying machinery, components or processes that are no longer discernable in the final product or service. As a result, the products lose their distinct identity or autonomy. How many hotel guests care about which software is used for making room reservations? It's "Fidelio" and when consumers buy a bottle of soda, do they stop to consider how the liquid got into the bottle or how the label was attached? Apart from specialist engineers, who knows that the interior surface of the cylinders in a combustion engine should not be perfectly smooth but slightly rough in order to achieve better lubrication? And that Gehring produces the best honing machinery to create these surfaces? What about perfumes? Does anyone stop to think that the scents come from hidden champions like Givaudan, Firmenich, IFF or Symrise?

Another reason why hidden champions remain concealed is that they avoid drawing attention to themselves. According to the CEO of the world's leading manufacturer of textile needles, "every unwanted public mention of our company counteracts our efforts to stay unknown." His company is not exactly a midget; it employs over 7,000 people. The head of a global leader in electronic connectors told me, "I welcome your research, but at the same time I am reluctant for our company to appear in your publications." He employs almost 10,000 people. And the CEO of a sensor manufacturer with over 4,300 employees said to me, "I'm sure I don't have to tell you that hidden champions are successful because they handle their success strategies with discretion." These comments are typical of the CEOs and owners of hidden champions who prefer to stay out of the public eye. Many of them explicitly shun contact with journalists, researchers or other interested parties. The CEO of the world's number one manufacturer of a key shock absorption component remarked to me, "We want neither our competitors nor our customers to know our true market share." In a similar discussion, the CEO of a service provider stated, "We have cherished our anonymity for years and feel very comfortable about it. Nobody has noticed our niche."

Keeping a low profile in the public eye, the media and the research sector offers advantages that should not be underestimated: it helps companies to focus on their business. Jim Collins makes a telling distinction between "show horses" and "plough horses." The plough horses do not put much time or effort into grooming their public image, so they save time and energy to concentrate on their true purpose: conducting good business.

Of course, this reserve does not mean that the hidden champions are not well known to their direct customers. The opposite is true. Most hidden champions have extremely strong brand names in their markets. Their brand awareness is high, they enjoy outstanding reputations, and competitors often see them as benchmarks.

In recent years, I have noticed that hidden champions are beginning to step out from behind the curtain more frequently. There are several reasons for this. One is that rapid growth and internationalization automatically attract attention. The number of hidden champions listed on the stock exchange or attracting private equity investors has risen sixfold in the last ten years. Increasingly, hidden champions are also enlisting the services of external consultants.

Who Qualifies As a Hidden Champion?

To qualify as a hidden champion, a company must meet the three criteria listed in Fig. 1.1.

Fig. 1.1: Criteria for a hidden champion

Who is a hidden champion?
- Number one, two or three in the global market, or number one on its continent. The market position is generally determined by market share. If a company does not know its exact market share, we use the relative market share (its own market share, revenues or number of units divided by the market share, revenues or number of units of the strongest competitor). As it is not possible to monitor every market, we rely on the market share information provided by the companies.

- Revenue below $4 billion.

- Low level of public awareness. This aspect cannot be quantified precisely, but over 90% of the companies included meet this requirement from the qualitative point of view.

Despite the substantial size of some of these companies, they typically aim to retain the strengths of midsize firms. Companies with annual revenues of more than $1 billion are generally classified as large corporations. Size is, however, relative. Wal-Mart Stores, the largest company in the world, posted revenues of $379 billion in 2007. Ten years earlier, Mitsubishi made it to the top with revenues of $184 billion. Even the smallest company in the Fortune Global 500 list achieved revenues of almost $17 billion in 2007.[5] The average Fortune Global 500 has 67,812 employees and is thus 33 times larger than the average hidden champion with 2,037 employees. The biggest of our hidden champions are still much smaller than the international top 500 and can be described as midsize.

Where Do the Hidden Champions Come From?

As we learned from the selection of hidden champions at the start of this chapter, these global leaders can come from all over the world. I found and encountered hidden champions in consulting projects, conferences and travel in dozens of countries. These companies exist almost everywhere. Several times after concluding a speech, I was approached by someone from the audience with the remark, "You just described our company. How is it possible that you are so familiar with us?" In most cases, I had never heard of the company in question. From these experiences, it became clear that the strategies, leadership methods, and cultures of hidden champions are similar throughout the world.

Before we analyze locations and country origins of the hidden champions in more depth, it is worth looking into the export performance of countries. Over the years in my speeches all over the world, I asked audiences "Which country has the highest exports in the world?" I presented four choices: China, US, Japan, and Germany. The answers have changed over time: 25 years ago, the US typically came out as number one, then in the 1990s Japan, and in recent years most listeners (almost always managers) name China as the presumptive number one. The truth is different. If we look at the most recent six years (2003–2008), Germany has consistently been the number one exporter. (Figure 1.2 shows exports for 2008, 2007, and the average annual exports for the six-year period 2003–2008).

Fig. 1.2: Exports in 2008, 2007 and in the five-year period 2003–2008 (average annual exports in billion US$)

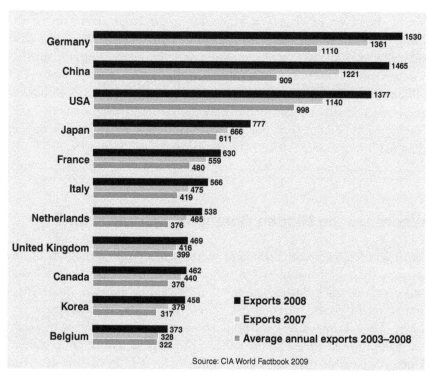

Germany: 1530, 1361, 1110
China: 1465, 1221, 909
USA: 1377, 1140, 998
Japan: 777, 666, 611
France: 630, 559, 480
Italy: 566, 475, 419
Netherlands: 538, 465, 376
United Kingdom: 469, 416, 399
Canada: 462, 440, 376
Korea: 458, 379, 317
Belgium: 373, 328, 322

■ Exports 2008
■ Exports 2007
■ Average annual exports 2003–2008

Source: CIA World Factbook 2009

How can it be that a relatively small country in Europe has sustained this position for so long? A large part of the explanation lies in the prevalence of hidden champions in Germany. Contrary to what most people believe, the export strength of a country is not determined by a few giant, highly visible corporations, but rather by a large number of midsize firms that are very strong exporters. When China overtakes Germany in the coming years, this truth will not change.[6] It also applies to China.

Along with export performance and the ensuing dependence on international markets, we observe that the interest in the topic of world market leadership varies strongly across countries. A Google search reveals a surprising pattern and confirms the strong attention that the idea of world market leadership receives in Europe. In a search with "world market leader" and country name, Germany, the leading exporter, is revealed as number one ahead of the US in absolute figures. Fig. 1.3 lists the countries with more than 20,000 entries. On a per capita basis, Switzerland, Austria, and the Netherlands top the list—all direct neighbors of Germany.

Fig. 1.3: Google pages that include "world market leader" and country name

Country	Entries	Entries per million of population
Germany	63,000	765
USA	55,200	183
UK	41,440	682
China	37,500	28
France	32,200	505
Japan	31,000	243
Netherlands	29,500	1,780
Italy	29,100	500
Canada	27,100	812
Switzerland	26,100	3,455
India	24,200	21
Australia	22,100	1,081
Spain	21,800	539
Austria	21,300	2,598

In the light of export performance and the high interest in global market leadership, it is no surprise that by far the biggest concentration of hidden champions is found in the German-speaking countries. My global list of hidden champions contains about 2,000 companies. About two thirds of them come from the German-language area. Scandinavia also has a sizable number, as does Northern Italy. For the US, my best estimate is between

300 and 500 companies, for Japan less than 100. Besides the higher prevalence in German-speaking countries, an additional reason for the lower numbers outside this region is most likely that I have not achieved the same coverage in the US or Japan as in Europe. But this is unlikely to affect the validity of the general pattern described here.

In line with the regional prevalence of hidden champions, the primary focus of this book is on hidden champions from German-speaking countries. As outlined above, I found the hidden champions remarkably similar across the world. I am convinced that this book captures the special spirit of these companies in an increasingly globalized world, regardless of their location. Anecdotal evidence and many cases from hidden champions outside the German language area underpin this tenet.

Knowledge and Data Base

An extensive pool of knowledge and data has accumulated since I first started investigating hidden champions more than 20 years ago. In this book, I draw on the following knowledge and databases.

1. The hidden champions list
   Collected over a 20-year period, the list of hidden champions contains about 2,000 companies throughout the world. Of those 1,174 are in Germany, 61 in Austria, and 81 in Switzerland, making a total of 1,316 in the German-speaking countries. The data includes company name, key product, revenues, number of employees, market, market ranking, and absolute and relative market shares.
2. Public information
   This source includes newspapers, magazines, books and the Internet, which has become the most important source of information on the hidden champions in the public domain.
3. Company information
   This category comprises annual reports, company websites, brochures, catalogs, anniversary publications, etc.
4. Questionnaire
   A questionnaire addressing a wide variety of relevant aspects (such as key figures, strategy, leadership, and market position) was sent to the heads of all hidden champions in the German language area. It was largely identical to a questionnaire I used in the 1990s study in order to

ensure comparability. I added a few recent aspects (new markets, globalization, Internet, etc.). A total of 147 questionnaires were returned, of which 134 were suitable for in-depth analysis. Given the extreme introversion of the hidden champions and the sensitivity of the questions asked, the response rate of over 11% is acceptable (less intrusive studies of this kind usually achieve response rates of 15%–20%). The responses can be viewed as representative for all hidden champions. If we use the median to exclude outlier effects, the difference between the overall list and the responding sample stands at only 1.3% for revenues and 1.9% for the number of employees.

5. Consulting projects, visits and interviews

   In the last three decades, I have had hundreds of opportunities in many different countries to gain first-hand impressions of hidden champions and the people who lead them. The deepest insights have arisen from my consulting projects. We have worked for numerous midsize global market leaders all over the world — not to mention the countless discussions, meetings, interviews, and visits with the managers of hidden champions.

Relative to these sources, management books and journals contributed little to this book. The phenomenon of the hidden champions is sparsely covered in management literature.

This book and its conclusions draw on all the above mentioned sources. In comparison with the first book, I pay greater attention to qualitative aspects. My intention is not to bombard the reader with as many statistics as possible. Instead, I aim to offer insights into why the hidden champions are so successful, how they are different from large corporations, and what we can learn from them. As far as possible, I skip discussions of methodology. In the interest of entrepreneurs and managers—the key target groups of this book—I will focus on the content and findings relevant to corporate management.

Structural Data on the Hidden Champions

The following structural data relates to our sample. Such detailed information is available for the sample only. In view of the broad range covered within the revenue limit of $4 billion and the very wide variance, all means should be treated with caution. They do not provide information on distributions and thus represent only part of the complex reality. Fig 1.4 shows selected key figures.[7]

Fig. 1.4: Hidden champions: key figures

Revenues	
Average	$434 million
Annual revenues <$70 million	24.8%
Annual revenues $70–$200 million	27.4%
Annual revenues $200–$700 million	29.9%
Annual revenues >$700 million	17.9%
Number of employees	
Average	2,037
<200	21.6%
200–1,000	32.0%
1,000–3,000	25.6%
>3,000	20.8%
Sector	
Industrial goods	69.1%
Consumer goods	20.1%
Services	10.8%
Export quota	61.5%
Equity ratio	41.9%
ROI before taxes	13.6%

On average, the hidden champions reported revenues of $434 million. This is more than three times higher than the figure of $130 million in the first *Hidden Champions* book ten years earlier. These figures reflect the hidden champions' rapid growth, which we will examine in greater detail in Chapter 2. It is instructive to look at the distribution of revenues shown in Fig. 1.4. Roughly one in four companies has revenues of less than $70 million, which is relatively small by worldwide comparison. Yet even these smaller companies can be truly global competitors and market leaders, as demonstrated by the organ builder Klais. Almost 18% of the hidden champions achieve revenues of more than $700 million. Many hidden champions have broken the dollar $1-billion revenue barrier in the last ten years.

As employers, the hidden champions play a key role. The average workforce size today is 2,037 compared with 735 ten years ago. Most of the new jobs have been created outside the home markets of the hidden champions. We will address this development in more detail in Chapter 9. By taking the figures from the sample and extrapolating them, we get accumulated revenues of $570 billion and a total workforce of 2.68 million for all hidden champions. These numbers illustrate the importance of the hidden champions for the economy in the German-speaking countries as a whole.

Fig. 1.4 shows that 69.1% of the hidden champions operate in the industrial goods sector. One fifth sells consumer products and 10.8% are service providers. A closer examination of the various sectors reveals that 35.6% of the hidden champions are in engineering, while the second-largest group (28.8%) belongs to the category "Other." This means that hidden champions typically serve smaller markets that are not listed separately in industry statistics. The electrical sector accounts for 12.1% of the hidden champions and metal processing for 11.4%. Chemicals are another important sector with 6.8%.

The age structure of the hidden champions is very interesting. Fig. 1.5 illustrates the distribution of companies founded in different time periods.

Fig. 1.5: Hidden champions: the founding years

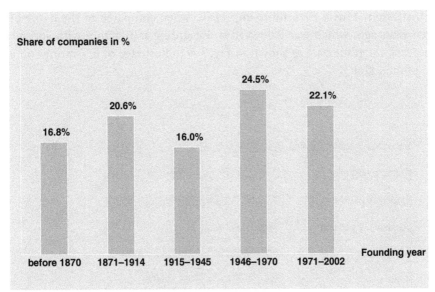

The distribution is fairly even across the periods selected. The oldest hidden champion, Achenbach Buschhütten (which produces three quarters of all aluminum roller mills in the world), was founded in 1452, making it 556 years old. The youngest, Carbon Sports (a leading manufacturer of carbon wheels and components for lightweight racing bikes), was established in 2002. The median age, avoiding outlier effects, is 61 years. About one third (32.1%) of the hidden champions are older than 100 years, which is a convincing demonstration of these companies' ability to survive. By comparison, only one of the companies originally listed on the Dow Jones Index back in 1897—General Electric—is still in this index today. About half (49.6%) of the hidden champions were founded after World War II, and 15.3% are less than 25 years old, which is very young for a global market leader.

How Successful Are the Hidden Champions?

What is success in business? The answer to this question depends on the goals. How do the hidden champions see their success? When questioned about overall satisfaction with business results in the past five years (based on a scale from 1 = not satisfied to 7 = extremely satisfied), more than half (51.9%) responded with the top two ratings, reflecting a high level of satisfaction. This is even more impressive when compared to the figure of ten years ago, which was below 30%. Regarding satisfaction with specific aspects, the results are as shown in Fig. 1.6 (percentage of 6/7 ratings on a 7-point scale):

Fig. 1.6: Satisfaction with selected performance aspects

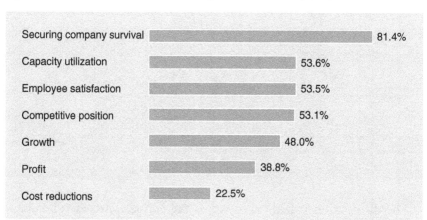

The levels of satisfaction are very different. Most respondents are very satisfied with how their company's survival is secured. On the other hand, significantly lower satisfaction ratings emerge when it comes to profit and, in particular, to cost reductions. It is important to keep in mind that satisfaction depends on the goals set.

The companies' low satisfaction with their profit situation seems astonishing. As shown in Fig. 1.4, those questioned named an average pretax ROI (return on investment) of 13.6% in the last ten years. If we assume a realistic tax rate of 30%, we obtain an after-tax ROI of 9.5% for the hidden champions. This figure compares with 3.5% for the Fortune Global 500 in 2007.[8] We can thus see that the hidden champions are very profitable vis-à-vis world's largest corporations.

Linking the ROI of 13.6% to the equity ratio of 41.9% and assuming borrowing costs of 6% results in a ROE (return on equity) of 24.2%—also a very high figure. This finding is consistent with the estimate of the hidden champions' profitability relative to that of the industry in general. All study participants answered this less sensitive question. Of the participants, 65.9% see themselves in the top third of the industry. Only 7.9% assumed that their returns were in the bottom third. A comparison of returns in revenues—albeit slightly speculative—also proves interesting. Based on the realistic assumption that in industrial companies capital is turned over about once per year,[9] a pretax return on revenues between 10% and 12% is obtained. This is about twice the average of 5.7% reported by industrial firms in Germany.[10] This margin also compares favorably with the Fortune Global 500, which achieved an after-tax return on revenues of 5.7% (thus a pretax margin of 7.8% in 2007) and with 3.7% for the U.S. Fortune 500 in 2008.[11]

How do the hidden champions deal with downturns and crises? The majority seems to actually profit from difficult conditions. Half of the respondents took the view that they survive downturns better than their industry as a whole. Most respondents said that this was definitely true of past downturns and that they expect no changes in this respect. Market shares are newly distributed in difficult market phases, not in favorable economic times. When times get tough, the weaker competitors tend to buckle under pressure. This in turn provides the stronger contenders with the opportunity to expand their market position. This model is similar to that propounded by the evolutionist Stephen Jay Gould. In his so-called "punctuated equilibria" theory,[12] *Fortune*, July 21, 2008, p. F-15, and *Fortune*, May 18, 2009. p. F-32. he asserted that evolution is not a continuous process, but rather occurs in leaps. There are long periods with minimal mutations followed by brief phases with abrupt changes. This hypothesis could well apply to markets in general and to the hidden champions in particular. A majority of those questioned confirm that the development of their company proceeded in distinctive leaps. To this end, I suspect that the recent phase of rapid globalization has put the hidden champions of the twenty-first century into a position in which they have been advancing their growth and their market position fast and decisively. In the same vein they may well profit from the current crisis.[13]

With regard to overcoming major crises, the picture is mixed. While 29% of the companies developed without a serious crisis, close to 30% experienced and survived a major crisis in their history. During my hidden champions speeches throughout the world, I am often asked how many of these companies have disappeared. I cannot answer this question in precise numbers, as my research looks at only existing hidden champions, i.e., survivors.

Ten years ago, my list contained 457 German hidden champions. I estimate that about 10% of those have failed in the last ten years[14]—a remarkably low percentage that proves the hidden champions' tenacity. A typical case of a failed hidden champion is Reflecta, former world market leader in slide projectors. This case reveals the danger of major changes in technology. In the age of digital photography, the electronic beamer has replaced the optical-mechanical slide projector.

In spite of their ability to survive, I would like to emphasize that the hidden champions are not miracle companies. They are not immune to crises or to the attacks of better competitors. As with most other companies, they must contend with the competition every day. For example, as suppliers e.g., to the automotive industry, they are exposed to enormous pressures. The vast majority emphasize that their competitors are also strong and that their success is not attributable to a magic formula. Rather, their success stems from the many little things they do slightly and consistently better. Theodore Levitt once expressed this tenet as follows: "Sustained success is largely a matter of focusing regularly on the right things and making a lot of uncelebrated improvements every day."[15] I am certain that most CEOs of the hidden champions would subscribe to this statement.

With this in mind, you as a reader should not interpret the following lessons as simplistic success formulas similar to a cookbook recipe. Instead, you should apply critical judgment as to which observations, experiences, and conditions can be transferred to your specific situation and, of course, which cannot. Take everything with a grain of salt and remain skeptical. Personally, I have learned enormously from the hidden champions. In building and managing our own company, Simon-Kucher & Partners, my partners and I have implemented the hidden champion strategy with the utmost determination. By observing these lessons over the past 20 years, we have become a small hidden champion ourselves. To a substantial degree, we owe the success of Simon-Kucher & Partners to the hidden champions.

Learning from the Hidden Champions

Every firm should be open to learn from successful companies. Until now, this process has mainly been a one-way street running from the large, well-known corporations down to the midsize and smaller firms. About 90% of all case studies deal with large corporations. In other words, only the big companies purportedly have something to teach. It is time to reverse this learning process. As we will see in this book, even large corporations have a lot to learn from the hidden champions. During the many years of my work with larger companies, I often saw that the unconventional strategies and surprising successes of the hidden champions spurred ardent discussions and led to specific and concrete improvements.

In the last ten years, strategic aspects such as focus, core competencies or closeness to customer have been more intensely observed. This new spirit frequently paved the way for radical restructuring in large corporations. Often, the newly formed business units are similar to the hidden champions. However, I continue to see considerable room for improvement in many firms. Companies of all sizes that are less successful can benefit from the hidden champions. They should compare their own strategies with those of the hidden champions and determine where the differences lie. From these audits, specific actions can be deduced. In Chapter 11 of this book, we present a hidden champions audit and a strategy system for companies of all sizes to examine their strategic positions. Such benchmarking processes not only facilitate new perspectives, but they also help in the implementation because they relate to real-world examples.

Finally, I believe that young people can gain valuable insights for their careers from the hidden champions. Most university graduates have a preference for working in large corporations. This stems partially from their limited familiarity with the real economy, combined with a dominating perception of well-known brands and the influence of their peers. Yet such perceptions and the ensuing preferences for certain employers don't do reality justice. Hidden champions are very attractive employers. Due to their focus and limited size, new employees can grasp the company structure and take on real responsibilities more quickly. Ultimately, with their global presence, the hidden champions offer highly attractive prospects for international careers.

The Goals of This Book

After more than a decade, the time has come to write a radically new hidden champions book. So much has changed. The disappearance of the Iron Curtain, the economic emergence of Asia, the liberation of world trade, and the diminishing costs of transportation and communication have opened a whole new world to entrepreneurs.

What is this book about? We strive for a better understanding as to why the hidden champions are so successful—both in the past and more so in the twenty-first century. We want to learn from them. What has changed in this increasingly globalized world? What strategies and methods of leadership lead to long-term success? Specific questions we will cover in this book include the following:

- How do the hidden champions approach goals and visions? How are these visions communicated and implemented?
- How do they define their markets? What role do focus and concentration play? How do the hidden champions deal with the challenge of diversification in the face of market saturation and their high market shares?
- What does globalization mean for the hidden champions? How do midsize and small companies react to the enormous demands posed by mental internationalization and the need for worldwide market presence? How do they see and approach the "markets of the future" such as China, India or Russia?
- What are the attitudes and strategies of the hidden champions with regard to closeness to customer, marketing, competitive advantages, outsourcing, and strategic alliances?
- What drives innovation? How do new hidden champions emerge?
- How do hidden champions finance their expansion? What has changed and what will continue to change?
- Which organizational structures and processes do they choose? How do they cope with centralization versus decentralization?
- What is the relevance of local business environments, industrial clusters, innovation centers, and training institutions?

- What characterizes their corporate culture? How do these companies achieve such high levels of identification and motivation among their employees? How is personnel hired, trained, and retained?
- What are the prevailing leadership styles? What characterizes the leaders? How are they selected?
- How can the findings be used for judging one's own position and honing one's own strategy?

A comprehensive program lies ahead of us. It will reveal surprising findings and perspectives.

Summary

A plethora of extremely successful companies remain hidden behind a curtain of inconspicuousness and secrecy: They are the hidden champions of the twenty-first century. With immense ambition and stamina, they are thrusting forward in a phase of rapid globalization. Yet the press, management experts, and the public continue to overlook these companies. And it is precisely these companies that reveal the strategies and leadership methods that will spell success in the twenty-first century. Traditional virtues and healthy common sense prevail over the latest management fashions and fads—and the teachings of modern management gurus.

The hidden champions of the twenty-first century dominate their markets worldwide, have noticeably grown in size, show a remarkable capability to survive, often specialize in low-profile products, have become truly global competitors, and are successful but are not miracle companies.

Everyone interested in management can learn immensely from the hidden champions. This even applies in no small degree to large corporations that often fail to take small firms seriously. I am very familiar with large and midsize companies worldwide. For exactly this reason, I am convinced that the hidden champions of the twenty-first century have much to offer as role models for modern business management and leadership.

Notes

1 Jim Collins, *Good to Great: Why Some Companies Make the Leap... and Others Don't*, New York: Harper Collins 2001; see also James C. Collins and Jerry I. Portas, *Built to Last: Successful Habits of Visionary Companies*, New York: Random House 1994.
2 Exchange rate: $1 = YEN 115

3 Exchange rate: $1 = CHF 1.1987 (average for 2007)

4 Fortune, February 5, 2007, p. 26.

5 Fortune, July 23, 2007, p. F-9.

6 Since the Chinese population is 17 times larger than the German population, China will overtake Germany when its per capita exports reach 6% of the German figure.

7 For the conversion of Euro into US Dollars, we use the average rate for 2007 of $1.37 per EUR for all years between 1995 and 2007. This rate is practically identical to the average rate of our base year 1995 of $1.36 per EUR. In case the reader would like to carry out calculations with the relevant $-rates for individual years, we list the average annual exchange rates for the years between 1995 and 2007:

1995	1.3641
1996	1.3007
1997	1.1274
1998	1.1118
1999	1.0658
2000	0.9236
2001	0.8956
2002	0.9456
2003	1.1312
2004	1.2439
2005	1.2441
2006	1.2556
2007	1.3705

8 *Fortune*, July 21, 2008, p. F-18.

9 With the Fortune 500 of 2008, the average asset-revenue-ratio was at 1.00; *Fortune*, May 18, 2009, p. F-32.

10 Institut der Deutschen Wirtschaft, Cologne, March 2008.

11 *Fortune*, July 21, 2008, p. F-15, and *Fortune*, May 18, 2009, p. F-32.

12 Stephen Jay Gould, *The Structure of Evolutionary Theory*, New York: Belknap Press 2002.

13 This should definitely be true relative to their weaker competitors.

14 In the same time 37% of the large corporations listed on the DAX index (the Dow Jones of Germany) have disappeared from that group.

15 Theodore Levitt, Editorial, *Harvard Business Review*, November-December 1988, p. 9.

Chapter 2
Growth and Market Leadership

Goals play a central role for the strategy and the leadership of an enterprise. The hidden champions pursue highly ambitious goals aimed above all at growth and market leadership. When and how are these goals formulated? How are they filled with content? How are they communicated? And how successful are the hidden champions of the twenty-first century at realizing these goals? In this chapter, we see that the hidden champions have grown strongly and continuously over the last ten years. In the process, they have strengthened their market position. This applies to both absolute and relative market shares. Hidden champions define market leadership not only in terms of market share, but see it as an extended claim to overall leadership in their markets. Their goals are truly long term.

The Inner Flame

A goal—or a vision—is the start of everything. This encompasses two aspects. A decision must be taken about what is to be achieved and the time frame for this achievement must be set. The second requirement is the energy it takes to achieve this goal. Successful entrepreneurs have bold goals and visions. At certain stages of development, an increasingly clear inner idea emerges of the long-term goals the entrepreneurs want to achieve with their enterprise. It is less relevant whether this idea is formulated in writing, explicitly communicated or thought through to the last detail. Initially, all of this is typically not the case. Goals and visions crystallize in the course of their realization: an entrepreneur learns, feels confirmed by his success, or is forced by setbacks to adapt his initial intentions. With time, he gains courage as a result of success and growth.

In this way, goals and visions become a powerful motor for entrepreneurial thought and action. Visionary entrepreneurs also inspire others. In the words of Augustine of Hippo, "The fire you want to ignite in others must first burn within you." The phrase "the boss's vision is the engine of our success" originates from a report on Wittenstein, a leading manufacturer of mechatronic drives.[1] Visions can be an effective means of creating successful companies, helping new technologies achieve market breakthrough, and changing society as a whole. Companies that not only formulate their visions but realize them become Schumpeter's "creative destroyers" and the drivers of progress.

If we look back at the history of the hidden champions, two goals in particular become very clear: growth and market leadership. The chicken-and-egg question of what comes first or which has the higher priority can be left unanswered. These two goals are conditions of each other and at the same time promote each other. Growth results in market leadership or strengthens it. Market leadership contributes to growth.

Growth, Growth, Growth

First of all, we will look at growth and growth-related goals. The hidden champions have grown enormously since our first investigation about ten years ago. With an average annual growth rate of 8.8%, they have increased their revenues by a factor of 2.3 on average. Today, they are on average more than twice their size of ten years ago. In the light of this annual growth rate, they double their size every 8.2 years. An enterprise with annual revenues of $1 billion in the 1990s has today become a giant, reporting annual revenues of $2.3 billion. In the past ten years, growth was significantly stronger than in the preceding five-year period. Between 1989 and 1995, the hidden champions achieved annual revenue growth of 6.5%. We thus perceive acceleration in the growth of the hidden champions of the twenty-first century.

This high growth rate is evident in all size classes. There is no significant correlation between the size of the companies and their growth rate.[2] This finding is surprising, because it could be assumed that the growth rates level off with increasing company size. Our random sample investigation refuted this hypothesis. The hidden champions' power to grow does not significantly depend on their size.

As always, the average figures are only of limited value. If we look at the top growth rates, we find companies that are now ten to twenty times the size they were ten years ago. This gave rise to about 200 new $-billionaires (i.e., companies with revenues exceeding $1 billion). Today, one tenth of all companies are at least five times the size and one quarter are at least three times the size they were a decade ago. However, there are also some firms that have not grown significantly, or have even shrunk. Interestingly, some of these deliberately choose not to grow. We will see below that this may well be a sensible strategy.

The growth in the number of employees is 4.7% annually, which is considerably lower than the growth in revenues of 8.8% annually. However, the cumulative growth of head counts over ten years is still enormous: on average, the number of employees has risen by 58%. The hidden champions created new jobs on a significant scale. However, only a small proportion of the increase in employment takes place in the home markets of the hidden champions. The majority of new jobs were created in foreign countries. We will analyze these aspects in more detail in Chapter 9. In view of the differences in the growth rates, revenues per employee rose to $219,253 today from $151,629 ten years ago.

There are several causes for the difference between revenues and employee growth. These include increases in productivity, shifts in the value chain and inflation effects. The annual increase in productivity was probably around a solid 4%. This is an impressive figure if we recall that the initial productivity level of the hidden champions was already high. The hidden champions obviously improve their productivity continuously and significantly. The depth of the value chain has been reduced by approximately 10%. As the majority of the hidden champions are active in the business-to-business sector, we can assume a relatively low rate of inflation. In spite of their market power, even the hidden champions are unable to completely escape the price pressure that dominates many supply markets (e.g., the prices for car parts suppliers have dropped regularly over the last few years by 3%–5% annually). In our sample, 24.2% of respondents said that their prices had dropped noticeably, whereas only 12.9% said that their prices had risen noticeably. However, a considerable majority of 62.9% reported that the price levels had essentially remained the same. Thus, we can assume an inflation rate close to zero or even slight deflation.

From Hidden Champion to Big Champion

Have you ever asked yourself how big companies come into being? The answer is simple: they originate from midsize companies that continually grow over a long period. In the course of the last decade, some of our hidden champions have soared well above the $4 billion revenue threshold and are therefore no longer "hidden" champions covered by the definition we use today. We thus call them big champions. Surprisingly, even the growth rates of the big champions are not significantly below average. Over the last ten years, the big champions have grown at a rate of 8.1% annually, which is similar to the hidden champions' growth rate of 8.8%. The big champions have also more than doubled their revenues.

Three case studies illustrate the rise to the large corporations' league. Ten years ago, Fresenius Medical Care, SAP and Würth were classic hidden champions with revenues of about $1—$3 billion. Today, their revenues are well above $10 billion.

Each of these three big champions is the world market leader in its respective market and has achieved the following revenues and growth rates:

Company	Main product	Revenues 2007 ($billion)	Annual growth rate 1995-2007
SAP	Standard software	14.03	18.2%
Fresenius Medical Care	Dialysis services	14.76	23.4%
Würth	Assembly products	11.63	11.9%

In the course of this development, SAP and Fresenius Medical Care have attained listing in the top stock market index and are included in the premier league of major German corporations. In spite of its size, Würth has remained a family-run enterprise.

SAP created the market for standard business software in its present form, and has systematically developed this market and its own market position over decades. During this period, all growth routes were consistently pursued, such as extension of software functionality, enlargement of the sector, internationalization, and the involvement of software suppliers. Growth was predominantly organic. Acquisitions did not play an important role as they did with competitors such as Oracle. SAP's impressive growth was accompanied by a high degree of continuity at the helm of this big champion. In its 36-year-history SAP has only had three CEOs.

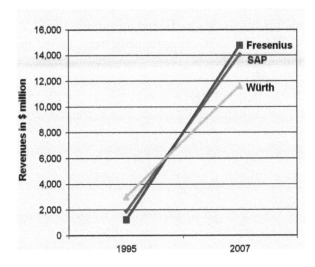

Fresenius Medical Care took advantage of increase in civilization-related illnesses and the progress in medical technology. The company decisively and courageously seized the chances for growth that resulted from these conditions. Internationalization in particular was pursued with great energy. Acquisitions such as the recent purchase of the American company Renal Care made decisive contributions to growth. Problems presented by integration were solved with great skill. The management became international at an early stage: today, FMC's seven executive board members are of four different nationalities.

While SAP and Fresenius Medical Care grew with their new markets, Würth predominantly operates its main business with assembly products in established markets. Würth is first and foremost a sales and logistics system trimmed to maximum efficiency. More than half of its employees work in sales. Motivation, incentives, sales targets, multiplication of the segments, and so forth, are the engines for growth in this context.

A closer look at the growth history of Würth Group, now a big champion, is illuminating. If we think about long-term goals and visions as instruments of leadership and drivers of growth, the path automatically leads to Reinhold Würth. Growth was always the core of his vision. For the nearly three decades that I have known him, Reinhold Würth has never stopped preaching about the benefits of growth. He often compares his company to a tree: as long as a tree grows, it is healthy. If it stops growing, it dies. Only growth keeps a company young, dynamic and agile. And Würth was not content with general appeals for growth. Instead he repeatedly set precise quantitative targets, which at the time seemed virtually unattainable, thus rendering his vision specific and measurable. Fig. 2.2 shows what has become of Würth's visions: the company has achieved more than 50 years of continuous growth.

Fig. 2.2: Würth Group 1954-2007 — from hidden to big champion

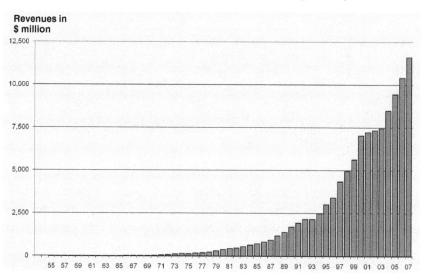

In the first two decades following 1954, revenues were at a level that is invisible on the scale necessary today. The size achieved—is as spectacular as the fact that the company grew every single year—year after year—for more than 50 years. It is not surprising that growth was stronger in some periods and weaker in others. A period of extremely high growth rates in the 1990s was followed by a respite at the start of the twenty-first century. As we can see from the most recent revenue figures, the old growth spirit seems to have revived recently.

It is well documented how Reinhold Würth kept raising the benchmark. In 1979, the company generated revenues of approximately $300 million, and then Reinhold Würth challenged his team to break the $700 million revenue barrier in 1986, followed by the target of $1.4 billion revenues for 1990. At the time, Würth commented, "It is astonishing how fast such targets develop a life of their own and become part of the corporate culture. Employees identify themselves with these goals and do everything to realize them." The $1.4 billion target was reached a year early in 1989 and Reinhold Würth did not hesitate for a second to set a new target exceeding the $7 billion threshold—for the year 2000. At the start of the 1990s, Würth made the following statement about this extremely ambitious target, "This new vision was accepted very quickly by the employees. Nobody thinks any longer about this enormous number today and no one has difficulty adapting his activities to this new target. I do not exaggerate when I say that this new vision created an almost magnetic attraction." Klaus Hendrikson, who was at the time managing director of Würth do Brazil, commented, "This is no longer a vision. It is a clear, achievable goal. The optimism that we can achieve these revenues is based on sober analyses." This last aspect is critical, because it determines the employees' acceptance of the target. Reinhold Würth admitted that a vision like this "cannot simply be presented out of thin air. The vision must be substantiated. All limitations must be investigated, the means tested—market, financing, employees, management capacity, etc. Such ambitious visions and goals can only be announced after the homework has been thoroughly done. When the foundations are solid, the vision will take care of itself."

Fig. 2.2 demonstrates precision success. The $7 billion revenue mark was achieved in 1999, just as had been envisaged ten years earlier. This exemplary realization of a vision is now a global enterprise with revenues of $12 billion in 2007 and more than 60,000 employees. The company reports above-average profitability when compared with the rest of the sector. Reinhold Würth has always stressed, "Growth without profit is lethal." And despite his age of 73 years, Würth's energy is not fading. In November 2007, he announced a revenue target of $30 billion for the year 2017. The flame continues to burn.

The Exploding Middle

The positive development of the big champions is diametrically opposed to the predominant mood of the last decade. We could argue that these companies are the famous exceptions to the rule, and that companies in general are suffering from competitive pressures, cutting jobs and displaying weaknesses in international competition. However, we will see that many midsize hidden champions have grown even faster than the big champions discussed above.

Why do these successes go unnoticed and fail to have an effect on the public mood? Presumably, the press and public attention are only focused on large corporations and even confine their attention to a few "well-known" big companies. A great number of these large corporations throughout such sectors as industry, banking, insurance, trade, and telecommunications have repeatedly announced massive job cuts. The 30 companies composing the DAX index, for example, reduced their workforces in Germany by 3.5% in the period from 2002 to 2006.[3]

The midsize hidden champions we will now discuss have grown enormously in the last ten years. This growth has produced almost 200 new companies with revenues of more than $1 billion in the German-speaking countries. Regardless of the yardstick applied, revenues exceeding $1 billion suggest a company size that can be classified as "large." With so many new large corporations evolving over the last ten years, it is fair to say that this type of company is characterized by unusually dynamic growth.

These new companies with revenues of more than $1 billion have grown at an average annual rate of 11.6% in the decade under review. This rate means that revenues have doubled in size in 6.3 years. Such a development is based on fantastic entrepreneurial performance. On average, the companies are now 3.7 times the size they were ten years ago. At that time, mean revenues were $811 million; today, they have reached $2.21 billion.[4] The sum of revenues of the new $-billionaires was $83.6 billion ten years ago and is now $227 billion, representing an increase of $143.4 billion. Judging by revenues of $151,629 per employee ten years ago and $219,253 today, these growth champions have created about 484,000 new jobs—naturally not only in their home countries, but throughout the world. Of the new jobs created by the hidden champions 30% are in their domestic markets. The contrast between the development of these midsize enterprises and that of the large corporations could not be more marked.

Numerous new companies with revenues in excess of a $1 billion will emerge from the ranks of the hidden champions in the future.[5] In 2007, an estimated further 20 companies have generated revenues exceeding $1 billion. A similar number achieved this in 2008. Revenue growth will feed the pipeline of future large corporations. Several selected announcements of targets for the forthcoming years underline this hypothesis and the ambitions behind it:

– Frank Asbeck, CEO of Solarworld AG, announced that he "wants to break through the billion barrier in 2010."
– Grohe, world market leader in high-quality sanitary fittings, reported breaking through the billion revenue barrier in 2007.

- Eckes-Granini, Europe's leading fruit juice producer, is close to revenues of a billion. CEO Thomas Hinderer plans to reach this level by 2010 at the latest.
- IDS Scheer, a leading software company, announced "IDS Scheer plans to become a company with revenues approaching one billion." In 2007, IDS Scheer's revenues were about $485 million. Growth is expected to come mainly in the US and Asia.
- Dorma, the world market leader in door technology, plans to achieve billion in revenues in three years' time.
- Karl-Heinz Streibich, CEO of Software AG, with revenues of $850 million in 2007 announced a revenue target of $1.5 billion for 2011.[6]
- Phoenix Contact, a leading manufacturer of electronic interfaces that are predominantly used in automation technology, broke the billion barrier in 2007 and is currently heading for its second billion.
- The flame also burns at EBM-Papst, the world market leader in industrial fans. CEO Hans Jochen Beilke promises to double the 2007 revenues of almost $1.5 billion, and thus to break the $3 billion threshold before 2015. Incidentally, Beilke is a direct neighbor of Reinhold Würth. Ambition is contagious.
- In the spring of 2008, Kion, currently the global number two and European market leader in fork lift trucks, announced its "Vision 2015." The core message: Kion aspires to become the global leader by 2015 and to push the mighty Toyota from the throne.

We will reexamine the midsize hidden champions, looking more closely at several extraordinary growth stories. Fig. 2.3 shows the revenue growth of three companies: Leoni, Enercon, and Cronimet. Leoni is the global leader in cable systems for cars and numerous other applications. Enercon is the global technology leader in wind power generation, and is also number three in terms of market share. Cronimet is a global leader in the recycling of raw materials for the steel industry. These three hidden champions have leading positions in what can be characterized as "new markets." Although metal recycling and cables have existed for a long time, technical developments and innovations led to a new growth phase during the last decade.

The three companies have shown excellent growth performances and are at least six times larger today than they were in the mid-1990s. Their common feature is their activity in rapidly growing markets. While expanding with their markets, they have given their growth additional impetus by consistent innovation, and internationalization.

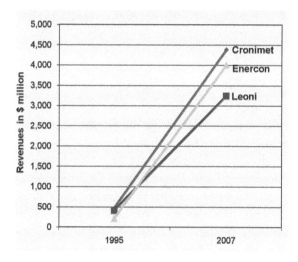

With the slogan "Energy for the World," Enercon aims to benefit from the global growth opportunities in wind power generation. Since 1995 (see Fig. 2.3), Enercon has increased its revenues to more than $4 billion in 2007 from less than $200 million. Enercon has more than 10,000 employees, an impressive achievement for a company that is only 24 years old. Enercon's wind turbines are installed in 31 countries. Sales subsidiaries are active in 16 countries, and the company's own servicing and spare parts service is available in all markets served. Growth is set to continue. To date, Enercon has supplied wind energy facilities with a total capacity of 13,700 megawatts. According to CEO Hans-Dieter Kettwig, this accumulated capacity will be doubled in the next 50 months. One megawatt corresponds to revenues of approximately $1.4 million, which means that Enercon's growth is set to continue and even to accelerate.

Leoni was founded 90 years ago. With its competencies in cable technology it has entered its latest growth phase since the mid-1990s. Cable systems today have little in common with cables 20 years ago. A look at Leoni's business units shows the range of its technological challenges and opportunities. Automotive, aerospace, machinery, medical, robotics, and wind & solar are industries and applications with different requirements for a cable specialist, and all are growing markets. Leoni is currently present in 34 countries and growth limits are not in sight.

Would you have expected metal recycling to be an explosively growing high-tech business? Cronimet is a persuasive witness to this allegation. In a market not exactly known for its obsession with quality "Cronimet stands for reliable quality of the highest standards." This value system seems to work. Founded only in 1980, Cronimet's revenue has grown to well over $4 billion in 2007 from $500 million a decade ago. The steep growth has been driven by incessant innovation and expansion into new markets. Today, the company is present on four continents.

It could be argued that growth in new markets is not surprising. However, midsize hidden champions even grow in markets that are considered mature and unlikely to produce growth. The three companies in Fig 2.4 impressively illustrate the growth in such mature markets.

Fig. 2.4: Growth even in mature markets

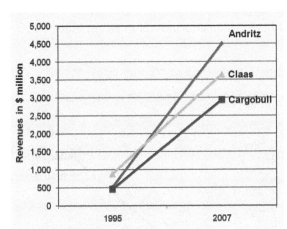

Hidden champion Andritz's main business is mechanical engineering for the paper industry, not considered a growth market. Cargobull produces semitrailers and has advanced to become market leader despite only modest growth in the overall market and stiff competition in recent years. Claas, a classic manufacturer of agricultural machinery, also operates in a market with very tough competition and mostly stagnating or cyclical demand. In spite of such relatively unfavorable conditions, these three hidden champions have achieved fast growth and have improved their profitability.

Claas chose the external growth route and acquired the tractor business from French car maker Renault. Cargobull focused radically on very few products, which led to a huge increase in productivity and competitiveness in all spheres. In spite of a significant and long-term price decline, the company succeeded in increasing its revenues to $2.9 billion from $500 million in the mid-1990s.

Andritz strategically repositioned itself at the end of the 1980s and has since then primarily grown through acquisitions. These included many complementary takeovers, such as refiner disks (Durametal Corporation, USA); equipment for wood processing (Kone Wood, Finland); animal fodder production facilities (Jesma-Matador A/S, Denmark); and cold rolling lines and treatment facilities (Sundwiger, Germany).

Growing Dwarves

If we proceed further down the size categories, we find innumerable "dwarves" that have grown enormously in recent years. Fig. 2.5 offers three cases.

Fig. 2.5: Growth of selected small hidden champions

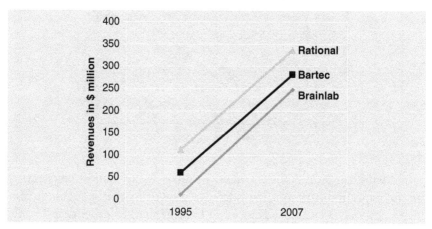

Bartec is the European market leader for explosion protection equipment. The enterprise was founded in 1975. Bartec has more than quintrupled its revenues since 1995. Ten years ago Bartec had 450 employees; today this figure exceeds 1,300—a shining example of job creation. Bartec's future growth markets are in Asia, and particularly in China, with the company's explicit aim to advance "from number one in Europe to number one in the world."

Brainlab develops and markets computer-controlled medical technology. The company was founded in 1989. In the sphere of computer-controlled surgery systems, Brainlab is one of the market leaders, having installed 3,000 systems in more than 65 countries. Worldwide sales are conducted through 15 offices in Europe, Asia, North and South America, as well as through distributors in 70 countries. Brainlab has more than 950 employees worldwide. Today, Brainlab is the global world market leader for image-supported navigation systems in operating theaters. According to CEO Stefan Vilsmeier, "no competitor can compete with us across the entire range."

Growth Is Not a Wonder Drug

As shown by our numerous case studies and the growth rates achieved, the typical hidden champions follow the mantra: grow or die. Reinhold Würth's statement about a tree that starts to die when growth stops illustrates this dictate of continually increasing in size. However, there are companies among the hidden champions that deliberately do not grow, refusing to submit to the growth imperative and preferring instead to remain small. Typically, such enterprises are characterized by craftsmanship and/or operate in small, limited niche markets that display low growth or high market volatility. The pattern is similar to that of a classic master craftsman, who works throughout his life with a more or less constant number of journeymen and apprentices and is successful. Considerations of risk contribute to this self restriction. In particular, we have found companies that choose not to grow in markets that have strong cyclical demand.

An example of this kind of company is Klais, the organ builders described in Chapter 1. In response to my question about the number of employees over the last ten years, I received the answer, "We have the same number of employees as we did 100 years ago." The enterprise was founded in 1882 and—apart from negligible fluctuations—has always had 65 employees. An important reason for this is that the value chain comprises ten individual workshops that must each have a minimum size. In addition, approximately a quarter of the workforce is always busy somewhere in the world, installing or servicing organs in teams that have a minimum number of employees. These circumstances define the minimum size of the workforce. Conversely, the strongly cyclical nature of the demand for world-class organs prevents the management from increasing the workforce in order to seize short-term opportunities. Continued employment could not be guaranteed at the onset of the next slump in demand, which would threaten the company's existence. In addition, because highly specialized employees are required (and are not readily available on the labor market, at least not at short notice), Klais has to train these specialists itself. The training process requires continuous, stable employment. Increased outsourcing is considered as a modern alternative, but implementation proves difficult. The firm has survived on this strategy for over 125 years. Growth is not automatic and is not always the best way. Klais' decision not to grow has not prevented the firm's globalization, as noted in Chapter 1.

Employee Growth Versus Revenue Growth

If we take the number of employees as the yardstick for growth, we will find a series of companies without any increase in employment figures over recent years, although the revenues have increased. This development is not only the result of increases in productivity but also of fundamental restructuring. In particular, this pattern is evident in industrial engineering and in the construction of plants. The hidden champion Achenbach Buschhütten was founded in 1452. Three quarters of all aluminum rolling mills in the world come from this company. This achievement is possible with just 300 employees, a number that has declined over the last 13 years. In spite of this, revenues rose to $140 million from $70 million. CEO Axel E. Barten explains the reasons, "We have transformed ourselves from an industrial enterprise into an engineering service business. We have handed the physical manufacturing of parts over to others. Now, only the pre-assembly takes place in our plant. Most of our employees are engineers and no longer production workers. For this reason, our employee numbers have fallen significantly over the long term when compared with the peak figure of more than 1,000 employees around 1960. At the time, we were an industrial enterprise, whereas we are now a provider of engineering services." Like most plant engineering companies, Achenbach Buschhütten operates in a cyclical market, so that the described self-restriction and the shifting of risk to suppliers constitute an intelligent strategy.

Drivers of Growth

The case studies of large, midsize, and small champions show that there is not one single or dominant driver of growth. However, globalization and innovation are the outstanding engines of growth, presumably in that order. As discussed previously, many of the fast-growing hidden champions operate in traditional markets and continue to grow, primarily by expanding regionally, through internationalization. We will investigate these growth strategies in more detail in Chapters 4, 5, and 7.

For other hidden champions, innovation is the primary engine of growth. Many of them have created their own markets and established themselves as the sustained market leader from the outset. Examples of this innovation are Brita for household water filters, Kärcher for high-pressure cleaners, SOS International for global rescue services, and Omicron for tunnel-grid microscopes. Innovation encompasses not only technical but also process innovations (e.g., sales). Numerous hidden champions have based their growth on such process innovations. Würth, world market leader in direct trade with assembly and fastening products; Bofrost, Europe's market leader in direct selling of frozen food; and WIV Wein International, the world's largest direct marketer of wine, all fit this pattern. Marketing innovations are also important in this context. Hipp's consistent organic image successfully contributes to helping it achieve supremacy in the baby and children's food market. This is not a superficial marketing gag but a true reflection of the deep and religious convictions of Claus Hipp, who has managed the company since 1968.

In contrast to the situation in the mid-1990s, diversification plays a considerable and increasingly important role as a driver of growth. It is the most dramatic change in the hidden champions' strategy at the start of the twenty-first century. For example, the broadening of the product range (takeover of Renault tractors) made a noticeable contribution to growth at Claas. However, genuine diversifications (new products—new customers) remain rare exceptions. Despite market share that is often already high, further development of the respective market position and the desire to increase market share retain their importance as engines of growth. Therefore, it is astonishing that most hidden champions have further increased their market share and improved their market leadership position. In the next section, we will discuss this aspect, which is important not only for the growth but also for the hidden champions' self-image.

What are the central messages from our analysis of the hidden champions' growth? Clearly, most of these little-known market leaders are growing fast. It is also surprising that the growth rates are similar across all size categories. We do not see any "growth boundaries" in the twenty-first century, even for larger midsize enterprises. This should encourage other midsize firms to set ambitious—or more ambitious—growth targets for themselves, even if they are not (yet) a hidden champion. Employees are strongly inspired by ambitious growth-oriented goals and visions. They prefer that their company grows rather than shrinks. Growth requires leaders with the courage to embrace visionary goals. It also requires the energy to achieve these goals. The growth successes discussed were only possible due to enormous commitment of all participants over many years, managers and employees alike. Lack of commitment and stamina, not of market opportunities, are the real factors limiting growth in affluent societies and in many companies.

We have also seen that growth is not a panacea in every case. Some hidden champions who deliberately limit their growth have a strong capacity for survival. Astonishingly, this does not have a negative effect on their globalization. Such exceptions show that each enterprise must choose its strategy with care. A uniform growth formula applicable to each and every one does not exist.

Market Leadership

For many hidden champions, market leadership is not just one goal among many, but an identifying characteristic. One hidden champion CEO told me, "The identity of our enterprise is defined by our leading position on the world market." RUD, the world market leader for industrial chains, claims "the clear leading position in the market segments we cover." Gelita, world market leader in gelatines, self-confidently states, "We are the leading edge in the gelatine market." 3B Scientific, the world market leader for anatomical teaching aids, says, "We want to become and remain the worldwide number one." The simple governing principle of Wacker, world market leader in silicone, is "We want to be first." A statement by Dräger, world market leader in anesthetic and respiratory protection equipment, documents a similar expectation, "Pole position: we want to remain at the top! We have always aimed for and occupied top positions. This applies to both technology and marketing leadership." Trumpf, the world market leader in industrial lasers, aims to "lead by world standards in each of our work areas, both technically and organizationally." Zimmer, American world market leader in orthopedic products, formulates its ambitions as follows: "Passion to be the best. To be the global leader in enhanced quality of life for orthopedic patients." Phoenix Contact, the world market leader in electronic interface technology, stakes a similarly ambitious claim, "Phoenix Contact achieves worldwide technological leadership in each of its business spheres." Chemetall says, "Our goal is the worldwide technological and marketing leadership in profitable niches of the specialty chemicals market." Chemetall is the global number one for cesium, lithium, and other special chemicals and metals. Even a young company like Brainlab stakes its claim to market leadership, "Brainlab intends to become the leading provider of software for minimally invasive therapies as well as for cancer."

Some companies use their world market leadership as an advertising message. For example, Wanzl, the worldwide leader for shopping carts, says, "The size of a world market leader creates security." Being the biggest, the first or the best has always been an effective advertising message.[7] Many hidden champions leave no doubt at all about their goal of maintaining or defending their leading market position. The head of a world market leader in the textiles machinery sphere states, "We want to keep our world market share at 70% or above. One of our rules was always that our profit should be higher than the revenue of our closest competitor." Ernst Tanner, group CEO of the Swiss chocolate manufacturer Lindt & Sprüngli, announced, "We have strengthened our position as a chocolate manufacturer of the highest quality across the world in all markets."

True ambitions start early. Even young, small companies do not shy away from announcing their claim to world market leadership. Niels Stolberg, founder and CEO of the heavy-duty shipping company Beluga Shipping, has guided his company to the number three spot on the world market since founding the company ten years ago. However, this does not satisfy his ambition. "We will reach for the top," he announced recently. He plans to increase his current fleet of 40 heavy lift vessels by an additional 26 ships. This means that Beluga Shipping would expand to become the clear number one on the world market for heavy duty transporters. Bard, one of the pioneers in off-shore wind parks, was founded in 2003 and has only 400 employees. The company is currently building a park with 80 wind towers 100 miles off the North Sea coast. Despite its young age and small size, Bard is determined to become one of the global market leaders in the new field of off-shore wind power generation.[8]

Anton Milner is also not shy of challenging global Goliaths for the top positions. Milner is CEO of the hidden champion Q-Cells, a photovoltaic company. The company, which went public in the fall of 2005, was at the time market leader in Europe, but only number five worldwide. Milner had set his sights on Q-Cells fast becoming one of the top three companies worldwide. It is worth noting who were the previous top three. Milner said, "The industry leader is Sharp. Kyocera is number two and BP/Solar is number three. We want to catch up with them."[9] Strengthened by the new capital in October 2005, Q-Cells has achieved this goal: in 2006, it became the world's second largest manufacturer of solar cells, thereby shortening Sharp's lead. In 2005, Q-Cells achieved revenues of $410 million and increased this to $740 million one year later in 2006. It even managed to generate $1.2 billion in 2007. Today, the company says it is the world's largest manufacturer of solar cells. Revenues are expected to increase 35% in each of the coming years.

We find similar statements expressing the goal of, or the claim to, market leadership with many other hidden champions. The overwhelming majority of today's hidden champions were already driven by such market leadership goals at an early stage. Naturally, such courageous visions are sometimes coined from hindsight. It is also certain that not all market leadership goals and visions propagated by ambitious entrepreneurs are fulfilled. The future will show which of the specified number one goals will actually be achieved. Many have failed in spite of their ambitions and many will fail in the future. Conversely, we can see that the early formulation and the examples of ambitious market leadership targets are effective driving forces towards their realization.

Peter Drucker impressively described the ultimate purpose of such targets, "Every enterprise requires simple, clear, and unifying objectives. Its mission has to be clear enough and big enough to provide a common vision. The goals that embody it have to be clear, public and often reaffirmed. We hear a great deal of talk these days about the 'culture' of an organization. But what we really mean by this is the commitment throughout an enterprise to some common objectives and common values. Management's job is to think through, set, and exemplify those objectives, values and goals."[10] This statement clarifies that the goals and visions can never be seen in isolation from the enterprise and the entrepreneur. They must fit with the history, culture, and identity of the respective entrepreneur and the company.

In addition to creating a common purpose shared by everyone, the most important effect of goals and visions is the activation of motivation and energy. Visions that employees can identify with and be energized by are required. They impart a sense of purpose to the work. The entire enterprise is carried along on a wave. The French writer Antoine de Saint-Exupéry described this, "If you want to build a ship, then do not gather men to find wood, award commissions and distribute work, but teach them to yearn for the wide, endless sea." Employees want a vision. A good vision grows out of a delicate balance between a sense of reality and utopia. It must not be so utopian that the employees do not believe in it, but should be utopian enough to pose a real challenge and mobilize energy. Vision involves what is only just possible!

The market leadership goals and visions discussed above are highly effective with regard to motivation and the mobilization of energy—perhaps even more effective than growth targets. Employees are happy to identify with visions that aim at being the best, the first, the friendliest or the fastest. Nobody wants to be average. Targets like catching up with or overtaking a competitor are very effective leadership tools. Nothing motivates more than a fight against a powerful opponent. For years, Pepsi-Cola was obsessed by the idea of defeating Coca-Cola. AVIS made the goal of beating market leader Hertz its corporate slogan "We try harder." The challenge of catching up with archrival Mercedes-Benz inspired BMW and Audi for decades. Cargobull and its strongest competitor, Krone, are located in close proximity and drive each other to maximum performance. Although Krone is only half the size of Cargobull, it has succeeded in growing at similar rates and—like Cargobull—has increased its market share at the expense of other competitors. The intense competition between competitors who are geographically close to each other is an extremely effective driving force.

Should visions like market leadership be formulated in qualitative or quantitative terms? Principally, goals and visions should not be too general or vague. Where systems of values, superior performance, quality, technological supremacy, and so forth, are concerned, qualitative statements are preferable. Goals involving growth, market share or return on investment, however, require quantitative precision to prevent a lack of commitment. The statement "We want to grow profitably" is not only less precise, but also less likely to result in binding commitment than the following statement: "We want to double our revenue every five years and achieve a return on equity of at least 25%." Reinhold Würth always formulated his goals for the next five or ten years in concrete numbers. The hidden champions tend to include both qualitative and quantitative elements in their goals. As we will see, their understanding of market leadership is not restricted to having the largest market share or the largest volume.

To conclude this part, we want to discuss the question of how early and how explicitly such market leadership goals should be formulated. In my discussions, many leaders of hidden champions said they started out with ambitious ideas from the very beginning. This may or may not be true. Doubts appear justified. It is difficult to find the truth in such cases, and I restrict myself to relating a story I personally experienced and influenced.

As with all autobiographical writing, the reader should be warned that the described incidents might be portrayed in too positive a light. In this case, occurrences from more than 20 years ago are viewed from the perspective of 2008. Simon-Kucher & Partners is today assessed by neutral third parties to be the world market leader in price consulting.[11] With revenues of close to $150 million and almost 500 employees in 2008, we are a small hidden champion. Did we aim for market leadership (or world market leadership) in price consulting when we were founded in 1985? The answer is no. Even ten years later this had not changed. Until 1996, our only office was in Bonn. Eleven years after the firm was founded we started expanding beyond Germany's borders and took the risky step of opening our second office in the USA. At this stage, the ambition to succeed in the largest and toughest consulting market in the world clearly played a key role. Otherwise, we would have opened our second office in Zurich or Vienna (i.e., in German-speaking, "easy" markets). From today's point of view, it is evident that certain roots and foundations for globalization and the current market leadership were laid early, although we only became aware of this later. All my former assistants, who are today partners at Simon-Kucher & Partners, and I had worked at top American universities. We knew the capabilities of the Americans as well as our own. Initial reserve about working abroad had been overcome. In 1996, we generated revenues of $12.6 million, less than one tenth of our current revenue. For the first time, we then explicitly formulated a vision and quantitative growth target for the next decade. We were determined to grow at a rate of 25% per year, which means doubling in size every three years. In 2008, we achieved revenues of close to $150 million, representing an annual growth rate of 21% over ten years. While this did not fully meet the target of 25%, it was not far from it.

In the words of Mintzberg, this represents an "emergent strategy," which is characteristic of many hidden champions.[12] Mintzberg talks about conduct that "crystallizes in a series of decisions." The strategy develops through a process in which the results of many individual actions flow into each other in sequential order. My knowledge of numerous hidden champions suggests that the "emergent strategy" is the predominant development pattern for these enterprises. It is in any case an accurate description of our own development.

Mintzberg defines a further strategy variant that he calls "entrepreneurial strategy." He describes it as follows: "An individual who personally controls an organization is in a position to transfer his vision completely to the enterprise. Such strategies are often found in newly founded or small enterprises. The vision supplies a general direction that leaves room for adaptation. As the planner is at the same time the implementer, this person can react swiftly to the results of actions as and when they arise, or in response to new opportunities or threats from outside. The entrepreneurial strategy leaves room for flexibility—at the expense of a precise description of the goals."

This strategy is less typical for the hidden champions than one might expect. An enterprise does not become world market leader by frequently changing directions. Some young and/or small enterprises in our investigation are exceptions to this. They create new markets, endeavor to better understand the needs of their customers and the opportunities offered, and have to be very flexible until they have found their long-term goal and their direction. The firm Weckerle is an example. It was founded in the 1970s and specialized in lipstick machines. Weckerle is currently number one in the world in this field. However, this market only offers limited potential. For this reason, founder Peter Weckerle sought out further growth opportunities at an early stage and started producing lipsticks for large corporations. Yet this too is a limited business, because the large cosmetic companies outsource only part of their production. Weckerle next established his own brands and distributed them through special channels. Today, revenues from the sale of machines and from the manufacture and sale of lipsticks are roughly equal. However, there is greater future growth potential in the production and sale of lipsticks. Different roads may lead to Rome and as shown, different routes to market leadership.

What Is Market Leadership?

Market leadership is normally defined by market share: the provider with the largest market share is the market leader. Yet even this simple definition is ambiguous, because it does not clarify whether we mean market share in terms of volume or value. There are valid arguments for both variants. In practice, there is often no precise distinction as to what is meant by market share or market leadership. Confusion abounds.

The hidden champions have a differentiated and comprehensive understanding of the concept of market leadership. They are clearly concerned with what "leading" a market means and how they define their leadership position. In response to the question "Why do you see yourself as market leader?" 75.8% answered that they were the provider with the largest revenues, and 42.5% answered that they sold the largest volume (the sum may be greater than 100 because an enterprise can be a leader under both criteria). The difference in the percentages is an indication that the value-related and not the volume-related domination of the market is more relevant.

A closer look at the implications of market leadership reveals interesting differentiations. Fig. 2.6 shows the attributes in which the hidden champions view themselves as market leaders.

Fig. 2.6: What constitutes market leadership?

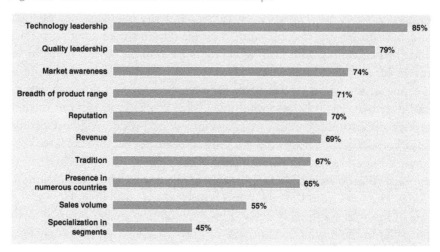

This list reveals that the hidden champions do not confine their view of market leadership to market share but take into consideration the content and causes behind it. They see themselves primarily as technology and quality leaders. In a study by one of the leading technology institutes, the same characteristics, i.e., "Innovation/Technology" and "Quality", top the list.[13] The highly rated attributes of market awareness, reputation, and tradition indicate that market leadership is based on long-term supremacy. In comparison, revenues and volume are only of average importance.

In this context it is revealing that the hidden champions have been market leaders in their respective fields for an average of 21.6 years—a very long time. The average CEO tenure in these companies amounts to 20 years—an interesting parallel.

In summary, market leadership is more than just the largest market share. Market leadership has to do with leadership in its true meaning. One of the CEOs I interviewed used the phrase "psychological market leadership." Siltronic, world market leader for wafers made of pure silicone, says, "We lead by anticipating our customers' expectations." Sick, one of the world market leaders in sensor technology, states, "Leadership means becoming the yardstick for others. This applies both to leaders who can inspire teams and to companies that set standards on the world market." Many hidden champions report that they define the standards in their sector. RUD, the world market leader in industrial chains, clearly says, "We set the new technological standards." Oerlikon, a leading high-tech industrial group in vacuum and engine technology, makes the following comments: "We set the standard for innovation and technologies." Standard-setters also include Otto Bock in orthopedic technology, Semikron in diodes/thyristors, Eppendorf in systems for biotechnology, Hauni in tobacco processing, and many more. Stabilus, the world market leader for gas-pressured springs, changed an important symbol. Within a year, the competitors throughout the world had also switched to the new symbol. I often heard that competitors liked to use the following sales argument "We are as good as ...", possibly with the addition "... but somewhat cheaper." If competitors refer to another company in this way, it is a sure sign that this company has taken over the leadership in a market. Many hidden champions lead their markets in this comprehensive sense—worldwide.

Market Shares

Until now, we have discussed market leadership without revealing the specific market shares of the hidden champions. Fig. 2.7 unveils the secret for the global and the European market.

Fig. 2.7: Market shares of the hidden champions

	Market Leaders	Absolute market share		Relative market share	
		ten years ago	today	ten years ago	today
World	65.9%	30.2%	33.0%	1.56	2.34
Europe	78.3%	36.7%	38.4%	1.76	2.84

The column "Market Leaders" shows that around two thirds are market leaders on the world market and more than three quarters are market leaders in Europe. Fig. 2.7 contains "absolute" and "relative" market shares.

The absolute market share corresponds to the percentage of the entire market. The relative market share is the firm's own market share divided by the market share of its strongest competitor. Thus, if you have a market share of 32% and your strongest competitor has a market share of 20%, your relative market share is $32/20 = 1.60$. Only the market leader has a relative market share higher than 1. For all other competitors, this number is below 1. In the example, the relative market share of your strongest competitors would be $20/32 = 0.625$.

The hidden champions' average absolute market share is 33.0% for the world market and 38.4% for Europe. It is astonishing that both figures have increased over the last ten years. Given the rapid progress of globalization and the associated expansion of markets, this was not expected. The picture is even more surprising when it comes to relative market shares, which reflect how the hidden champions have developed in relation to their strongest competitor. The strong supremacy of ten years ago has increased further. Even on the world market, the average relative market share is now about 2.34, up from 1.56 ten years ago. The hidden champions today are more than twice as large as their strongest competitors. This is simply unbelievable! In Europe, the market position in relation to the strongest competitor is even better, with a relative market share of 2.84.

The hidden champions have not only been successful in an expanding world market, but have actually left their competitors far behind. They have increased both their absolute market shares and their lead over their strongest competitors. Their superior competitive strength has improved significantly over the last ten years. The hidden champions have proven that they need not fear their competitors throughout the world. The reverse is true. The competitors should fear the hidden champions.

Market Share and Profitability

The hypothesis that a large market share leads to higher profitability has dominated the discussion in management theory and practice since the start of the 1970s. This is presumably one of the biggest management misunderstandings of our time. For decades, managers have been told by their superiors, colleagues, professors, consultants and other experts that the achievement and maintenance of the largest achievable market share is the answer to everything. In 2006, two younger partners in our firm and I took a decided stand against this misconception in a book entitled *Manage for Profit, Not for Market Share.*[14] Is this title a contradiction? How can the position "not for market share" be brought into line with my praise of market leadership in the current book?

There is no contradiction. In the first edition of *Hidden Champions*, I found no correlation between market share and return on equity.[15] This finding has now been confirmed. As regards the hidden champions of the twenty-first century the correlation between margin and market share is again not significant. This applies both to the absolute and the relative market share. Naturally, the objection can be raised that our sample involved only firms with high market shares and that the variance of the variables is small. At least for the relative market shares this is not true. They vary considerably.

I will refer very briefly here to the origins of the hypothesis "high market share leads to high profits" and the arguments against it. In *Manage for Profit, Not for Market Share* we explain in great detail why this theory tends to be misleading. I refer to this book for further information.[16] The best-known origin of the market share thinking is the PIMS Study, which revealed a strong correlation between market share and profit margin.[17] A second source is the experience curve. According to this concept the cost position depends on the relative market share: The larger the relative market share, the lower the unit costs when compared to the competition, and consequently the higher the margin. The famous matrix of the Boston Consulting Group with the two dimensions "market growth" and "relative market share" also propagates driving up the relative market share. The last and particularly influential propagator is Jack Welch, who after becoming CEO of General Electric announced in 1982 that his company would withdraw from markets where it could not become number one or number two in the world.

Recently, belief in the magic of market share has increasingly been questioned and in part refuted.[18] Interestingly, even older sources with a similar argumentation can be found. The core question is whether the connection is pure correlation or a genuine causal relationship. I deliberately express my thoughts on this in a simplified way in order to get to the heart of the problem and the hidden champions. Market share and market leadership are not decisive as such. The relevant issue is whether the market share and market leadership are "good" or "bad." "Good" market shares are "earned" by innovation, superior performance, excellent service, and so forth. Under these circumstances market leadership is not attained by price reductions that ruin margins, but in a way that is supportive of prices and margins, or even increases margins, by providing added value to the customer. "Bad" market shares are achieved through price reductions and aggressive promotions to drive up volume without correspondingly lower costs—this condition is decisive. "Bad" market shares are not earned in the long term, but obtained quickly in the short term by unsustainable price concessions. They lead to low profits and frequently losses because the costs are too high when compared with the prices offered (or conversely: the prices are too low in relation to the costs). In many modern markets, we find "bad" market shares. A striking example is the American automotive market, where the domestic car manufacturers have reached the brink of bankruptcy in spite of high market shares and market leadership in numerous segments. We see similarly catastrophic consequences of market share obsession among airlines, in retail, consumer electronics, tourism, and many other sectors. It should be clear that the price level as such does not define a "bad" market share. If, despite very low prices, sufficient margins can be realized, these are "good" market shares. Southwest Airlines, Wal-Mart, IKEA, and other discounters have high market shares and low prices and still earn excellent profits because the costs are extremely low and the margins are right. Yet General Motors, Ford, Sony and similar companies fail to earn money in spite of high market shares, because they engage in aggressive price wars that do not yield sufficient margins due to the high costs involved.

How do the hidden champions fit into this picture? With few exceptions, the hidden champions do not gain their market shares with low or aggressive prices, but with superior performance. They "earn" their market leadership by being the best in technology, innovation, quality, reputation, and so forth. In most cases, their superior performance permits them to charge significantly higher prices. In my experience and as a result of many conversations, I estimate that the typical price premium of a hidden champion versus the market average is 10%–15%, sometimes even higher. Even in cases with high price pressure (e.g., large-scale projects, large customers), hidden champions can maintain price premiums between 5% and 10%. Almost always, the market shares of the hidden champions are "good" market shares with healthy margins. The hidden champions are not only market leaders, but also charge the highest prices. As described above, the result is a satisfactory profit. The key to this success is not the size of the market shares as such, but whether the market shares are "good" or "bad."

The hidden champions "earn" their market leadership and market share positions through performance and not through price aggression. For this reason—and not because of a magical correlation—they have "good" market shares with high values. The market share mania observed in many other markets, in which "bad" market shares are acquired or defended regardless of profit, is atypical for the hidden champions. Their claim to market leadership is based on performance and a solid foundation and, thus, consistent with the aim of generating profit.

If we consider growth and market position together, the picture in Fig. 2.8 emerges. It illustrates the extremely positive development of the hidden champions in the past ten years vis-à-vis market leadership and growth. They have considerably increased their revenues, have grown faster than in the preceding period, and have significantly improved their dominant market position in relation to their strongest competitors.

Fig. 2.8: Ten-year comparison of growth and market position at a glance

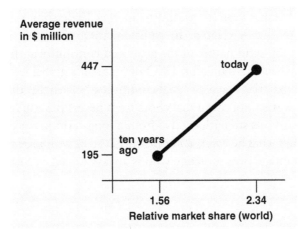

Long-Term Goals

One of the most controversial discussions in management theory relates to the time horizon of goals. One extreme is the fixation of many public companies on quarterly results. The hidden champions are at the other end of the scale. Alfred T. Ritter, head of Ritter Sport chocolate manufacturers, expresses this in a way representative of many others, "We do not think in years, but rather in generations." Dr. Karsten Ottenberg, CEO of Giesecke & Devrient, a global leader in security papers, made a similar statement, "We don't think about producing good figures in the next quarter. We are more concerned with sustainability over generations." O.C. Tanner, world leader in employee recognition programs, eschews short-term thinking and the "making the numbers" mentality that public companies face. Before his death, the former CEO, Obert C. Tanner, placed the company in a trust. As the president of O.C. Tanner, Dave Petersen, explains, this left senior management with two options, "We either operate the company well and profitably for the benefit of our associates, our clients, and our community, or we fail and go out of business. There is no other option. We can't think short term." Hermut Kormann, CEO of Voith, world market leader for water turbines, asks himself how the company will survive the next 100 years. This is the horizon in which Voith operates. It is clear that long-term thinking is easier to find in family enterprises than among investors seeking quick profits.

The long-term nature of the goals must be viewed in context. Building up a global market presence is a process that normally requires several generations. It takes years to ascend to market leadership, unless a completely new market is created. In addition, there is a close relationship between the long-term nature of the goals and continuity at the top of the company. Michael Schwarzkopf, CEO of Plansee, a global leader in high-performance materials, talks of "goal continuity." Naturally, the long-term nature of goals does not mean that short-term necessities can be neglected. However, enormous strengths derive from a long-term perspective. Someone who knows what he wants and pursues his goals with incessant stamina has a big advantage over someone who is always forced to focus on short-term results.

Summary

In this chapter, it has become clear that goals and their consistent implementation play a central role in the strategy and development of the hidden champions. The following aspects should be kept in mind:

- Growth and market leadership are the dominant goals of the hidden champions.
- These goals are often extremely ambitious and are formulated early.
- Entrepreneurial flexibility is not sacrificed in the pursuance of these goals.
- In the last ten years, the revenues generated by the hidden champions have more than doubled, with growth rates surprisingly similar across companies of different sizes.

- In this way, numerous midsize firms have become "revenue-billionaires," (i.e., their revenues exceed $1 billion).
- The claim to market leadership is not confined to market share but includes performance attributes such as technology, innovation, quality, and reputation. Market leadership is more than just market share.
- Absolute market shares have increased in comparison over the last ten years, which is astonishing in view of fast-growing world markets. In addition, even the relative market shares increased strongly, and the hidden champions have become significantly more competitive in their respective markets.
- The hidden champions earn their market shares by superior performance and not through aggressive pricing. These "good" market shares are fully consistent with the profit target.
- Communication of the goals is generally clear and unequivocal. Strategy implementation is characterized by persistence. The will to be or become number one never ends.
- The goals are long-term and extend over generations rather than quarters. Long-term goals give a company great strength. However, short-term necessities must not be neglected.

The messages of this chapter are simple. Great successes always start with ambitious goals. The hidden champions of the twenty-first century pursue above all growth and market leadership goals. These goals provide a joint sense of direction and motivate employees. It is essential that the goals are effectively communicated and lived. The hidden champions have realized their visions in the last ten years with long-term orientation, persistence, and never-ending energy and in doing so have grown into new dimensions. They have improved their market positions relative to their strongest competitors. They teach us what is possible in the age of globalization. In this way, they can be shining examples for many other companies.

Notes

1 *VDI News*, March 2, 2007, p. 9.

2 The correlation coefficients are extremely low (with revenues 1995: -0.133; with revenues 2005: -0.041) and at the 10% level insignificant.

3 The 500 largest family-run enterprises have increased their employee numbers by 10% in Germany over the same period. See the study of the Bonn Institut für Mittelstandsforschung 2007, *Frankfurter Allgemeine Zeitung*, May 8, 2007, p. 12.

4 It is important to note that the statement in this sentence and the preceding sentence is not a contradiction, because "on average 4.3 times the size" contains no weighting.

5 This is the EUR1 billion threshold, the equivalent of $1.37 million.

6 *VDI-News*, September 5, 2008.

7 See Hermann Simon, *Goodwill und Marketingstrategie*, Wiesbaden: Gabler 1985.

8 *Frankfurter Allgemeine Zeitung*, September 4, 2008, p. 16.

9 *VDI News*, 23 September 2005.

10 Peter F. Drucker, "*Management and the World's Work*," *Harvard Business Review*, 66, September 1988, p. 76.

11 "Simon-Kucher is world leader in giving advice to companies on how to price their products." *Business Week*, January 26, 2004, "Simon-Kucher is the world's leading pricing consultancy." *The Economist*, 2005, "Simon-Kucher is the leading price consultancy in the world." Eric Mitchell, President Professional Pricing Society, 2003.

12 See Henry Mintzberg, *Die Strategische Planung: Aufstieg, Niedergang und Neubestimmung*, Munich-Vienna: Hanser 1995, and Henry Mintzberg and James A. Waters, "Of Strategies, Deliberate and Emergent," *Strategic Management Journal*, 1985, p. 257–272.

13 See Steffen Kinkel and Oliver Som, *Strukturen und Treiber des Innovationserfolges im deutschen Maschinenbau*, Karlsruhe: Fraunhofer-Institut für System- und Innovationsforschung ISI, No. 41, May 2007, p. 3.

14 Hermann Simon, Frank Bilstein, Frank Luby, *Manage for Profit, Not for Market Share: A Guide to Higher Profitability in Highly Contested Markets*, Boston: Harvard Business School Press 2006.

15 See Hermann Simon, *Hidden Champions*, Boston: Harvard Business School Press 1996, p. 25.

16 Hermann Simon, Frank Bilstein, Frank Luby, *Manage for Profit, Not for Market Share: A Guide to Higher Profitability in Highly Contested Markets*, Boston: Harvard Business School Press 2006, p. 8-13.

17 See Robert D. Buzzell and Bradley T. Gale, *The PIMS Principles: Linking Strategy to Performance*, New York: Free Press 1987.

18 See in particular the following reader: Paul W. Farris and Michael J. Moore (Eds.), *The Profit Impact of Market Strategy: Restrospect and Prospects*, Cambridge (UK): Cambridge University Press 2003, and Richard Miniter, *The Myth of Market Share: Why Market Share Is the Fool's Gold of Business*, London: Crown 2002.

Chapter 3
Market and Focus

The selection and definition of a market are the starting point for strategic planning. How do the hidden champions define their markets? How do they conduct their businesses in these markets? The hidden champions usually focus on narrow markets. Many of them do not feel restricted by customary market boundaries, but define their markets autonomously as part of their strategy. In doing so, hidden champions often achieve high market shares with sometimes monopolistic positions; thereby establishing effective barriers to entry. But high market shares in narrow markets can limit the opportunities for growth. Considering the hidden champions' ambitious growth targets, this is a serious problem. To cope with this dilemma they do not abandon their growth targets, but instead choose the route of "soft" diversification. This is the greatest shift in strategy in the last ten years. Nevertheless, the hidden champions endeavor to maintain their traditional strengths. One way to achieve this is through consistent decentralization.

Market Definition and Market Share

Until now, we have discussed "market share" and the market leadership of the hidden champions as if these terms were self-explanatory. However, "share" must always relate to a specific "market." Market size and market share do not exist in absolute, clear forms. Instead, the definition of a market determines its boundaries and size and, thus, the market share. This definition can cause great practical difficulties. It is possible for a company to define the market so narrowly that it automatically becomes

H. Simon, *Hidden Champions of the Twenty-First Century*,
DOI 10.1007/978-0-387-98147-5_3, © Hermann Simon 2009

market leader, or to choose a wide definition that results in a huge market but only a tiny market share. Let us consider Rolls Royce's market and market share. We could justifiably take the view that the market is defined solely by existing Rolls Royce buyers. The market share would then be 100%. This definition would be correct if there are no new customers and existing Rolls Royce buyers never consider buying a different automobile brand—an allegation certainly not true of all Rolls Royce buyers. Even the British Royal Family broke a 50-year Rolls Royce tradition and changed to Bentley after Rolls Royce was taken over by BMW.[1] Some of the hidden champions define their market in this sense and have a 100% market share. For example, Suwelack no longer has any competitors in the collagen market since the only competitor bowed out. If an alternative market definition for Rolls Royce included all automobiles that cost at least as much as the least expensive Rolls Royce (the Phantom model cost $350,000 plus VAT in 2007), the resultant market would be far larger and Rolls Royce's market share would drop to about 10%. If we define the market even more broadly by including cars like the Mercedes S-Class, Audi A8, BMW 7 Series or Maserati, as well as brands like Maybach and Bentley, the market is many times larger and Rolls Royce would have a market share below the 1% level. If we go yet a step further and consider the entire automobile market, the market size becomes immeasurable and Rolls Royce's market share melts to approximately 0.0001%. Such a wide market definition makes little sense for strategic considerations, because a Rolls Royce does not compete with a Chevrolet or a Toyota Corolla. Similar thought processes can be applied to almost any market.

In view of this complexity, arbitrariness and wishful thinking may easily have an influence on the definition of a relevant market by a company. As indicated in Chapter 1, we have to rely on the statements made by the hidden champions about their markets and market shares, because individual investigations of this issue would be impossible. Some hidden champions may be trying to delude themselves, their competitors and their customers, but such cases seem rare. In addition, competition is a very effective means of control. I received a letter from the CEO of a hidden champion that first attained world market leadership in 2005 and publicly announced this achievement, "This was followed by a competition suit filed by the former world market leader. Yet the facts exchanged within the course of the proceedings evidenced that we had generated considerably higher revenues than the competitor." Competitors do not tolerate simple assertions of world market leadership without proof.

Hidden champions often refuse to employ customary or traditional market definitions. Instead they define their markets in autonomous and innovative ways. Such idiosyncratic market definitions can affect the value chain, the choice of segments, the product portfolio, and may lead to decisive differences in strategy. "Defining the business—or the market," in Derek Abell's[2] words, is not just the starting point, it is the core of strategy.

Narrow Markets

The classic hidden champion is a one-product, one-market company. One of our most important findings in our first study ten years ago was the hidden champions' narrow definition of markets. This results in markets being relatively small. For the world market, we calculated an average market size of $489 million at the time.[3] Today's figure of $1,096 million is 2.2 times higher. Over the past ten years, the typical world market size has changed to a similar extent as have the revenues of the hidden champions.

Fig. 3.1 shows the distribution of the size of the world markets. Roughly a quarter of the companies (exactly 26.0%) operate in markets with a volume of less than $400 million (i.e., specialized niche markets). By contrast, almost one fifth (exactly 19.8%) operate in markets larger than $4 billion. Even this size is relatively small when compared with very large markets

Fig 3.1: Size of the world markets of the hidden champions

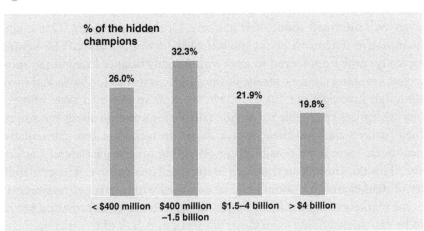

like the automotive or telecommunications markets. Unsurprisingly, hidden champions tend to operate in small markets. For the smaller firms this is true without exception, but it also applies to a large extent to the bigger hidden champions.

When compared to the 1990s, it is remarkable how dramatically the proportion of small markets has declined. Then, almost 50% of the world markets in which the hidden champions operated were less than $400 million, whereas this only applies to 26% today. Almost 80% of respondents said that their markets have grown, and 42.1% even assessed the growth in their markets as extremely strong. However, 9% report a stagnation of their markets and 12% say that the market size today is smaller than ten years ago. A differentiated view is therefore necessary. In spite of the strong overall growth of the world markets—and regardless of China, India, and so forth—there are shrinking segments among the hidden champions' markets, as in any dynamic economy.

During in-depth discussions, we repeatedly found that the definition of market boundaries and the assessment of market sizes are unusually difficult. This can be illustrated by our own experience. Does Simon-Kucher, as the world's leading price consultancy, know the size of the market for price consultancy in the world? Of course not, and nobody else does either. Such strong fragmentation is typical for the hidden champions' markets. It is not unusual for a hidden champion to compete in individual segments with companies who in turn are market leaders in their respective special fields or niches. We will see that the definition of the markets is not one-dimensional but multidimensional. It is our impression that firms try to define their markets adequately. Nevertheless, the assessment of the size of a market remains full of uncertainties.

In spite of these circumstances, the hidden champions are comparatively well informed about their markets. Of the respondents, 72% made quantitative statements about the size of their world market. The figures typically come from several sources with roughly balanced weighting: subjective estimates account for 46%, third party statistics for 54%, and own thorough investigations for 61%. However, as in our own case, numerous enterprises are unable to provide reliable information about the size of their markets and thus their market shares. In many markets, particularly new ones, there is no possibility of obtaining precise data about market size. This does not mean that such markets are unattractive. The availability of market statistics should not be confused with market attractiveness. Some markets that are difficult to pin down in terms of information prove to be extremely attractive on closer inspection. A lack of transparency can have its advantages. Albert Blum, founder of ABS Pumps, once told me, "If you don't know the size of your market and your market share, you need not fear the Japanese." I will not attempt to answer as to whether this statement also applies to the Chinese. However, my impression is that, in contrast to the Japanese, the Chinese also venture into markets for which they cannot obtain reliable statistics.

Closeness to the market and to customers is an effective way to overcome gaps in objective and quantitative market information. This closeness is one of the hidden champions' greatest strengths. It helps them to accurately and timely recognize trends in the market and to adapt to them, even without sophisticated statistics.

How Hidden Champions Define Their Markets

There are numerous ways to define a market or a business. The oldest version is based on the product: "We operate in the market for dishwashers." This product-oriented definition was heavily criticized by Theodore Levitt in the groundbreaking article *Marketing Myopia* in 1960.[4] Levitt's criticism of the American railroad companies has become famous. According to Levitt, their definition of their market as "railroads" and not "passenger transport" meant that they overlooked the emerging competition from airlines. He argued that the airlines ultimately squeezed the railroads out of the market and drove them into bankruptcy, because they were competing in the same market, namely passenger transport. If the market definition had been adequate, the railroad companies would have launched into air travel or built high-speed railroads at the time. A historical footnote to the story was that the first legislation on airlines in the USA was contained in the Railroad Act of 1934.

The market definition demanded by Levitt is based on customer needs or application. "We make clean dishes our business" would be a needs-oriented definition for a dishwasher manufacturer. In addition, markets can be determined by reference to customer or target groups. Staying with our example, this would be: "We supply hotels and restaurants with dishwashing systems." For example, the CEO of Brother, Seiichi Hirata, made the following precise market definition according to target group, "Our main target group is the segment of small offices, home offices and small and midsize companies. We know this business very well and focus on it.

Our competitors cover all segments. We don't."[5] Brother achieved market leadership with its office machines in this segment as a result of the narrow market definition.

Similar price or quality levels can also be used to define the relevant market: "We only offer systems in the price category starting at $15,000" or "We are only active in the top quality class." Not least, regional market definition has great significance in practice: "We serve the Japanese market."

Fig. 3.2 shows the importance of the criteria that the hidden champions apply in defining their markets.

Fig. 3.2: Importance of market definition criteria

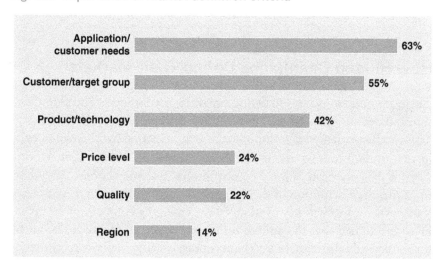

"Application/customer needs" comes first, at 63%. Ted Levitt would have liked this. A further customer-oriented criterion, "customer/target group," follows in second place. "Product/technology" also has considerable weight, with 42%. By contrast, "price level," "quality," and "region" play a lesser role as market definition criteria.

With their market definitions the hidden champions of the twenty-first century generally show a very modern understanding of the market. Customer needs and target groups clearly top the list. A large percentage includes product/technology and the core competencies behind them in their market definition. By contrast, regional market definition is of negligible significance to these global firms. The hidden champions have grown beyond the narrow boundaries of their regions of origin. They view the world as their market, not their country or region.

The sum of the percentages in Fig. 3.2 is greater than 1, namely 2.2. This shows that the hidden champions do not use one single criterion for the definition of their markets, but on average 2.2 criteria. Their market definition is not one-dimensional but multidimensional. Netstal, a leading worldwide manufacturer of plastic injection molding machines,[6] has specialized in the market for PET bottles (application), primarily with the beverage industry in mind (customer group), and sells only relatively expensive machines (price level) with corresponding premium performance (quality). In this case, all criteria apart from region are involved in the market definition. This example shows how fragmented a market can be and how a typical hidden champion defines its market in an active, targeted way in order to build a position of superiority. In a complex market like plastic injection molding machines, there is no place for "general" market leadership such as that of Microsoft in standard software for PCs. Heterogeneous, fragmented markets and a market leadership strategy require a differentiated definition of markets and their boundaries.

Focus, Focus, Focus

If we asked a hidden champion selected at random to state the key to its success, the most likely answer would be "We specialize in . . . ." I have encountered similar statements hundreds of times:

- "We concentrate on what we do best."
  The former CEO of Krupp, Gerhard Cromme, extended this phrase slightly, using it as Krupp's motto, "We concentrate on what we do best. Worldwide." Here we have evidence that even large corporations are willing to learn from the hidden champions. The link between focus and global orientation is key.
- "We supply a niche market." This statement is frequently used by the hidden champions, often supplemented by the addition of ". . . and plan to keep it that way."
- "We are deep, not broad." This means that a deep value chain is offered, but for a narrow, not a broad market. We will investigate this important facet of strategy in several case studies.
- "We stick to what we do," or "no diversification." This maxim continues to apply to most hidden champions. They haven't had the need to diversify or have withstood the temptation to do so. Yet we also find that

some larger hidden champions face growth restrictions in their narrow markets. Consequently, recent diversification attempts of different kinds can be observed.

Generally, focus and concentration remain dominant. Allegiance to the respective market and sphere of competence is normally very strong. As we have learned in Chapter 2, the hidden champions have been market leaders for an average of 21.6 years. Two thirds of the companies made their last significant decision about strategic direction at least five to ten years ago, and more than half of them made their last decision about basic technology more than a decade ago. The focus on one market sheds light on the high concentration and continuity of the hidden champions. They signal strong commitment to their customers, who in turn can depend on the hidden champion's reliability. "We always had one customer and will only have one customer in the future: the pharmaceutical industry," says Uhlmann, the world market leader for pharmaceutical packaging systems. This focus is expressed in a brief motto, "We only do one thing, but we do it right." Jake Burton, founder and chairman of Burton Snowboards from Burlington, Vermont, would certainly agree with this statement. He says, "Stick to your game. I saw how others who had made it in the ski industry were parlaying into golf. I swear I'd never go that route."[7]

Depth or Breadth

One aspect of market definition closely connected with focus relates to the breadth or depth of the product portfolio. Here, we look at the product range and/or the value chain. Breadth refers to the number of different products a company offers. Electrical appliances are an example. A product range encompassing dishwashers, washing machines, and refrigerators is broader than just dishwashers. A trailer manufacturer offering 50 models has a broader portfolio than one with only four models—like Cargobull. The concept of breadth can be transferred to markets. A company that sells dishwashers both to consumers and to commercial customers and also sells to various target segments within these groups has a broader field of operation than a firm that only supplies the market for hotels and restaurants.

By contrast, depth relates to the number of variants of the same product, the completeness of a problem solution, or the value chain covered. For example, a manufacturer of dishwashers can offer different models or extend its range to include consumables and services for dishwashers. The number of articles may well be similar for "broader" and "deeper" suppliers. However, the strategies behind these two options are fundamentally different.

Among the hidden champions, we predominantly see a deep value chain coupled with a narrow definition of the relevant market. A suitable case to illustrate this strategy is Winterhalter Gastronom, a manufacturer of commercial dishwashing systems. Winterhalter's strategy is illustrated in Fig. 3.3.

Fig. 3.3: Depth instead of breadth—Winterhalter Gastronom's strategy focuses on hotels and restaurants

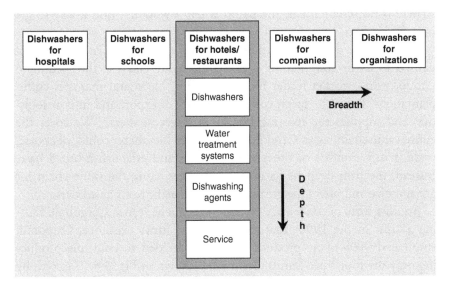

There are numerous submarkets for dishwasher systems; e.g., schools, hospitals, canteens, barracks, prisons, and finally hotels and restaurants. The market potential in this entire breadth is correspondingly large. However, customer requirements in the various market segments are very different. Years ago, Winterhalter commented: "We analyzed the entire market for commercial dishwashers and found that our world market share was well below 5%. We were an insignificant follower. This prompted us to completely realign our strategy. We tailored our services to serve hotels and restaurants exclusively. We even changed the company's name to Winterhalter Gastronom. We now define our business as 'providing services for clean glassware and chinaware in hotels and restaurants' and take full responsibility for this. We have extended our range to include water treatment systems and our own brand of dishwashing agents. We offer excellent, round-the-clock service. Our world market share in the hotels/restaurants segment is now 15%–20% and increasing. In this market segment, we are always first choice."

BHS Tabletop has chosen a similar focus to that of Winterhalter. When Hans Beckmann took over the management of BHS in 1995, the company was generating losses of $21 million. He made a radical cut and made the enterprise's least-known product line its core business. BHS Tabletop decided to focus exclusively on the high-quality catering industry worldwide, a strategic move that has made BHS the world market leader for hotel chinaware. As with Winterhalter, the entire strategy from product policy to sales concentrates solely on this segment. Beckmann sums up, "There is no restaurant in the world where I wouldn't find a way to get into the kitchen."

Idiosyncratic definition of markets requires creativity. One example of narrow focus in conjunction with a deep value chain is the Neumann Group, world market leader for green coffee. Neumann manages coffee plantations, treats the green coffee, takes care of export and import logistics, and supplies the roasting houses in target markets. "We cover the entire value chain," says CEO Peter Sielmann. Neumann could, of course, trade in any number of other raw materials and establish a broad base. Instead, the firm deepens its range of services along the value chain for green coffee and offers the greatest possible benefit to its customers.

Another form of concentration and focus can be seen at Cargobull. During a crisis in the 1990s that threatened the firm's existence, Cargobull eliminated 90% of its product range and decided to continue producing only the four basic semitrailer models shown in Fig. 3.4. "Growth by streamlining" was the catchphrase at the time.

The target was to sell at least 5,000 of each of these four basic models in Europe every year, a very high figure. In the ten years since, this focus resulted in massive improvements in all areas. Productivity has quadrupled; the quality is now premium, and sales have more than quintupled. Thanks to the brand's strength, Cargobull is in a position to insist that the customers tolerate the clearly visible brand name on the back of the semitrailer. Customers unwilling to accept this are not supplied. Although the prices dropped about 30% during this period, Cargobull was able to increase its margin to 7% from 2%. Fig. 2.4 showed the development in revenues to $2.9 billion today from about $450 million in the mid-1990s. In 2001, Cargobull became European market leader and today has a market share of 20%. The former market leader gave up and left the mar-

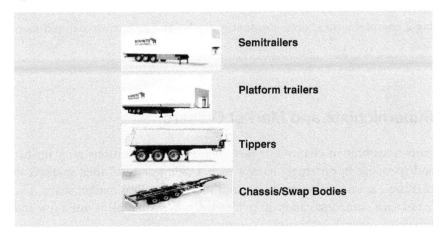

ket. The goals for the future are no less ambitious: the intention is to more than double capacity to 80,000 trailers in the near future from 36,400 trailers in 2006, and to increase the revenues to more than $4 billion. This vision is backed by a strategy of extreme focus and concentration. The case of Cargobull shows that focus occasionally results from a crisis.

The terms breadth and depth are often used in ambiguous ways. This can lead to confusion. We illustrate this with two cases. Brasseler offers the "world's largest, broadest and deepest program for rotating dental instruments" under its "Komet" brand. These drills are sold in more than 120 countries in the world. In our terminology, we would say that Brasseler is focused on dental drills, is therefore narrow and not broad, but that within this segment considerable depth is offered. The performance promise made by Plansee, the world market leader for high-performance powder metallurgy materials, sounds similar, "The product range offered by Plansee covers the entire temperature scale between 800 and 3,000 degrees Celsius—ideally suited to the mechanical, thermal and chemical uses by customers." Again, in our terminology Plansee is deep, not broad. We also find a wide variety in the product range offered by Bosch Rexroth, which says, "We have a very broad spectrum. In this way, we can offer all drive and control solutions." Bosch Rexroth is the world market leader in hydraulics, ahead of the US company Parker. In the hydraulics sphere, the firm actually offers everything its customers need, from hydraulic components for agricultural and building machinery to stationary hydraulics in industrial automation and hydraulic solutions for harbor gates, bridges, or stages (such as the Bolshoi Theater in Moscow). These examples are typical for the hidden champions. As with Brasseler with dental drills, Plansee with high-performance materials or Bosch Rexroth with hydraulic solutions,[8] they focus on offering a comprehensive, deep product range for their narrowly defined markets.

Supernichists and Market Owners

Numerous hidden champions take their market definitions even further and specialize in extremely narrow niches. Some "create" their markets so that there are no real competitors and they have 100% market share. The list of such companies adds up to hundreds. We will look at just a few and briefly examine them by way of example.

With its market share of over 90%, PWM has equipped virtually all German gas stations with electronic price display boards. PWM is number one in all other countries except the US, and the plan is to penetrate this market too. "We are the world market leader and the only global supplier," says CEO Max Ferdinand Krawinkel. And since we're on the subject: Hiby supplies all of the gas pump nozzles for German gas stations. This hidden champion is also the clear number one in Europe. The French world market leader in food and environmental analyses, Eurofins, has the reputation of being "such a strong market leader in Europe that competitors hardly have a chance."[9]

Polar-Mohr specializes exclusively in high-speed cutting systems for the paper industry. There are only six enterprises in the world in this market niche. Poly Clip generates $120 million in revenues from its clips for sausage skins and the required machines and is world market leader in this special area. Kugler-Womako is an expert for passport production lines. Koenig & Bauer produces 90% of all banknote printing machines in the world. Karl Marbach in Heilbronn is the world market leader in punching moulds for packaging materials. Kolbus concentrates exclusively on bookbinding machines and has a "very pleasing global market share well above 50%," reveals CEO Kai Büntemeyer. He sums up his strategy in few words, "We are small and focused." Robbe & Berking produces silver cutlery and has a world market share of 40%. Kässbohrer practically generates its entire revenues with one product, the PistenBully vehicle, and is the clear world market leader in this niche. The CEO, Gebhard Schwarz, emphasizes that the company cannot afford extensive product development. Focus really has the greatest relevance from the R&D perspective. Small companies are well advised to concentrate their limited development budgets. It is the only way to leadership in innovation and to world class.

Several years ago, Karl Mayer, the world market leader for warp knitting machines, said, "We only have competitors for 10% of our revenues." However, China may have changed this situation. The example shows that there is no protection of the status quo even for "market owners."

The "market owners" include many smaller hidden champions that manufacture products that are unknown to the layperson and occasionally appear exotic or bizarre. The Mitec Group presents itself as the world market leader for "mass compensation systems for noise reduction in combustion engines." The former screw manufacturer August Friedberg has removed standard screws from its portfolio and now leads the world market with a focus on "connecting technology used in the wind energy sector." In this area, characteristics such as utmost resistance, lasting stability capable of withstanding wind and weather, as well as standing up to tremendous force, are required—a far cry from traditional screws. Tente concentrates on casters for hospital beds and has become the world market leader in this segment. On a world scale, even a superniche like that can have an attractive volume. The Swedish firm Poc does not aim for the far larger market for protective motorcycle helmets, but has deliberately concentrated on the small segment of protective ski helmets. On the motorcycle helmet market, the company wouldn't stand a chance against strong market leaders like HJC from Korea, but Poc is set to become the global number one in protective ski helmets. Ismet Koyun says, "There is no competition for our technology in the world." His company Kobil Systems, founded in 1986, makes a hardware component that secures banking transactions. Rupp + Hubrach Optik concentrates on glasses for sports eyewear and is one of the world market leaders there. The hidden champions Nivarox (90% world market share for regulating parts in wristwatches) and Universo (world market leader for watch hands), which were mentioned in Chapter 1, are further "market owners." While the motorcycle manufacturer KTM is "only" number seven in the world for the motorcycle market, it is number one in the small segment for so-called enduro machines (motocross motorcycles which are also licensed for road traffic). The company is number three for off-road motorcycles, which are normally not licensed for road traffic. BBA, an English textile company with hidden champion characteristics, includes a corresponding statement in its company philosophy: "Our tactic is to dominate our market niches by transforming general markets in which we are a nobody into market niches where we are somebody!" This statement convincingly demonstrates that a company seeking to become market leader should not accept existing market definitions and boundaries. The possibilities to newly define or redefine a market differ from case to case. The refusal to accept existing market definitions and the determination to create new ones form a promising prerequisite for market leadership.

Supernichists and market owners can also be found in consumer goods markets. One example is Hein, manufacturer of the popular Pustefix soap bubbles for children. Managing director Gerold Hein explains, "Pustefix does not compete with other products of this kind, it competes with chocolate bars, sweets and other things children buy." The product is exported to more than 50 countries. The USA and Japan are the most important markets. The small size of such a superniche makes it unattractive for competitors, and several patents protect the product. McIlhenny has the market for Tabasco to itself, it's a self-defined market. World market leaders like Pöschl (snuff), Müller (shaving brushes) or Aeroxon conform to a similar pattern. Aeroxon's main product, flycatchers, has remained unchanged for 90 years and has a world market share of 50%.

An interesting example for successful superniche policy is the former world-class equestrian rider Paul Schockemöhle. He has specialized in breeding extremely high-class thoroughbred race and show horses, and has a unique position in this market worldwide. While excellent horses are sold at auctions for $70,000, premium horses from Schockemöhle are sold for several hundred thousand dollars, and even for up to $1 million in exceptional cases.

Market owners who have created their very own markets are often companies that offer collector's items. The Ritzenhoff glass manufacturer began to develop its own market in 1992 when the milk board asked Ritzenhoff, then a mass producer of glass, to create a promotion product for a glass for milk. Contributions by the best designers worldwide were intended to make milk more attractive. Today, Ritzenhoff glasses are sold in more than 50 countries. More than 280 renowned designers like Alessandro Mendini and Roger and Philippe Petit-Roulet contributed their designs for glasses, the range of which now encompasses more than 70 collections. In addition to milk glasses, the company offers designer collections of champagne glasses, clocks, espresso cups, Christmas decorations, ashtrays, table lanterns, and bags. On its homepage the company has established its own online trading service for the millions of Ritzenhoff fans throughout the world. Swarovski, the world market leader for crystal jewelry, also uses the collector's instinct to consolidate its market position. The initiation of the "Swarovski Crystal Society" marked the establishment of a world-wide collectors' club that is intended to "launch a new pioneer phase in the company's history."[10] Model railways by Märklin are likewise coveted collectors' items. Stuffed animal manufacturer Margarethe Steiff has established the collectors' "Steiff-Club."

Fig. 3.5 shows a selection of further hidden champions with world market shares of 70% or higher. This table illustrates that such market positions exist in numerous and very different markets.

Fig. 3.5: Hidden champions with world market shares of 70% or more

Company	Main product	World market share
Dr. Suwelack	Collagen	100%
SkySails	Towing kite wind propulsion systems	100%
Gerriets	Theater curtains, stage equipment	100%
Ulvac	LCD panel coating	96%
G.W. Barth	Cocoa processing systems	90%
GKD – Gebr. Kufferath	Metal fabrics	90%
Kirow Leipzig	Railway cranes	85%
alki-Technik	Special screw systems	80%
Delo	Adhesives for chip modules on smart cards	80%
Nissha	Small touch panels	80%
ScheBo Biotech	Biotech in in-vitro diagnostics	80%
Kern-Liebers	Springs for safety belts	80%
Weckerle	Lipstick machines	80%
TEXPA	Home textile processing machines	75%
Achenbach Buschhütten	Aluminum rolling mills, rolling mill filtration systems	70%
Karl Mayer	Warp knitting machines	70%
Omicron	Tunnel-grid/tunnel-probe microscopes	70%
Tente Rollen	Casters for hospital beds	70%
Wirtgen	Road-recycling machines	70%

Market domination strategies adopted by supernichists or market owners are not easily imitated by normal companies, just as it makes no sense for an average violinist to compete with Anne-Sophie Mutter or Itzhak Perlman. The simplest way for a company to own a market is to create that market itself. Ideally, such a market does not yet exist and is created or defined by the new product. In addition, the uniqueness of the product must be sustainable. Imitation or the establishment of similar markets must be prevented at all costs. The product's outstanding position must be continually renewed and defended over time. Various instruments can be used to maintain a product's uniqueness:

- Patent protection,
- powerful trademark or logo,
- intensive relationships and familiarity with customers, and
- artistic designs with frequent updates.

At times it is necessary to deliberately make a product scarce. Luxury goods manufacturers implement this strategy. Limited editions are one of the most effective means of keeping the value of a product high. The difficulty to obtain such a product is intentional. Its scarcity is an essential element for the most faithful customers. However, scarcity also means that the supernichists or market owners voluntarily refrain from exploiting their full growth potential. Exclusivity can only be maintained if volume expansion is controlled.

Market owners teach us valuable lessons in relationship marketing. They have been spoiling their loyal customers for years, initiating clubs and collectors' movements long before these concepts were discovered by the marketing literature. They also organize exchanges through which coveted older items can be traded. Margarethe Steiff, maker of teddy bears, holds a series of auction records. The most expensive Steiff teddy bear was sold at an auction for almost $300,000 in 2000. Market owners often have a loyal following of customers who are fanatical about their products and willing to pay very high prices. Those who enjoy sustained success are wise enough to stay specialized and secretive, and to keep their markets small. These can be important lessons for other companies.

Superniches limit growth opportunities and make the deliberate decision not to grow, which we discussed in Chapter 2, an obvious choice. Size and niche can conflict with one another. Jürg Zumtobel, chairman of the supervisory board of the world market leader in lighting systems, which bears the same name, expressed this dilemma from the customer's point of view, "We were too large for a niche and too small for international business." At the same time, superniches can offer effective protection against competitors.

For Better or Worse

It is evident that the strong focus of the hidden champions harbors risks. After all, it means putting "all the eggs in one basket." Are the hidden champions too highly dependent on their narrow markets, just a handful of customers, and the business cycles they cannot compensate elsewhere? And are they not exposed to a high risk of technological change due to their confinement to one product? Indeed, the hidden champions' dependence on their main market and product is high. On average, 70% of their revenues are generated in this market, and presumably an even higher proportion of their profits. It is therefore not surprising that 93% of the respondents answered that this market is very important for their company; 56% even expect this importance to increase in the future. This indicator of market dependence is higher than ten years ago, when half of the respondents forecast that the core markets would increase in importance in future—a prediction that has come true.

The hidden champions are committed to their markets for better or worse. The risks of this dependence should not be underestimated. Whether specialization goes too far can only be determined on an individual basis. Focus is simultaneously the foundation of strength and a source of risk.

There are essentially three types of risks:

- Dependence on one market ("all eggs in one basket").
- An upscale market niche can be attacked by standard products (risk of losing the premium position).
- The niche's small market volume or high costs may erode customer acceptance and/or price competitiveness.

We will deal with the last two risks in later chapters.

Dependence on one market is an obvious risk. A company with a very high market share faces great difficulties when a crisis occurs in its core market. Its very existence may be threatened. It is useless to build the best steam locomotive in the world if nobody today wants to buy it.

A second risk for the hidden champions is the threat from competitors who achieve superiority in the same or a closely related technology. Setting a clear focus can most likely reduce this risk. Fig. 3.6 compares the market risk with the competitive risk.

The comparison clearly shows that the choice is not between higher or lower overall risk, but between higher market and lower competitive risk, and vice versa. There is no straightforward answer as to whether a focused or a diversified strategy is superior. The hidden champions clearly favor a focused strategy. Hans Riegel of Haribo, the world market leader in gummi bears, says, "Risk is actually reduced if you focus on what you are really good at." Another interview partner commented: "Isn't it less

		Market risk	
		low	high
Competitive risk	low		Focused strategy of the hidden champions
	high	Diversification strategy (typical of large companies)	

risky being a big fish in a small pond than being a small fish in a big pond infested with sharks?" In view of the high number of failed diversification attempts, a focused strategy may actually be less risky than a diversification strategy.[11]

Simple structures regarding both products and customers are one of the hidden champions' keys to success. The hidden champions avoid the risk of distraction from their core business, a mistake that is frequently fatal for diversified companies. The hidden champions rarely sell off businesses. Focus on the core business and the risks associated with it force the hidden champions to keep a close eye on their market and to defend their position by swift reactions to changes in customer needs or to new technological developments. The dependence on their market makes them ferocious defenders and great innovators.

Trumpf, world leader for precision sheet metal cutting machines, is a perfect example. Traditionally, sheet metal cutting was done mechanically. In the early 1980s, laser technology began to invade this field, a very serious threat for Trumpf. By staying focused and developing its own lasers Trumpf not only defended its leading market position in sheet metal cutting, but also became one of the top companies for industrial lasers.

A second example is the lock and fittings industry concentrated in the vicinity of Dusseldorf. This cluster involves about 150 companies from a purely mechanical tradition. Several of these companies are world market leaders and eventually had to defend their position by integrating electronics into their lock systems. Their focus and inextricable commitment to the locks business made it possible for them to take this leap in technology and to survive. The threatening situation caused by changing technological requirements mobilized unexpected energy reserves and led to a wave of innovations. Companies with a clear focus do not give up easily and strongly rise to such a challenge.

A welcome side-effect of increasing internationalization is broader risk diversification. However, this only applies if the business cycles of the regional markets are not synchronized. Dürr, world market leader for automotive paint shop systems, benefits from the different investment cycles in the automotive industry in America, Europe, and Asia. But there are also synchronized global markets, such as electronics. The market for automatic stocking equipment for electronic boards slumped worldwide almost 70% between 2000 and 2002, and even a global presence could not offset this risk. Such correlations are decisive to the effect of international expansion on risk diversification. Of course, internationalization harbors additional risks, such as failure, copycatting, currency fluctuations, and so forth (see Chapter 4).

Soft Diversification

Focus dominated in our first study. At the time, we found only a few hidden champions that had diversified or taken steps in this direction. Since then, the number of hidden champions choosing this route has risen sharply. The most important reason is that the combination of narrow markets and high market shares restricts growth opportunities. In their search for new ways to grow, quite a few hidden champions have initiated a change of strategy and embarked into new markets. Does this mean that they will become normal diversified corporations? Or will they be able to retain the traditional strengths of the hidden champions? And how do they proceed?

Hidden Champions in Diversified Corporations

Before we look at more recent examples of soft diversification, we will consider several hidden champions that have always belonged to diversified corporations. Our current study revealed that 16.1% fall into the category of hidden champions belonging to diversified corporations, a percentage that was even higher ten years ago (21%). Some diversified corporations' portfolios comprise few, others many hidden champion units, and these cases show that the hidden champions' strategy may well be practicable and successful within the framework of a diversified enterprise. Heraeus, a technology conglomerate, has always had a distinct preference for niche markets coupled with market leadership. CEO Helmut Eschwey says, "If we see a business turning into a mass market, we quickly seek an alternative, ideally a niche within a niche."

The Körber Group began to diversify at an early stage while remaining true to the hidden champion principles. On the basis of the very strong world market position of its main business Hauni (90%–95% world market share for cigarette machines, the only complete provider of tobacco processing systems) and the realization that the cigarette market would stagnate in time, diversification into paper, grinding, packaging technology, as well as electronics, took place as early as the 1970 s. Körber pursued a decided hidden champion strategy—with great success. The division Körber PaperLink now includes several world market leaders. E.C.H. Will is the global number one in small-format cutters. More than half of the school notebooks in the world are produced on E.C.H. Will machines. Kugler-Womako is the world market leader for passport production lines. Winkler + Dünnebier is the global market leader for production machines for envelopes and tissues. The Körber Schleifring Group, which in turn comprises several companies, is the world market leader for grinding machines. We will look more deeply at the organization of the Körber Group in Chapter 8. A few hidden champions had embarked on diversification even before our first study in the mid-1990s, but they were rare exceptions at the time.

Motives for Soft Diversification

One big surprise found in our current study is that a considerable number of larger hidden champions are venturing into diversifications. The main motive for such extension of the field of business is not only—or not primarily—risk diversification. A more important goal is overcoming growth barriers expected in the future. If a company has a very high market share in a narrow market, revenue growth becomes increasingly difficult.

Resistance from competitors increases. In addition, some hidden champions anticipate increased pressure from new competitors in the future (e.g., from China), so that even maintaining the high market share can become questionable; particularly, if this can only be achieved by price concessions, which damage margins.[12] If, in addition to the strong market position, market growth is slow (e.g., with cigarettes), the earnings from the established core market cannot be fully reinvested. The only remaining alternative is to diversify into other markets or products in order to continue realizing ambitious growth targets and acceptable returns on equity.

Better exploitation of existing competencies and know-how potentials are another important motive for diversification. Trumpf, for example, traditionally the world market leader for laser cutting machines for metals, has recently successfully applied its expertise in metal processing for the medical field.

Sometimes another, somewhat, controversial motive comes into play. Entrepreneurs who have been very successful in one market tend to believe that they can repeat this success in other markets. Successful people in particular are susceptible to surges of anything-is-possible. They then plunge into new, seemingly attractive markets hoping to prove themselves to the world yet again. However, it is extremely rare that the same person achieves world championship or wins the Nobel Prize in two disciplines. Danger looms just around the corner if the new activity is too distracting and the core business is neglected.

We will now look at selected cases of hidden champions that have extended their business. Igor Ansoff introduced the concept of diversification in 1964. Ansoff's distinction between the dimensions "products" and "market/customers," either one "old" or "new," results in a matrix with four cells. We speak of diversification in the genuine sense when both the product and the market/customer are new. The other options are termed market penetration (old product and old market), market development (old product, new market) and product development (new product, old market). Note, that when we discuss new markets/customers, we expressly do not consider purely regional expansion (i.e., entry into new country markets with the same product or customer group).

The hidden champions' diversification attempts often cannot be clearly categorized according to the Ansoff matrix, and there is frequent overlap between the cells. We therefore talk about "soft" diversification. "Soft" means that the new units stay close to the traditional business, both in terms of technology and market. Würth, world leader in assembly products, has, among other things, added an insurance company, a bank, and a leasing firm to its portfolio alongside its core business "assembly products" and its core target group "handicraft businesses." The idea was to sell banking and insurance services to the traditional Würth customers ("product development" according to Ansoff) and to also attract target groups that Würth has not yet attended to ("diversification" according to Ansoff).

Fig. 3.7 provides a compilation of numerous cases of soft diversification. Hard, or true, diversification in the Ansoff sense remains the exception.

Fig. 3.7: Selected cases of soft diversification

Company	Existing business		New business		Method	Success/Failure
	Main product	Core target group	Product	Target group		
Claas	Harvesters	Farmers, contractors	Tractors	Farmers, contractors	Acquisition	+
Wirtgen	Road recycling machines	Construction companies	Road makers, rollers	Construction companies	Acquisition	+
Leitz	Woodwork tools	Wood processors	Metal tools	Metal processors	Acquisition	+
Dürr	Automotive paintshops	Automobile industry	Systems supplier	Automotive industry	Acquisition	-
Trumpf	Lasers, metal cutters	Metal processors	Medical technology	Health sector	Organic growth	+
Doppel-mayr	Cableways	Cableway operators	Transport, cable cars	Transport companies	Organic growth	?
			Inhouse transport	Industry	Organic growth	?
Groz-Beckert	Needles	Textile industry	Ceramic punching components	Computer industry	Organic growth	?
Gelita	Gelatine	Food/pharmaceutical industry	Health care	Consumers	Sales cooperation	?
Bofrost	Direct frozen food distribution	Consumers	Frozen food	Bulk consumers	Organic growth	?
Weckerle	Lipstick filling machines	Cosmetic industry	Lipsticks	Cosmetic industry	Organic growth	+
Rittal	Switchboxes	Industry	Air conditioning equipment	Industry	Organic growth	?
EGO	Hotplates	Household appliances industry	Catalytic converter sensors	Automotive industry	Organic growth	?
Otto Bock	Orthopedic products	Health sector	Plastic components	Automotive industry	Organic growth	?
Huf Haus	Prefabricated houses	Building principals, architects	Financing	Building principals	Cooperation	+
Bauer	Civil engineering equipment	Construction industry	Civil engineering services	Building principals	Organic growth	+
Plansee	High-performance materials	Industry	High-performance tools	Mechanical engineering	Cooperation	+
			Powder metallurgical products	Automotive industry	Cooperation	+
G&D	Printing of banknotes	Central banks	chipcards	Electronics industry	Organic growth	+

Claas has traditionally focused on harvesting machines. It is world market leader in field shuttles, number one in Europe for combines, and a worldwide leader in technology. However, the growth potential in this market is limited. In addition, Claas saw a risk in letting the distance between the leading agricultural machinery manufacturers John Deere, Case New Holland, and Agco become too great. When a joint venture with Caterpillar in the tractor business did not bring the desired success, Claas took over Renault's tractor business in 2003 with the aim of full integration. This integration has since been successfully completed, and today the tractors are sold under the Claas brand. The target group continues to be farmers and contractors, whereas the tractor as a product is new for Claas. This business expansion has given Claas a strong growth boost (see Fig. 2.4).

Wirtgen, the dominant market leader in its core business of road-recycling machines with a market share of 70%, has taken a similar route. Wirtgen's customers, usually road construction companies, do not only need recycling machines, but also tarmac-makers and steamrollers for road renewal. Wirtgen acquired Vögele and Hamm, two companies with excellent reputations in these products. In 2006, Wirtgen also bought Kleemann, which produces machines for the treatment and recycling of building materials. The Wirtgen Group now offers a complete program for road and mineral materials technologies. In contrast to the previously described case of Claas, the acquired companies continue to operate under their established brand names. Fig. 3.8 shows that all four companies of the Wirtgen Group have been able to realize a successful growth strategy under their joint management. The revenues of Wirtgen, Vögele, Hamm, and Kleemann do not comprise the total revenues of the Wirtgen Group, because there are additional foreign subsidiaries. Since 1995, the Wirtgen Group increased its revenues to $1.945 billion from $247 million. Wirtgen would not have been able to achieve this spectacular growth without the acquisitions.

Leitz, the world market leader for wood processing tools, has chosen a similar strategy. To overcome the limited growth potential of the wood tooling market, the Leitz Metalworking Technology Group was established as a second pillar. "We wanted more diversification," comments Leitz's CEO, Dieter Brucklacher. Brucklacher's intention was to retain the flexibility of a midsize enterprise at all costs. In contrast to Claas and Wirtgen, it is worth noting that, Leitz approached a new customer group, namely metalworkers. There, the name Leitz was virtually unknown. For this reason, renowned specialists such as Fette, Boehlerit, Kininger, and Bilz were acquired. All these companies continue to operate under their own names within the organizational structure of the Leitz Group.

The cases of Claas, Wirtgen, and Leitz could lead us to believe that the takeover of companies as a means to extend the product range or the market bears comparatively few risks. This conclusion is not justified. Dürr, in its core business the world market leader of automotive paint shop systems, had the drive to become a systems provider for the automotive industry to accelerate its growth. To achieve this, Carl Schenck was acquired in 2000, a company that operates in various automation and processing

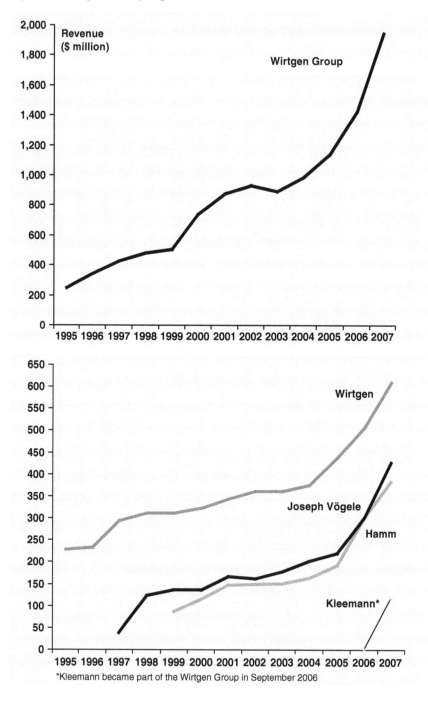

*Kleemann became part of the Wirtgen Group in September 2006

technology markets and also sells its products outside the automotive industry. Taking over Schenck catapulted Dürr into a new dimension. In 2000, revenues increased 54% to $2.59 billion. But in subsequent years the earnings situation deteriorated rapidly. The takeover of Schenck turned out to be a mistake that endangered Dürr as a whole. In 2005, after numerous changes in the top management, Dürr sold off a good portion of the businesses it had acquired. It kept Schenck RoTec, the world market leader in balancing and diagnosis technologies for the automotive industry. Under Ralf Dieter, the CEO since 2006, Dürr has returned to its established automotive focus. Schenck RoTec contributes about 10% to Dürr's revenues, which amounted to $1.48 billion in 2007 and 90% of which come from automotive customers.

Jenoptik experienced a similar development, yet from a very different starting point. Jenoptik is a leader in photon technologies (i.e., in the use of "light as a tool.") This includes three fields of competence: "creating light—lasers," "forming light—optics," and "sensing light—sensors." Under the management of the former CEO Lothar Späth, Jenoptik embarked on rapid expansion and acquired M+W Zander, world market leader for turnkey cleanroom systems. In 2004, revenues reached more than $3.4 billion, 85% of which were generated by the "cleanroom systems" business. However, in the course of this extreme expansion the company plunged into the red. In 2005, Jenoptik made a radical move and sold off the cleanroom systems business, reducing its revenues by 75%. "We focus our activities on profitable growth, not on growth at all costs,"[13] the annual report explains. The results confirm this strategy. Although the revenues declined to $713 million in 2007 from $2.6 billion in 2005, the $95 million loss in 2005 was turned into earnings before interest and taxes (EBIT) of $48 million in 2007. The plan is to once again reach a revenue of $1 billion and an operative return on sales of 10% within three to seven years. Refocusing on the core business not only ensures survival, but also opens up a new growth and success route for Jenoptik.

Failed diversification, as with Dürr and Jenoptik, is not only dangerous with regard to the unfulfilled hopes of the new businesses, but it also impedes the development of the core business due to the strain on the financial resources. This side-effect, which is difficult to quantify, is illustrated by automotive giant Daimler.[14] Where would Daimler be today if it had invested into its Mercedes core business the many billions that have over the years been plowed into AEG, Fokker, Mitsubishi, and Chrysler, as well as the establishment of a wide-ranging technology group? If this question is put to Daimler managers today, eyes shine. Given the limited financial resources of the hidden champions, this problem deserves even higher attention.

By contrast, consider Doppelmayr, world market leader in ropeways that have been installed in 77 countries. As the growth opportunities in this business are limited, the company explored the possibility of new business areas in the 1990s, seeking to build on its technical competencies. "We only make things with cables. That is our core competency—and everything else is not our business. We have no expertise there," says Michael Doppelmayr. The subsidiary Doppelmayr Cable Cars (DCC) was formed to manufacture cableways for inner city transport in 1995. The first reference project, a link between three casinos, was realized four years later in Las Vegas in 1999. In 2006, a second project followed in Las Vegas. In total, Doppelmayr has sold six cable liner systems. In-house material transport is another new line of business. The subsidiary Doppelmayr Transport Technology was founded for this purpose in 2006, and has installed four systems to date. In both new fields of business, Doppelmayr addresses new customer groups. "We have made ourselves a name in cableways, but not yet in the two new fields of business," says CEO Michael Doppelmayr when explaining the challenge. Doppelmayr is an exemplary case of soft diversification. While sticking to its core competency, Doppelmayr cautiously moves into new spheres.

Transitions from the B-to-B market to the B-to-C market, or vice versa, often prove especially difficult (as seen with Bofrost and Weckerle), although there are also counterexamples. Gelita, world market leader in gelatine, has traditionally supplied only food and pharmaceutical firms. In 2004, the newly founded Gelita Health Products launched a consumer and joint protection product called CH-Alpha. A cooperation partner sells CH-Alpha through pharmacies. The product has been introduced in several European countries and the USA, and is on its way to becoming a success.

Bauer is pursuing a rare form of business expansion by not only manufacturing special deep drilling equipment, but also providing the corresponding drilling services. In 2005, these services earned 62% of the company's $1.1 billion revenue. This forward integration brings a significant expansion in markets and revenues. An interesting side effect is that the company's own drilling activities provide ideas for product development. The customer is in the same company.

Huf is a further example of value chain extension, and thereby of market extension. Traditionally, Huf only built modern timber-frame homes. Recently, Huf started to offer the financing for such houses in cooperation with a bank. In addition, further house components such as sanitation, heating, climate control, flooring, and so forth have been systematically brought in-house by acquiring suppliers or founding new subsidiaries. These steps made a significant contribution to the rapid growth over the last few years. The other cases in Fig. 3.7 serve to illustrate the variety of diversification moves.

The following conclusions can be drawn from the soft diversification attempts to date:

- While diversification was a rare exception among the hidden champions in the past, this form of business expansion has recently increased significantly.
- Larger hidden champions are particularly disposed toward diversification, as well as smaller hidden champions that experience low growth in their niche markets.
- In addition to maintaining growth momentum in the face of future market saturation with a high market share, motives for diversification are risk reduction and a better use of technological skills. Entrepreneurial ambitions extending beyond the traditional core business also play a role.
- The diversification results to date are mixed, even for companies that have long since chosen to diversify. The Körber Group has been successful in all divisions with its consistent hidden champion strategy of staying close to mechanical engineering.[15] By contrast, Würth's intentions to sell financial services to its craftsmen customers in addition to assembly products were not particularly successful. In most cases, the jury is still out.
- It is not surprising that the greater the distance of new ventures to existing fields of competence the lower the likelihood of success. The transition to a new target group seems riskier than the launch of a new product for the existing target group. The same difficulties for new customer segments exist for accessing new sales channels.
- Takeovers of existing companies are promising but not risk-free options, as the experiences of Dürr and Jenoptik prove. The strategy of retaining company names and brands often seems advisable. The cases of Körber, Wirtgen, and Leitz support this option. However, the successful brand integration of Claas shows that other alternatives exist.

Diversification involves a break with traditional strategy and changes the character of a hidden champion. Highly focused one-product, one-market companies become small conglomerates that are active in various fields. This increases the risk that the strengths and philosophy of the hidden champions, particularly focus, may be lost. The greatest risk is the distraction from the core business. Being or remaining world class in several fields is anything but easy. Diversified hidden champions are aware of this risk, and they respond to it by applying the hidden champion philosophy on the next lower level. The new business units emerging in the course of soft diversification are organized and managed like hidden champions. This means decentralization without compromise and is the recipe for success applied by Heraeus and Körber. We will look at the organizational implications of soft diversification in more detail in Chapter 8. The relentless decentralization with which the hidden champions accompany diversification provides valuable insights for other companies, not least for large diversified corporations.

Summary

Most hidden champions of the twenty-first century remain true to their focus and continue to define their markets narrowly. However, we increasingly find cases of soft diversification, particularly among the larger hidden champions. With regard to market definition and the associated focus or diversification, the following points should be noted:

- Hidden champions typically define their markets narrowly and build up strong market positions in these markets.
- The narrow market definition means that the hidden champions' world markets are and remain relatively small.
- However, these markets have predominantly grown strongly and have on average more than doubled their volume in the last ten years.
- In spite of the fragmentation and the fuzziness of many of their markets, the hidden champions are relatively well informed about them. As a result of their specialization and pronounced closeness to their customers, the hidden champions typically have an excellent intuitive understanding of their markets—even in the absence of precise data.
- In defining their markets, the hidden champions primarily apply customer-oriented criteria such as application and needs. Product and technology are often additional elements of market definition. Typically, several criteria are used to define a market.

- Hidden champions often do not accept the market boundaries customary in their industry, but view market definition as a strategic parameter that they apply in an autonomous way.
- Focus leads to deep problem solutions or value chains for a narrow market. The value chain served is accordingly narrow and deep. Out of this focus specialized competencies and perfection evolve that are difficult for competitors to match.
- Many hidden champions are supernichists operating in very small markets with global market shares as high as 70%–100%. This can limit growth but, at the same time, establishes high entry barriers for new competitors.
- For better or worse, hidden champions strongly depend on their core markets. This dependence is not one-sided, but applies to the customers as well. Dependence on a single market increases the market risk but reduces the competitive risk, due to the full concentration of all resources on the core market. The balance between both risks must be judged for each individual case.
- Once the hidden champions have selected a market, they show a strong and lasting commitment to it. Fundamental redefinitions of the market and changes in basic technology are rare and occur only every 10–15 years.
- The most important motive for soft diversification is not the desire to minimize the risk stemming from concentration on a narrow market, but to overcome growth barriers, to better employ existing competencies or to realize greater entrepreneurial ambitions.
- Although the jury is still out, hidden champions seem to diversify most successfully when they stay true to their philosophy. The new units should have a decentralized management and in turn strive for leadership in their markets.

Finding the right market definition and focus are demanding challenges. The hidden champions have become and have remained market leaders with a narrow market definition and a strong focus. World-class performance is not the result of spreading resources broadly, but of sustained concentration. Every company should bear this in mind for its own strategy development. The risk of specialization seems less serious than the risk of dissipating talent and energy. The specialist frequently beats the generalist. However, we also have to face the fact that narrow markets coupled with high market shares limit further growth and only confine investment opportunities as of a certain point. A promising route to continued growth in this situation is soft diversification. The new units should again have a narrow market definition and a clear focus. In this way, the hidden champion strengths can be most effectively transferred to new businesses and open future growth avenues.

Notes

1 Shortly afterwards Bentley was acquired by Volkswagen.

2 Derek F. Abell, *Defining the Business: The Starting Point of Strategic Planning*, Englewood Cliffs (NJ): Prentice Hall, 1980.

3 See Hermann Simon, *Hidden Champions*, Boston: Harvard Business School Press, p. 42, in order to avoid outlier effects, we use the median here as with the new figures.

4 See Theodore Levitt, "Marketing Myopia," *Harvard Business Review*, July-August 1960, p. 45–56.

5 *VDI News*, January 26, 2007, p. 20.

6 Netstal belongs to the MPM Group (Mannesmann Plastics Machinery), which is overall world market leader for plastic injection molding machines with numerous brands like Krauss-Maffei, Demag Ergotech, Netstal, Billion. Some of these subsidiaries are in turn world market leaders in their segments. Engel in Austria and Arburg in Germany are also leaders in some segments.

7 *Fortune*, April 2, 2007, p. 19.

8 Bosch Rexroth also offers comprehensive solutions for industrial automation, but hydraulics is the core business.

9 *Frankfurter Allgemeine Zeitung*, March 5, 2007, p. 18.

10 INTES (Eds), *Familienunternehmen heute: Jahrbuch 2007*, Bonn, 2007.

11 See C. K. Prahalad, G. Hamel, "The Core Competence of the Corporation," *Harvard Business Review*, May-June 1990, p. 79–91; Gary Hamel, C. K. Prahalad: *Competing for the Future*, Boston: Harvard Business School Press, 1994.

12 See Hermann Simon, Frank Bilstein, Frank Luby, *Manage for Profit, Not for Market Share*, Boston: Harvard Business School Press, 2006.

13 *Frankfurter Allgemeine Zeitung*, January 30, 2007, p. 15.

14 See Peter Brors, Michael Freitag and Dietmar Student, "Die Quittung von Daimler", *Manager Magazin*, April 2007, p. 34–48. This article estimates the sum of the losses resulting from failed diversification and acquisitions at Daimler to be at least $billion.

15 However, not everything went smoothly at Körber. In 2003, a plant of the subsidiary Topack had to be closed due to lack of market success.

Chapter 4
Globalization

How does a company ascend to world market leadership? Certainly not by staying at home and waiting for customers to call on it. Instead, the hidden champions venture into the world and offer their products wherever their customers are. This process of globalization typically takes generations and requires unending stamina. In the preceding chapter we learned that the hidden champions operate in narrowly defined and therefore relatively small markets. To expand these markets, the hidden champions have chosen globalization as the second pillar of their strategy besides focus. This means that they are narrow in the substance of their business and wide in the regional dimension. The hidden champions' world markets are far larger than their respective home markets. Ten years ago their main markets were in Western Europe and North America. In the current process of rapid globalization the hidden champions increasingly expand their scope into Asia and Eastern Europe. They are simultaneously confronted with numerous attractive new markets that makes setting priorities very difficult. In the decades after World War II, entries into new markets were executed in a very entrepreneurial manner (i.e., the entrepreneur made the decision and sent his troops into the new country without much instruction). The current generation of hidden champions managers relies on a more professional and systematic preparation. Mental internationalization is at the same time a precondition for and a consequence of successful globalization. The participants themselves (i.e., leaders, managers, and employees) change in this process. Increasing knowledge of foreign languages and cultures gradually removes the shortage of internationally experienced and versatile personnel that was characteristic of the early stages. In a globalized economy Western Europe is in a geostrategically advantageous location. From Europe companies in all important countries can be reached within

H. Simon, *Hidden Champions of the Twenty-First Century*,
DOI 10.1007/978-0-387-98147-5_4, © Hermann Simon 2009

normal office hours, and global travel times are considerably shorter than from Asia or America.

Globalization: The Second Pillar

As noted in Chapter 3, narrow focus, the first pillar of the hidden champions' strategy, makes a market small. Winterhalter's confinement to hotel and restaurant dishwashing systems defines a market that is far smaller than the overall market for all commercial dishwashing systems. By focusing on protective ski helmets, the Swedish firm Poc only reaches a small fraction of the entire market for protective helmets. Similarly, Enduro motorcycles, the specialty of the hidden champion KTM, account for less than 1% of the total motorcycle market. The consequences of narrow market definition are even more pronounced for supernichists and market owners. Even in large countries, niche markets can become tiny. The hidden champions would be doomed to remain small without the possibility of regional expansion. Consequently, globalization is the second pillar of their strategy. We have already indicated in previous chapters that this second pillar is a source of enormous growth surges.

The narrow market definition based on application, technology, target group or other criteria is coupled with a wide market definition regarding the regional dimension. These are the two major pillars of the hidden champion strategy: specialization in product and know-how combined with breadth in the regional market coverage, normally on a global scale. Manfred Fuchs of Fuchs Petrolub, the largest independent manufacturer of lubricants worldwide, describes this strategy, "Our development was driven by the early recognition that—relative to the large, vertically integrated mineral oil corporations—Fuchs Petrolub could only create genuine competitive advantages if we pursued specialization and niche strategies. This narrowed down the potential demand, so that internationalization became a mandatory correlate of product specialization. The volume of national or even European niche markets is limited, and the larger global framework is required to recover our research and development costs."[1] Otto Bock, world market leader in orthopedic technology, provides a similar rationale for its global strategy, "We couple our outstanding innovativeness and technological leadership with global presence of our sales and service network." And Heinrich Weiss, CEO of SMS, the global leader for flat steel plants, contends that "a midsize company in industrial engineering can only be successful if it concentrates on a narrow market niche, operates worldwide and endeavors to be or become number one on its market."[2]

Fig. 4.1 shows the two pillars of the hidden champion strategy: specialization coupled with global marketing.

Fig. 4.1: The two-pillar strategy of the hidden champions

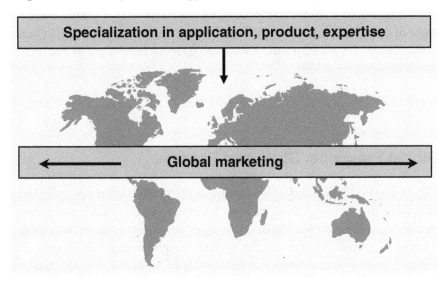

The only way towards world market leadership is to venture out into the world. In the modern age, globalization is not confined to large corporations, but a realistic option for companies of all sizes. Mike Eskew, CEO of UPS, the world's largest parcel dispatch service, shares this view, "Globalization started as a trend for large multinational companies, but it is increasingly becoming the same for the small and mediums. We see that small and midsize companies push harder to go global. They look as big on the Internet as anyone else."[3] Harting, one of the world market leaders in electronic interface systems, sums up its vision in one sentence, "We want to become a world company."

When did the two-pillar strategy develop? Did it emerge after the hidden champions had grown to a certain size or was it there from the very beginning? Our findings show that in most cases the latter applies. Of the respondents 74.4% said that they started exporting "right from the outset," and 33.9% said that they established their first foreign subsidiaries right after company foundation. Tecmen, a specialist in drives, entered the Chinese market only a year after it was founded and now employs more personnel in China than in Germany, its home country. Manfred Fuchs of Fuchs Petrolub comments, "Our company wouldn't be as successful today if we had not committed ourselves to rigorous internationalization from the very beginning."[4] By 2007, Fuchs Petrolub had 40 plants in all important industrialized countries. "The backbone of our success is our worldwide fully owned sales and service network in currently more than 55 countries," says Hans-Joachim Boekstegers, CEO of Multivac, world market leader in thermoform packaging machines with a global market share of over 50%. Early and consistent internationalization is the logical consequence of the ambitious visions and goals of the people at the helm of the hidden champions.

Global Presence: State and Process

Where do the hidden champions stand in the globalization process? And how have they reached their current positions? Today's hidden champions have on average 24 subsidiaries in other countries, a surprisingly large number for midsize companies. An average of eight foreign subsidiaries are active in both manufacturing and sales, while 16 subsidiaries are pure sales and service organizations. The hidden champions clearly favor going it alone when they enter foreign markets. More than three quarters (exactly 77.1%) state that they do not cooperate with other firms for this purpose. Only 16.8% said they frequently use partnerships or joint ventures when entering new markets. The foreign subsidiaries are almost always owned 100% by the hidden champion parent. Two thirds of the hidden champions consider themselves the company with the largest number of international subsidiaries in their market.

This impressive coverage of numerous country markets is the fruit of extraordinary entrepreneurial achievements. Once a company has been established and is functioning smoothly on a global scale, this situation appears rather effortless and natural, as if it had always been like this. In an age where so-called "born global" companies or products[5] shoot out of the ground in markets like information technology, telecommunications or e-business, it is easy to ignore the tremendous efforts, stamina, and frustration tolerance necessary to build a global enterprise in a market that is not "born global."

To illustrate such a process, Fig. 4.2 shows the international expansion of Kärcher, world market leader in high-pressure cleaning equipment.

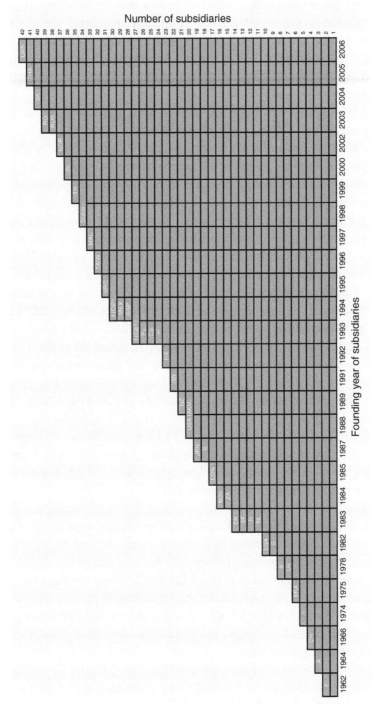

Fig. 4.2: The globalization process—the case of Kärcher

Number of subsidiaries

Founding year of subsidiaries

Kärcher was founded in 1935, but things were quiet in terms of internationalization during World War II and the reconstruction of Germany in the 1950s. The first subsidiary outside of Germany was established in France as late as 1962, and in the following years three more foreign subsidiaries were founded. The initial process moved hesitantly and with great caution.

After the founder's death, his widow, Irene Kärcher, took the helm. A more decisive globalization phase started in the 1970s. It is interesting that Irene Kärcher spoke five languages, had previously worked as a secretary for the executive vice president for sales at Mercedes-Benz, and was familiar with international business practices. From 1972 onwards, she initiated a determined globalization process in cooperation with the new und young CEO Roland Kamm, who was then 31 years old. Figure 4.2 shows that this process has gone on without interruption until today, and it is most likely that it will continue for many years to come. Since 1975, Kärcher has entered one or several new country markets virtually every year. By the end of 2008, the company had its own subsidiaries in 44 countries. The expansion will continue under the leadership of the young CEO Hartmut Jenner, who took over from Kamm in 2001. There is still a long way to go. There are, after all, more than 200 countries around the globe.

WIKA, world market leader in pressure and temperature measurement, pursued a similar route. WIKA plans to enter into two new foreign markets every year and proceeds very systematically, as CEO Alexander Wiegand stresses.

Molex, based in Chicago, Illinois and a market leader in interconnect products, operates 59 manufacturing plants all over the world. Gore, based in Newark, Delaware and market leader for Teflon (PTFE)-based products, has 45 facilities throughout the world.

These cases show that building up a global market presence typically takes several generations and calls for never-ending tenacity. The road to market globality is anything but smooth. Setbacks and disappointments, particularly on the personnel front, are the rule and not the exception. If even giant groups fail, such as Wal-Mart in Germany and Korea in 2006, it must be evident how much harder the globalization process is for a midsize company. As discussed in Chapter 2, clear visions and ambitious goals are the foundation and necessary precondition for successful globalization over such extended periods of time.

If the number of subsidiaries is any indication, Kärcher is well ahead of the average hidden champion regarding globalization (44 versus 24 foreign subsidiaries), yet Kärcher doesn't belong to the top group by any means. Many hidden champions have a higher number of foreign subsidiaries: Fig. 4.3 shows selected companies with revenues reaching at least $750 million.

Company	Main product	Revenues in $ million	Number of foreign subsidiaries
Knauf	Gypsum	5,343	ca. 130
GfK	Market research services	1,284	120
Andritz	Paper/cellulose facilities	4,497	>100
RHI	Refractories	1,643	100
Manroland	Web offset printing systems	2,419	ca. 100
SEW-Eurodrive	Drive technology	1,644	80
Dräger	Anesthetics/respiratory protection	2,233	65
Rittal	Industrial enclosures	2,329	63
Bauer	Deep drilling equipment	1,129	60
Plansee	Powder metallurgy	1,850	58
Hillebrand	Wine shipment	789	56
Wirtgen	Road-recycling machines	1,137	55
Festo	Pneumatics	1,918	55
Dorma	Door-lock systems	1,051	54
Giesecke & Devrient	Banknotes	1,692	51
Westfalia Separator	Centrifugal separation technology	822	50
Fuchs Petrolub	Lubricants	1,633	48
Givaudan	Aromas/fragrances	2,421	46
Logitech	Computer peripherals	1,545	44
AL-KO	Mobile home chassis	967	41

It is also striking that even smaller hidden champions have a very strong international presence. Fig. 4.4 lists selected examples.

International presence is not necessarily restricted to a company's own subsidiaries. The hidden champions use many different means to establish a global presence to reach their customers. JAB Anstoetz, the world's leading fabric editor, has showrooms in more than 70 countries. Hillebrand, the number one in the shipment of wine and alcoholic beverages, has 73 offices in all relevant countries, 56 of which are its own. Utsch, world market leader in security license plates, operates in more than 120 countries. In summary, we find that the hidden champions—independent of their size—have an impressive international market presence. They are on their way towards genuine globality. In spite of their small size and limited resources, many of them have become truly global enterprises, the hidden champions of the twenty-first century. The world is their market and they are increasingly present with their own subsidiaries in this world.

Company	Main product	Revenues in $ million	Number of foreign subsidiaries
Germanischer Lloyd	Ship certificaion	436	171
Multivac	Thermoformers, tray sealers	450	55
Semikron	Diodes/thyristor modules	370	35
Binzel	Welding torches	110	30
Netzsch	Pump/grinding technology	296	28
Heraeus Electro-Nite	Sensors for steelworks	411	23
Balluff	Sensor technology	274	23
KTR	Clutches	151	19
Utsch	Security license plates	200	17
Kleffmann Group	Agricultural market research	18	17
Brainlab	Surgical software	247	16
Simon-Kucher	Price consulting	140	14
Taprogge	Water circuits	69	8
Uniplan	Corporate communication	96	7

Globalization of Brands

Presence in international markets, ideally in the form of fully owned and controlled subsidiaries, is one aspect of globalization. Establishing and maintaining a presence in customers' heads throughout the world is often the more difficult challenge. Naturally, many hidden champions have the ambition to establish global brands. When discussing this aspect, it is important to differentiate between different kinds of markets. Although most hidden champions are unknown to the general public, they often have a strong or even unique brand franchise with their target groups. Hidden champions in global markets with few customers (e.g., the automotive or aircraft industry) have no serious difficulty globalizing their brands. They are in direct contact with their few customers who can judge the performance of their suppliers well. With larger and more fragmented target groups and more indirect distribution the establishment of a brand becomes increasingly difficult, expensive, and time-consuming.

Once again, focus helps. A consumer goods manufacturer operating in a narrowly defined market segment faces an easier task in building a global brand than in a mass market. Some focused consumer goods manufacturers have achieved impressive brand positions on a global scale. A case in point is Miele, the leading producer of high class appliances. Reinhard Zinkann, Co-CEO of Miele, says, "We have succeeded in exporting the value proposition of our brand into markets where no one before knew us. Miele is now a worldwide synonym for high-end products. We stand for quality and status." Sales director Horst Schübel adds, "Miele is well positioned on all five continents as the top brand." Increasingly, Zinkann and Schübel meet Australian, Chinese, and Japanese real estate developers who equip their luxury apartments in Asia's megacities with Miele electrical appliances. With revenues of $3.8 million, Miele is a small player in the global market for household appliances (by comparison, Whirlpool generates revenues of $19.4 billion, Electrolux $17.5 billion, Bosch-Siemens $12 billion). However, Miele is a true global player, possibly the only one in this field. It has 42 foreign subsidiaries and generates 73% of its revenues outside its home market, an unusually high percentage for an appliance maker.

In the same vein, hidden champions such as Kaldewei, Villeroy & Boch, Grohe or Hansgrohe are well-known brands in the sanitary sector across Europe or the globe. Today, Kärcher is an established brand in cleaning equipment around the world, and its Formula 1 sponsoring is intended to further promote its global brand franchise, especially in Asia, where Formula 1 races are increasingly popular. JAB Anstoetz, the world's leading fabric editor, is a well-known brand among experts on all five continents and always true to its motto "JAB Anstoetz does not simply sell fabrics, but a lifestyle." Aquarium enthusiasts around the world are familiar with Tetramin. Young people looking for unusual ring tones for their cell phones know Jamba in more than 30 countries. Stihl is renowned worldwide for its chainsaws. And every professional camera team knows ARRI cameras and Sachtler tripods.Likewise, top singers and sound technicians appreciate the microphones made by Sennheiser and Neumann.

Gore-Tex is a particularly interesting case. Both sides of the Gore-Tex membrane are covered with additional layers so that no one can actually see this "performance fabric." Nevertheless, Gore, Inc. has succeeded in establishing a very strong global brand, not unlike the far larger Intel in the computer domain. Gore invests large sums into the maintenance and further strengthening of its brand.[6]

Branding is also becoming more important for industrial suppliers, within the spare parts business in particular. Sachs is one of the few automotive suppliers whose name is well known to the general public.

According to the former CEO, Hermann Sigle, this turned out to be a great advantage in the internationalization of Sachs' spare parts business. Master mechanics in car repair shops exert a strong influence on the choice of the spare part, and Sachs has an excellent image among this target group, particularly in Asia. The origin of this brand awareness lies in Sachs' original equipment business (i.e., the direct sales to car manufacturers). Sachs has successfully extended this brand franchise to the much broader automechanics target group all over the world.

Whenever a product addresses large numbers of sales agents, craftsmen or service providers, branding is of utmost importance. Building a global brand is one of the biggest challenges in the globalization process. Many hidden champions have made excellent progress in this realm. Essential ingredients for building a strong brand are market leadership and time. On average, the hidden champions have been market leaders for 21.6 years. A brand is "time coagulated."

Globalization as the Driver of Growth

How much does globalization really contribute to growth? Is globalization more than hype? Do some of the numerous foreign subsidiaries eke out only a marginal existence? In face of the difficulties and the time required to successfully enter a foreign market, these are pressing questions. What does the second strategy pillar of regional expansion mean and how do the revenue portfolios of the hidden champions change in this process?

For individual companies it is easy to answer such questions, as their home markets play marginal roles at best. Ziemann, world leader in brewery plants, gets 98% of its revenues from outside its German home market. For Koenig & Bauer, global number one in money printing presses, it is 95%. These are no exceptions but quite representative examples.

It is hardly possible to overestimate the importance of globalization and its contribution to growth. If we ask which megatrend has changed our lives the most over the past 50 years, the generally accepted answer is "information technology." If we ask the same question in 50 years' time, the answer will probably be "globalization."[7]

Let us look at selected statistics. Exports of goods are an obvious and valid measure but by no means the only indicator of globalization. Exports of services and direct investments are indicators of similar importance. Fig. 4.5 shows the development of world exports per capita of the world population.[8]

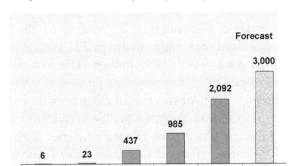

Fig. 4.5: Development of world exports per capita of the world population

In 1900, the figure was $6. By 2000, global per capita exports had risen to nearly $1,000. The astonishing facet in this development is that half the rise took place in the last two decades of the twentieth century. After the two World Wars and the global economic depressions in the first half of the last century, international trade was effectively reduced to nothing and had to be completely re-established after World War II. The development since 2000 is even more surprising. In seven years, per capita world exports have increased more strongly than in the preceding 20 years. Despite an ever increasing world population it seems realistic to forecast that per capita exports will reach the $3,000 mark by 2020.

In absolute figures, this means a rise in the international trade in goods to $13,619 billion in 2007 from $9.9 billion in 1900 (when the world's population was 1.65 billion[9]). This means that international trade in goods is today more than a thousand times higher than a century ago. The effects of direct investment and the export of services (e.g., financial services, software development or call centers in India) are not even included in this calculation. Their inclusion would presumably again double the growth that has taken place. Although these figures are not adjusted for inflation and should generally be interpreted with some caution, they clearly point to spectacular tendencies and dimensions. The message could not be clearer. Between 2000 and 2007 alone, the global export volume increased by about $7,000 billion.[10] Countries and companies participating in this secular expansion reap huge benefits. Another significant indicator is the international container transport, the volume of which grew

10.8% per year between 2000 and 2005 with a further growth expected for the mid- and long-term future. This means that the number of containers shipped around the world doubled every seven years.

If we look at exports from Germany, Austria, and Switzerland, it becomes evident that the hidden champions make an unbelievably large contribution. In the last decade, the hidden champions' export ratio (exports as percentage of their revenue) has risen to 61.5% from 51.1%, clear proof that globalization is a growth driver. The average hidden champion today exports goods worth $275 million. The respective figure ten years ago was $105 million. Of the absolute increase in revenues of $270 million, $170 million (63%, or two thirds) come from export growth.

In total, the 1,316 German, Austrian, and Swiss hidden champions contribute $361.4 billion to the exports of their countries. This figure represents 26.8% of the entire exports of Germany, Austria, and Switzerland[11] and confirms the tenet from Chapter 1 that a rather small number of strong midsize firms are vitally important for the outstanding export performance of the German-speaking countries. Viewed from another angle, it is evident that the opening of the markets in Eastern Europe and Asia, the disappearance of trade barriers, and the reduced costs of transport, travel, and communication, in other words "globalization," are tremendously important drivers of growth for the hidden champions—and all internationally active firms.

Fig. 4.6 illustrates the expansion of the hidden champions' markets when they thrust forward into internationalization. Here, we consider Germany as a starting base and index the German market size as 100.

The hidden champions perceive an enormous expansion of their accessible markets through Europeanization and globalization. The step from

Fig. 4.6: Expansion of markets in globalization (German market = 100)

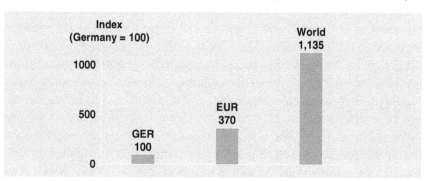

Germany to Europe almost quadruples the size of the accessible market. For the world, the accessible market potential is more than 11 times higher than for Germany. We should remember that Germany is the third-largest economy in the world. These numbers corroborate our statement from the beginning of the chapter that even narrow markets—such as those usually served by the hidden champions—take on considerable volumes on a global scale. A simple calculation illustrates to what extent globalization can expand a market. Let us assume that a midsize company has only been active on the German market and has a market share of 50% and revenues of $100 million. This implies that the total German market volume is $200 million. It is likely that a continuous increase of the already high market share in Germany will provoke strong resistance from competition. If this firm expands into other European countries, it can access a market potential of $740 million. Its European market share would be only 13.5%, meaning that in theory 86.5% of the European market would be available for growth. If this company takes the plunge into the world market, the market potential increases to $2.3 billion and its global market share shrinks to a tiny 4.4%. If the company is competitive in the global sphere, internationalization opens virtually unlimited growth opportunities. The progression from the limited German market to the huge global market offers spectacular growth avenues. If a company's home market is a smaller country, the multipliers are correspondingly higher. If we apply the numbers from Fig. 4.6, the world market is 103 times larger than the Austrian market. The multiplier for Switzerland is 79, for Sweden it is 87, and 18 for Italy. Even relative to the US market the world market is 2.5 times larger for the typical hidden champions' product portfolios. Regardless of their size, companies all over the world encounter unlimited growth potentials if they globalize with determination and long-term orientation.

Regional Shifts

Entries into new markets and growth rates that differ across regions have resulted in strong regional shifts of the hidden champions' revenue shares in the last ten years. Fig. 4.7 shows the revenue shares and their changes.

The hidden champions can still be referred to as "transatlantic companies." Western Europe and the US remain the regions with the highest revenue shares. Together, they currently contribute 68.1% to revenues. But Asia is rapidly catching up with the US. Despite the increase in the US's

Fig. 4.7: Regional shifts in revenue shares

Region	Revenue shares ten years ago (in %)	Revenue shares today (in %)	Change (in %)
Western Europe	61.9	50.6	−18.3
USA	14.9	17.5	+17.4
Asia	10.1	16.9	+67.3
Eastern Europe	3.6	8.1	+125.0
Rest of world	9.5	6.9	−27.4

revenue share, the importance of the transatlantic region has declined as a whole. A decade ago, Western Europe and the US contributed 76.8%. The Western European share has declined sharply to 50.6% of revenues. One sixth of the European hidden champions get less than a quarter of their revenues from Europe. By contrast, revenue shares of Eastern Europe and Asia have increased sharply. These two regions have grown 125% and 67.3% respectively, and already today contribute a quarter to the revenues of the hidden champions. If this development continues with the same growth rates, the hidden champions will generate almost 30% of their revenues in Asia and close to 20% in Eastern Europe in ten years. In view of the ongoing growth in Asian countries, this vision does not seem unrealistic. Some hidden champions announce clear targets regarding the regional distribution of their sales. Mahr, the worldwide number three in dimensional measurement technology, aims for equal shares according to the triad concept of Kenichi Ohmae[12] and says, "At Mahr, we think in triads. In the medium term, sales, revenues and earnings should be generated in more or less equal proportions in Europe, America and Asia." Indeed, 25 years after Ohmae first published his triad concept, the vision seems to be coming true. And the hidden champions are leading the pack.

The decrease in the rest-of-world revenue share does not necessarily mean that the absolute revenues from these regions have declined. The sum of the shares can only be 100, and the decline of the rest of the world-share is an unavoidable consequence of overproportional growth in Asia and Eastern Europe. Given the enormous demands of international expansion on the human and financial resources of the hidden champions, it makes sense that they focus on the most important growth regions. The challenges posed by the rapidly expanding markets in Asia and Eastern Europe test the limits of what the hidden champions can handle. Shifts towards the East and away from the transatlantic region and the southern hemisphere are likely to proceed.

Strategic Relevance of Individual Country Markets

Size and contribution to revenues are only two facets of the strategic relevance of markets. The customer types, the competition, and the environment in a country have a strong impact on the choice of markets and the deployment of resources. Internationalization is not least a learning process in which a company gets increasingly fit for global competition. Why did we, at Simon-Kucher & Partners, open our own first foreign office in Boston and not in Zurich or Vienna? The reason is very simple. We wanted to prove ourselves in the largest and toughest consulting market in the world. For us, this seemed to be the most effective way to gain experience for the world market. We hoped to acquire "global fitness" more effectively and faster in the US than in a small country. Otto Bock, world market leader in orthopedic technology, says, "Our global attitude is a big competitive advantage, because it enables us to establish stable relationship networks across the world. It increases our flexibility and balances out regional economic trends. We strive for close partnerships with our customers in all markets. This closeness is crucial for us to understand the needs of our customers in different regions." Today, everyone knows that customer needs vary across countries and cultures. Globalization makes it necessary to go beyond pure export and to invest into development and manufacturing capacities abroad. Ultimately, and in the long term, this is the only way to adapt products and services to customer needs in the respective countries. For example, in the American catalog of Häfele, a global market leader in furniture fittings, 85% of the products cannot be found in the company's German catalog. Trox, a leading manufacturer of components for air conditioning equipment, trims its products to operate at a minimum noise level. However, knowing that American customers are accustomed to "hearing" the hum of air conditioning, Trox adjusted its products to generate the noise level Americans prefer.

How do the hidden champions see their customers in various regions? Fig. 4.8 shows where the hidden champions have the most, the largest, and the most demanding customers.

Fig. 4.8: Customer profiles according to region (ranking)

	Most customers	Largest customers	Most demanding customers
German-language area	1	2	1
Rest of Europe	1	4	3
USA	3	1	4
Japan	5	5	2
Rest of world	4	3	5

The largest number of customers can be found in the German-speaking region and in the rest of Europe. By contrast, the hidden champions' largest customers in terms of purchasing volume are in the US. The most demanding customers in terms of quality reside in the German-speaking region and in Japan. Japanese clients are famous for their high-quality expectations. The hidden champions' experience is well in line with a statement made by Yves Carcelle, president of Louis Vuitton luxury goods, "What happens in Tokyo today happens in the rest of the world tomorrow. The most demanding customers in the world live there."[13]

Fig. 4.8 also indicates that it is advantageous to conduct business in different regions of the world. Europe offers access to significant and demanding customers. To reach the largest customers in the world, a company must be established in the US, where almost one third (exactly 153) of the Fortune Global 500 companies are located. Japanese customers can make a valuable contribution to quality management because they are very demanding in terms of quality, and service in particular. A license to supply Toyota is deemed an indication of world class. Although not directly related to revenues and growth, such lessons from customers are critical facets of globalization. The customers in individual markets have different profiles and requirements. The hidden champions view this not only as a challenge to meet the various needs, but also as an opportunity to learn.

Markets of the Future

The years since the fall of the Iron Curtain have brought a radical shift in the attractiveness of markets. We already discussed the changes in revenue shares. In the course of the last 20 years, the Eastern European and, even more strongly, the Asian markets have attracted the attention of companies throughout the world. In this process, patterns of trade, investment flows, traffic, and communication have not only grown, but have been dramatically redirected. How do the hidden champions judge the future attractiveness of certain markets? In view of their extensive experience in these markets, these judgments are to be taken very seriously.

Fig. 4.9 reflects the future attractiveness of selected markets as seen by the hidden champions (percentage of 6/7 on a 7-point-scale, with 7 = highly attractive).

Fig. 4.9: Future attractiveness of markets as seen by the hidden champions

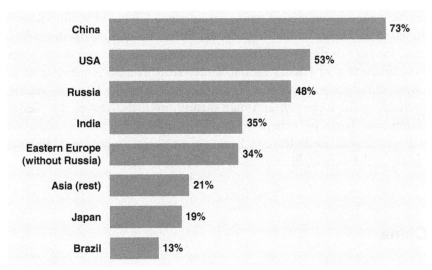

The surprising aspect is not that China is first in rank, but the significant difference between it and the US in second place. Only a few years ago the US clearly was the most attractive market for these firms. Today, the hidden champions view China as by far the most attractive market of the future. Whether this assessment will prove valid and whether this optimistic view of China will come true is not the issue here. The figure simply and clearly shows how the leaders of the hidden champions assess the Chinese market today—not more and not less.

The US continues to be attractive, but only ranks a few percentage points above Russia. Russia's significant future attractiveness is based partly on the fact that many hidden champions are industrial suppliers and equipment manufacturers, who anticipate excellent growth opportunities in view of the enormous investment requirements in the Russian Federation. India follows at a distance, but is doubtless on its way up. For some time I have been observing that the avant-garde within the hidden champions are increasingly investing in India. Typically, these are firms that had entered the Chinese market at a very early stage and have had a rather long presence there, often with several offices or subsidiaries. Now they are turning their attention towards India. It would not come as a surprise if in ten years' time India were vying with China for one of the two leading ranks as shown in Fig. 4.8.

Japan and Brazil are assessed with caution. The popular view of the attractiveness of the entire BRIC quartet (Brazil-Russia-India-China) is not shared by the leaders of hidden champions. In assessing the emerging markets, the hidden champions instead prefer a CRI triad (China-Russia-India, in this order and with graduated differentiation). CRI, not BRIC, is all the rage in the eyes of the hidden champions. The somewhat skeptical assessment of Japan's future market attractiveness is puzzling as all objective indicators support a high attractiveness of the Japanese market, particularly for high-tech and high-quality products. Yet for the hidden champions, Japan is at the bottom of the future attractiveness scale. We will discuss this conundrum in a subsequent section, where we look more closely at the individual markets of the future.

China

For the hidden champions, China is by far the most attractive market of the future. In the past years, I have repeatedly seen that this view is not mere perception or lip service, but is backed by decisive action. I am often asked, "How many of the hidden champions are already in China?" My standard answer is "All of them." While this may not be true in a verbatim sense because there are a few exceptions, it is true in terms of a rough generalization. Quite a few of the hidden champions have even decided to make China their second home market. A well-known case is Danfoss, the

Danish world market leader in components for refrigeration and air conditioning with revenues of $3.4 billion. CEO Jørgen M. Clausen explains and constantly repeats, "China will be our second home market." Clausen is willing to do anything to make this vision reality. He is challenging his teams: "We're growing by around 35% in China and we're making good money, but are we doing enough?" Clausen has even brought the Danish royal family to China, thereby deeply impressing the Chinese. Audi, the premium car manufacturer, also declared China its "second home market." Karl Mayer, world market leader for warp knitting machines, generates 50% of its revenues in China, so there is some justification that it might be considered the company's "first market." For SMS, world market leader in plants for flat steel, China has been the most important market for many years. Tecmen, founded in Germany in 1997, is today more Chinese than German. Tecmen started operating in China one year after it was founded. The company builds special clutches, drives and brake systems for nuclear power plants, cable cars, and waterworks. Tecmen says that the company achieved breakeven in China after only a year and a half. Vollmer, one of the market leaders for sharpening machines, says, "We see China not only as a target market, but as a location with highly qualified employees."[14]

For several years, our consultancy has been involved in the development of a high-tech industrial park. This new park, which has a huge surface of 40 square miles, is located in Wujin, part of Changzhou, a city with a population of 4.5 million, approximately 100 miles from Shanghai. To attract hidden champions as investors we have organized an annual China Investors' Day for several years in a row and have been in contact with hundreds of potential investors. It turned out that, more or less independent of their size, nearly all of them already had established a presence in China. "China is a giant that attracts small companies,"[15] was the catchphrase. "In principle, no midsize company can afford not to be active in China,"[16] was the comment from the German Chamber of Industry and Commerce. For years now, the Wujin High-Tech Industrial Zone has attracted numerous hidden champions as investors (e.g., Bosch Rexroth, world market leader in hydraulic solutions; Karl Mayer, world market leader in warp knitting machines; Stabilus, world market leader in gas springs and hydraulic vibration dampers; Mettler Toledo, world market leader in precision balances and adjoining fields; MAN Turbo, one of the leading companies in turbo engines; and Leoni, world market leader in automotive cable systems). The older industrial zones of Wuxi and Suzhou, located nearby, are also very popular among the hidden champions as manufacturing locations, and many of them have plants there. The hidden champions' presence in China is nothing less than impressive.

We often hear that China will become the "factory of the world," an assertion that will probably come true. But hardly anyone asks the ensuing question, "Who builds this factory of the world?" The answer is "The hidden champions!" These little known midsize firms play a key role in constructing the "factory of the world." China is "the" market of the future for industrial suppliers, engineering companies, and equipment manufacturers. A French study views China and Germany as the prime beneficiaries of globalization: China as supplier of consumer goods, Germany as supplier of industrial equipment.[17] Since most hidden champions operate in industrial goods, China is the most attractive market for them.

But how are the perspectives for consumer goods in China? After all, 30% of the hidden champions are not in industrial goods and yet consider the Chinese market highly attractive. I had a revealing experience years ago when I walked through the main street of the Chinese city of Wuhan and realized that all the well-known stores of the world were present (Adidas, Nike, Gucci, and so forth), and with the same high prices as anywhere else. How was this possible in inner China, in a city with a per-capita income of only a tiny fraction of the income in highly developed countries? The explanation is simple: Wuhan and its surroundings have a population of over 12 million inhabitants. Even if only 2% of this population is willing to pay $100 for a pair of Adidas or Nike sneakers, this means 240,000 potential customers. In view of China's population, even small market shares can mean gigantic sales volumes. This becomes even clearer if you combine the sheer numbers of potential buyers with the preference of the Chinese for status and prestige brands. The piano builder Bechstein, market leader in Germany, builds more pianos in China than in Germany (6,000 versus 5,100). In China, a total of 250,000 pianos are sold each year, 12,500 in Germany—5% of the Chinese portion. Zwilling Henckels, world market leader for premium cutlery, has its own network of shops in China—even one on the main street of Wuhan—and is very successful. China is therefore just as interesting for hidden champions that sell highly priced prestige consumer goods, as for manufacturers of industrial goods. It is obvious that cities and provinces with a high income should be the initial focus of attention for the providers of consumer goods.

The presence of the hidden champions in the Chinese market is truly astonishing. Many of them already have several manufacturing facilities in different locations and a large workforce. CEAG, world market leader for cell phone chargers, has 270 employees in its German headquarters but

18,000 employees in its five plants in China. Würth, the global number one in assembly products, owns 17 subsidiaries in China. Würth's electronics division alone employs 4,200 people there. Netzsch, a market leader in special pumping, grinding, and dispersion technology, with revenues of "only" $348 million, has more than 14 locations in China. IBG, a hidden champion in welding technology, has eight manufacturing facilities, and AL-KO Kober, world market leader for trailer chassis, has four factories in China.

Increasingly, manufacturing companies are not alone in their enthusiasm for China, service and software providers are joining them: The Dussmann Group, an industrial service provider, has a work force of 2,700 employees. Business Objects, world market leader for business intelligence software, is very active in the People's Republic. The business was established both organically and by acquisition. As early as 1999, Deutsche Messe founded Hannover Fairs China Ltd—Shanghai to acquire exhibitors and organize trade fairs on site. Other exhibition companies are similarly active in China.

Despite all this, the profitability and the risks of doing business in China are still cause for concern. With regard to profitability the picture is mixed. Until now, many foreign companies reap either losses or only low profits in China. Some claim that their profit situation is satisfactory. I am unable to paint a representative picture in this respect. The hidden champions are not immune to the risks and the challenges of the Chinese market.

It is well known that the foremost risks of doing business in China are copycatting and the violation of intellectual property rights by Chinese companies. However, copycatting is not confined to companies that manufacture in China. The simplest way is for an imitator to buy a product somewhere in the world and to reengineer it. Of course, setting up a manufacturing operation in China considerably increases this risk, because factory espionage is made easier and employees can be lured away or can set up their own production facilities. Legal protection remains a problem. In some cases, relatively effective protection for industrial property rights has been achieved within the province where the plant is located, because provincial party authorities protect the highly welcome foreign investor. However, the power of a provincial governor or secretary-general in China ends at the province's border.

The case of Eginhard Vietz is a telling example. The CEO of the world market leader for special pipeline construction machinery experienced a disaster in Asia when the Chinese joint venture partner copied the high-tech products and caused considerable losses for Vietz. As a result, Vietz moved hundreds of jobs from China back to Germany. These circumstances are changing slowly and are preventing quite a few hidden champions from transferring their core competencies to the People's Republic. Some managers of hidden champions plants in China told me, "We can do everything here that our parent company in Germany can do." Indeed, when I visited hidden champion subsidiaries there, I was impressed quite often by their technological competencies. However, some hidden champions explicitly refuse to produce in China. One case is toymaker Playmobil, which declared China as a manufacturing location taboo zone. Playmobil plans to export to the Chinese market, but does not manufacture there.[18] Enercon, the technology leader in wind power generation, is also reluctant to manufacture in China.

In spite of their impressive presence, most of the hidden champions are still in the fledgling stage in China. With a surface of 9.6 million square kilometers, the country is huge (in comparison, the US and Alaska together measure 9.8 million square kilometers; without Alaska the US has 8.1 million square kilometers), and the distances are so vast (the longest railroad distance from Harbin in Manchuria to Ürümgi in Western China is 5,162 km or more than 3,200 miles) that most companies will need several locations in China. Building a distribution and service network across China poses long-term problems even for the largest corporations. "China is the market of patience,"[19] says the East Asian Union. As the first major foreign company, Toyota hopes to establish a China-wide distribution system by 2015. Perhaps the hidden champions can lead the way for the giants. World market leader Demag Cranes is a case in point. Between 2004 and 2006, Demag opened 21 new sales and service offices across China. Demag now has a total of 26 such offices.

Although many hidden champions have been in China for more than ten years, the activities there are yet young. The positions they have reached in this huge country are little more than bridgeheads for further and higher investments in the future. The continuing demands of the Chinese activities also have implications for India and other emerging markets, all of which compete with each other for the limited financial and human resources of the hidden champions.

In summary, I have been deeply impressed by the determination and energy with which the hidden champions have set out to conquer the Chinese market. Recognizing the key role of this market they have acted at an early and decisive stage. The numerous cases leave no doubt that most hidden champions continue to believe in China—both as the "factory of the world" and as a market where they can sell huge volumes and which may well become their "second home market," as it has for Danfoss. I would not be surprised if this determined bet on China became the next significant engine of growth for many hidden champions of the twenty-first century. However, high and continuing investments as well as a lot of patience are required.

India

India is not China, even if these two giants are often cited in tandem. Similarities in population size and growth rates appear to be the reason why they are put in the same boat.[20] But these are the only substantial resemblances they bear. From a purely economic point of view, we could argue that China and India had more in common 30 years ago than they do today. The per-capita incomes of both countries were at similar levels in the 1970s. Today, China's per-capita income is eight times higher than in the 1970s, whereas India's has only quadrupled. Consequently, China's per-capita income in 2008 was, at $6,100, about two times India's per-capita income of $2,900, and thus is ca. 100% higher. Is India catching up? Not really! Or not yet! In the eight years between 2000 and 2008, the difference between the two countries actually widened, both as a percentage and in absolute terms. In each of these years, the real growth rate of China's gross domestic product was higher than India's. In 2000, the absolute difference in per-capita incomes was $405; by 2007, this difference had more than sextupled to $3,200. But isn't India the global software and IT competence center of the future? This aspect must also be assessed realistically, at least from today's perspective. Of the 524 million Indians who are actually employed and paid on a regular basis, only 2.2 million or 0.3% work in information technology.[21]

The differences in foreign trade are also eye-opening. In 2008, China exported goods with a value of $1,465 billion. India's exports in the same year amounted to only $163 billion, approximately one eighth of the Chinese figure. Whereas China has a positive balance of trade of $296 billion, India had a negative trade of $89 billion. The figures show that the integration of these two giant countries into the world economy is fundamentally different. Even if we take the exports of services into consideration, the picture does not change significantly.

The similarity in population size can be misleading. China has a population of 1.3 billion and India 1.2 billion. Yet in India, 363 million people

(31%) are under the age of 15, whereas this figure is "only" 252 million (19%) in China. China is aging rapidly. India is young and the population will continue growing quickly. In just a few decades, India's population will be larger than China's. With regard to the sheer number of people, India is the prime market of the future, not China. However, the differences in human resources reach deeper. Only 9% of China's population is illiterate, whereas 39% of all Indians cannot read and write. Conversely, India probably has the edge in top university education. Approximately 4,000 "Bachelors of Technology," selected from 200,000 applicants, graduate from the seven Indian Institutes of Technology every year. A large portion of these graduates migrate to America and fill the pipeline for academia there. I estimate that in fields such as operations research, statistics, or marketing, about one third of today's professors in America originate from India, a large-scale supplier of world-class intellectual capital. The same does not apply to China. This Indian competence can gain great significance for the future establishment of research and development centers within the country, a clearly recognizable trend. Examples can be found in the automotive industry, in engineering, and in wind power generation.

On the other hand, China has a substantial head start in building a modern infrastructure. In megacities like Mumbai (Bombay), Chennai (Madras) or Bangalore, traffic is on the point of collapse. India suffers from a dearth of modern motorways and railroads, and it may already be "too democratized" and decentralized to realize large infrastructure projects. The same applies to private large scale investments. In the fall of 2008, local protests hindered the realization of the manufacturing plant for the globally announced Nano car to be built by Tata, one of India's leading firms. Constructing the railroad corridors and the huge industrial sites such as the ones that were cut into European cities in the nineteenth century could no longer be realized in India's current political environment.*

Many hidden champions already are in India, but typically with smaller operations than in China. Groz-Beckert, world market leader in needles, opened its factory in India in the 1960s. Volkmann, with a global share of 35% market leader in twisting machines, entered a joint venture in India in 1981. Some hidden champions went to India first (e.g., IBG, world market leader in welding technology) or started in India and China at the same time. Marquardt, world market leader in switches for electrical tools and keyless car systems, entered both markets simultaneously in 1996. The

---

*Land ownership marks a big difference between the two countries. In India most of the land is privately owned, in China the government owns large chunks of land.

emphasis is gradually shifting to India from China. Claas, the harvester hidden champion, pays special attention to the Indian market. Claas has been manufacturing rice combine harvesters in India for many years. In 2007, a second combine harvester factory was opened in the north. In addition, one of Claas' two global purchasing platforms is located in India (the other is in Hungary). Claas India coordinates all purchasing from India and China. Semikron, world market leader in diodes/thyristor modules, plans a massive expansion of its manufacturing facilities in India, which have been operating for more than 20 years. India is also a focus market for Plasser & Theurer, the world market leader in machines for railroad track construction. The company founded its Indian manufacturing subsidiary in 1966 and the Indian railroad authority has used the machines produced by Plasser & Theurer ever since.

In the medium term, a hidden champion aspiring to stay or become world market leader must establish a strong market position in both China and India. These may well become the world's largest economies in the decades to come, ahead of the US.[22] In China, many hidden champions have built a solid bridgehead. In India, most are still at the outset. As both markets require further high investments and strenuous efforts, it remains a challenge to get the priorities right.

Eastern Europe and Russia

As we have seen, Eastern Europe and Russia are considered attractive markets of the future for the hidden champions. However, the situation is quite different from China or India. For companies from Western Europe, and to a certain degree even from North America, Central/Eastern Europe and even the European part of Russia form part of the extended home market. Many American companies have a strong presence in Western Europe that they use as a launching pad for their East European activities. In this sense, their starting point is not fundamentally different from that of European companies.

On the other hand, the still-limited size of the Eastern European markets should be kept in mind. In spite of strong growth in recent years the gross domestic products (GDP) of even the largest countries are small compared to Western countries. In 2008, Russia had a GDP of $1,757 billion, Poland $567 billion, the Czech Republic $217 billion, and Ukraine $198 billion. Thus, the Russian GDP is one tenth of the US GDP with $14,330 billion and not much bigger than the exports of Germany with $1,530 billion. While the long-term aspects of the region appear good, one has to be realistic about the short-term prospects.

In Eastern Europe/Russia, a clear distinction should be made between the role as manufacturing location and that as target market. A large amount of hidden champions have manufacturing operations in those East European countries that are now members of the European Union and NATO. A division of labor between parent and subsidiary is typical. Core competencies and the production of critical parts remain with the West European parent. Cost-sensitive and simpler parts are manufactured in the factories in Eastern Europe or Russia. Shorter distances and lower logistics costs (compared with China) make this division of labor highly lucrative for hidden champions originating from Western Europe and, to a certain extent, from North America.

Knauf, one of the world market leaders in gypsum, has grown very rapidly in recent years. One of the reasons is Knauf's early market entry into Eastern Europe and Russia. This midsize manufacturer of gypsum alone has 18 subsidiaries in the countries that emerged from the former Soviet Union. In these countries, Knauf is the second-largest German investor after the giant Siemens the revenue of which is 13 times larger. Western Europe, in particular the German-speaking countries, and Eastern Europe are rapidly growing into one economic zone. The European Union and NATO provide the political framework for this zone, which will be an increasingly attractive market for hidden champions from all over the world.

Japan

Japan is a highly developed and mature market. With a gross domestic product of $4,844 billion in 2008, it is the second-largest economy in the world. However, for many hidden champions from America and Europe, Japan is still a market of the future. The hidden champions' relationship with Japan remains contradictory. As discussed in connection with Fig. 4.9, the future attractiveness of the Japanese market is assessed as relatively low. On the other hand, Japanese customers are considered highly demanding. Big Japanese corporations are world leaders in large markets such as automotive, electronics, and cameras, and should therefore be key accounts for the hidden champions. Not being a supplier to the top Japanese firms is like a missing jewel in the hidden champions' crown. On the consumer side, Japan has a very high per-capita income and Japanese consumers value expensive consumer goods of high quality and luxury—precisely those products hidden champions have to offer. Thus, it seems the perfect match. In addition, the hidden champions with long-term presence in Japan are very successful and profitable—other than in China. Examples are Merck with liquid crystals, Heidelberg with printing presses, and Weinig, world market leader in wood processing machines. Bosch, the world's largest automotive supplier, is also very successful in Japan and one of the largest foreign companies there, with about 10,000 employees. Its strong presence in Japan forms one of the pillars for Bosch's ambition to further extend its world market leadership in automotive electronics.

I have visited Japan regularly during the past 25 years and have noted with surprise that little has changed since the early 1980 s regarding the market presence and success of the hidden champions.[23] The companies that are successful in Japan today are the same as 25 years ago. Few new companies have joined their ranks. One recent success story is Brainlab, world market leader in surgical software, which generates 10% of its revenues in Japan. Kern-Liebers, world market leader in springs for safety belts, and Scherdel, world market leader in valve springs, have both successfully entered the Japanese automotive market. Why do so many hidden champions shy away from Japan in spite of these positive experiences? It is a well-known fact that market entry into Japan is extremely difficult and time consuming. The biggest challenge is to be admitted as a supplier to the leading Japanese groups such as Toyota or Mitsubishi. However, it is also common knowledge that once acceptance has been achieved, a very lucrative long-term business relationship is likely to develop. This ratio between high initial investment and long-term rewards should be attractive, especially to companies such as the hidden champions who deliberately opt for a long-term orientation. Patience and perseverance are indispensable in Japan.

A major difference to emerging markets such as China or India is the systematic preparation required for entry into the Japanese market. In emerging markets, an entrepreneurial, down-to-earth approach is often the best way, given the lack of reliable data, the under-developed market structures, and the insecurities with regard to distribution and procurement. In Japan, all of these market features are well structured, so that market segments, performance levels, and distribution channels must be carefully selected and planned. Highly effective information networks among Japanese customers mean that an initial error can have lasting negative repercussions. In a recent case a fatal accident occurred in an elevator supplied by a leading foreign manufacturer. During a week's stay in Tokyo practically all my Japanese contacts reported this incident to me, even though it had occurred several months before my visit. In Japan, companies get only one shot and must avoid errors at all costs. This requires a very careful preparation for market entry into Japan.

In summary, the hidden champions that have been seriously committed in Japan over an extended time period are successful and earn high returns. The only advice to those who have not yet braved the Japanese market or only have a "foot in the door" is to finally take the plunge into Japan and ensure very professional preparation of their market entry. World market leadership without an appropriate presence in the Japanese market is like an unfinished symphony.

Latin America

German hidden champions have been traditionally strong in Latin America. Sao Paulo is the location with the largest number of German subsidiaries in the world. It is all the more surprising that Brazil ranks relatively low in the assessment of future market attractiveness as shown in Fig. 4.9. In this regard, Brazil can be considered representative for the subcontinent. More than 560 million people live in the countries of Latin America. Hidden champions' views of this region are mixed: They see the enormous wealth of raw materials and the vast agricultural resources that fuel strong growth today and will continue to do so in future. The cultural proximity to Europe is also perceived as an advantage. However, there are grave concerns about the inequality of income distribution and the social conflict potential resulting from this. The hidden champions also view the standard of education among the general population in Latin America as a problem, because they need highly qualified personnel. Assessment is always based on comparisons. In a global age, each region is compared with others around the world, and weaknesses are revealed without compromise.

Implementing Globalization

How exactly do the hidden champions proceed when entering new markets? The step into a foreign environment is an enormous challenge for a company with little international experience. Naturally, there are no easy and always applicable solutions. In my own experience, entry into a new market is always a risky endeavor. Although we, at Simon-Kucher, have entered more than a dozen countries, I don't have a standard formula for success.

Simplifying somewhat, we can distinguish between two forms of market entry. I call the first type the "old trooper approach." It is typical for founder-entrepreneurs and was widespread in the post World War II years. Several case studies from the 1960s serve to illustrate this pragmatic approach. Hermann Kronseder, founder of Krones, today the world market leader in bottling systems, describes his entry into the American market: "In 1966, an American businessman called me. Four weeks later I flew to the US, accompanied by my nephew who spoke English and acted as an interpreter. It was my first visit to the US and I was overwhelmed. We visited New York, Chicago, Detroit, and finally Milwaukee. I came to the conclusion that we needed our own subsidiary in the US. Two days later, we founded Krones Inc. in a room at the Knickerbocker Hotel in Milwaukee. Another two days later we had our first order from a Milwaukee brewery." It took about five years for the new subsidiary to function smoothly, and staff had to be replaced several times.

The entry of Brita water filters into the US market is another example of the old trooper approach. Founder Heinz Hankammer recounts, "Somebody in Salt Lake City expressed interest in our products. I flew over to see whether Brita water filters could be sold in the US. I went to a drugstore and asked whether I could install a table. I started to make tea with Brita-filtered water and talked to passing customers, and I sold my filters. After three days, I knew what works in America, and what does not. That was ten years ago. Today, our revenues in the US are more than $150 million. Four weeks ago, I was in Shanghai and did exactly the same. Last week, I was in Tirana, the capital of Albania. I want first-hand experience of new markets."

The decisive will to internationalize the company creates a situation of readiness in which even coincidental chances are seized without much hesitation. Heinz Hankammer, Brita's founder, describes another experience: "I sponsor a soccer club which was visited by a Russian team. I met the mother of one of the Russian players. She spoke English and seemed to think like an entrepreneur. She started our business in Russia, and only one year later, the company had 25 employees and revenues exceeded $1 million. Not a bad start!"

Manfred Utsch is the global "king of license plates," which he sells in more than 120 countries. Like an adventurer he has toured the whole world peddling his plates. His adventures in Libya, Kuwait, Belarus, Turkmenistan, and other distant places are legendary.

In the post-war years, the founders of the hidden champions typically did not have a higher education and didn't speak foreign languages. This did not prevent these "old troopers" from venturing beyond the boundaries of their home country to create worldwide empires. Education has improved significantly over recent decades. Today, the young founders of the hidden champions generally have a university degree and have gained experience abroad during university studies, internships or professional work. At Simon-Kucher, for example, all partners of the first and second generation had studied or worked abroad before starting as consultants. Market entries into new countries today are planned and implemented much more systematically and professionally. The hidden champions increasingly gain experience during the internationalization process and use it to avoid mistakes when accessing new markets.

However, the risks remain unpredictable. The bottleneck in the globalization process is people. The right individuals must be involved or found. Jim Collins expresses this as follows: "Excellence in corporations seems to stem less from decisions about strategy than decisions about people."[24] This remark hits the nail on the head with regard to internationalization. The multiplication of hidden champion subsidiaries from country to country relies more on key persons than on systems. This explains why this process takes so many years—as in the case of Kärcher (see Fig. 4.2). In the initial phase, international experience is very limited. A company has little personnel it can deploy to establish foreign subsidiaries. Gradually, more managers and employees become familiar with these activities and the process can be accelerated. Once a high level of experience is reached, hidden champions typically internationalize with increasing speed. It is clear that such complex processes do not always run smoothly and without setbacks. Frequently crises are encountered and top personnel needs to be exchanged.

The impulse for internationalization can have different origins. A customer takes the initiative as in the Krones case. An opportunity is perceived as with Brita water filters. An adventurer like Manfred Utsch conquers the world. Ultimately the process is target and will driven. The critical feature is that the hidden champions pursue their globalization with decisiveness and energy once they have acquired a taste for it. The process is slow in the initial phase, because management and financial bottlenecks limit the pace toward internationalization. In time, the process accelerates.

Mental and Cultural Aspects of Globalization

International business has always broadened the cultural horizons. This is both a precondition and a consequence of internationalizing a business. Such experiences date back to the Phoenicians and to Marco Polo and were repeatedly confirmed by history. Anton Fugger, whose trade empire spanned the known world in the sixteenth century, said, "The best language is the customer's language." Internationally successful entrepreneurs were always urbane characters who spoke foreign languages and became familiar with the cultures of other nations.

Today, these requirements apply more than ever, particularly for world market leaders like the hidden champions. Let us first look at foreign languages. Our data is only for foreign language skills within Europe. Fig. 4.10 reveals large differences among selected countries. The figures give the percentage of each population that speaks the respective language.

Scandinavia and the Netherlands clearly top the list with skills in English as a foreign language. Germany and Austria have average ranks, but are well ahead of France, Italy, and Poland. Knowledge of French and German also differs strongly between the countries. Today, English is indispensable for most hidden champions. Many have defined English as their company's working language. However, hidden champions who really strive for a genuine global culture are not satisfied with English alone. Barth, world market leader in hops, requires its managers to speak four languages. CEO Peter Barth explains: "Our philosophy is that each manager should speak at least three foreign languages. This is important because of the psychological effects. In learning a foreign language, one gains an understanding of the foreign culture. This is the very foundation for our superior relationship with our customers throughout the world and no

Fig. 4.10: Foreign language skills in selected European countries[26]

Country	English (%)	German (%)	French (%)
England	100	9	23
Sweden	89	30	11
Netherlands	87	70	29
Belgium	59	27	48
Austria	58	100	13
Germany	56	100	12
France	36	8	100
Italy	29	–	14
Poland	29	19	–

doubt our main competitive advantage. We happen to be located in Germany. Mentally, however, we are international."

Here, we find the seed and the soil for truly global growth. Thomas Lindner, CEO of the needle manufacturer Groz-Beckert, even says, "I am probably the last management generation who gets away with speaking only English as a foreign language."[27] Foreign language skills should not be restricted to management. Balluff, a leading manufacturer of sensors, runs special language programs for all employees. These programs have even been awarded innovation prizes. Assembly, service, and maintenance employees of hidden champions are constantly deployed to distant coasts and have to work in foreign language environments. In recent years, Huf, a leading manufacturer of premium prefabricated houses, has achieved its strongest growth abroad. Huf has realized projects in numerous European countries and in places as far as Siberia and Qingdao in China. The internationalization induced Huf to develop special language training programs for its 400 employees and to hire coaches. Participation in the language courses is mandatory for all employees. Needle manufacturer Groz-Bekert goes one step further and shows that the statement of CEO Lindner cited above is taken seriously: The company finances Chinese lessons in schools at its location. "We reap genuine benefits when a high school graduate who has learned Chinese joins our company, we train him and he then takes up a post with us in China," says Nicolai Weidmann, human resource manager at Groz-Beckert.

Another form of international exposure and a mental basis for globalization develops from traveling abroad—even if only as a tourist. Someone with international travel experience tends to be more open to work abroad than an employee who has never left his or her home country. Anyone who has seen how difficult it is for employees without international experience to embrace foreign assignments will confirm this. The pool of hidden champion employees willing to work abroad is relatively large. Reinhard Wirtgen, founder of Wirtgen, world market leader in road-recycling machines, said many years ago, "I frequently need a team which can be deployed anywhere in the world at short notice. With enough people who have been abroad, we can put together such a group within a short period of time, be it for Alaska or the Sahara. From an international point of view this is a great competitive advantage." Krones, world market leader in bottling equipment, always has several hundred service technicians at work around the world. Even very small companies such as the organ builder Klais, with 65 employees, are able to realize projects worldwide. Depending on the number of orders, every fourth or fifth Klais employee is posted somewhere in the world for several months. In the globalization process, there is a constant shortage of employees who feel comfortable wherever in the world they might be needed. Developing these competencies usually takes years and cannot be initiated soon enough.

International experience as a student forms another valuable foundation for globalization. The absolute number of foreign students has multiplied significantly since 1980, but the proportion of students who gain international experience during their studies is still relatively small. Graduates with international experience are very attractive candidates for the hidden champions. Work permit restrictions can be a hindrance. Normally it would be sensible to train new employees at headquarters for several years before they return to their home countries. Companies, including the hidden champions, have different methods for international personnel development. The companies that explicitly require international experience for management or consider this requirement indispensable for promotion to higher positions are still a minority. I encourage all companies with international ambitions to make this a prerequisite for promotion to higher levels—and to stick to it. I have never found a company that complained about having too much international talent, but a huge number where such a deficit led to grave errors and constituted a serious obstacle to globalization.

Global strategy is a buzzword that sounds modern and attractive. Yet its realization depends on employees who think, feel, and act internationally. Mental and cultural globalization is therefore an indispensable precondition for the successful implementation of a global strategy and must precede it, often by years.

Geostrategic Locations

The long-term consequences of globalization are beginning to show. Manufacturing and sales locations shift all the time and will continue to do so. The flow of goods, capital, and people will change with the locations. Regions and places must be reassessed in view of geostrategic aspects. By this I mean the unchangeable geographic features of the earth rather than the transitory political, legal, and fiscal frameworks. Globalization will increasingly encompass all facets of the value chain. Attracting the best talent from different countries, developing international teams in management as well as in research and development, establishing centers of competence and the cooperation between them are just some of the new challenges. In any case, communication, the exchange of knowledge and information, travel and cooperation across the time zones will intensify. Today, companies are sending development projects along with the sun, traveling around the planet to speed up the innovation process. Call centers are established in far-off countries. When I recently called Lufthansa from the US, a person in Cape Town, South Africa, answered the phone. It is always daytime somewhere in the world, and this fact is put to good use.

The worldwide communications infrastructure making all this possible has improved beyond imagination in recent years. Today, telecommunications, the Internet, and air travel give us access to the most remote parts of the world. Fax, e-mail, and voicemail make unsynchronized communication possible, simultaneous office hours are no longer necessary. Telecommunications costs have become negligible. This means that the advantages of the international division of labor can be exploited to a previously unknown extent. Distances, time differences, and borders have lost part of their traditional meaning. There is widespread euphoria about the evaporation of distances and time differences. In his bestseller *The World is*

Flat, Thomas Friedman postulates that spatial distance is no longer important for business.[28]

However, this euphoria is not just premature: it is fundamentally wrong. In their paper "It's a Big World After All," the Dutch economists Steven Brakman and Charles van Marrewijk refer Thomas Friedman's theories to the realms of fantasy.[29] They show, for example, that trade between two countries decreases 9% if the distance increases 10%. Increasingly, physical and practical barriers toward globalization are becoming apparent. Some of these barriers are based on immutable circumstances. The world is and remains a globe, it is not flat. Day, night, and time zones have not disappeared and will not disappear. There is a limit to the human capacity for adaptation to distances and time differences. In most businesses, a certain amount of direct personal communication remains necessary. Regular telephone conversations can become a burden in everyday business life if the time difference between two locations is 11 or 12 hours. The speed of travel on long-distance routes has not increased significantly since the 1960s, when air travel by jets was introduced. The age of the supersonic aircraft, which in any case only flew on very few routes, is long over. Supersonic travel at a reasonable price remains an illusion. Boeing has abandoned the plan for the Sonic Cruiser, a faster jet designed to fly just below the speed of sound. High-speed trains are irrelevant for intercontinental travel and will remain so. Traveling has even become more tedious and cumbersome due to crowded airports, waiting times in the air and on the ground, and increasingly stringent safety checks and unforeseeable strikes. This tendency will probably continue.

These circumstances cause great strain on the people involved in the global game. An executive vice president of a large car manufacturer told me about his numerous intercontinental trips and the negative effects on his physical condition. The CEO of an electronics supplier complained about his constant journeys to customers in Japan and the Silicon Valley. He was in his mid-forties, but looked nearly sixty. People seldom admit to these problems, but they are ever-present for managers who travel around the globe frequently. After all, world market leadership by definition means that the market spans the world. Hidden champions strive for a high degree of closeness to their customers. Even top managers frequently visit their international clients. These conditions make worldwide travel and communication indispensable.

In view of this, locations gain a new meaning in the geostrategic framework. The various continents face very different circumstances. Western

Europe is in a particularly favorable geostrategic position. Fig. 4.11 illustrates this in terms of time differences and flight times.

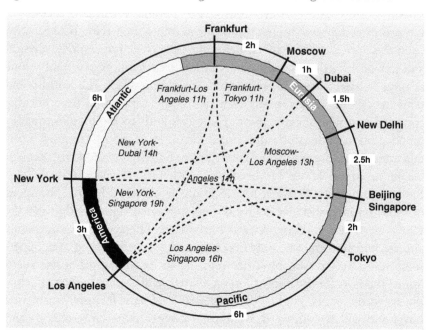

From Europe, it is possible to make telephone contacts with the whole of Eurasia (including Japan) and America (including the West Coast) within slightly extended office hours (nine hours) due to the "triangle character" of the earth. The Eurasian landmass, Transatlantica (Western Europe to the West Coast of the US), and the Pacific form the three sides of this triangle. Western Europe is right in the middle of the two "land sides" of the triangle. By contrast, communication between New York and New Delhi, Hong Kong, Beijing, Seoul or Tokyo is more difficult because the time differences are ten to twelve hours. The same applies in the other direction. The West Coast of the US is in a similar position. While Tokyo and Hong Kong are within the eight-hour boundary, the time difference to New Delhi, Moscow, Teheran and Cairo is between 10 and 12 hours. Although the unsynchronized communication technologies mentioned above (letter, fax, E-Mail, voicemail) ease the time discrepancies, they cannot fully replace synchronous, direct two-way communication (telephone, video conferences, telepresentations with questions and answers).

Europe's geostrategic advantage also applies to travel. Both Tokyo and San Francisco can be reached by air in about 11 hours. Los Angeles to New Delhi can only be flown with a stopover; the journey takes at least 20 hours, including the time required to change planes. The longest nonstop flight is from New York (Newark) to Singapore and takes a tortuous 18 hours and 40 minutes. From Europe, the economic centers in the Northern hemisphere can be reached without crossing the Pacific Ocean or the North Pole. In principle, the same applies to the Southern Hemisphere. Africa is in the same time zone as Europe. Johannesburg can be reached from Frankfurt or London in less than ten hours.

Hans Hess, a manager at T-Systems, described his respective experiences: "I am program manager for three almost simultaneous IT projects. These projects are located in the US/Mexico, Brazil, and China/Singapore. The necessary travel is relatively easy from Frankfurt. In addition, project conferences can easily be organized from Frankfurt, supported by active e-mail communication. In the early hours of the morning, I can communicate with Shanghai or Singapore, and in the afternoon with the US (East and West), Brazil, and Mexico. I am currently in China; here I no longer have the regular opportunity to reach my American business partners and colleagues interactively."[30]

Similar considerations apply within Europe as on the global scale. The German-speaking countries are once again in the middle. From Frankfurt, Vienna or Zurich virtually all major European cities can be reached by plane in about two hours. By contrast, a flight from Moscow to Lisbon takes five and a half hours, and from Helsinki to Madrid four and a half hours. Traveling time from St. Petersburg to Lisbon or Dublin to Athens takes more than six hours, including stopovers. The geostrategic position may be one explanation why so many of the world's hidden champions are located in Europe. Access to the world market is so much easier than from other regions on the globe.

Summary

In this chapter we have learned that the hidden champions have become truly global companies or are heading in that direction. The world is their market and they are working hard to extend their leading market position to as many countries as possible. In the course of this process, they have gained experiences that are valuable and useful for many companies:

- While focus on narrow markets comes first, globalization is the second pillar of the hidden champions' strategy. Globalization makes even narrow markets large and thus contributes to the realization of sufficient economies of scale.
- Globalization is the dominant driver of growth for the hidden champions. Every company with the ambition to grow should seize this opportunity.
- The foundation for the success of this strategy is that customers in the same industry tend to have similar needs across countries. The experience of the hidden champions underlines that it is better to expand regionally in a narrowly defined market than to enter different markets in the same region.
- The hidden champions favor an early entry into foreign markets and prefer going it alone. The pioneer advantage and the direct customer relationships made possible by fully owned subsidiaries are considered critical success factors.
- Globalization takes several generations and requires long-term goals as well as perseverance. Occasional setbacks are normal, and having to put up with considerable frustration is necessary.
- The globalization process involves a regional shift in revenues. Companies that have generated the major part of their revenues in Transatlantica in the past will develop a broader base with America, Asia, and Europe as main revenue sources. This requires drastic reorientation regarding culture, personnel, and so forth.
- The early and strong presence of the hidden champions in China is impressive. If this serves as a rule, international companies must be present in China. However, India is also becoming indispensable for companies that aspire to world market leadership.
- The "old trooper" approach that was formerly used to conquer new markets is increasingly replaced by a more professional and systematic approach. Internationalization itself should be understood as a learning process and executed in a targeted way.
- Broadening cultural and mental competencies is simultaneously a precondition and a consequence of globalization. Language skills, international experience as scholar, student, tourist or professional, and the integration of foreign employees pave the road toward globalization.
- The earth's structure favors Europe as a location, a vantage point for easiest communication and travel.

The world is the market. The hidden champions have proven that this statement equally applies to large, midsize, and even small companies. The wider global perspective discloses unseen avenues for growth. The companies that seize them can grow into new dimensions. However, experience also shows that globalization is a long-term process requiring incessant stamina. It depends on entrepreneurs and employees who transcend their national and cultural boundaries and, in this process, become global citizens. The hidden champions can be role models for other companies that want to embark on the journey to globalization.

Notes

1 "Kundennähe auf fünf Kontinenten: Weltmarktführerschaft in strategisch bedeutsamen Nischen", *Unternehmer-Magazin*, September 2006, p. 28.

2 *VDI News*, December 22, 2006, p. 12.

3 "What's Next," *Fortune*, February 5, 2007, p. 26.

4 "Kundennähe auf fünf Kontinenten: Weltmarktführerschaft in strategisch bedeutsamen Nischen", *Unternehmer-Magazin*, September 2006, p. 28.

5 "Born global" describes markets or products that are global from the outset. Global standards, "effortless" dissemination, e.g., through the Internet, or massive deployment of capital, drive the fastest possible worldwide penetration of the product. Recent examples are Microsoft, Google, Wikipedia or the Apple iPod and the iPhone. John Naisbitt says about iPod: "Apple's iPod has become the world's most successful global product." John Naisbitt, *Mind-Set* !, New York: Harper Collins, 2006. Dylan Jones, editor of the magazine, *GQ*, commented, "The iPod is fundamentally international, a machine that is truly pan-global." By spring 2007, 100 million iPods had been sold worldwide. Hidden champions' products are seldom born global, because they need explanation, require the establishment of distribution and service systems, and financial and human resources are limited.

6 See *US Today*, October 2, 2007, p. 5B

7 Biotechnology also has a good chance of becoming the megatrend of future decades. Today, we are not yet able to identify the megatrend of the next 50 years. Half a century ago, few would have identified information technology as the megatrend up until 2000.

8 Sum of the exports of all countries divided by the world's population. Source: Our own calculations.

9 See Carl Haub, *Dynamik der Weltbevölkerung* 2002, Berlin Institute for World Population and Global Development, Berlin 2002.

10 Year 2000: world population 6.057 billion, therefore exports 985×6.057 billion=$5,966 billion, for 2007 $13,619 billion according to the same calculation.

11 Exports between the three countries have not been deducted. For this reason, the calculation is somewhat speculative, because the stated export quota may also contain exports from other countries and not just those from the home market. We have no detailed information on this.

12 Kenichi Ohmae, *Triad Power: The Coming Shape of Global Competition*, New York: The Free Press 1995.

13 Think: act content, Erfolgreich in Japan, 2006.

14 *VDI* News, September 26, 2008, p. 14.

15 *Frankfurter Allgemeine Zeitung*, February 6, 2007, p. 16.

16 *Frankfurter Allgemeine Zeitung*, February 6, 2007, p. 16.

17 Luis Miotti and Frédérique Sachwald, *Commerce mondial: le retour de la "vieille économie"*? Paris: Institut Français des Rélations Internationales 2006.

18 General-Anzeiger Bonn, February 2, 2007, p. 21

19 *Frankfurter Allgemeine Zeitung*, February 6, 2007, p. 16.

20 For a very informative comparison of the two countries: see Wolfgang Klenner, *China und Indien: Zwei Entwicklungswege und ihre Synergieeffekte, Orientierungen zur Wirtschafts- und Gesellschaftspolitik* (Ludwig-Erhard-Stiftung), Vol. 1, 2007, p. 67–72.

21 See *Frankfurter Allgemeine Zeitung*, May 3, 2007, p. 11.

22 See Wolfgang Klenner, *China und Indien: Zwei Entwicklungswege und ihre Synergieeffekte, Orientierungen zur Wirtschafts- und Gesellschaftspolitik* (Ludwig-Erhard-Stiftung), Volume 1, 2007, p. 67–72.

23 For my first comments on this: see Hermann Simon, *Markterfolg in Japan*, Wiesbaden: Gabler-Verlag 1985.

24 *Fortune*, June 27, 2005, p. 50

25 European Commission, *Europeans and their Languages*, Brussels: Special Eurobarometer 2006, p. 13.

26 European Commission, *Europeans and their Languages*, Brussels: Special Eurobarometer 2006, p. 13.

27 Elisabeth Dostert, "Chinesisch in Schwaben: Die Ausbilder von Albstadt," *Süddeutsche Zeitung*, April 21, 2007.

28 See Thomas Friedman, *The World Is Flat*, New York: Farrar, Strauss, and Giroux 2005.

29 See Steven Brakman and Charles van Marrewijk, *It's a Big World After All*, CESifo Working Paper No. 1964, April 2007.

30 Personal e-Mail dated March 28, 2007.

Chapter 5
Customers, Products, Services

The hidden champions have extremely close relationships with their customers, due to the complexity of the products and services they offer. Three quarters of the companies practice direct sales. Five times as many employees in hidden champion companies have regular contact with customers than in large corporations, leading to the pronounced closeness.

Hidden champions are not marketing professionals by nature. It is a competence they have to work on once they become larger. A significant percentage of the hidden champions depend on only a few customers. This is not a one-sided dependence, but rather a symbiosis. Many hidden champions cooperate very closely with their top customers and benefit from them as drivers of performance and as references. The customers' demands are aimed primarily at high performance rather than at low prices. The products and services supplied by the hidden champions offer not only top quality with high-tech content, but also increasingly comprehensive advice and systems solutions. Prices are clearly above market level.

This simplified proposition describes the typical hidden champion. There are numerous variations and exceptions, and it is important to thoroughly understand each individual case. In the following analysis of various cases we will see that the hidden champions' relationships with their customers are much more differentiated and intricate than the modern management buzzword "closeness to customer" initially suggests.

H. Simon, *Hidden Champions of the Twenty-First Century*,
DOI 10.1007/978-0-387-98147-5_5, © Hermann Simon 2009

Close Customer Relations

The hidden champions' relationships with their customers are close and interactive. The main reason is that, in general, they offer complex product and service programs, often even systems solutions. Such programs cannot be sold off the peg, but require detailed consultation processes. In line with this, direct sales dominate: 82.6% of the hidden champions say they engage in direct sales while 29.5% sell via intermediaries. The sum of 112.1% is explained by the fact that some companies engage in both types of distribution. Approximately 70% of the hidden champions only sell directly and maintain intensive, lasting relationships with their customers. For this reason, they prefer entering foreign markets with their own subsidiaries rather than through importers or agents, as we have seen in the chapter on globalization.

The close relationship is clearly evident from numerous indicators. Of the buyers, 71% are regular customers. In the future, 86% of the respondents expect further concrete transactions with their existing customers. More than 70% of the customers depend on a product offered by the hidden champion. However, only 20% of the hidden champions say that their customers are completely dependent on them; 40% say that they have, at some point, "been through difficult times" with their customers. A relatively high proportion of 68% responded that they "benefit very strongly from the relationship with the most important customers." Apparently customers rarely put pressure on their suppliers. Only 31% of the hidden champions say that this occurs.

From the customer's point of view, the following indicators cast light on the supply relationship. In each case, about two thirds of the customers

- regard the purchase of the relevant product as important;
- enter into a long-term commitment with the supplier;
- show great familiarity with the product; and
- require a high level of information and advice from the supplier.

Routine purchases and infrequent purchases seem to carry similar weights. This is because the product programs of the hidden champions encompass the entire spectrum from regular deliveries to investment goods that are purchased infrequently. This spectrum is also reflected in the life span of the products. Almost half the hidden champions (exactly 48.1%) offer products with a life span of more than ten years. Only 12.9% sell nondurable consumer goods.

All these aspects are reflected in the customer-oriented strengths profile of the hidden champions as shown in Fig. 5.1 (percentage of 6/7 on a scale of 1-7, with 7 = very strong).

Fig. 5.1: Customer-oriented strengths of the hidden champions

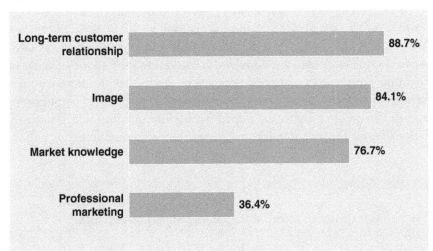

The hidden champions regard the long-term customer relationships as their greatest strength. This applies not only to the market-related attributes recorded here, but also in comparison with internal strengths such as employees' qualifications or loyalty. No other attribute was rated higher. Groz-Beckert, world market leader for sewing needles, says, "Our customer philosophy: the focus is the customer. When we talk about corporate philosophy, we mean our customers. The expectations and the success of our customers define our business."

Second place, as shown in Fig. 5.1, is image, which can be interpreted using the results of past performances. This includes the subject of brands. Hidden champions may be little known to the general public, but they are very well known and have an excellent reputation among their direct customers. This applies even on a global scale, because many of them have built up strong world brands in their narrow markets. Hidden champions also consider their market knowledge good. Market knowledge is not confined to quantitative data, but includes the "feel" for the market, its trends, and customer needs. Sick, one of the world market leaders in sensor technology, says, "We use our knowledge of customer needs to anticipate future developments." This matches the following statement by Jürgen Hambrecht, CEO of BASF, the world's largest chemical company:

"A successful innovator not only knows what the customer can do, but also what he cannot do." Although the markets of the hidden champions are typically fragmented and difficult to measure in numbers, the hidden champions acquire a deep understanding of these markets through their close customer relationships.

In contrast to these characteristics, "professional marketing" is viewed as a weakness by a majority of the hidden champions. Only 36% believe they are strong in marketing. Even in the twenty-first century, the hidden champions do not (yet) regard themselves as marketing professionals. Many of them do not conduct systematic market research; they do not have marketing departments or employees with marketing titles. Large corporations almost always have highly developed marketing functions, but frequently lack closeness to customer. Fig. 5.2 shows this "contradiction."

Fig. 5.2: Closeness to customer versus marketing professionalism

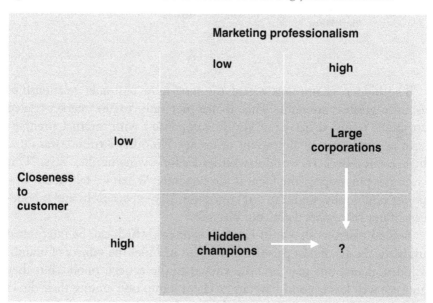

If we measure closeness to customer by the percentage of employees with regular customer contact, the following assessment emerges: The proportion is usually between 5% and 10% in large corporations, and with the hidden champions the percentage lies between 25% and 50%.[1] This means that the hidden champions' closeness to customer is five times higher than in large companies, and it is not surprising that a clear majority of those questioned, namely 60.6%, strongly agreed with the statement "Our most useful source of information is talking to the customer on site."

An interesting question is how the positions shown in Fig. 5.2 will change with strong future growth. The hidden champions will professionalize their marketing strategies as they increase in size, a development that appears indispensable. In the course of globalization, complexity rapidly increases and it becomes more difficult to keep track of the numerous markets, particularly if new markets and/or products are added within the framework of a soft diversification strategy. The increased complexity makes it much harder for the entrepreneur to intuitively understand the market. In the previous chapter, for example, we pointed out the difficulty of setting the correct priorities among the various future markets. A sound data and decision-making basis is required for such choices. Is this necessary professionalization of marketing a threat to the closeness to customer, the hidden champions' traditional strength? The company leaders seem to think so, and they repeatedly emphasize that the close relationship to the customer, swift reaction, flexible response to customers' wishes, and hands-on experience must not suffer in the course of expansion. As already mentioned, many appeal to the genuine and only effective means: decentralization and delegation of authority to the people on the job. But I have also observed cases in which too many decisions are still made by the head office and where the increasing size threatens the closeness to customer.

Large corporations have long since initiated movements to deal with this danger. CEOs are aware of the situation and try to counteract the lack of closeness to customer; every large company has programs to enhance it. However, these programs remain ineffective if they are not accompanied by a genuine decentralization of competencies. A large organization automatically presents a deep hierarchy to the customer. The average distance of an employee to the customer is much larger than in midsize companies. The far-reaching division of labor in large companies prevents customer contact and makes a comprehensive treatment of a customer's needs and problems difficult. Large corporations must face these facts, and the hidden champions should take care that their growth does not distance them from their customers.

The hidden champions and their customers often develop relationships similar to a symbiosis. The hidden champions are very close to their customers and consider this long-standing relationship their greatest strength. Growth brings the new challenge of maintaining this closeness to customer despite increasing size and complexity.

Customer Requirements

The hidden champions' customers are very demanding and have complex requirements. Fig. 5.3 shows the importance of 13 performance attributes.

Fig. 5.3: Importance of customer requirements

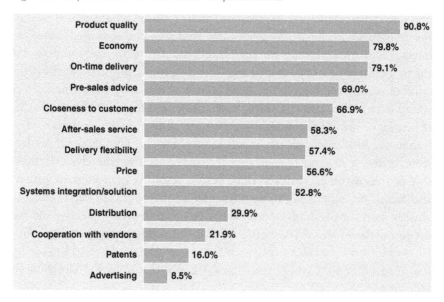

Product quality is by far the most important attribute. More than 90% of the hidden champions categorize the importance of product quality in the top two brackets (6/7 on a scale of 7). This result shows that the hidden champions' customers are very demanding. Economy takes second place, more or less equal in importance to on-time delivery. Supplementary services such as pre-sales advice, after-sales service, and delivery flexibility also have above-average weight. Price and systems integration lie just above the mean of all attributes. The findings indicate that the hidden champions do not have to compete primarily through price. Their customers are far more interested in quality and economy. It is no surprise that advertising, cooperation with vendors, and distribution (due to direct supply to customers) do not play a significant role. The customer is interested in the actual products and services he receives, and not how these products and services reach him. The high percentages for many of the attributes in Fig. 5.3 mean that the hidden champions are faced with taxing and complex demands. How well they meet these demands is not only a question of their absolute performance, but above all of how this performance compares with that of their competitors. We will discuss this aspect in depth in Chapter 7.

Dependence on the Customer and Risk Aspects

In Chapter 3, "Market and Focus," we have learned that the hidden champions are bound to their narrow markets for better or worse. While this can result in an increased market risk, the inherent concentration or focus may reduce the competitive risk. In Chapter 4, it has become clear that while globalization brings risk diversification (when market cycles in different regions do not correlate), it can also harbor additional risks (exchange rates, setbacks, knowledge drain, and so forth.). With regard to the customer structure, an equally differentiated view of the inherent risks is indicated. The composition of the customers can lead to varying degrees of dependence and is therefore a risk determinant. If a small number of customers account for a large proportion of revenues, stronger dependence and higher risk can be presumed than if the revenues are generated with numerous customers. In extreme cases, the loss of one single customer can endanger a company as a whole.

Revenue according to customers is very heterogeneous among the hidden champions. Fig. 5.4 shows the distribution of the revenue shares of the five largest customers.

Just over 10% of the hidden champions generate more than half their total revenues from the five largest customers. The printing technology supplier Technotrans, for example, earns 60% of its revenues from the three leading printing press manufacturers Heidelberg, Manroland, and Koenig & Bauer. This means high dependence on very few customers, although this dependence is not necessarily one-sided. Companies in this group are mainly vendors to sectors with a high degree of concentration, such as the automotive industry, aerospace, wind power equipment, cosmetics or beverages (beer, soft drinks). The second group, where 20%–50% of the total revenues are generated with the five leading customers, is significantly larger, at 28%. Again, we observe high dependence on just a few important customers, but the customer sectors are more fragmented here than in the first group. Mechanical engineering, general industry, medical technology, electronics, or chemicals are examples of typical customer industries. This category also contains numerous consumer goods

Percentage of revenue with five largest customers	Percentage of hidden champions
More than 50%	10.3%
20% – 50%	28.3%
5% – 20%	37.0%
1% – 5%	18.9%
Less than 1%	5.5%

manufacturers. This may be surprising, but the retailers, not the final user, are the direct customers of consumer goods manufacturers in most cases. And retailers are strongly concentrated in many areas (food, DIY stores, drugstores, electronics). Consumer goods manufacturers are frequently dependent on a small number of large retailers.

In the hidden champions group that generates less than 20% of its revenues with its five-largest customers, we find an extremely broad spectrum of products and services. These companies sell to more than one target group. Their focus is on product, technology or competence, not on the target group. Their customer markets are often highly diversified. Some examples in this category include the following:

- GfK, Europe's number one in market research, serves many different sectors;
- Effertz, Europe's market leader in fire protection rolling doors that are installed in all kinds of industrial and office buildings;
- SGL Carbon, world market leader in carbon products used in numerous different end-products;
- Plansee, specialist for powder metallurgy materials used in the automotive, electronics, and mechanical engineering sectors. No Plansee customer accounts for more than 2% of its revenues.

In the group in which the five largest customers contribute less than 5% of the revenues, we mainly find large to very large numbers of customers. Typical examples include the following:

- Bruns-Pflanzen-Export, European market leader in nursery plants. The customers are plant-buyers, nurseries, flower shops, garden and DIY stores, organizations;
- B. Braun Melsungen, market leader in infusion products sold to countless hospitals and medical practices;
- Schenck RoTec, world market leader in balancing machines needed by every car repair shop and tire dealer;
- Smiths Heimann, world market leader in baggage inspection systems used in large numbers at airports all over the world;
- Tracto-Technik, a hidden champion whose drilling equipment for trenchless pipe laying is required by every construction company that lays pipes.

These cases show that dependence on customers and the associated risks cannot be generalized. A significant number of hidden champions depend on a few key accounts. On the other hand, many hidden champions have a strongly diversified customer portfolio. This situation can even be very different within one company. In the two divisions of Demag Cranes, the situation is as follows: Gottwald Port Technology, world market leader in mobile harbor cranes with a market share of 45%, generates 39% of its revenues with the ten most important customers, which are the world's large container ports and large container shipping companies. The division responsible for industrial cranes, Demag Cranes & Components, one of the two world market leaders in industrial cranes (Finnish competitor Konecranes is about the same size), has more than 100,000 customers in different industries. No customer contributes more than 2.6% to the revenues, and only 8.8% of the revenues come from the ten largest customers. Similar structural differences arise with the two hidden champions in the Dürr Group. The contribution to revenues of the five largest customers is in the second-highest category (20%–50%) for automotive painting systems, whereas the five most important customers for balancing machines contribute less than 10%.

Demag Cranes and Konecranes illuminate a further facet of risk reduction in spite of a narrow focus. Demag generates 18.4% of its $1.4 billion revenues from service. This is backed by a vast installed base of 650,000 cranes, 40% of which are serviced by Demag. The plan is to raise this proportion to 50%. Konecranes generates 39% of its revenues from servicing and is number one in the world with earnings of $558 million in this area. Konecranes calls itself a "fully integrated company" and offers "superlative servicing" irrespective of the crane manufacturer. The company has servicing contracts for more than 240,000 cranes in 41 countries, 80% of the cranes are not from Kone. Konecranes does not view service as an adjunct to its product business, but as a business of its own. A high proportion of such services can make a considerable contribution to reducing risk, because the servicing business is not as cyclical as new business with products. This applies particularly to cranes, because regular inspections are stipulated by law. Many hidden champions work in service-intensive industries, offering opportunities to compensate business cycles and reducing risk.

We should not forget the other side of dependence. In many cases, the customers strongly depend on the hidden champions as suppliers. To a certain extent, customers are almost automatically dependent on a company with a very high market share—even if this is only capacity-related. This is a certain insurance against risk, because the customer would have difficulty replacing the supplier. When Schefenacker, world market leader for car rear-view mirrors, had financial difficulties, it was not only a problem for the company and its shareholders, but for the entire automotive industry. Schefenacker makes approximately every third rear-view mirror in the world. Flabeg, world market leader with a market share of 60%, makes the glass part of the mirror.[2] The rear-view mirror may not be a technologically sophisticated or particularly valuable component of the modern automobile, but no car can be delivered without one. A gap caused by the pending loss of one third of the global production capacity cannot be closed at short notice. The large automotive manufacturers had to help solve the problem.[3] There are more than enough examples in the automotive suppliers' industry in which the car manufacturers had to intervene to keep their own production lines rolling. Too much pressure on the suppliers' prices can therefore backfire. Differences according to sectors and customers seem apparent. Rumor has it that retailers such as Wal-Mart or Aldi are tough negotiators, but remain fair to their suppliers, leaving a margin necessary to survive.

In summary, close differentiation appears necessary with regard to dependence on customers and the associated risks. The hidden champions are very heterogeneous in this respect. Even within one company conditions for different segments may vary significantly. Taking into account the risk-reducing customer dependence on the vendors, the general claim that the hidden champions are exposed to greater risks in their customer structure than large corporations or less focused enterprises is unfounded. Focus and market leadership do not automatically mean higher risks.

An assessment of the customers' risks requires a profound understanding of the market structures and the relationship between customers and vendors.

Achieving Closeness to Customer

Since the publication of *In Search of Excellence*, closeness to customer has been one of the most intensely discussed topics in business and marketing.[4] But the implementation of the closeness to customer concept is still difficult for most companies. At the beginning of this chapter we saw that customer closeness is one of the biggest strengths of the hidden champions—especially compared to large corporations.

How do the hidden champions get so close to their customers? In the following pages we will present views and case studies to discuss this question. Clearly, the hidden champions have a natural advantage when it comes to closeness to customer, namely their manageable size. While not every small or midsize company is automatically close to its consumers, and not every large company is correspondingly remote, a certain tendency cannot be denied. It is more difficult for larger companies, with a pronounced division of labor and a complex organization, to be close to the customers. It is easier for smaller companies. The percentages of employees with regular customer contact as reported in the context of Fig. 5.2 are a clear indicator. But size alone is not the decisive factor. In addition, the hidden champions use a whole range of organizational, procedural, and cultural instruments to achieve a high degree of closeness to customer, and to maintain it in spite of their strong growth.

Closeness to customer by means of decentralization

The formation of decentralized units is particularly important and effective. Many hidden champions are structured in smaller departments, often even independent firms directed at special customer segments. The Plansee Group, market leader in powder metallurgy, comprises three divisions. Plansee attempts to get as close to the target groups as possible from an organizational point of view. The business units are designed thus to encompass the entire value chain (e.g., development, manufacturing, and sales). To achieve that, the energies of the entire value chain are focused on fulfilling the customers' needs, as done in a small company. This division-alization often takes place at an early stage of a company's development. Würth, world market leader in assembly products, had formed divisions for wood, construction, metal, and automotive as early as the 1980s, when it realized that the customers' needs in these segments differed. At Simon-Kucher, we started introducing industry-oriented divisions in the 1990s, five years after the company was founded. Segmentation has taken place ever since, with the aim of even better orientation toward the relevant customer target group.

Decentralization can even be implemented on the project level. A project is run like a small, autonomous company. Klaus Grohmann, founder-CEO of Grohmann Engineering, a leading producer of assembly lines, describes his system, "We consciously do not employ salespeople. Our managers have full responsibility for their projects: they sell, submit the proposal, develop the solution, and implement the project. These project leaders have all the competencies of a general manager for their projects. We assign a team to each project and this team acts like a small company. Everyone adopts a holistic view of the project. This approach guarantees an incredible closeness to the customer."

Chemetall, world market leader in cesium and lithium, practices a similar system. Sales engineers have full technical and business responsibility for their negotiations with customers. At Simon-Kucher, we have learned from the hidden champions and grant our partners full authority in dealing with clients. This delegation of responsibility at the customer interface creates not only a high degree of closeness to customer, but adds significantly to process efficiency. Time-consuming clarification with headquarters or management becomes largely obsolete. However, a holistic entrepreneurial view by all participants is indispensable to make sure that these decentralized systems of closeness to customer function.

The high degree of closeness to customer and detailed knowledge of many hidden champions' top managers are impressive. More than three quarters of the respondents (exactly 75.6%) strongly agreed with the statement "Our top management has intensive personal contacts with our customer." Direct customer contacts are considered an important management responsibility, even if this requires constant travel. Wolfgang Pinegger, owner and CEO of the Austrian company DMT Technology, one of the market leaders in biaxial film-stretching systems, says, "I know and have visited every one of our customers around the world. The direct relationships I build up when making these visits are invaluable."

I once read an article in a local newspaper in the US-Midwest about the difficulties an automobile manufacturer was having in the paint shop. The workers in the region used a hairspray with metallic particles that settled on freshly painted surfaces. I cut out the article and sent it to the CEO of Dürr, world market leader for automotive painting systems in Stuttgart, Germany. The CEO replied: "I know about this problem because I have been to that plant. The current equipment is from a competitor who cannot solve the metal particle problem. We have developed a solution. I am optimistic that we will get the next project assignment from this car company." This is an outstanding example of top management's closeness to customers. The CEO of a billion-dollar enterprise with headquarters 5,000 miles away not only knows about a specific problem in the paint shop of a customer near Detroit, Michigan, but has actually been there and has found a solution, although a competitor supplied the current equipment.

In large corporations, programs for the improvement of management's customer orientation or closeness to customer have become popular. For example, managers are required to spend a certain number of days a year with customers or to see them at specific intervals. The seriousness of these efforts is sometimes underlined by bonus payments linked to their fulfillment. Such programs may be sensible, and they mainly serve two purposes: First, managers whose everyday work is far away from the customers are guided to develop a better feeling for what happens at the gateway to the customer. One important effect of customer visits is that direct experience has a stronger impact on behavior than abstract data and market research.[5] Reinhold Würth, a great champion of direct customer contact, says, "In my experience, one day on the front is a hundred times more valuable than a whole week at clever conferences. Contact with customers produces a vast amount of ideas and creativity." A second effect is that the presence of top management on the customer front signals to the employees that customer orientation and closeness are taken seriously. This is a strong source of motivation. However, we should also be aware that top managers, especially in large diversified companies, can rarely provide the individual customer with qualified information because they are not familiar enough with the details of the product, the technology, or the relevant business.

The hidden champions' far stronger focus means that they usually do not need such programs. Most hidden champion top managers are continuously in touch with their customers, and their detailed knowledge makes the contacts so valuable. We have already seen that the percentage of employees with regular customer contact is about five times higher than in large corporations. Closeness to customer at all levels is effectively built into the hidden champions' business processes.

But there are exceptions to this rule among the hidden champions also. Michael Schwarzkopf, CEO of Plansee, regrets that he is rarely in touch with customers. "We supply products and components (e.g., cutting tools) that are not of great interest to the top management of our customers. For the specialists among our customers, by contrast, I am not a technically competent discussion partner." This example, once again, shows that even in hidden champion companies, there are no patent recipes for how to deal with customers. Deep understanding of the business processes is always required. Standard answers do not help, even with buzzwords like customer orientation and closeness to customer.

Manifold interaction with customers

Many business relationships are not restricted to the supplier and the customer, but include other influencers such as sales intermediaries or multipliers. The management of such networks involves special challenges to realizing closeness to customer. Eckart Schmitt, director of sales control at Zumtobel, the world market leader for lighting equipment, describes the situation, "We are particularly close to our customers because we work together in many ways: When an internationally acclaimed architect drafts a new lamp for us, we market it, stating the name of the designer. We help a customer with the technical realization of an innovative concept by providing a special solution. If it is successful, this solution leads to a standard product for us. We organize exhibitions together, in which we explain the architect's concept and our technical solution. We treat other customer groups in a similar way, depending on their specific situation and their needs." Zumtobel manages such networks with great skill. Its homepage lists and provides links to numerous partners and associations with which this hidden champion cooperates. Hettich, one of the worldwide market leaders in furniture fittings, also cooperates intensively with all participants in the buying process. Architects, planners, carpenters, the furniture industry, retailers, and the end-user are all involved. Gore, from Newark, Delaware, best known for its Gore-Tex fabric, has a similarly comprehensive view of the whole value chain. I remember a workshop where, besides Gore-managers, several retailers from various countries participated, including the maker of the raw material and vendor to

Gore (a Swedish company), a leading manufacturer of outdoor garments (a German company), and a maker of hiking boots (a British company). Gore's aim with this project was to fully understand the whole industry network from raw material to end customer. The network character of complex markets has been strongly emphasized and investigated by Swedish researchers.[6] This network character of closeness to customer is very important for the complex business processes of many hidden champions, and is consequently attracting top management attention.

Orientation toward top customers

A conversation with Klaus Grohmann, founder and CEO of Grohmann Engineering, drew my attention to a specific aspect of the hidden champions' customer orientation, namely the attention they give their top customers. These customers are extremely demanding, have set the highest standards, and constantly drive their suppliers to improve their performance. Also, they are excellent references. Grohmann himself explicitly pursues the top customers in his target sectors, irrespective of where they are located. Evidence of the ability to satisfy the most demanding customers in the world eases access to the rest of the market. Grohmann formerly concentrated on the electronics industry and won practically every leading company as customer. In 2006, Grohmann was the only European company to receive the "Continuous Quality Improvement Award" by Intel. Today, Grohmann's customized production systems are used in the automotive, consumer electronics, and biotechnology sectors. Fig. 5.5 shows Grohmann's success in gaining top customers in these sectors. Jake Burton, founder and chairman of market leader Burton Snowboards from Burlington, Vermont, describes a similar approach, "Listen to the pros: we gather top snowboarders about every six weeks for what we call 'the process.' The importance of listening to that kind of feedback is a lesson I had to learn."[7] Fig. 5.5 lists selected hidden champions that serve large top customers in various industries, although they themselves are relatively small.

The CEO of a hidden champion describes his top customers as follows: "We don't love them, but we know that they will always drive us to better performance." The conscious use of customers as internal performance drivers is an interesting aspect. It may be easier to approach less difficult customers first, but companies only become or remain world

Fig. 5.5: Case studies of orientation toward top customers

Company	Main product	Top customers
Grohmann Engineering	Production systems	Intel, Bosch, Siemens, Tyco Electronics, Boston Scientific, Pfizer
M+C Schiffer	Tooth brushes	Industry: Procter & Gamble Retailers: Schlecker, DM, Rossmann, Aldi, Plus
Becker Marine Systems	Rudder systems	Leading shipyards such as Hyundai, Daewoo, Samsung
Doppelmayr	Cableways Cable cars	Las Vegas casinos, Venice, Mexico-City, Toronto
BWT	Water purification	Intel, AMD, Infineon
Qiagen	Molecular analysis sets	US Army (protection against biological attacks)
Stengel	Rollercoasters	Disney World, Six Flags, Phantasialand
Lantal	Aircraft interiors	Singapore Airlines Raffles Class, Lufthansa Business Class, Boeing, Airbus
Scherdel	Valve/piston springs	Toyota, Porsche, BMW, Honda, Audi
Winterhalter	Dishwasher systems for hotels/restaurants	McDonald's, Burger King, Häagen Dazs, Tchibo, Hilton Hotels, Maredo
Ziemann	Turnkey brewery plants	Heineken, Sapporo, Tsingtao, Grupo Modelo (Corona), Inbev
Euro-Composites	Honeycomb components	Boeing, Airbus
Hero-Glas	Glass building constructions	Harrod's London, CNN-Studio New York, yacht of Bill Gates

market leaders by attracting and retaining the top and the most demanding customers. Once this has been achieved, business can be established with less demanding customers, or it may even be possible to do without them. Orientation toward top customers means following them everywhere. Many hidden champions became global by sailing in the wake of top notch customers.

Product and Service Spectrum

Up to now, this chapter has concentrated on the relationships with customers, their demands, the dependence on them, and their role as references and drivers of performance. The other side of the coin is the product and service spectrum that the hidden champions offer their customers. We will examine the following subsections in this area: products, services, systems integration, and price. The product service spectrum should never be considered in absolute terms, but always relative to the competitors. The question of the competitive advantages and disadvantages that are decisive for success in the market is examined in detail in Chapter 7 and will be skimmed only briefly here.

Products

Where do we place the products of the hidden champions on the low-tech, high-tech scale? The answer could hardly be clearer. Four out of five respondents (exactly 78.9%) categorize their products in the high-tech segment. Surprisingly, about 70% (exactly 69.7%) claim the technological development stage is mature, meaning the typical hidden champions' products are high-tech, but no longer in the experimental phase.

The assessment of the stage in the product's life cycle appears consistent with this technical categorization. Fig. 5.6 shows the percentages according to life cycle stages.

Fig. 5.6: Position of products in the life cycle

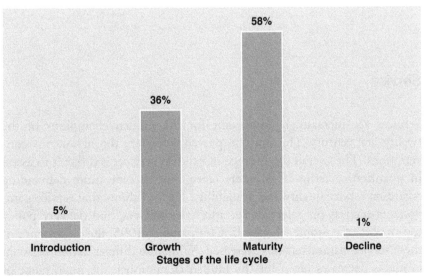

Few products are found in the two extreme phases of introduction and decline. More than 90% of the products are in the growth or maturity stage. This means that few hidden champions are active in completely new markets. Perhaps this is a consequence of our definition. In very new markets, a distinct market leader does not yet become apparent. Sometimes these markets cannot be defined within clear boundaries. Fig. 5.6 also shows that the hidden champions are not threatened by the disappearance of their markets. In contrast to the opinion generally voiced in literature, the life cycle of a product does not inevitably end in decline.

The hidden champions with mature products (which is the majority) are not about to enter a phase of decline. If we look at the list of products, few of them are dispensable. Of course, future technology may make these products obsolete, which raises the question discussed in Chapter 3, whether the hidden champion is successful in making the transfer required by such a new technology (e.g., as Trumpf has done regarding mechanics—laser technology; or the Italian hidden champion Durst that shifted from photographic magnifying devices to special ink jet printers). As explained in Chapter 4, globalization provides excellent growth opportunities even in seemingly mature markets. On a global scale, saturated markets hardly exist. The life cycle portfolio in Fig. 5.6 supplements our earlier assessment of a relatively low life cycle risk. The hidden champions are not threatened by the decline of their markets, and are only marginally exposed to the high risks of the introduction phase. The majority operates on a relatively stable life cycle base. More than one third deem themselves in a phase of strong growth.

Service

Services are increasingly important for the hidden champions of the twenty-first century. This opinion proved consistent throughout my conversations. The overall significance of product services is difficult to assess in quantitative terms. Customers constantly become more demanding regarding service quality and availability. Fig. 5.3 shows that service components such as pre-sales advice, after-sales services, and delivery policy top the list of customer demands. Compared to 1995, the importance of these service parameters has increased. While the differentiation between products decreases (even for the hidden champions), the importance of services increases. In addition, they are an integral part of the growing area of systems solutions. We will look into this in the following section.

One indicator of the importance of services is their contribution to revenues. However, many services are not billed separately and do therefore not lead to service revenues. Not counting approximately 10% of those companies that do not report service revenues, revenues for service and spare parts contribute an average of 14.6% to the total revenues of the hidden champions. With an average of $447 million in revenues, this adds up to $65.2 million. It is important to note that services usually involve a far higher profit margin than the sale of products.

Enercon, the world's number three in wind power equipment, offers a perfect example for service in the twenty-first century. The "Enercon Partner Concept" (EPC) guarantees a consistent high availability for the first 12 years. All eventualities are covered in just one contract, from continuous collateral security to maintenance and repair. This service offer is very popular with Enercon's customers. More than 85% of them sign a contract according to the EPC concept.

Hako, number two in the world and number one in Europe for professional cleaning equipment, only generates 20% of its revenues from the sale of machines. The far greater proportion of revenues derives from a comprehensive service package comprising leasing, maintenance, property planning, and advice. Hako offers programs for property-related cost calculation and guarantees the calculated costs (i.e., shares the entrepreneurial risk). In the words of Executive Vice President Bernd Heilmann, Hako is no longer an industrial enterprise, but rather a "service provider for service providers."

Training is an increasingly important part of services. Reasons are the increased complexity of products as well as the entry into countries where the qualification standards of the employees are relatively low. Hidden champions operate thousands of training centers worldwide and offer countless seminars. Some companies have turned such training activities into autonomous business units. Years ago, Festo, world market leader in pneumatics for industrial automation, formed the company Festo Didactic, which describes itself as "a leading worldwide training provider in automation technology." and offers its courses in more than 100 countries. The training content is broad-based (i.e., not restricted to Festo products), and is even available to companies who are not Festo customers.

A worldwide service presence and international service networks are becoming more and more important. Prime examples for excellent service in demanding markets existed as early as the 1970s. Heidelberger, world market leader in printing presses, or Weinig, world market leader in wood processing machinery, both established extensive service networks in Japan at a very early stage and have acquired an excellent reputation. Groz-Beckert, world market leader in needles, promises that its services will be "fast, direct and reliable on all continents. Wherever our customers work, that's where we are." Today, such service networks are essential for success in highly developed markets. In China and India, however, even large corporations, not just the hidden champions, will need years to reach this stage. The example of Demag Cranes that opened 22 new service centers in China within three years sets benchmarks. However, demands on services in the twenty-first century go beyond mere presence in the respective countries. It is crucial to ensure availability for service customers at all times and from anywhere in the world. One example is the sales partnership between Häfele, one of the world market leaders in furniture fittings, and Dorma, world market leader in door-lock systems, which received an order for the Burj Dubai, the tallest building in the world at a height of more than 800 meters. Dorma supplies the lock systems and Häfele "contributes the international problem-solving competence of its worldwide advisory project service, irrespective of the brand." The Korean company Samsung is the general contractor for this high-rise, and the order will be coordinated simultaneously by Häfele Korea and its subsidiaries in Dubai and Hong Kong. A company offering such cross-border services has an obvious competitive advantage.

More and more multinational companies require services at uniform standards throughout the world. Such demands have been well known to advertising agencies and auditing firms for a long time and are increasingly made in other markets. In addition, there are network advantages when a provider can offer the same services everywhere and be interconnected across borders. The following examples illustrate such new offers and the benefits to customers, as well as the barriers to market entry faced by competition:

- Since customers often rent offices in several countries, Regus, world market leader with over 750 office service centers in more than 60 countries, arranges framework agreements for the whole world.
- International SOS, the world market leader for medical rescue missions based in Singapore, helps its customers anywhere in the world during emergencies and also evacuates them by air.

- Belfor, world market leader for the removal of fire, water, and storm damages, is the only company that can carry out such services worldwide.
- Micros Fidelio supplies the world's leading software for hotels and restaurants. Hotel companies and their employees naturally appreciate standardization in this area.
- Netjets, world market leader in fractional ownership aircraft, offers its customers worldwide access to 700 private jets. Netjets belongs to the Berkshire Hathaway Group of the famous investor Warren Buffet. The advantages of a private jet are available for roughly the price of a first-class ticket. More than 370,000 flights take place each year in over 140 countries.

All these examples combine new types of service content on a global scale and use network economies to optimize customer benefits and costs. Services in the twenty-first century must increasingly offer a comprehensive content in a global network.

Providing consistent and fast worldwide service is a major challenge for midsize companies. Unlike large corporations, they cannot always afford to keep a complete, competent service team in each country and have to compensate for this disadvantage by being fast and flexible. Hermann Kronseder, founder of Krones, world leader in bottling systems, describes this challenge, "At all times, we deploy 250 service and installation technicians around the world. Sometimes they cannot return home for weeks or even months. Coordinating all of them is an almost impossible task for the customer service department and its manager. But I am proud to say that I am told time and again that our service is the best worldwide. This is the foundation of our success, and we owe it all to our 250 customer service specialists, many of whom have ten or twenty years of experience." Kronseder continues describing his spare parts delivery system, "We store the data for each machine, totaling 20,000, in our central computer. These data are accessible at every one of our locations in the world within half a minute. The data are fed directly into the numerically controlled machines, and the spare parts are manufactured immediately, day and night. Parts that are ordered before 7 a.m. are usually sent out by truck in the afternoon to Frankfurt Airport; from there they are air-shipped the same evening to their country of destination. At the same time, our subsidiary receives the flight and freight number so that the shipment can be cleared through customs without delay." No wonder that a company like this gets top service grades from its customers.

Today, even the smallest companies must be able to offer their services worldwide. Let us consider Klais, the organ builders. Although this enterprise has only 65 employees, it is able to install or renovate its organs anywhere in the world. Depending on the order book, every fourth or fifth staff member is out working somewhere in the world, sometimes for months at a time. A global enterprise must bear in mind that the customer does not care where the supplier is based. Customers want service where they need it.

Systems integration

Systems integration is one of the most important trends in the ever-changing service spectrum of the hidden champions. The term systems integration itself is a vague description for a wide variety of forms that might better be called "comprehensive problem solutions." There are many reasons for the increasing importance of systems integration:

- Reduction in the number of suppliers. This reduction is achieved by buying modules or subsystems instead of individual products. The consequence is a hierarchical structure of the supply chain (first tier, second tier, and so forth). A first-tier supplier must offer systems. This is the model that dominates the automotive industry and, increasingly, the aerospace industry today.
- Reorganization of production and supply chain. Former manufacturers become pure engineering service providers that take on the role as systems integrators and leave the manufacturing to other companies. Companies such as Achenbach Buschhütten, world market leader in aluminum rolling mills, or SMS, world market leader in flat steel works, have long since embarked on this route.
- Development of one-stop shopping. On its homepage, Groz-Beckert, world market leader in needles, explains its own development ". . . from being a pure manufacturer of knitting and hosiery machine needles to becoming the most important systems supplier of precision components in the field of textiles and beyond. Step by step, the company has branched out into the business sectors of needles for sewing machines, felting, structuring, and tufting—complemented most recently by the important sector of weaving machine parts." In the latter division, the Swiss world market leader for weaving machine accessories, Grob

Horgen, was acquired in 2000, followed a year later by the acquisition of the German company Schmeing.

- Provide full turnkey projects. While industrial vendors used to supply only parts for plants or only the hardware, we see more and more turnkey providers today. A case in point is Ziemann, world market leader in brewery plants. CEO Joachim Gunkel describes the new situation, "Traditionally, a brewery had 200 engineers and technicians. Today it employs only 20 technical experts." This is possible because Ziemann assumes responsibility for the planning, the construction, the software, the test runs on its own pilot plant and other activities. No other competitor offers the same comprehensive service as the market leader. This is obviously appreciated by the brewers. In the last three years Ziemann has more than doubled its revenues. In some cases the engineering company even runs the operations of a new plant it built. Voith, the global number one in paper machines, runs several customers' plants as a service provider.
- Increased complexity. This form of problem solution can be higher technical complexity, such as the coordination of hardware and software. The IT service provider Bechtle offers comprehensive problem solutions encompassing both components. Increased technical complexity can create new market opportunities. Festo has reacted to the higher training requirements originating from industrial automation by offering a systems solution for both product and training. Similar trends can be observed with pure service providers, for such as the Neumann Group, world market leader in green coffee. As discussed in Chapter 3, Neumann operates coffee plantations, processes green coffee and takes care of the import and export logistics.
- Added value for the customer. Greater added value for the customer can arise through better coordination of the components of a system. Winterhalter not only offers special dishwashers for the hotel and restaurant industry, but also provides its customers with water treatment systems, its own dishwashing agents, and service around the clock. Enercon guarantees extensive availability of wind energy plants and even shares the entrepreneurial risk. Kannegiesser, world market leader in laundry technology, began to view the "laundry as an overall system" as early as the 1980s, heralding the end of an era in which the manufacturers of ironing and other machines operated separately. Instead, Kannegiesser developed an integrated complete program for industrial laundry technology and rose to world market leadership in this domain. Lantal, world market leader in cabin designs for commercial aircraft, offers the airlines a

comprehensive service system that includes the design of the entire interior according to the customer's specifications as well as the production of seat covers, curtains, wall coverings, headrest protectors, and carpets.[8]

- Implementation of new solutions for problems previously unsolved or solved unsatisfactorily. The American hidden champion Biomet is one of the world market leaders for orthopedic implants. The implantation of artificial joints involves an operation, hospitalization, and rehabilitation. With its "Joint Care" program, a registered service brand, Biomet offers hospitals and health insurance companies a completely new process, in which all therapy and rehabilitation steps are carefully planned in advance. "Joint Care" reduces the average stay in hospital to 7 days from 14, and rehabilitation periods are also shorter. The pilot hospital increased the number of annual operations by 50%, with corresponding effects on the profits. In the Netherlands, where "Joint Care" was first introduced, 40% of all hospitals already operate with this program. As the costs are about 10% lower than with traditional methods, the health insurance companies also save money. Patients benefit by having to pay only half of the usual copayments. Biomet offers the program to hospitals free of charge if they use the knee and hip implants made by this hidden champion. The systems solution creates a win-win effect for all participants.

- Promotion of certification and liability standards. Here again, Lantal is an appropriate example. Extreme safety standards are applied to aircraft interior coverings. Lantal is authorized by the European Aviation Safety Agency (EASA) and the American Federal Aviation Agency (FAA) to issue official test certificates for materials and carpets. Every airline prefers dealing with only one supplier, instead of several, when it comes to certification and liability issues.

- Implementation of safety and efficiency standards. One-stop solutions can mean greater safety and efficiency for the customer. The Australian company Orica, world market leader for commercial explosives, offers the operators of stone quarries one-stop problem solutions. Orica not only supplies the explosives, but analyzes the rock and carries out the drilling and the explosions. In this new system model, Orica supplies the customer with broken rock and charges according to performance. As this is a customer-specific solution, the price becomes less transparent, revenues per customer, efficiency, and safety increase. The quarry operator is no longer involved in the explosion process and is effectively tied to the supplier. Changing to another provider becomes more difficult.

- Integration of new business models. GE Aircraft Engines, world market leader in jet engines, was the first company to practice a business model in which airlines were offered thrust power that was charged by operating hours. In this business model GE takes care of everything. Business models that only charge the performed services also fall into a similar category. Dürr, number one in automotive paint shops, cooperates with BASF, world market leader in automotive paints, to offer car manufacturers the painting of a vehicle for a fixed price.

These cases show that systems integration can be based on a combination of several products, a merger of product and service, shifts in the value chain, or completely new business models. The hidden champions take advantage of all these options. The strategic significance of this expansion of the product and service spectrum can hardly be overestimated:

- Systems integration usually involves a deepening of the value chain. The growth potential resulting from this is an obvious implication. "We cover the entire value chain," says Neumann's CEO, Peter Sielmann.
- Systems integration opens up the opportunity to noticeably increase the benefit for the customer and above all the retention of the customer. It has been proved often enough that customers who buy several products or entire systems from one supplier change their suppliers less easily and less frequently than customers who only buy one product.
- Entry barriers for new competitors are significantly higher with complex systems solutions than with single products. Systems integration is a very effective means of raising the barriers to market entry and reinforcing a company's own market position.
- The market leader is in an ideal position to offer systems solutions. Customers believe the market leader is most capable of mastering the strongly increased complexity.

For these reasons, systems integration and system offers are highly lucrative opportunities for the hidden champions of the twenty-first century. However, warning must be given that systems integration involves complexities and risks. I have repeatedly seen cases in which the transition to system offers caused great organizational difficulties. A company organized in divisions that wants to offer cross-divisional solutions to its customers automatically faces the problems of a matrix organization, no matter what the specific structures, processes or incentives look like in practice. Product businesses and service businesses are subject to different processes, for example with regard to the degree of centralization or predictability. Hako, market leader in professional cleaning and care equipment, is no longer a typical industrial company, but has placed most of its employees in local branches that provide service to their customers. Systems selling and cross-selling often fail due to a lack of employee training or motivation. The hidden champions in particular face the risk that systems offers threaten their clear focus and the strengths derived from it. My advice is not to naively follow a fashion, but to carefully consider the option of offering systems solutions and to devote the greatest attention to its organizational implementation.

Price

The discussion to date has made it clear that the strategy of most hidden champions is directed toward high value to customer, not toward low prices. With few exceptions, the respondents said that this positioning is an integral part of their corporate strategy. "We sell high value, not low prices" or "quality counts for us, not the price" are typical comments I have heard frequently.

The extreme price pressure that dominates many markets (e.g., automotive, electronics, retail) and leads to continuous price decreases appears not to affect the hidden champions to the same degree. When asked about price changes over the last ten years, the average rating was about 3.7, close to the mean on a scale of 7. A clear majority of 62.9% said that the price level fundamentally remained the same. Almost a quarter (24.2%) reported that their prices had declined somewhat. Only 12.9% said that their prices had perceptibly risen (i.e., every eighth company was able to charge considerably higher prices.).

Understandably, hidden champion CEOs do not want to be quoted on specific price premiums. The hidden champions charge prices that are generally 10%–15%, often 20% above the average price level of the respective markets. Even for price-sensitive products or target groups, the price premium is between 5%–10%. The observation that the market leader's prices are above average is not new. Competition in most markets is not between commodities, but between differentiated products. Accordingly, the customers' willingness to pay is also differentiated, and price differences are normal. Superior product or service value is reflected in a higher price. If most customers give high quality a priority over low prices, high market shares come along with high prices. This is the typical situation of the hidden champions. This observation is not contradictory to the negative slope of the price-demand curve from economic theory.

An above-average price level does not at all mean that the hidden champions are exempt from price competition. Although they have a certain latitude in pricing (which is called "pricing power" in economics), the usual price mechanism sets in once they go beyond that latitude. We found that half the customers would withdraw when facing a price difference of 28%. Within this range, the price elasticity is 1.78 (=50/28). In other words, the percentage decrease in sales is 1.78 times as high as the percentage price difference. This is a medium, not a high price elasticity. In spite of the price premiums we mentioned, the hidden champions do not overstretch their scope for price increases. The opposite is probably true: they do not fully exploit their pricing power. There is considerable potential for improved quantification of the value to customer (which should always be the basis for price setting) and in a refined price differentiation. The pricing processes also deserve greater attention. As most hidden champions are active in business-to-business markets, actual transaction prices are almost always negotiated. We know from numerous projects with hidden champions that there is considerable potential for process improvement regarding argumentation, information, the quantification of relative power positions, application of game theory, and incentives for sales personnel.

There is a small group of hidden champions that does not use the premium price strategy described above, but instead offers low, sometimes even aggressive, prices. Cargobull has cut its costs to such an extent (see Chapter 3) that the company was able to increase its margins strongly despite a price drop of 30% in the last ten years. Fielmann, European market leader in the distribution of eyeglasses, applies a pricing strategy with aggressive characteristics compared with regular opticians, and does so successfully. The automotive parts supplier A.T.U. says, "We are one of the cheapest quality suppliers on the auto after-sales market" and advertises with the slogan "everything, except expensive." Suspa, a leading manufacturer of gas springs for office chairs, emphasizes "cheap prices" and "price advantages." Likewise, 3B Scientific, world market leader in anatomical teaching aids, advertises with its "extremely competitive cost-effectiveness." Kaldewei, European market leader in steel bathtubs, is proud of its high efficiency and low prices. Böllhoff, a leading producer of screws, also considers itself fully competitive with Asian suppliers vis-à-vis cost and prices due to a high degree of automation.

Hidden champions offering or advertising low prices remain the exception. Profits can only be earned with low prices if a company can manufacture at lower costs than the competition over a sustained period of time. Generally, few companies and very few hidden champions fulfill this condition.

Summary

This chapter has shown that the hidden champions maintain very close relationships with demanding customers and target their product and service spectrum to the needs of these customers. Closeness to customer forms a central element of their strategy. Our detailed findings and the recommendations for other companies are as follows:

- The close relationship to customers is reflected in all indicators. The complex products that are typical for the hidden champions require close and continuous interaction with customers.
- This requirement is best met by direct sales, practiced by more than three quarters of all hidden champions.
- Hidden champions are characterized by their pronounced closeness to customer. The percentage of hidden champion employees with regular customer contact is five times higher than in large corporations. Unlike many large corporations, most hidden champions are not marketing professionals. With increasing size, both marketing professionalism and retaining closeness to customer receive continuous attention from the hidden champions' top management. Large corporations should aim for greater closeness to customers.
- Closeness to customer is easier to realize in view of the hidden champions' small size and the less stringent division of labor. In addition, many of these companies are decentralized according to target groups.
- Top management values continuous direct customer contact and practices this on a regular basis. This conduct has positive effects with regard to their own information as well as to employee motivation.
- The risk profile regarding customers requires a differentiated view. Many hidden champions are dependent on a small number of customers, but this dependence is not one-sided. Customers also depend on the hidden champions. A symbiosis emerges.
- Customer requirements are performance rather than price oriented. Customers around the world are becoming more alike.

- Companies that want to become or remain market leaders must attract top customers and satisfy them on a long-term basis. Therefore, many hidden champions direct their primary attention strongly toward top customers. This has two advantages. The top customers function as internal performance drivers, and they have a high reference value. Continued market leadership is normally only possible if a company is supplier to the top customers.
- The product and service spectrum is designed to meet the customers' exact needs. The products are highly sophisticated, with well-established technology. More than 90% of the products are in the growth or maturity stage of the life cycle without danger of going into decline.
- Service is becoming increasingly important for the hidden champions' strategy. Extended offers such as comprehensive service packages, training, worldwide presence, and networking are becoming indispensable in the twenty-first century.
- Numerous (particularly younger) hidden champions use network economies by offering services the value of which increases due to global presence.
- The trend toward systems integration can be observed with many hidden champions. Systems solutions can improve the value to customer and raise entry barriers for competitors. The market leader appears predestined to introduce these complex offerings. However, we should not forget that the transition from products to systems solutions increases organizational complexity and threatens the hidden champions' focus. Every business extension of this kind should be carefully considered.
- Apart from a few exceptions, the hidden champions do not compete through price. As are their superior products and services, their prices are typically above market level. However, they are not immune to price competition and should professionalize their pricing with regard to knowledge of price elasticities, price differentiation potentials, and pricing processes.

These insights and recommendations largely correspond to common sense. However, their observation and practical implementation prove difficult. The greatest differences between large and midsize enterprises become apparent when they deal with customers, customer relationships, and closeness to customer. The hidden champions succeed in structuring their customer relationships in a way that is advantageous for themselves and for their customers. This is possible because of their manageable size and arrangements such as decentralization and regular customer contact by top managers. They practice closeness to customer in their conduct and their organization, and apply it to their spectrum of products and services, as well as, increasingly, systems solutions. When it comes to customer relations the hidden champions are excellent role models.

Notes

1. There are cases, like the big champion Würth, where more than half of all employees work in the field. Würth's competitor Berner even has 4,200 of a total of 6,500 employees in the sales force. The same applies to direct sales companies like Bofrost. Service-intensive companies also have a high proportion of employees with direct customer contact. The service division of Demag Cranes has 1,612 employees, 28.4% of the entire workforce of Demag Cranes. Services contribute 18.4% of Demag Cranes' revenues and this percentage is to be increased in the future.

2. Flabeg is an abbreviation for the German word "Flachglasbearbeitungsgesellschaft," meaning flat glass processing company. The company produces automobile mirrors in Germany, Brazil, UK, US, and China. Flabeg also has a leading market position in solar mirrors. The company is the only supplier of curved solar mirrors worldwide.

3. See *Frankfurter Allgemeine Zeitung*, February 10, 2007, p. 16

4. Thomas J. Peters and Robert H. Waterman, *In Search of Excellence: Lessons from America's Best-Run Companies*, New York: Harper & Row 1982.

5. Edward F. McQuarrie, *The Customer Visit: A Tool to Build Customer Focus*, San Francisco: Sage Publications 1993.

6. See Hakan Hakansson and Jan Johanson (eds.), *Business Network Learning*, Kildington, UK: Elsevier 2001; Mats Forsgren and Jan Johanson (eds.), *Managing Networks in International Business*, Langhorne, PA: Gordon & Breach 1994.

7. See *Fortune*, April 2, 2007, p. 19.

8. See *Neue Zürcher Zeitung*, February 5, 2007, p. 7.

Chapter 6
Innovation

We have already seen that excellent performance with regard to goals, globalization, and closeness to customer is a necessary requirement for becoming a hidden champion. However, in most cases innovation is the foundation for success. Achieving and maintaining world market leadership requires outstanding and continuously innovative performance. The innovations of the hidden champions are in no way restricted to technologies and products; these companies also demonstrate tremendous innovative drive in processes, systems, marketing, and services. Various indicators such as R&D intensity, number of patents, and revenues coming from new products prove that the hidden champions are extremely innovative. How do these midsize companies achieve such innovativeness in spite of their limited resources? In this chapter, we will see that the hidden champions differ from large corporations in the way they handle several key factors for success in innovation.

It is no exaggeration to speak of a massive wave of innovation at the start of the twenty-first century. In Chapter 4, we identified globalization and the associated market expansion as the dominant growth driver for the hidden champions. In addition, these companies have increased their market shares, as we saw in Chapter 2. Innovation is the main reason for the hidden champions' considerable improvement of their competitive position in the last ten years, in terms of both absolute and relative market shares.

What Does Innovation Mean?

Innovations must either improve the value to customer or provide an existing value at a lower cost. Ideally, they do both. The word "innovation" is primarily associated with technology and new products, and technology is in fact the key factor behind most hidden champions' innovativeness. As shown in Fig. 2.6, 85% of the hidden champions see themselves as "technology leader," (i.e., the technically most innovative and progressive company in their market). According to RUD, the world market leader for industrial chains, "Leadership in technological innovation has always been a key component of our business strategy and our vision." Technology leadership frequently means a considerable head start over competitors. Günther Blaschke, CEO of Rational, the clear world leader in cooking technology for large-scale kitchens with a global market share of 52%, estimates that competitors would need six to seven years to reach his company's technical level. Norbert Nold, CEO of Omicron, world market leader in tunnel-grid microscopes, reports, "We create value not in manufacturing, but in innovation and development. Our customers honor our technical head start." To retain this lead in the future, Omicron employs about 40% of its people directly or indirectly in research and development. Fischer, the world leader in wall plugs, made innovation the core of its slogan, "If you look for innovation, you'll find Fischer." More than 2,000 patents prove that this is by no means an empty phrase.

Innovation applies not only to technology and products, but to all business processes at the hidden champions. Process innovations are very important. They involve more than cost reduction and often lead to improvements in quality, shorter cycle times or greater convenience, and thus higher value to customer. For many hidden champions, process innovations are more important than product innovations. CEO Jürgen Thumann describes the role of process innovations at Heitkamp & Thumann, the world market leader in battery cans and other components, "My company is process-driven. Our expertise lies in the ongoing improvement of processes rather than in product technology."

Innovations in distribution, sales, and marketing are abundant. Many hidden champions were born out of such innovations or derived their growth from them. The core competency of Würth, for example, is a highly efficient sales and logistics system that incorporates a device called the ORSYMAT (an acronym for order, system, and automation), which is installed in the workshops of Würth's larger customers. The ORSY-MAT is connected online to Würth's local branch and filled with the items the customer needs. When a drawer is opened and an item removed, the next order is automatically placed and the invoicing is initiated. On his or her next visit to the customer, the Würth representative refills each compartment. The customer no longer has to take care of hundreds of small items because the stock management is handled by Würth. Taking a similar approach, Bofrost offers maximum convenience by delivering products straight to the customer's deep freezer, ensuring that the cooling chain is never interrupted.

Aenne Burda was responsible for a groundbreaking innovation in 1952, when she began publishing cutting patterns in the fashion magazine she had launched two years previously. This made it possible for her readers to sew the clothes shown in the magazine at home. Cutting patterns have existed since the nineteenth century, but their real breakthrough came when magazines began to publish them. By 1961, Burda Moden had become the largest fashion magazine in the world. Today, it is translated into 16 languages and published in 89 countries.

Festo, the world market leader in pneumatics, is highly innovative in both technology and marketing. Its general catalog was replaced by specialized catalogs for individual industries when the organization was restructured along industry segments. As a result, the company is able to target customers in each industry much more effectively, because these customers regard Festo as a specialist for their industry. In 2005, Festo even introduced individualized catalogs that take into consideration the past order patterns and the needs of the customer in question. As a result of modern information technology, such approaches are possible without having to invest a great deal of time, effort, and expenditure.

Assist Pharma has developed a complex process innovation with enormous market potential: different medications to be taken by one patient are packaged together and delivered through pharmacies. This innovation could radically reduce life-threatening errors made by older patients with multiple diseases when taking their medication, and thus to save money and lives.

Innovations often serve to lengthen an existing value chain. Bosch Power Tools, the worldwide number one in its field, introduced the shop-in-shop concept in large DIY stores and now operates 700 of these shops. Bosch's revenues in these DIY stores have increased 30%. Globetrotter, Europe's leading supplier of outdoor equipment, creates new types of adventure landscapes in its stores to whet customers' appetites for new adventures. The company employs only people with a real passion for outdoor activities.

We do not normally think of pricing as an area for innovation, yet there are innovations here, too. Ryanair, the European market leader in no-frills flights, charges its passengers $15 per checked-in item of baggage. Previously unheard of in the aviation industry, this innovation was justified with the argument that it enabled a 9% price reduction for passengers who do not check in any baggage. Enercon, meanwhile, is an exemplary innovator not only in technology and service, but also in pricing. The price for a service contract within the Enercon Partner Concept described in Chapter 5 depends on the earnings of the wind energy plant in question. Enercon's pricing for its service contracts therefore contains a strong element of entrepreneurial risk. In addition, Enercon covers half of the service fee for the first six years of the 12-year contract.

For some hidden champions, design is an important, if not the most important, aspect of innovation. Combining function and appearance is always a particular challenge. "Our task is to incorporate the technology into the design," states Klaus Grohe, CEO of the leading bathroom fittings manufacturer Hansgrohe. His company employs top designers such as Philippe Starck, Antonio Citterio, and the Bouroullec brothers, and Grohe himself heads the 103-strong development department. In 2007, Hansgrohe filed 310 applications for patents, registered designs, and trademarks, a very large number for a company with 3,250 employees and revenues of $907 million.

The systems integration discussed in Chapter 5 offers starting points for more unusual innovations. Behr, the world market leader in engine cooling and vehicle air conditioning, works with partners to develop and produce comprehensive systems modules for the automotive sector. HBPO—the joint venture of Behr, the lighting specialist Hella, and the French company Plastic Omnium—is a case in point. Its innovative IFP front-end project achieves unparalleled integration by combining lighting, cooling, aerodynamics, pedestrian protection, and crash management. Such comprehensive systems solutions provide not only greater customer value, but also simplified processes and lower costs, Behr-Hella Thermocontrol (BHTC), another joint venture, is the innovation leader in air-conditioning control. Its new control concept enables the vehicle climate to be regulated to a previously unattained degree, placing the focus squarely on increased customer benefit.

Simplification is a further route to innovation. The simplicity of Ikea's products, for example, enables customers to assemble the products themselves. The resulting cost advantages in manufacturing are then passed on to the consumer. In spite of aggressive prices, Ikea achieves unusually high margins of about 10%. Most manufacturers of photovoltaic equipment, meanwhile, focus on improving the efficiency of their solar cells, but tend to neglect construction and assembly problems. "Until now, hardly anybody has tried to make it simpler to install photovoltaic equipment," reports Christian Kirschning, founder of Sunclip. His company has chosen another innovation route and concentrates on simplifying assembly, which accounts for a significant proportion of the total costs of a solar panel system. Overall, it is expected that solution simplification will gain importance in the future. Parallel to the concept of lean manufacturing, the aim of lean engineering is to develop radically simplified products that perform just as well as more complicated equipment, but cost less, are less susceptible to disruptions, and are simpler to operate and service. This approach offers the hidden champions a wide range of innovation opportunities. Karl Mayer, the dominant world market leader in knitting machines, has been successful in pursuing this route. One constraint in implementing lean engineering could be the attitudes of engineers who tend toward complex rather than simple solutions—a phenomenon called "overengineering."[1]

Innovations are also important in the service sector, even if they cannot be patent protected. We described several case studies in Chapter 5. Belfor, for example, has established a global system for handling fire, water, and storm damages and has become the world market leader in this field. The hidden champion International SOS from Singapore is the world's largest medical assistance company, operating a global network of ambulance aircraft, emergency centers, and hospitals. Netjets, the world market leader in private aviation, has created a new market by introducing partial ownership of private jets. Services such as these are groundbreaking innovations.

These cases illustrate that the hidden champions approach innovation from many different vantage points. The innovative activities of the hidden champions vary widely, but these companies all appear to have embarked on a phase of pronounced innovativeness. We will look more closely at this aspect in the following section.

High Level of Innovativeness

Various indicators such as expenditure on research and development, the number of patents, and the proportion of revenues generated by new products can be used to measure a company's capacity for innovation. However, even economic experts probably have misleading ideas about companies' activities in this area. A study of 3,171 companies from all sectors conducted by the German Economic Institute had revealing results.[2] The study made a distinction between innovators and non-innovators. To be classed as innovators, respondents were required to have introduced new products or processes in the preceding three years. About 30% of the participating companies were categorized as non-innovators, so only 70% qualified as innovators. This finding is surprising because it shows that innovation is by no means a matter of course in business. About one third of companies do not innovate at all, and three quarters of the non-innovators conduct no R&D activities. Even among the innovators, 26% occasionally engage in research and development, and only 40% do so continuously.

R&D intensity

Across all companies in the German Economic Institute study, average R&D spending as a percentage of revenues stood at 1.8%. In judging this R&D intensity it makes more sense to look only at companies that actually engage in R&D. For them, the figure is 3%, while non-innovators spend only 0.5% of revenues on innovation. Another study showed that in the engineering sector, the average R&D intensity was 3.5%.[3] In a worldwide study, management consultants Booz Allen Hamilton examined the 1,000 publicly listed corporations that spend the most on R&D in absolute terms.[4] On average, these 1,000 companies spent 4.2% of their revenues on research and development.

Such figures are relevant benchmarks for the hidden champions. These companies spend 5.9% of revenues on research and development (i.e., twice as much as the average innovators in the German Economic Institute study and almost 50% more than the top 1,000 R&D companies in the world). For one fifth of the hidden champions, the R&D intensity actually exceeds 9%, more than three times the typical figure for German companies. Fig. 6.1 lists selected hidden champions the R&D intensity of which exceeds 10%. The figures from the studies mentioned above are also shown.

The R&D intensity of the hidden champions far outstrips that of average companies. The hidden champions invest

- double the share of revenues spent by average companies,
- 68% more than mechanical engineering companies,
- and almost 50% more than the global top 1,000 in research and development. Many hidden champions' R&D intensity exceeds 10%.

Results of studies	R&D intensity
German Economic Institute (3,171 companies)	1.8%
German Economic Institute (with R&D)	3.0%
German engineering sector	3.5%
Booz (global top 1,000)	4.2%

Hidden champions		
Average	*Main Product*	*5.9%*
ScheBo Biotech	Biotech in in-vitro diagnostics	20%
Windpilot	Wind steering systems for sailing yachts	20%
Geutebrück	Surveillance systems	15%
Heidenhain	Length and angle measurement	15%
Binder	Thermal cupboards	13%
Brainlab	Medical software	11%
Vitronic	Industrial vision	>10%
Zöllner	Warning systems for track building sites	>10%
Carl Zeiss SMT	Wafersteppers	>10%
Firmenich	Aromas/perfumes	10%
Jenoptik	Light as a tool	10%
Omicron	Tunnel-grid microscopes	10%
alki-Technik	Screw systems	10%
JK Ergoline	Professional sunbeds	10%
Kontron	Embedded computers	10%
Lobo Electronic	Laser and multimedia systems	10%
Qiagen	Molecular analysis sets	10%
Söring	Ultrasound tissue destruction	10%
Dr. Suwelack	Collagen	10%
TEXPA	Home textiles equipment	10%

However, we note that the absolute R&D budgets nevertheless remain modest, because the hidden champions' revenues are significantly smaller than those of large corporations.

Patents

R&D expenditure reflects an input-oriented view, but it is even more interesting to examine results. One relevant way of measuring them is the number of patents held by a company. Before we analyze patent statistics, however, we should remember that the significance of patents differs greatly from sector to sector. According to the German Economic Institute study cited above, only one third of all companies have any patents, and three quarters of those patents are used commercially. Even in industries and companies dominated by technology, the use of patents differs widely. According to a study by the European Patent Office, two thirds of the small and midsize companies that actively engage in research and development do not protect their innovations through patents.[5] Smaller companies are often deterred by the red tape, costs, or time required to obtain patents. Further reasons for the reticence are doubts about being able to enforce patents against large competitors or in legal proceedings abroad, or about disclosing expertise. "We do not apply for patents because we do not have the people to do it and we hate the bureaucracy," explains Klaus Grohmann of Grohmann Engineering, a highly innovative company. "In any case, innovation in our sector is very fast compared with how long it takes to obtain a patent. Patents would not help us anyway, because we could not enforce them. Our development would outpace the patent before we received it. Patents move at horse speed, we're flying at jet speed." Quite a few hidden champions share this view, even if they are very innovative. Speed is a serious problem in the patent application process. The average waiting period for a patent decision is 2.2 years at the German Patent Office and 2.6 years at the American Patent Office.[6]

Patents can be registered not only for a company's own use but also to block the competition. These two motives received roughly equal weighting in the study mentioned above. A total of 60.2% of respondents said that their exclusive own commercial use was important, and 56.4% viewed a blockade of competitors as relevant for their patent policy.[7] A relatively new aspect has emerged in the US, where patents are registered not with the intention of using them in products, but rather to enforce compensation claims against "patent infringers." The Canadian company Research In Motion (RIM), manufacturer of the BlackBerry and world market leader in this area, bore costs for patent disputes amounting to $202 million in 2006; 27% more than RIM's R&D budget and about 10% of its revenues. Some of the companies that sued RIM have yet to introduce any products, but have embarked on numerous lawsuits. Among them is the software company Visto, which has for ten years been financed by venture capital funds and has sued six companies since 2003, including RIM and Microsoft. Hidden champions can be more easily threatened by such attacks and are more susceptible to them than large corporations. RIM feared that the sale of the BlackBerry in the US could be stopped and accepted an unfavorable settlement.

Patents traditionally play a lesser role in the service sector and in the software industry, and the introduction of service patents has changed little in this regard. A differentiated view is therefore appropriate here. Our survey respondents from these sectors illustrated the heterogeneity: 17% said that patents were relatively unimportant to them, while 29.2% considered patents to be a pronounced strength of their companies.

Among the hidden champions that consider patents to be very important for their competitive strategy, we consequently find a high patent intensity. About one third of the hidden champions belong to this category. Claas is a case in point: "Since the company was founded in 1913, we have on average applied for one patent every week." In its history of almost 100 years Claas has held over 4,000 patents. Of the 50 largest patent applicants at the German Patent and Trademark Office (DPMA) in 2005, 12 were hidden champions. It is revealing to compare the hidden champions' patent intensity with that of the largest patent applicants. To do this we take the number of patent applications filed at the DPMA and put it in relation to the size of the workforce and the R&D expenditure of the company in question. Fig. 6.2 lists the results for selected hidden champions and large corporations with a high patent intensity.[8]

Fig. 6.2: Patents of selected hidden champions and large corporations

	Company	Patent applications	Employees in thousands	Patent applications per thousand employees	R&D expenditure ($ million)	R&D expenditure per patent ($ thousand)
Large companies	Siemens	2,398	461.0	5.2	7,062	2,946
	Bosch	2,149	251.0	8.6	4,210	1,959
	Daimler	1,899	382.0	5.0	7,739	4,076
	Volkswagen	859	344.9	2.5	6,265	7,293
	BASF	631	80.9	7.8	1,458	2,310
	Average	*1,587*	*304*	*5.8*	*5,347*	*3,717*
Hidden champions	Voith Paper	325	10.0	32.5	86	264
	Behr	233	18.0	12.9	295	1.265
	Koenig & Bauer	200	8.0	25.0	75	378
	Giesecke & Devrient	187	7.5	24.9	92	489
	Manroland	136	9.0	15.1	119	875
	Sick	90	4.4	20.5	73	882
	Heidenhain	62	2.4	25.8	79	1.282
	Brainlab	61	0.7	87.1	19	316
	Qiagen	51	1.6	21.9	40	780
	Tracto-Technik	15	0.5	30.0	11	715
	Average	*136*	*6.2*	*30.6*	*88.9*	*725*

Fig. 6.2 shows the excellent innovation performance of the hidden champions active in the patent sphere compared to large corporations that are leaders in technology. The finding that small companies have a higher patent intensity per head is fundamentally nothing new. What is astonishing, however, is the extent of the difference. On average, patent intensity is more than five times higher for the hidden champions. The number of patent applications per 1,000 employees is 5.8 for large corporations and 30.6 for the hidden champions. R&D expenditure per patent application is $724,730 for the selected hidden champions, but $3.55 million for the

large corporations—around five times higher. The value of these patents is unknown, but the assumption that the patents of large corporations have a higher value is not confirmed. According to the study, "larger companies do not have more valuable patents, as might be assumed."[9]

Some hidden champions regard innovation protected by patents as their core competency. One example is Enercon, the technology leader in wind power generation. Aloys Wobben, the founder of Enercon, has incessantly focused on innovation since the foundation of the company in 1984. Although Enercon now has more than 10,000 employees, Wobben is still personally involved in improving existing products and developing new ones. Enercon's website resembles a technical handbook. The company holds more than 40% of the world's patents in wind power generation and is the undisputed technological leader in this field. Even giants such as Siemens and General Electric have to rely on licenses from Enercon. Tellingly—and typically for many hidden champions—Enercon has chosen its own route for technical solutions by developing turbines without gears, in contrast to nearly all of its competitors. This means shorter startup times as well as lower vulnerability to disruptions and wear and tear. Enercon's products are thus regarded as the "Mercedes" of the wind power sector. Enercon has its own fleet of cargo ships for transporting its wind towers, and it is relying on its outstanding technological expertise by building a rotor freighter that, in addition to conventional diesel engines, has four "Flettner" rotors developed by Enercon. These rotors are 27 meters high, have a diameter of four meters, and house rotating cylinders. One Flettner rotor generates 10–14 times more thrust from wind than a traditional sail with the same surface. The potential reduction in fuel consumption is expected to be 30%–40%. If this technology proves successful, Enercon has a good chance of revolutionizing sea transport.

Another extremely innovative company with a highly professional patent strategy is Sennheiser, the world market leader in stage microphones. Sennheiser systematically protects its products by at least one and often by five or more patents. By contrast, large manufacturers such as Philips and Sony that serve mass markets instead of the top segment have a quota of patent-protected products of less than 20%. Imitators can relatively easily copy their products because effective protection is hard to enforce without patents.

Among the hidden champions, the critical role of patents is also reflected in the allocation of responsibility. In many cases, the CEO personally assumes the responsibility for patents. In large corporations, this area is usually handled by staff departments. Experts assume that even the heads of patent departments seldom have direct access to top-level managers. Patents have a maximum life of 20 years, which corresponds more closely to the planning horizon of a hidden champion than that of a large corporation. Incidentally, it is also as long as the average tenure of the hidden champions' CEOs.

Patents measure the technical outcome of innovation endeavors, but not their economic success. After all, the number of patents says very little about their actual use and even less about their economic significance. Invention does not always equal innovation. According to the study cited, 75.6% of the patents are actually used in products,[10] which means that almost a quarter remain unexploited. The value of an unused patent is estimated to be about $200,000. At small companies, the lack of sufficient financial resources is an important reason for the failure to use patents. At larger companies, patents often remain unused because products or markets are not ready for them. Experienced patent lawyers estimate that the quota of used patents is much higher in small companies than in large corporations. These figures support the assumption that smaller companies like the hidden champions work more efficiently and effectively than large corporations, not only in terms of patent intensity and costs, but also regarding the exploitation of R&D and patents.

New products

An innovation can be considered a success only if it has proved itself on the market. So how do the hidden champions fare on the market with their new products? The contribution of new products is difficult to quantify and compare. It is common to measure the significance of new products by the percentage of revenues generated by products that are less than three, four or five years old. From this point of view, many hidden champions are extremely innovative. Whereas the industry study cited found that 23% of revenues were generated by new products, the overall percentage is far higher among the innovative hidden champions. Kärcher, for example, reports that 85% of its revenues is accounted for by products that are less than four years old. AL-KO, world market leader in mobile home chassis, says that hardly any of its products are older than four years. Putzmeister, the world market leader in concrete pumps, earns 80% of its revenues from products that have been on the market for less than five years. At Wittenstein, a market leader for mechatronic drives, this figure is as high as 85%. CEO Manfred Wittenstein describes his innovation program with the abbreviation MINI, standing for miniaturization, integration, network capability, and intelligence. More than half the products of Vitronic, a leader in industrial image processing, are less than three years old. And at Bosch, the world market leader in power tools, more than 40% of the tools sold were introduced in the last two years.

The comparability of such innovation indicators is not clear, because there is no single definition of a "new product." Calculating percentages of new products makes little sense for companies that produce individually rather than in series, such as builders of technical plants. For these companies, every product is by definition new, because it differs to a certain extent from its predecessors. Usually, improvements are made continually, so each product is a partial innovation. This would mean that 100% of revenues came from "new" products, but it would not do justice to the spirit of our comparison. In spite of this difficulty in measuring the significance of new products, we clearly see that the hidden champions are very innovative on the product side. This applies both to markets in the growth phase and to mature markets.

The following cases illustrate selected innovations in markets at different stages of development. Skysails, founded in 2001, became the first company to develop functioning towing kite wind propulsion systems for commercial shipping and luxury yachts. Skysails systems can reduce annual fuel costs about 10%–35%. The first system to be installed on a large freight ship was a freighter from Beluga Shipping in 2008.

Carl Zeiss SMT supplies chip manufacturing plants with lithography optics and opened the most advanced factory in the world for lithography systems in 2006. The Dutch hidden champion ASML incorporates SMT's products in its machines. With its innovations, SMT has gained a world market share of 55% in recent years.

There is a wealth of groundbreaking innovations in microelectronics and nanotechnology. One example is a coated bonding wire that makes it possible to connect semiconductor chips at room temperature—a world sensation. According to the product description, "The entire technology, in particular the wire coating, is unique and delivers absolute peak performance."

The German company Sennheiser and its American competitor Shure are competing for world market leadership in high-performance microphones with breakthrough innovations. Another significant innovation is the lightweight bicycle wheels produced by Carbon Sports. These were developed by the toolmakers Rudolf Dierl and Heinz Obermayer, who previously worked for two aerospace companies. Carbon Sports' website states, "They made their wheels in absolute secrecy. All of the windows were darkened and the doors remained closed. The workshop was hermetically sealed off from the outside world. And this workshop was the birthplace of numerous high-tech product legends." The same original tools and procedures are still in use today. Once the first world cycling champion won his title on lightweight wheels in 1996 and Jan Ullrich won the Tour de France with these wheels in 1997, the inventors were deluged with demands from cycling professionals. The website reports, "They were besieged by the best cyclists in the world. Even long delivery waiting times of a year, and the fact that even a world champion or Tour de France winner had to pay the full price for his set of wheels, did not deter buyers from all over the world." All of the Tour de France winners in recent years have raced to their victories on Carbon Sports wheels.

An innovation from GKD Kufferath, the world market leader in metal fabrics, has opened up new possibilities for the use of buildings for advertising purposes. Light-emitting diodes (LEDs) that can be controlled individually are set into a steel fabric affixed to the facade, enabling videos or graphics to be shown around the clock. The fully transparent and nonflammable stainless steel fabric at the same time offers protection against wind and sun.

The speed of development in orthopedic technology has accelerated rapidly. Otto Bock, number one in the world market, recently introduced numerous groundbreaking innovations, such as myoelectrically operated arm prosthesis and a new leg prosthesis system. Myoelectrics is the science of how humans can operate a prosthesis by brain waves.

Even in mature markets, we see a wave of innovations that are setting new standards. Claas' Lexion model is the most innovative and powerful combine harvester in the world. With a cutting span of 12 meters, the Lexion harvests in one hour the daily requirement of a city of 350,000 inhabitants. Packed with high tech, the Lexion is steered by onboard computers via satellite navigation. All the driver has to do is monitor the vehicle's progress. The Lexion also exemplifies the potential global scope of an innovation. It was designed for the vast agricultural areas in North America and Eastern Europe, but not for Western Europe, where the fields are too small for this huge machine. Russia alone has more agricultural land than the entire European Union. Practically all of the innovations that Claas has launched on the market in the past two years have set new world records. This applies both to forage harvesters, for which Claas is the world market leader, and to mowers and balers. The orientation of product development toward international markets that we observe at Claas applies to the majority of the hidden champions. While the development activities of 56.1% of respondents focus closely on foreign markets, only 9.9% are driven primarily by their home markets in this regard.

Another company with an impressive track record in innovation is Herrenknecht. In just 25 years, this company has become the unchallenged world market and technological leader in tunnel-drilling machines. New standards are continually being set in tunnel-building technologies, such as with the construction of the world's longest tunnel, the Swiss Gotthard tunnel, which will be completed in 2015, and with the world's largest tunnel-drilling machine at the Yangtze tunnel in Shanghai. A new subsidiary, Herrenknecht Vertical, was founded in 2005 to pursue innovative concepts for deep drilling to a depth of 6,000 meters (about four miles) for geothermic purposes. This completely new market is expected to harbor tremendous potential.

We could add to this list of groundbreaking innovations. The examples mentioned confirm that the hidden champions have embarked on a spree of massive innovation. The spirit of innovation appears to have been unleashed once again. In many fields, the hidden champions are now the technological leaders, and the enormous research and development efforts of recent years are beginning to pay off. This is probably the key explanation for the growth in absolute and relative market shares we observed in Chapter 2. At the start of the twenty-first century, the hidden champions are stronger than ever in technological terms and have every reason to look to the future with optimism.

Driving Forces of Innovation

The simplest distinction for driving forces of innovation is between company-external and company-internal stimuli. Customers are the most important external stimulus. Suppliers, competitors, and cooperation partners also contribute ideas for innovation, sometimes without even meaning to. Internal stimuli come primarily from top management and the R&D department. The study mentioned above investigated the importance of these different sources as impetus for innovation.[11] Fig. 6.3 shows the findings.

These results demonstrate that both sides play a critical role in providing impetus for innovations. In our own study, we asked whether companies

Impulse	Percentage very important/important	
	internal	external
Top management	93%	
Customers		92%
Other company departments	67%	
R&D department	64%	
Competitors		61%
Affiliated enterprises		54%
Suppliers		44%
Science		40%

were technology- or market-driven, or whether both driving forces were equally important. For the purposes of comparison, we also posed this question to selected large corporations. Indicators such as R&D intensity and patent statistics discussed above could lead to the presumption that the hidden champions are primarily technology-driven. Fig. 6.4 shows that this hypothesis is refuted.

Exactly half of the large corporations answered that they were market-driven. This could be a politically correct answer in accordance with the modern belief that this is what a company should be. Just under one third of the big players (31%) said that technology was their dominant driving force. Only 19% saw both market and technology as equally strong driving forces of innovation. The picture is entirely different for the hidden champions. About two thirds (65%) consider market and technology to be equally important driving forces. Only 21% contend that they are primarily market-driven, and just 14% say they are technology-driven. It is revealing how the percentages have shifted among the hidden champions in the last ten years. The proportion of primarily market-driven companies has fallen 11%, while the percentage with balanced driving forces has increased to 65% from 57%.

There is an ongoing discussion in corporate strategy literature between the "resource-based" and the "market-oriented" schools of thought. The resource-based school of thought postulates that the strategy of a company

Fig. 6.4: Driving forces of innovation in large corporations and in the hidden champions

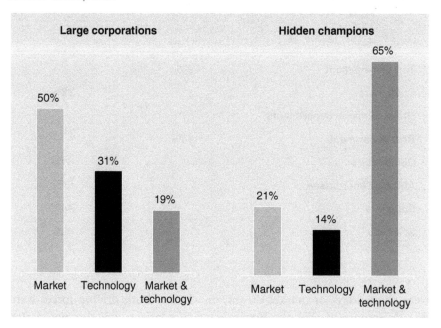

should be driven from within (i.e., by its resources). Consequently, the focus of interest is on competencies and skills, on their origin and their improvement.[12] By contrast, the market-oriented school of thought focuses on the opportunities offered by the market and requires strategies to be developed in line with market needs. Here, attention is paid primarily to recognizing unserved market niches, better satisfying the customers' requirements, and creating competitive advantages.

What do the hidden champions teach us in relation to these competing schools of thought? The answer could not be clearer. In contrast to the large corporations, 80% of which belong to one of these competing schools of thought, two thirds of the hidden champions reject the mutually exclusive attitude. Instead, they practice a both-and-strategy that incorporates market and technology as equal driving forces. Wanzl, the world market leader in shopping carts, expresses this both-and-school of thought as follows: "We rely both on product orientation and on customer orientation for expansion and future growth." According to Alberdingk Boley, the European market leader in water-based coatings, "We achieve optimal synergies between internal expertise and external market opportunities by involving both market and technology." Gelita, the clear world market leader in gelatines with a market share of 27%, states, "We are the leading edge of the gelatine market and are fully customer-oriented." There are many reasons why such integrative approaches are superior to any one-sided market or technology view. It seems obvious to interpret market or technology orientation not as mutually exclusive opposites, but rather as two sides of the same coin.[13] Norbert Gebhardt of Netzsch, a market leader in pumping and grinding technology, accurately describes this position, "We need both market and technology orientation to do business with our customers. The salesman is lost when it comes to technical details and the technician is not a communication specialist. We are aiming for the 'golden' combination."

A one-sided focus on the market or on internal resources, i.e., the lack of an integrative approach, has led to many strategy disasters. With the benefit of hindsight, it is difficult to explain how BASF, today the world's largest chemical company, became involved in the music business, Kodak in the pharmaceutical market, Exxon in office systems or Daimler in electronics. The problem in each case was not the market. The markets were growing and companies that successfully entered them earned a lot of money. The weakness and the problem was the lack of the right expertise. None of the companies came even close to matching the level of competency of the leading competitors. The mobile phone market is growing and is very attractive, as demonstrated by the ongoing success of Nokia and Samsung. Yet Motorola and Siemens have withdrawn from this market, because they do not see their core competencies in the marketing of short-lived, fashionable consumer goods such as cell phones. Even the semiconductor market would appear to be attractive, because the semiconductor companies Freescale and NXP, spinoffs from the giants Motorola and Philips, have recently been bought by investors for exorbitant prices. However, Siemens, Philips, and Motorola were right to withdraw from this market when they realized that they lacked the necessary expertise. This insight often comes too late—sometimes only after billions of dollars have been lost.

And yet an exclusive focus on internal resources or competencies is equally dangerous. The corporate graveyard is full of companies with excellent know-how that became obsolete because the market for their products disappeared. Even the company that builds the best and most efficient steam locomotive is doomed because no one buys steam locomotives any longer. Competencies, however excellent, are only valuable in relation to a given market, as shown by NSU for motorcycles,[14] Faber-Castell for slide rules, Reflecta for slide projectors, and Kodak for chemical film and photo prints. These considerations show that the integrative approach practiced by the majority of the hidden champions is indispensable and superior.

However, the integrative approach also complicates strategy development. A one-sided orientation allows for a linear approach based on either the market or the competencies involved, whereas the integrative strategy requires frequent changes of perspective. The starting point for strategy development is usually on one side, but at an early stage of the analysis the following questions must be asked:

- Do we have the competencies for this potentially attractive market or can we develop them?
- Or on the flip side, is there a market for our competencies or can we develop one?

In the following cases, we find that one particular initial perspective swiftly gave way to the integrative approach. Some of the cases address the circumstances that led to the foundation of a company. A look at the origins of the hidden champions is fascinating.

The Origin of Innovations

The origins of innovations and of the hidden champions themselves are so diverse that they elude all attempts at classification. Luck or chance often played a role. Sometimes the recognition of unsatisfied customer demands was the starting point. In other cases, new technology or expertise emerged as a solution without yet having a problem to solve. But in each case, market and technology met relatively quickly. This connection often characterizes the core of the innovative entrepreneurial achievement.

While visiting a factory of the cosmetics company Avon in 1972, engineer Peter Weckerle, who was working for the American machine tool manufacturer Cincinnati Millacron, noticed the large proportion of manual work in lipstick production. Convinced that this could be better organized, he designed a lipstick machine. Avon bought his prototype. The breakthrough came when the Russians wanted to increase lipstick production for the Moscow Olympics in 1980 and visited the Avon factory. They saw the Weckerle machine and ordered 23 of them at once. Today, at least three quarters of all lipstick filling machines in the world are produced by

Weckerle, and the company is also the largest independent manufacturer of lipsticks. This is a typical case of how a customer problem was identified and how technology was used to solve it, both personified by the entrepreneur Peter Weckerle.

In the 1960s, Bayer, one of the world's largest chemical corporations, developed an ion exchanger but saw no market for it. Heinz Hankammer, who at the time sold furniture, heard about this innovation from a friend. He began to sell the product to gas stations, where it was used for producing water for batteries. This was the start of Brita, today the world market leader in table water filters. It all began with a technical innovation for which the entrepreneur Hankammer found different markets and entered them. Technical expertise and products were also the starting point for Gore. Founder Bill Gore worked in a laboratory of the large chemical company DuPont and was involved in the development of Teflon (PTFE). In 1958, he founded his own company with the aim of developing markets and applications for PTFE. Since then, Gore has introduced an uninterrupted stream of PTFE-based innovations in fields such as leisure clothing (the famous Gore-Tex brand), electronics, and environmental and medical technology, and in many of these areas the company is now world market leader. Today, Gore employs 8,000 people at 45 locations across the world and generates revenues of $2 billion per year.

Many hidden champions' innovations originate from problems the founder experienced in his or her own life and for which there was no satisfactory solution. Claus Hipp, who founded the world market-leading supplier of organic baby food, recalls how the business was born out of an emergency, "My grandmother could not breastfeed her twins. Her husband Josef Hipp, a master confectioner, wasted no time and mixed a porridge of milk, rusks and water. The twins survived and the rusk mixture became popular with consumers. Neither of my grandparents could have foreseen that this product discovered by chance would become the origin of the top baby food manufacturer."[15]

The story of Tetra is similar. Its founder, Ulrich Baensch, wrote his doctoral thesis on tropical fish and discovered that it was very difficult to breed these fish because there was no suitable fish food on the market. He developed his own ready-to-use fish food and founded Tetra in 1955. Today, the company is the world market leader in the aquarium segment with a world market share in excess of 50%. At both Hipp and Tetra, everything started with a problem that the founders, drawing on their own skills and know-how, solved in an innovative way. Again, customers' needs and competencies met to create something new.

Recognizing a customer need is often the starting point of a company. O.C. Tanner detected employee recognition as a business opportunity. "One fascinating thing about our business is that everything we make or sell is purchased to be given away," said Clark A. Campbell, the company's current senior vice president of administration. O.C. Tanner helps thousands of companies design programs to recognize their employees for reaching milestones or achieving other forms of success in their day-to-day work. It has also expanded into consulting services to help companies understand how appreciating great work helps to grow a company's people, its brand, and its bottom line. While O.C. Tanner continues to explore and understand the power of appreciating great work, the physical manifestation of that appreciation still matters. O.C. Tanner ranks as one of the largest buyers of jewelry-grade diamonds in North America, and to this day it continues to manufacture customized emblems and awards at its Salt Lake City headquarters. The company also designed and produced the medals for the 2002 Winter Olympics in Salt Lake City.

Occasionally, innovations arise purely by chance. CEO Seiichi Hirata relates how Brother Industries started manufacturing typewriters, "We started with sewing machines. So how did we get involved in producing typewriters? An American customer approached us one day and asked whether Brother could supply typewriters, because he had a very large customer and if Brother were able to manufacture typewriters, he could sell them to this customer. We have been producing typewriters ever since."[16] How did Brother become successful in the hard-fought market for typewriters with strong competitors and rise to become the global market leader? What technology formed the basis of this success? "We possessed the technology to satisfy the customers in the new field," replies Hirata. "We developed everything from scratch. The secret is our machine tool competency—we produce the forms and tools for our products ourselves." The connection of a random market opportunity and a technical competency created a world market leader in this case.

The most serious challenge for innovation management comes from radical changes or breakthroughs in technology. In some cases, the companies already have the market, but still have to develop the new technological competencies to serve it. In previous chapters, numerous examples (including Trumpf, Otto Bock, and Durst) showed how such challenges were successfully mastered. On the other hand, there are numerous cases of failure to make the transition to a new technology. Prominent examples include Reflecta with slide projectors and the European typewriter manufacturers Olympia, Olivetti, and Triumph Adler. These companies were the world market leaders in the 1960s, but they were unsuccessful in making the transition to electronics and personal computers. The market existed and the companies even had a strong market position, but they lacked the competencies in electronics and computer technology.

Two lessons can be learned from these case studies:

- Innovations can be controlled to only a limited extent.
- An innovation is successful only if internal competencies are brought together with external market opportunities.

These cases should not, however, create the impression that the hidden champions' innovations are predominantly successful due to chance, luck or entrepreneurial instinct. The majority of innovations by hidden champions are results of systematic research and development.

Leadership and Organizational Aspects of Innovation

Specific leadership and organizational features characterize the innovation processes of the hidden champions.

Role of top management

As illustrated in Fig. 6.3, top management generally plays a key role in providing stimuli for innovation. This applies even more so to hidden champions. Innovation is a top management concern for many of these companies, not only in the initial and early phases but throughout the entire process. Managing partner Peter Zinkann was the innovation driver *par excellence* at Miele for decades. Hans Riegel, CEO of Haribo for more than 60 years, is now 85 years old, but remains an important source of inspiration for innovations. Aloys Wobben has made Enercon the technological leader in the wind energy sector and continues to contribute new ideas. CEOs often climb into the ring themselves when it comes to innovations and improvements.

The following passage from the biography of Hermann Kronseder, founder of Krones, the world market leader for bottling systems, sums up this role: "Service technicians' feedback from the field can be quite unpleasant for the design engineers because I am present when the technicians report their findings to them. They clearly state the difficulties they encountered, what has gone wrong, what should be changed and improved. These service people generally have an excellent understanding of such problems. Although they know exactly what went wrong, they cannot translate it into new concepts or drawings. In most firms, the technicians don't have enough opportunities to bring their complex experiences directly to the designers. Sometimes the two groups simply don't come into contact with each other. The reason I have made it a point to be present at these meetings is that if I were not, the technician doesn't stand a chance. Designers and engineers who enjoy a stronger position, are smarter and have a better education, push technicians to the wall. The technician usually resigns himself to the inevitable in such a situation, thinking, 'Do what you want, it's not my business.' Technicians, who are not good at writing and spelling, dislike having to present written reports, which are first read by secretaries who correct the errors like schoolteachers. This is poison for the technicians, who feel humiliated. So they don't have to write reports. Not at Krones!"

The devil is in the details, and Kronseder's experience proves that communication between the market and the technological people is full of traps. Ultimately Kronseder's practice may make all the difference between successful and unsuccessful innovations.

Innovative ideas are frequently born when companies observe how their customers work. Reinhold Würth, the guru of assembly products, stumbled on such an idea during a visit to a construction site, where he heard a worker grumbling about how hard it was to read the size number of tools and the corresponding screws, which, stamped into the metal, were barely legible. Würth subsequently replaced the numbers with colored rings so that workers need only match the colors of screws and tools. This trademark-protected system has become a huge success. Würth also, during such visits, heard workers complaining about soreness in certain muscles and sinews. Nobody had thought about the question of whether standard tools like pliers and screwdrivers were ergonomically optimized. Würth discovered that some tools had not changed their shape for more than a hundred years, so it was unlikely that they were at maximum handling efficiency. He initiated a research project with a university that resulted in a whole set of new tool designs, some of which reduce critical stress by more than 30%. They became a great success.

The active involvement of the head of a company in the innovation process requires in-depth and detailed knowledge and many years of familiarity with the problems. A sense of focus facilitates this closeness to the business and to technology. In Salt Lake City where I visited O.C. Tanner, the world leader in employee recognition products, the production manager, Mike Collins, gave me a tour of the manufacturing plant. Whenever we stopped at one of the hundreds of machines, all of which are made in-house, Collins was able to explain the most intricate details of this machine to me. In large corporations with many different types of business, it is difficult to imagine a top manager getting involved in this way. It seems unavoidable that the involvement of the top people declines as a hidden champion grows and its business is broadened. As repeatedly mentioned and explained in our case studies, the hidden champions work against this tendency by means of deliberate decentralization. The heads of the decentralized units can once again achieve sufficient focus and depth and thereby continue to supply important impetus for innovations.

Heads more important than budgets

It is always impressive to see the innovations that the hidden champions produce with relatively small R&D budgets and teams. Where large corporations tend to "throw money at the problem," small companies generally have to cope with limited funds and few people. Even if they spend large percentages of their revenues on research and development, as shown in Fig. 6.1, the absolute budgets remain relatively modest. Vitronic is one of the leading names in industrial image processing and has supplied Toll Collect, the ground-breaking European truck toll collection system, with its products. Although Vitronic invests more than 10% of its $63 million revenues in R&D, this results in only a small budget of approximately $7 million. However, according to Vitronic's founder Norbert Stein, the company "probably has the greatest concentration of specialists in our field." Fig. 6.2 showed that the hidden champions get far more out of their R&D dollars than large corporations. The quality of the employees affects not only the final result, but also the speed of innovation. Booz' study of the global top 1,000 R&D companies concluded that "superior results seem to be a function of the quality of an organization's innovation process rather than the magnitude of its innovation spending."[17]

At the hidden champions, innovation is more a question of the quality of people than the size of the budget. But how can individuals or a handful of people make a company a worldwide technology leader? The explanation lies in two aspects: focus and continuity. Berthold Leibinger, long-time CEO of Trumpf, the world leader in laser cutting machines, specifies three success factors: "Innovation, internationalization, and continuity." In large corporations, R&D work is often only an interim step to higher career levels. At the hidden champions, we frequently find experts whose life's work is dedicated to improving their product. They stay tuned and never give up in order to further improve the fruits of their focused minds. Replacing such a key innovator can, however, cause the same difficulties as succession at the top of a company.

Shared values and strategy

If the team wholeheartedly backs the values and the strategy of its company, friction is reduced. I have often asked managers in midsize companies how much of their energy is used up in overcoming internal resistance. Most of them answered "20%–30%." In large corporations the answer to the same question is typically "50%–70%." Wolfgang Niehoff, head of R&D at Sennheiser, comments, "We have no time for vanity and power games between departments. We have to compete with Sony and Philips. We can't afford to mess around." If it is true that implementation accounts for 90% of a strategy's success, the hidden champions have an important strength in innovative capacity. "The hidden champions generally know better than larger companies what they really want in the medium and long term," explains Klaus Goeken, a patent attorney with extensive experience with both hidden champions and large corporations. "This sharing of a vision makes it easier to adopt a well-aligned innovation strategy. Less friction means higher efficiency and an advantage over competitors."

If the strategy is understood and shared by all employees in technology and sales, there is greater openness toward suggestions coming from the other side. The same applies to the relationship between centralized and decentralized units. The "not invented here" syndrome is less prevalent among the hidden champions. In large corporations with a strict division of labor, we often see departments at war with each other. Technology, manufacturing, and other internal functions are viewed as enemies by sales—and vice versa. Warlike relations often prevail between head office and foreign subsidiaries. It is evident that such conflicts do not have a positive influence on the innovativeness of a company. By contrast, a strategy accepted by all employees leads not only to more substantive solutions but also to swifter implementation.

Cooperation between functions

CEOs of the hidden champions repeatedly emphasize how strongly their innovation success depends on cooperation between research and development and the other business functions. This applies particularly to innovations in manufacturing and sales processes. Kern-Liebers' first rule is "Success is born not by chance, but through the cooperation of everyone involved." Kern-Liebers has 5,800 employees and is the world market leader for springs in safety belts.

"In order to remain the world market leader, we need constant cooperation between manufacturing on the one hand and research and development on the other," states Jürgen Thumann, CEO of Heitkamp & Thumann, the world market leader for battery cans. "Research in the ivory tower must remain an exception. Closeness to production is vital for us." The same applies to cooperation between technology and sales in order to ensure that an innovation really does address customers' needs. Susanne Seidel, head of marketing at Sennheiser, comments, "The smooth and timely handover of a project from research to development to production to marketing to sales is crucial for our success." Having worked for General Electric before joining Sennheiser, Ms Seidel is in a position to make comparisons. Her company's head of development, Wolfgang Niehoff, supports her view, "We need close interaction between R&D on the one hand and sales and marketing on the other."[18] Stihl, the world market leader in chain saws, develops so many innovations each year that the former head of sales, Robert Mayr, was unable to launch them all. "We have so many innovations that I really don't know whether the customers need, want, or accept them," he remarked. "All the ecological novelties are great. But do the customers understand and appreciate the advantage and are they willing to pay for it? My first task is not to push these innovations into the market too fast but to learn what customers are willing to accept and report the information back to our company so as to achieve an appropriate level of innovation. Because we are so inventive, we have to be more customer-driven. Attaining that goal is not an easy task." The Booz study confirms the importance of interfunctional interaction: "Successful innovation requires an exceptional level of cross-functional cooperation among R&D, marketing, sales, service, and manufacturing. Collaboration failures can have a devastating impact on the success of the innovation process."[19]

Their manageable size and less division of labor mean that the hidden champions have a natural advantage over large corporations when it comes to cooperation. The greater closeness to customers and the deployment of manufacturing and R&D employees to the customer front, such as in service jobs, strongly contribute to a better understanding among different functions.

Development with customers

As shown in Fig. 6.3, the customer can be an extremely valuable source of ideas for innovations. MIT Professor Eric von Hippel has been propagating this message for decades.[20] His mantra is "Listen carefully to what your customers want and then respond with new products that meet or exceed their needs." Joint development with customers is extremely important to many hidden champions. In sectors such as engineering and industrial components, virtually every product requires joint development activities. Closeness to customer, long-standing relationships, and the trust that has grown out of them can foster these cooperations and make them more effective. Close R&D collaboration, for example, is advantageous not only for the vendor, but also for the customer, because it improves the quality of the end-products and shortens development times. A study by J.D. Power, the American automotive market research firm, strongly corroborates these advantages.[21] As Siltronic, the world market leader for pure silicon wafers, contends, "We interact with our customers right from the outset when we develop new products, and our close cooperation continues down to the serial production of the wafers." Brainlab, the world market leader in positioning software for surgery, collaborates closely with surgeons and oncologists. "The relationship Brainlab has with medical professionals has been a catalyst for transforming great ideas into great products. Effectiveness, ease of use and innovations are the result of close cooperation with experts in the medical field. That way, we are able to garner continuous customer feedback at all stages of the development process. Their comments also help us adapt our product to clinical workflows and refine our training programs." Hidden champion Diametal invites its customers to "knock on the door" at a very early stage of development. Diametal is the technology leader in high-precision tools for the production of cog-wheel drives for clocks. If the customer's request is made early enough in the R&D process, Diametal suggests innovative solutions for the design of the clock or the manufacturing process. In these cases, the company even assumes process responsibility for the manufacturing times and quantities that can be achieved with its tools. Deutsche Mechatronics, meanwhile, develops and produces modules and subsystems for mechanical engineering. "If we get involved in the development of the subsystems at an early stage, we can cut the costs for our customer by over 20%," comments Karlheinz Sossenheimer, Mechatronic's CEO. The key factor here is to coordinate R&D and manufacturing, which in turn requires very close cooperation between the supplier and the customer. Schott is the global market leader in ceramic cooking surfaces with its brand Ceran, and offers several thousand types of Ceran cooktops. An R&D team at Schott continually works on improvements together with the manufacturers of household appliances, cookware, and cleaning agents, as well as with designers. The story of Ceran is an uninterrupted chain of innovations, to which all participants have made a contribution. Schott is at the center of this network.

In cooperation with architects, Zumtobel, the market leader in lighting technology, developed a system that allows the greatest possible flexibility in lighting infrastructure. For modern properties, the aim is to make the rooms highly adaptable, as it is initially often unclear whether they will be used as offices, for retail purposes or as a fitness center, for example. Aside from the issue of lighting, building technology has long addressed customers' flexibility requirements by means of modules. Zumtobel turned this problem into an opportunity and developed a "dimming on demand" solution in workshops conducted with planners and architects. The new solution comprises light management modules that can satisfy very different demands. Only the basic function is initially activated. This can be done for a reasonable price, and more sophisticated lighting options for specific room purposes can be added for a surcharge at a later date. Hako, number two in the world for cleaning machinery, supports its customers (professional cleaning companies) early in the project and proposal phase, and guarantees the estimated costs, as does Diametal.

Joint development projects require a great deal of mutual trust to prevent an outflow of know-how to competitors. For the hidden champions, this comes full circle back to their greatest strength, the long-standing customer relationships.

Ongoing improvement versus breakthrough innovations

When we talk of innovation we typically think of radically new products and procedures. Breakthroughs such as the iPod and the Segway attract attention and become the darlings of the media. However, breakthrough innovations are rare in the real word. Berthold Leibinger of Trumpf, for example, observes real breakthroughs only once every 15 years in his high-tech sector. The typical innovation process involves smaller improvements that do not make the headlines. Many hidden champions rely on con-tinual improvements rather than groundbreaking innovations. Wanzl, the world market leader for shopping carts, says, "The history of Wanzl is a story of continual innovations," referring to exactly this process of ongo-ing improvement. Breakthrough innovations in shopping or baggage carts remain an exception. Of Sennheiser it has been said, "Evolution, not revo-lution, has made the company strong. Even many technical breakthroughs were the result of a development policy of small steps."[22] Swarovski, the global market leader for cut crystal, still propagates the slogan of its founder, "Constantly improving what is already good." The maxim of Miele, market leader in premium household appliances, is "Always bet-ter." This simple slogan expresses the determination to deliver the absolute top product in every market in the world. Eduard Sailer, who is in charge of technical development at Miele, explains, "All the products we develop and produce are built to last for 20 years." Continual innovation is the foundation for success at Miele. The repurchase rate of Miele products is a sensational 90%. Hidden champions' superiority is often based on doing many small things better than their competitors. Their products and ser-vices are closer to perfection, and this is the result of a never-ending series of improvements rather than single breakthrough innovations.

Speed of R&D

Many hidden champions emphasize that they have to be faster in innova-tion than their larger competitors—and they actually achieve this. The rea-sons are the smoother cooperation with other business functions we have already described, focus, less division of labor, shorter coordination pro-cesses, and swifter decisions at the top. Employee expertise plays a key role when it comes to speed. "We benefit from the long-standing experience of our fine opticians," says Dieter Kurz, CEO of Carl Zeiss, of his SMT semiconductor division. "An insane innovation speed such as we see in chip equipment is achievable only if you have excellent people. New markets always open up the opportunity to attain market leadership. But speed and the right time are often decisive." Westfalia Separator achieved a world market share of 80% on the new market for biodiesel centrifuges because of its speed. Its success is based on "putting the right innovation on the market at the right time." Gardena, the market leader in garden watering and equipment, is proud of its swift development process. CEO Martin Bertinchamp sees this as a decisive competitive advantage arising from the fact that Gardena, like many other hidden champions, builds its own manufacturing machines parallel to their product development.

Summary

Innovation is one of the key pillars on which the market leadership of the hidden champions is based. It definitely applies to pioneering innovations that created a new market and are the sources or origins of numerous hidden champions. In addition, the hidden champions make continual improvements that help them defend the market position they have worked hard to achieve. At the start of the twenty-first century, the hidden champions have embarked on a phase of massive innovations. Innovations are the main reason for the increase in their relative market shares and lead us to expect further consolidation of the hidden champions' market positions. The following findings are worth keeping in mind:

- A company only becomes and remains a world market leader through innovation. Mere imitation is insufficient.
- Innovation must contribute higher value to customer and/or lower costs. To this end, innovation activities should not be restricted to product and technology. All aspects of a business offer opportunities for improvement and should be exploited.
- The type and relevance of innovations differ from sector to sector. An in-depth understanding of the specific circumstances of an industry is necessary, and the indicators for innovative performance must be adapted accordingly.
- In the sectors in which product innovations, R&D, and patents play an important part, the key figures back up the hidden champions' out-

standing innovation performance in comparison with the industry as a whole and with large corporations in particular.

- The hidden champions are outstanding innovators in process-oriented industries and the service sector as well. However, there are no clear indicators as with product innovations (such as patents).

- Two thirds of the hidden champions use market and technology as equal driving forces for innovation, while four fifths of large corporations view either the market or the technology as the dominant driving force. Successful innovation requires the convergence of market/customer needs and technical competencies.

- An integrative strategy is therefore necessary and superior. The dispute between the resource-based and the market-oriented schools of thought should be abandoned in favor of an integrated strategy view.

- Innovation is much more than spectacular breakthroughs. Many hidden champions are successful precisely because they keep introducing small innovations one step at a time.

- Innovation should be a top management concern. Management should be a strong and active source of impetus and the chief promoter of innovations. This role requires managers to remain close to the business and its intricacies.

- Values and strategy shared by everyone and smooth cooperation between functions ease and accelerate the innovation process and lead to better results in process innovations.

- For innovation success, heads are more important than budgets. Continuity is indispensable for achieving continual improvements and, ultimately, perfection.

- Customers are a very important source of ideas and should therefore be closely involved in the innovation process. This requires a relationship of trust.

In spite of their limited resources, the hidden champions prove to be extremely successful innovators. They apply practices that differ significantly from those of large corporations. While globalization is the most important driver of their growth, their superior innovative performance has above all strengthened their competitive position as measured in market shares. At the start of the twenty-first century, they are excellently equipped for innovative competition with a global outlook.

Notes

1 Günther Schuh, Thomas Friedli, Michael A. Kurr, *Reengineering ist einfach nicht tot zu kriegen*, Munich: Hanser 2006.

2 See *Institut der Deutschen Wirtschaft, Forschung und Innovation*, Panel Report 2/2006, Cologne: IdW-Verlag. See also Oliver Koppel, *Das Innovationsverhalten der technikaffinen Branchen*, Opinion for the VDI, Cologne: IdW-Verlag, April 2006.

3 See Steffen Kinkel and Oliver Som, *Strukturen und Treiber des Innovationserfolges im deutschen Maschinenbau*, Karlsruhe: Fraunhofer-Institut für System- und Innovationsforschung ISI, No. 41, May 2007.

4 Barry Jaruzelski, Kevin Dehoff, Rakesh Bordia, "Money Isn't Everything," Booz Allen Hamilton, *Strategy + Business*, Winter 2005, p. 54 ff.

5 See *Frankfurter Allgemeine Zeitung*, December 2, 1994, p. 15.

6 See *VDI News*, February 16, 2007, p. 6.

7 Oliver Koppel, *Das Innovationsverhalten der technikaffinen Branchen*, Cologne: IdW-Verlag, April 2006.

8 See Annual Report 2005 of the German Patent and Trademark Office, Munich 2006. Four of the largest 6 German patent applicants are also among the 12 largest patent applicants worldwide. In a typical year, Siemens has the highest number of patents worldwide.

9 Oliver Koppel, *Das Innovationsverhalten der technikaffinen Branchen*, Cologne: IdW-Verlag, April 2006, p. 22.

10 Oliver Koppel, *Das Innovationsverhalten der technikaffinen Branchen*, Cologne: IdW-Verlag, April 2006.

11 See Institut der Deutschen Wirtschaft, Forschung und Innovation, Panel Report 2/2006, Cologne: IdW-Verlag. A study by *Wirtschaftswoche* magazine came to similar conclusions, see *Wirtschaftswoche*, March 26, 2007, p. 94.

12 For a many-faceted description of competence-oriented strategies, see Robert Zaugg (ed.), *Handbuch Kompetenzmanagement: Durch Kompetenz nachhaltig Werte schaffen*. Bern: 2006.

13 See Barry Johnson, *Polarity Management: Identifying and Managing Unsolvable Problems*, Amherst, MA: HRD Press 1992.

14 In 1957, NSU owned the largest motorcycle factory in the world, but the market in Europe collapsed. Automobiles replaced motorbikes as the primary means of transport.

15 See *Frankfurter Allgemeine Zeitung*, January 27, 2007, p. C3.

16 See *VDI News*, January 26, 2007, p. 20.

17 Barry Jaruzelski, Kevin Dehoff, Rakesh Bordia, "Money Isn't Everything," Booz Allen Hamilton, *Strategy + Business*, Winter 2005, p. 54 ff.

18 Thomas Ramge, *Klingt gut!*, brand eins, 7/2006.

19 Barry Jaruzelski, Kevin Dehoff, Rakesh Bordia, "Money Isn't Everything," Booz Allen Hamilton, *Strategy + Business*, Winter 2005, p. 54 ff.

20 Eric von Hippel, *The Sources of Innovation*, New York: Oxford University Press 1994; see also Stephan Thomke and Eric von Hippel, "Customers as Innovators: A New Way to Create Value," *Harvard Business Review*, April 2002, p. 74–81.

21 See *Harvard Business Review*, November-December 1994, p. 177.

22 Thomas Ramge, Klingt gut!, brand eins, 7/2006.

Chapter 7
Competition

How do the hidden champions compete? Which competitive strategies do they apply? What competitive advantages do they have? We will address these and similar questions in this chapter. The hidden champions operate predominantly in oligopolistic markets, and even on a global scale, they face only a limited number of competitors. However, competition is fierce. Their strategy is oriented to superior performance, not low prices. Their long-standing competitive advantage of product quality continues to form the core of their market leadership. They also offer excellent service. More recently, they have developed superior positions in softer parameters such as advice and systems integration. As these parameters are based on internal competencies, they are difficult to imitate and therefore sustainable. Today, barriers to entry for a new competitor are likely to be higher than they were ten years ago. In spite of these advantages, the hidden champions must keep tight control of costs as the balance between superior performance and price premium is a delicate one. When it comes to new markets with previously unknown segments (e.g., extremely low-priced products), unconventional strategies directed towards radically simplified products and radically lower costs must be adopted. In spite of globalization, competitors in geographical proximity continue to be crucial sparring partners for remaining competitively fit. However, excessive orientation towards competition should be avoided.

Competitive Structure and Conduct

The typical hidden champion faces a limited number of competitors. On average (median),[1] the hidden champions have six serious competitors on

H. Simon, *Hidden Champions of the Twenty-First Century*,
DOI 10.1007/978-0-387-98147-5_7, © Hermann Simon 2009

the world market. Almost 60% (exactly 59.8%) have fewer than ten competitors worldwide and only 12.8% have more than 20 competitors. However, there are also hidden champions that have thousands of competitors (e.g., A.T.U. for automotive parts or Würth for assembly products).

The great majority of hidden champions operate in oligopolistic markets in which we can expect behavioral interdependence between competitors. Only a small number of hidden champions operate in polypolistic markets where the individual company has little influence on the conduct of its competitors. The oligopolistic situation is not unusual. Even in large markets (e.g., cars, aircraft, power stations, telecommunications equipment or computers), there are rarely more than 10–20 serious competitors worldwide.

It is obvious that the number of competitors has an influence on market share. We have measured this correlation for the market leaders. A nonlinear hypothesis produced the best results:[2]

Market share $= 55.3$ x number of competitors$^{-0.34}$

The exponent -0.34 is a so-called elasticity, expressing that the market share of the market leader decreases 0.34% if the number of competitors increases 1%. If the number of competitors increases 10%, the market share would accordingly decrease 3.4%. Fig. 7.1 shows the correlation

Fig. 7.1: Dependence of market leader's market share on the number of competitors

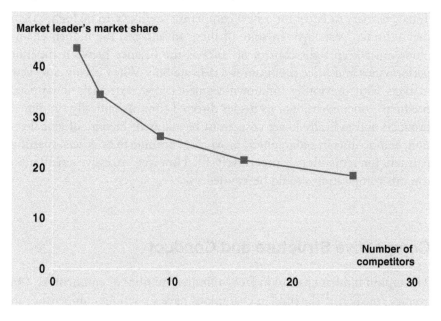

between the market share of the market leader and the number of competitors.

The outstanding competitive position of the hidden champions is reflected in the following answers:

- Of the hidden champions, 84.1% report an increase in their market shares over the last ten years, and only 11.9% a decrease.
- Only 7.6% report volatile market shares, whereas 30.3% report a stable market share situation.
- Of the hidden champions, 61.7% face the same competitors over and over again.
- Almost half (exactly 46.2%) have been in the market much longer than their most significant competitor.
- Only 7.5% of the hidden champions have experienced frequent entry of new competitors into their market.
- Of the hidden champions, 28.1% consider the entry of new competitors in the near future likely or very likely.
- About every 13th hidden champion (exactly 7.5%) sees such an entry as a threat to its own company, whereas 37.6% do not perceive an entry as a threat.

In which countries do the hidden champions see their most important competitors? Fig. 7.2 shows the figures for today and ten years ago.

Compared to ten years ago, there has been a marked shift in the locations of the most important competitors. The lower percentage for Europe can be seen as the logical consequence of globalization. The clear rise of the US as home of the strongest competitors is surprising. I see two reasons for this change: The increasing internationalization of American midsize companies and the stronger activity of European hidden champions in high-tech markets in which American companies play a strong role. As a training ground, the US is indispensable. Strong new competitors are emerging there. Nevertheless, some hidden champions continue to shy away from the US. Japan's importance as a location of strong competitors has declined. Today, Japanese companies are less relevant as competitors than they were ten years ago. This corroborates the earlier finding that there are relatively few midsize world market leaders in Japan. For the most part, internationally active, successful Japanese firms are large corporations. A new finding is that 4.7% of the hidden champions locate their most significant competitor in China, and for the first time India made the list of further tough competitors. The sum of the percentages in Fig. 7.2 is

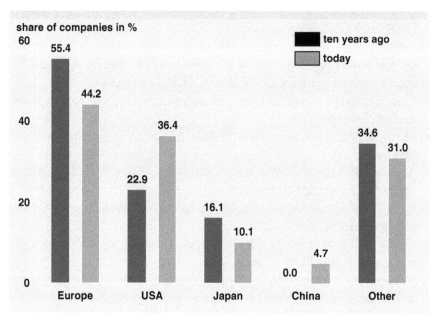

larger than 100 (122.2%) because some respondents stated that they have important competitors in more than one country. The competition in the hidden champions' markets is truly global. A total of 69.0% said that their most significant competitor (or one of their most significant competitors) is a foreign company.

How similar are the hidden champions to their competitors? One may assume that the similarity is quite high—a presumption that is not confirmed, as we see from the following answers:

Similarity regarding. . .	Very similar	Very dissimilar
• Ownership structure	30.3%	40.1%
• Technological competence	18.3%	25.1%
• Product and service offering	14.5%	27.5%
• Size of company	5.3%	45.8%

These results are truly surprising. They confirm again that the hidden champions are very different from one another and operate in heterogeneous competitive environments.

The small number of competitors and their dissimilarity might lead to the presumption that the intensity of competition in the hidden champions' markets is relatively low. The opposite is true. In spite of the limited number of competitors and the low threat from new competitors, the hidden champions' markets are characterized by fierce competition. Almost two thirds (exactly 63.2%) report very intense competition. Only a negligibly low percentage of 4.5% considers competitive intensity to be very low. In my interviews, the hidden champion CEOs repeatedly emphasized that their competitors are strong, frequently even excellent, and that it would be very dangerous to consider one's own market leadership as safe for the future. Windmöller & Hölscher, which has a world market share of 70% in machines for the manufacturing of paper bags, says, "The number of competitors is very small, but this does not mean that the fight for market shares is less tough." I rarely encountered hubris with regard to a company's market power. My experience with large corporations is slightly different. Large corporations often are confident about their market position; whereas the awareness that market leadership has to be fought for and defended every day is widespread among the hidden champions.

The Hidden Champions in the Light of Porter's "Five Forces"

It is interesting to assess the competitive strategy of the hidden champions in the light of Porter's "Five Forces."[3] Porter's perspective encompasses both the competition between established providers and the potential competition from new providers and substitutes. This view, known as "potential competition," has for a long time been common in industrial economics. Porter goes one step further and includes the "competition" along the value chain, because both the vendors and the customers compete with the company for a share of the added value. Porter distinguishes five competitive forces: (1) competition among established competitors, (2) with new competitors, (3) with substitutes, (4) with suppliers, and with (5) customers. These five forces determine how well a company fares, and particularly how profitable it can be.

In the light of these five competitive forces, the hidden champions' situation is as follows:

- Competition between established providers is very intense, but relates primarily to performance and innovation, less to price;

- New competitors and substitutes do not play a decisive role (as shown above);
- Likewise, vendors are also not dominant forces in most cases.
- For customers the "picture" is differentiated (see Chapter 5). Hidden champions may well depend on their customers, but this dependence is not necessarily one-sided.

This is basically the situation of a typical hidden champion with regard to the Five Forces. While this picture is consistent with a healthy profit situation, there are deviations. Automotive suppliers, for example, have to deal with very powerful customers, and there is stiff competition between established competitors, largely due to overcapacities. Occasionally, strong suppliers (new competitors) enter the markets (e.g., Japanese suppliers following Toyota and Co. into western markets, European suppliers such as Bosch and Valeo into Asian markets). Supply shortages and price increases for steel and aluminum have increased pressure on suppliers. With such a combination of several negative factors, it is not surprising that, despite their strong market position, many automotive suppliers have considerably lower profit margins than the average hidden champion, or even incur losses. This situation can be improved only if the automotive suppliers as a whole control their capacities better, and if there is a shift from volume orientation towards profit orientation.[4] On the other hand, there are industries in which established suppliers adopt intelligent policies with regard to capacity and price. In these industries, the individual customer and the individual supplier tend to be weak and new competitors or substitutes do not constitute a threat. Many of the markets in which the hidden champions have world market shares of more than 50% belong to this category. Since these market leaders earn high margins, they are able to invest in innovations and to strengthen their leading positions. This does not mean that competition is weak in such markets, but that it focuses on performance and innovation. Aggression that ruins margins and price wars remain the exception in the markets of the hidden champions.

It is interesting to assess the hidden champions in view of a further concept by Porter, the so-called "diamond" of international competitiveness. This "diamond" includes production factors, competition, demand and supporting industries in a country.[5] Porter's central tenet is that all these determinants contribute to the success of a sector or a company. He attributes an outstanding role to competition: "Among the strongest empirical findings from our research is the correlation between rigorous domestic rivalry and the creation and persistence of competitive advantage in an industry. Nations with leading world positions often have a number of strong local rivals."[6] Our study contains numerous examples of sectors in which this tenet applies, despite the regional shift in the most important competitors already described. Fig. 7.2 shows that the locations of the most important competitors have in some cases shifted. This means that the hidden champions must regionally broaden their competitive perspective—which they are doing. Just as top customers must be followed all over the world (see Chapters 4 and 5), the hidden champions must prevent competitors from quietly establishing a bastion elsewhere in the world from which they can then conquer the world market.

We come to the conclusion that the typical hidden champion has only a limited number of competitors worldwide. The markets of the hidden champions are usually oligopolistic, even on a global scale. Competition is intense and focuses on performance and innovation rather than on price. Increasingly, the fiercest competitors are spread across the whole world. This means that local competition will lose some of its historical significance. A company striving to achieve a top position in the world market should actively seek, not avoid, competition with the best companies in the world. The toughest market environments must be used as training grounds for remaining competitive fitness. Greatness on a global scale is attained only by confronting the best—wherever they may be.

Competitive Advantages

As a framework for the analysis of competitive advantages, Ohmae proposed the so-called "strategic triangle" composed of the company, the customer, and the competition.[7] Ohmae postulates that offering the customer a substantial benefit is insufficient in modern markets, because there will always be competitors that also offer good performance at competitive prices. The decisive factor is to supply the customer with a clear advantage when compared with the competition. Such a "strategic" competitive advantage must fulfill three criteria: it must be

1. important for the customer;
2. actually perceived by the customer; and
3. sustainable/difficult to copy.

If, for example, the packaging of a product is unimportant for the customer, it is unsuitable as a competitive advantage. If a product has a particularly long life span, but the customer is not aware of this advantage or does not perceive it, this advantage cannot influence the customer's decision to purchase and does not help the supplier. If a company ruins its margin by reducing a price, the low price advantage cannot be sustained.[8] Simultaneous fulfillment of the three criteria "important, perceived, sustainable" is a significant challenge.

Frequency of competitive advantages

What are the hidden champions' competitive advantages? Fig. 7.3 shows the percentages of companies that stated they had a clear competitive advantage in the respective attribute. The attributes were specified in the question (closed question).

Fig. 7.3: Competitive advantages of the hidden champions

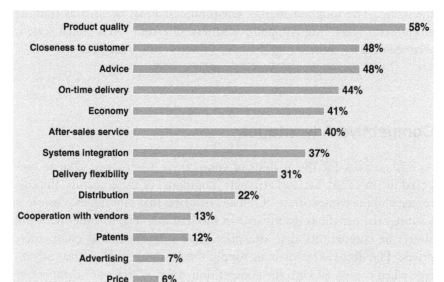

Product quality is the most frequently cited competitive advantage. This finding is consistent with Fig 2.6, which revealed quality leadership to be one of the fundamental characteristics of the hidden champions. The next most frequent competitive advantages are oriented around softer factors such as closeness to customer, advice, delivery, and service (i.e., factors surrounding the product). Marketing instruments such as advertising and price are the least frequently named competitive advantages.

The answers to the open question about competitive advantages (without specification of the attributes) and the changes in the last ten years are also revealing. Product quality remains, by far, first in the open question. A total of 39% of respondents listed quality as a competitive advantage. This percentage is almost identical to the 38% ten years ago. Service/advice came second, which is consistent with the closed question. However, we observe marked shifts in several attributes. The four competitive parameters with the strongest increase are shown in Fig. 7.4.

Fig. 7.4: Change in frequency of competitive advantages (open question)

Performance attribute	Increase in percentage points compared to ten years ago
Advice	+10
Systems integration	+8
Ease of use/simplicity	+8
Technology	+6

Advice increased the most, with 10 points. Systems integration and ease of use/simplicity follow closely with 8 percentage points. It is interesting that ease of use did not even appear in the open question ten years ago, while 8% of the respondents list it as a competitive advantage now. The other attributes as shown in Fig. 7.3 are largely unchanged compared to ten years ago. In the 1980s, Levitt proposed the concept of the "augmented product."[9] In the broader sense, this idea involves an extended service spectrum. This includes product-related services, software, and information. Systems integration also means an extension of the product. The extended service spectrum has become enormously important for the competitive position of the hidden champions.

Fig. 7.5 contains a selection of open answers relating to specific competitive advantages. This selection illustrates the variety and complexity of hidden champions' competitive advantage.

Company	Main product	Description of competitive advantages (selection)
Germanischer Lloyd	Ship certification	Worldwide 24/7 availability of service
Veka	Plastic profiles for windows and doors	Large product range, solutions for all problems
Tente	Castors	Better qualified employees
SEW-Eurodrive	Drives/gears	Comprehensive service portfolio, worldwide availability
DMT Technology	Bi-axial film-stretching machines	Short adjustment periods, broad use
Schwan-Stabilo Cosmetics	Cosmetic pencils	Highest innovation level in chemistry and packaging
Märklin	Model railways	Compatibility over decades, collectors' topics
ColArt	Artists' materials	Largest variety in application, highest innovativeness
Sick	Sensors	Widest product range

These advantages shed light on the so-called "opportunity principle" of competitive strategy: there are as many opportunities to create a competitive advantage as there are (important) competitive parameters, which makes the list of potential competitive advantages quite long. The hidden champions typically use several of these opportunities and do not confine themselves to one competitive advantage.

Matrix of competitive advantages

Until now, we have considered competitive advantages from the point of view of frequency. Importance to the customer was the first criterion for a competitive advantage. The importance profile from the point of view of the customer was shown in Fig. 5.3. In Fig. 7.6, we connect both aspects, the importance from the customer's point of view and the relative competitive performance, in the so-called matrix of competitive advantages. The importance from the customer's point of view is shown on the vertical axis; the competitive performance is shown on the horizontal axis. Left-of-center positions mean that the company is weaker in these attributes than the strongest competitor; right-of-center positions say that a company is stronger than its strongest competitor in this attribute. Positions

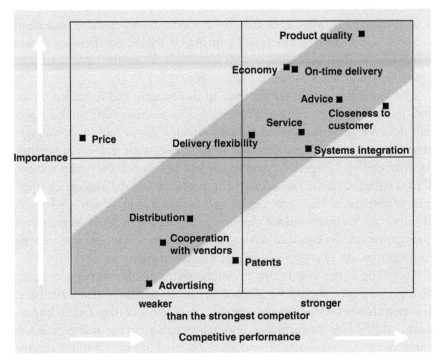

right of the center line therefore indicate competitive advantages. However, only the parameters in the top right quarter (i.e., those regarded as particularly important by customers), give rise to a "strategic" competitive advantage.

The matrix of competitive advantages contains highly condensed information and provides a comprehensive view of the hidden champions' competitive position at a glance. This position must be assessed as outstanding. It is evident that the hidden champions have not only one but several strategic competitive advantages. At least five of these, namely product quality, closeness to customer, on-time delivery, advice, and cost effectiveness, are characterized by a combination of above-average importance and above-average competitive performance. The hidden champions rank way ahead of the competition in service and systems integration.

The position of price is, however, completely different. At slightly above-average importance, competitive performance is extremely weak here. Price is the strategic competitive disadvantage of the hidden champions. This is consistent with our statement in Chapter 5 that the hidden champions pursue predominantly premium strategies and do not compete through price. However, the weak competitive position regarding price is in principle—if not necessarily to this extent—acceptable, because it is compensated for by numerous performance-related competitive advantages. The fact that cost effectiveness (i.e., value for money) is judged positively also indicates a balanced relationship.

The remaining attributes decrease in importance and furthermore are not characterized by strong performance. The position with patents naturally does not apply to each individual company. We are looking at averages here. The position is very different in industries with numerous patents. As discussed in Chapter 6, patents do not play a role in many sectors. This is reflected in the low degree of importance and the average competitive performance. The same can be said of advertising, which is relatively unimportant for many hidden champions as they are in direct contact with their customers. By contrast, advertising is very important for fast-moving consumer goods. Averages tell only part of the truth.

According to the consistency principle of competitive strategy, competitive performance should be aligned to the importance of an attribute. Top performance must be the aim for parameters of significant importance, while lower performance appears acceptable if a parameter is less important to the customer. The shaded diagonal in Fig. 7.6 illustrates the consistency principle. It is striking how well the hidden champions adhere to this consistency. Importance and competitive performance are generally well matched. When compared with thousands of other such competitive advantage matrices that we at Simon-Kucher have analyzed, the hidden champions' consistency is remarkable. The only strong divergence is in price. As explained above, this is not a fundamental problem in view of the high performance in numerous other attributes. Still the extent of the divergence of price from the consistency corridor is striking. This must be interpreted as a warning signal. Hidden champions should observe the competitive disadvantage in price carefully. We will return to this subject later.

Once again, the ten-year comparison is interesting. What has changed? The competitive advantages in product quality, closeness to customer, service, and cost effectiveness have fundamentally remained the same. The competitive performance in on-time delivery has improved noticeably from a neutral position to a clear strategic competitive advantage. This is the result of the enormous efforts in logistics and supply chain management that many hidden champions have undertaken in recent years. In contrast to on-time delivery, there has been no progress in delivery flexibility. The neutral position of this performance parameter has been maintained. The greatest changes are evident in advice and systems integration, as already shown in the answers to the open question (Fig. 7.4). The importance of both attributes has strongly increased and the hidden champions have managed to produce superior competitive performance in these parameters.

Sustainability of Competitive Advantages

In addition to importance from the customer's point of view and perception of the superior performance, sustainability is the third criterion for a strategic competitive advantage. What is the hidden champions' competitive position in this regard? We look at Fig. 7.7 to discuss the sustainability of competitive advantages and its origins.

Fig. 7.7: Sustainability of competitive advantages and its origins

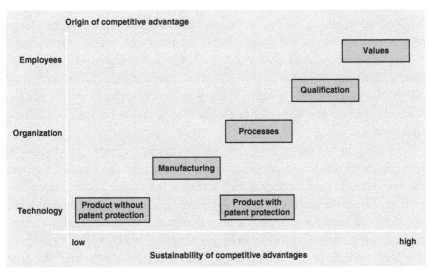

Competitive advantages built (solely) into the product are easiest to imitate. Competitors often need only a few weeks or months for reverse engineering to copy a product. This is different if the product is patent-protected and the protection can actually be enforced, which in turn depends on the relevant jurisdiction. It is significantly more difficult to copy manufacturing or organizational processes. For example, it would require much more time and money for a competitor of Caterpillar to achieve the performance level of Caterpillar's worldwide spare parts logistics system than to copy the latest Caterpillar bulldozer. The competitive advantages hardest to imitate, and thus the most sustainable, are those rooted in the qualifications and value systems of the employees. Such internal skills and values are hard to copy. This category includes the new competitive advantages of the hidden champions, such as advice or the capability for systems integration, that are based on employees' superior qualifications.

A look at the changes in the matrix of competitive advantages in Fig. 7.6 in the light of sustainability leads to interesting insights. The position of product quality remained stable. Contrary to the ongoing discussion, we cannot see a general threat to the sustainability of product quality as a competitive advantage. But views differ from company to company. In response to the question whether it will be easier or more difficult to achieve quality leadership in the future, 25.4% answered that it would be more difficult and only 3.8% said that it would be easier, but a clear majority of 70.8% chose a middle category by saying "neither much easier nor much more difficult." The findings about the enormous wave of innovations presented in the last chapter indicate that many hidden champions see a strengthened sustainability of their competitive advantages. A lot of them have increased their head-start on the competition. However, a significant number of companies say that Chinese competitors have caught up. To ensure their superior quality in the coming years, the hidden champions from the West definitely have to keep an eye on the Chinese competition.

The findings about competitive advantages in extended products and services are clearer. In particular, we have seen that the importance and the competitive performance have increased for advice and systems integration. These competitive advantages have their origins in the employees' competencies and the company's value systems, and therefore show a particularly high degree of sustainability. The improvements of the competitive performance in on-time delivery and closeness to customer also lead us to assume a higher sustainability of these competitive advantages. Better performance in these intangible factors means that the hidden champions have raised the barriers to entry for new competitors. It is probably harder to enter the hidden champions' markets today than it was ten years ago.

We cannot support the widespread opinion that the hidden champions' competitive position is in greater danger than in the past. On the contrary, we come to the conclusion that the sustainability of the hidden champions' competitive advantages has actually increased. More than ever, their superiority is based on factors that competitors find difficult to imitate.

Demonstration of Competitive Superiority

Market leadership, in particular on the world market, places pressure on companies to fulfill high expectations. The "world champion" is expected to demonstrate competitive superiority, top performance, pioneering achievements, new "world records" and solutions to unsolved problems. The champion is more likely to be given the opportunity to participate in high-visibility projects and to prove its outstanding competency. If the champion successfully masters these challenges, the result is a very effective demonstration of competitive superiority. Ideally the company is perceived as the one and only provider for high-visibility projects—a unique communication message. However, we should be aware that spectacular projects also harbor risks because they are the focus of attention in the sector and among the customers. If such a project goes wrong, grave damage can be done to a company's image and reputation—the flipside of fame.

The hidden champions demonstrate their competitive superiority through an impressive number of high-visibility projects. Fig. 7.8 shows a selection of case studies that demonstrate competitive superiority or even uniqueness.

Being the best, the number one, the market leader, are excellent communication messages both for the market and for the employees. The statement: "We are number one" is clear and comprehensible for everyone. Such spectacular projects prove to the target group that the company is simply the best, creating a sense of pride among employees. These opportunities are only open to the best provider(s); only they can send out the message that they are number one. The demonstration of superior performance and the effectiveness of communication form a virtuous circle. Access to prestigious projects is obtained only through past performance. The prestigious projects in turn make the communication more effective and strengthen the perception of the competitive advantages, giving rise to new opportunities. This performance-communication-opportunities cycle can be maintained for as long as a hidden champion defends its superiority over the competition.

Fig. 7.8: Demonstration of competitive superiority by high-visibility projects

Company	Main product	High-visibility projects
Klais	Organs	The only bamboo organ in the world/ Philippines; Petronas Concert Hall, Kuala Lumpur; Cologne Cathedral; Beijing National Theater; Concert Hall Tokyo; Cologne and Munich Philharmonic Halls
Josef Gartner	High-rise facades	Taipeh 101, the world's highest building till 2009; Burj Dubai, tallest building today
Putzmeister	Concrete pumps	Record of 600 m pipe length in Gotthard Tunnel; record distance tranportation at 1,661 m in drinking water tunnel, Barcelona; world record in concrete height transportation (532 m), Riva del Garda power station, Italy; largest concrete pump in the world with 62 m mast for Chernobyl reactor rehabilitation
Arnold & Richter	Professional film cameras	12 technical Oscars
Belfor	Fire and water damage removal	Restoration of 100,000 books after a large fire at the University of Vienna; removal of damage caused by hurricanes Catrina and Rita in Mississippi and Louisiana
Herrenknecht	Tunnel-drilling machines	Gotthard Tunnel measuring 2x57 km, from 2015 on the longest traffic tunnel in the world; world's largest tunnel-drilling machine with 15.43 m diameter for the Yangtse crossing near Shanghai
Sennheiser	Stage microphones	Beyoncé, Nena, Superbowl, Lisbon World Exhibition, Olympic Winter Games in Turin, technical Oscar, Emmy Award, technical Grammy Award
Glasbau Hahn	Glass cases	All famous museums in the world
Sport-Berg	Sports equipment: discus, hammer	Supplier to the Olympic Games and world championships
Von Ehren	Large living trees	Trafalgar Square and the National Gallery in London; Euro-Disneyland; Munich airport; Kurfürstendamm in Berlin
Gerriets	Stage curtains,	Metropolitan Opera, New York; Opéra Bastille, Paris; Operas in Taipeh and Istanbul; Wang Center, Boston
Otto Bock	Prostheses	Paralympics Beijing; service for all brands
Kärcher	High-pressure cleaners	Spectacular cleaning actions: Statue of Christ in Rio de Janeiro; Statue of Liberty, New York; Presidents' Heads at Mount Rushmore; coast of Alaska after Exxon Valdez catastrophe
Dorma, Häfele	Door-lock systems	Burj Dubai, more than 800 m high
Sick	Sensors	Sick sensors protect the Mona Lisa, Louvre
Robbe & Berking	Silver cutlery	Sultan of Brunei, first-class hotels and restaurants
McIlhenny	Tabasco sauce	Special supplier to U.S. Navy and Marine Corps. Also used in space (Skylab, International Space Station)
Trox	Components for air conditioning systems	Burj al Arab; Madrid airport; Luthuli Hospital in Durban
Bosch Rexroth	Hydraulics	Beijing National Theater; Bolshoi Theater Moscow; world's largest ferris wheel in Beijing
Knauf	Plaster	Reichstag and Federal President's Office, Berlin; Italian museums
Carbon Sports	High performance cycles	Numerous Tour de France and world championship successes
Ziemann	Turnkey brewery plants	Largest brewery in the world, in Piedras Negras, Mexico
Utsch	Security license plates	9 million license plates for Egypt, 2008, largest order ever, most expensive license plate bought by sheikh in Abu Dhabi in 2007

Tradition can have a similar effect on the perception of a competitive advantage—and cannot be imitated. Faber-Castell, the world market leader in pencils, was founded in 1761 and presents a long list of famous customers. Bismarck wrote with Faber-Castell pencils, Vincent van Gogh praised the company's "famous black," and Max Liebermann called them simply "the best." No marketing or advertising money can buy such unique selling propositions. The following dispute between Faber-Castell and Staedtler-Mars, its strongest competitor, sheds light on the value of traditions. The company Staedtler-Mars was founded in 1835, although the first pencil was created by Friedrich Staedtler much earlier, in 1661. In 1994, Staedtler organized a retailers' competition to mark the 333rd anniversary of the production of the first pencil by Friedrich Staedtler. Faber-Castell retaliated defending its reputation as the oldest company in this trade. The Lyra pencil factory, founded in 1806, also claims to be older than Staedtler-Mars. The situation became even more complex in 1978 when Staedtler-Mars acquired the American company Eberhard Faber, which had been founded in 1904 by a black sheep of the Faber family. Tradition obviously has a very great value in the market. Interestingly, Faber-Castell, Staedtler-Mars, and Lyra are close neighbors in the Nuremberg region.

An unusual indicator for competitive superiority and a high degree of recognition is when a product or company name becomes part of a language. The verb "roentgen," to X-ray, is an example in German, just as "to hoover" has become a synonym for vacuum cleaning in English. Recently, the verb "to google" has been adopted. Kärcher, world market leader in high-pressure cleaners, has become part of the French language. The strict language guardians of the Académie Française have even recognized the verb "kärcheriser." The current president of France, Nicolas Sarkozy, said during civil unrest in Paris that the streets of the suburbs would have to be "kärcherised"—a questionable compliment for Kärcher, but evidence of the degree of recognition and competitive strength of the brand. In such cases, the company must, however, take precautions that the brand does not become a generic name.

Competitive Edge and Costs

In Porter's system of generic strategies, the hidden champions' competitive strategies typically fall into the category "differentiated focus" (i.e., they practice a combination of narrow target market and superior performance in one or more parameters).[10] In our discussion of price positions (see Chapter 5) and competitive advantages (see Fig. 7.6), it became clear that the prices are higher than those of the competitors. General cost leadership as defined by Porter, in other words an offer to the entire market at the lowest price or cost, is rare among the hidden champions. Fielmann, European market leader in the distribution of eyeglasses, fits this pattern. Focused cost leadership, in which the cheapest products are provided for a market segment, is slightly more frequent. Kohlpharma, Europe's leader in parallel imports of pharmaceuticals, explicitly aims for cost leadership in its core business. Cargobull (semitrailers), 3B Scientific (anatomic teaching aids), Suspa (gas springs) or Böllhoff (screws) consistently emphasize their cost and price competitiveness. However, even in these cases we can ask whether there is pure price/cost leadership, because quality is also always emphasized by these hidden champions. If we compare this with radically cost-oriented strategies like those applied by Southwest Airlines, Ryanair, Wal-Mart or Aldi, we come to the conclusion that hardly any hidden champion pursues a strategy of pure cost leadership.

However, this in no way means that the costs can be neglected in the hidden champions' competitive strategies. First, the intensity of competition forces the hidden champions to increasingly concentrate on costs and to constantly rationalize. Second, there is the latent risk of a company edging itself out with premium positioning with regard to economies of scale and absolute price levels. Performance, prices, and costs must always be viewed in relation to each other. The following comment by a Dutch customer to the CEO of a German engineering company sheds light on the problem, "Your price is $1.6 million. The price quoted by an Italian company is $1 million. While I acknowledge that your product is better, it's not 60% better. So I won't pay 60% more." The Dutch customer bought the Italian product.

Our impression is that the best hidden champions continuously and seriously work on their costs. Bernd Hoffmann, CEO of Cargobull, has energetically driven up productivity for years. In the last ten years, the cycle time for a semitrailer has been reduced to 24 hours from three weeks. Hoffmann says, "Given our wage levels, we are damned to continuously increase productivity. If the costs per unit fall we can offer lower prices. In this way, we become more competitive and increase our sales and market share. This is reflected directly in profit and margin." Despite a price decline of 30% in the market, Cargobull's return on sales has increased to more than 7% from 2% in this period.

Hoffmann, however, emphasizes that Cargobull does not pursue a "low-price strategy." Instead, he talks about a "hybrid strategy" that combines "innovations, highest product quality and strong customer orientation" on the one hand with "cost leadership, economies of scale, efficiency and strict control of fixed costs" on the other hand. Trumpf, world market leader in laser cutting machines, aims for a very ambitious combination of performance differentiation and low costs. CEO Nicola Leibinger-Kammüller comments, "We must become faster, better and cheaper in all areas. Production time for a machine has been shortened from twelve to five weeks. We are one of the few mechanical engineering companies that have changed the entire final assembly work to assembly line processes." Hans-Joachim Boekstegers, CEO of Multivac, global number one in thermoform packaging machines, says, "Our move into more standardized and therefore less costly solutions lets us reach new customer groups and applications."

Some hidden champions apply a second-brand strategy to be price competitive in lower segments. Winklhofer markets its high-performance steering chains under the brand name Iwis and has a second product line under the name Eurochain, which is positioned much lower with regard to costs and prices. The JK Group, world market leader in professional sun beds, has a high-price brand Ergoline and a second brand, Soltron, which is priced less expensively to appeal to a younger clientele. Binder, world market leader in thermal cabinets for medical and biological research, has armed itself against cheaper competitors by founding a subsidiary, called Advantage Lab, offering thermal cabinets at lower costs and prices. "Nobody should be in a position to manufacture such equipment more cheaply than us," emphasizes CEO Peter Michael Binder.

A company that continues to produce in high-wage countries, either by choice or out of necessity because the required expertise is only available there, must pay highest attention to cost management, even if it is a hidden champion. In spite of these pressures, the competitive advantage of the hidden champions is not shifted to the cost and price side. Instead, the task of rationalization is primarily to prevent pricing oneself out of the market despite superior performance.

The calls for lower costs and prices become tougher in markets where quality requirements are low. Premium position and high costs in such markets involve two risks. The first risk is missing a large proportion of the market because the price is too high; the second risk involves competitors with low costs and prices improving their quality and attacking from below. This has happened, and continues to occur, in countless markets, as evidenced by the examples of motorcycles, cameras, automobiles or generic pharmaceuticals after the expiry of patent protection. A good example is the Chinese market for plastic injection molding machines. The structure of this market at the beginning of the twenty-first century is shown in Fig. 7.9.

Fig. 7.9: Market structure for plastic injection molding machines in China

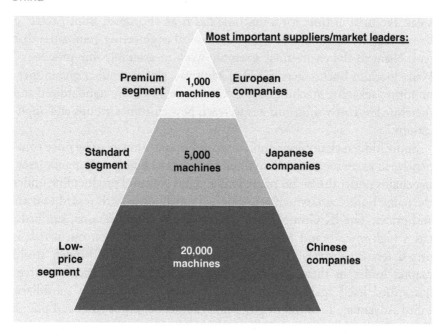

The premium segment, with approximately 1,000 machines per year, is mainly served by world market leaders of European origin such as Engel from Austria, Netstal from Switzerland, and Krauss-Maffei, Demag Plastics Group or Arburg from Germany. The middle segment comprises approximately 5,000 machines and is the domain of Japanese suppliers. The low-price segment, which is four times the size of the middle segment comprising 20,000 machines, is dominated by Chinese companies. What strategy options are open to a premium hidden champion in such a market? For a world market leader, restriction to the top niche, which in this case only accounts for 4% of the units sold, cannot be a realistic long-term option. Even in a market such as China, the premium niche is too small. A study concluded that "machinery and engineering companies must radically simplify their product concepts to conquer growth markets such as China and India."[11] In addition, there is the significant danger that suppliers with far lower prices but acceptable quality will attack from below. Essentially, the only answer is entry into cheaper products, which means that manufacturing has to take place in China. Many hidden champions follow this pattern to be able to compete in medium- and low-price segments. Many years ago, Nicolas Hayek, creator of the Swatch watch and former CEO of Swatch, warned against abandoning the lower market segments to competitors from low-wage countries. The most effective defense strategy for the premium segment is often to become cost-competitive in the segments below it, a strategy that an increasing number of hidden champions are pursuing. Sick, one of the market leaders in sensor technology, has resolved to avoid overengineering at all costs. "I can't bear frills," said the CEO and former head of development Robert Bauer. Professor Günther Schuh, director of the machine tool laboratory at the Aachen Institute of Technology,[12] says, "With a suitable product range and efficient processes, German mechanical engineering can operate profitably in the growing middle segment."[13] Professor Horst Wildemann, of TUM, Technical University of Munich, talks about a printing press for which the manufacturing costs were reduced by 32% without a reduction in performance. Bühler, the Swiss world market leader in milling technology, took over a Chinese company to keep up with costs and for reasons of simplicity. According to CEO Calvin Grieder, this enabled a better alignment between the product and the customer's expectations than would have been possible with the more complex Swiss originals.

Karl Mayer, the warp knitting machine manufacturer with a dominant 75% world market share, pursues an interesting double strategy. The aim is to consolidate both positions in the premium and standard segments. For this purpose, CEO Fritz Mayer issued the following development objectives:

1. Same performance in the standard segment with a cost cut of 25%.
2. Better performance of 25% in the premium segment for the same price.

According to Fritz Mayer, these highly ambitious goals were achieved by 2008.

These approaches lead to further considerations. Do the hidden champions have a chance to beat really cheap competitors? We do not strive for a final answer here, but instead offer the thought-provoking case of motorcycles in the Vietnamese market and the company Honda. With $96 billion in revenues,[14] Honda is not a hidden champion but, in contrast to typical large Japanese companies and despite its size, the company has remarkable similarities with hidden champions. Honda is world market leader in motorcycles and is the global number one in small internal combustion engines (production 21 million units, mainly small motors), in power generators, and also has a leading position in lawnmowers. In the 1990s, Honda dominated the motorcycle market in Vietnam with a market share of 90%. Its main model Honda-Dream was sold for the equivalent of $2,100. Chinese competitors increasingly encroached on the Vietnamese market and priced their motorbikes at $550–$700, somewhere between a quarter and a third of the price of a Honda. In 2000, the Chinese sold one million motorcycles with their extremely aggressive price strategy, while Honda's sales dwindled to 170,000 units. In this situation, most companies would have given up or withdrawn to the premium niche. Instead Honda, as a short-term reaction, reduced the price of the Dream model to $1,300 from $2,100—a level that could not, of course, be sustained on a permanent basis and was still double the Chinese prices. Next, Honda developed a new model called Wave α, which combined acceptable quality with low costs. Honda's comment on the new model sold from January 19, 2002 onwards was "The Honda Wave α has achieved a low price, yet high quality and dependability, through using cost-reduced locally made parts as well as parts obtained through Honda's global purchasing network." The new model was introduced at a price of $732 and won back the Vietnamese market for Honda. In 2003-2004, most Chinese suppliers withdrew from Vietnam.

This case points our attention to a new market segment in the emerging countries. This is an ultra low-price segment unknown in this form both in the highly developed and the emerging countries so far. Vijay Mahajan, a professor who teaches at the University of Texas, describes this new development in his book *The 86% Solution—How to Succeed in the Biggest Market Opportunity of the Twenty-first Century*.[15] The 86% in the title of the book refers to the fact that 86% of humanity had a family income of less than $10,000 at the time of publication. People in this income category cannot afford the typical products of highly developed countries (e.g., automobiles, body care, and so forth.). However, fast growth in countries such as China or India means that many millions of consumers break through this magical $10,000 barrier every year and therefore become relevant target groups for industrial products, though in the lowest price categories.

There are very specific developments with regard to such super cheap products in Eastern Europe and particularly in Asia. The French automobile manufacturer Renault is very successful with the cheap automobile

Dacia Logan, which is produced in Romania and Russia. This automobile is available for less than $10,000 and Renault has sold over one million of this model since its market launch in June 2005. The price for a typical compact car today is about twice as high. However, super cheap cars in emerging countries will be far below the price of a Renault Dacia Logan. In 2009, the Indian manufacturer Tata attracted worldwide attention with its introduction of the small car Nano. In India, the Nano is referred to as the "one Lakh car." "Lakh" means 100,000 and refers to the price threshold of 100,000 rupees, approximately equivalent to $2,000. A total of 10 million super cheap vehicles are already being sold worldwide. By 2015, this figure is set to rise to 27 million. This segment is growing twice as fast as the automotive market as a whole. Automotive manufacturers and suppliers, including many hidden champions, cannot afford to ignore the lowest price segment. In addition to large suppliers such as Bosch (with a supply proportion of more than 10% of the value of the Nano), Continental, and ZF, the hidden champions Behr, Freudenberg, and Mahle also contributed parts to the Nano. You could say that the Nano is as much a hidden champion car as it is an Indian car. This example shows that hidden champions can keep up in the lowest price segment. Renault-Nissan has announced its intention to launch a cheap car for less than $3,000 along with the Indian three-wheel manufacturer Bajaj. However, the biggest challenge in this segment is not to generate revenues, but to make a profit.

The case studies Honda and Nano are thought-provoking. There is no room for naïve generalizations. We see that radically new, simpler products are required to compete with ultra cheap contenders. Honda's new model is an example of the "lean product concept" suggested by Professor Schuh. A lean product must naturally be manufactured and distributed at the lowest possible cost. Whether this goal can be more effectively achieved by manufacturing in low-wage countries, or by a high degree of automation, remains to be seen. Quite a few hidden champions are expecting a massive breakthrough in automation. These changes are likely to have strong effects on the competitiveness of advanced and emerging countries. In Vietnam, Honda used its enormous process know-how and its brand. With the Nano, the hidden champions directed their massive innovative forces towards simplification. These new strategies deserve serious consideration. The either-or decision between product differentiation and cost leadership postulated by Porter has the charm of simplicity and apparent intellectual clarity, but the real world is not always that simple. In spite of all superiority with regard to performance, the hidden champions cannot afford to neglect the costs. In the changed competitive environment of the twenty-first century, unconventional strategies such as those of Karl Mayer, Cargobull, Honda or the Nano-suppliers must be employed to build or defend world market leadership.

Sparring Partners for Competitive Fitness

Earlier in this chapter, we discussed Porter's theory about the interdependence between "rigorous domestic rivalry and the creation and persistence of competitive advantage in an industry."[16] Rivals who fight for the same business are at least partially caught in a zero-sum game; yet they are also voluntarily or involuntarily sparring partners for competitive fitness. This does not imply that they have good relations with each other, but companies that compete with each other simply cannot avoid becoming better if they want to survive and operate profitably. This relationship is comparable to top athletes pitted against each other. Even if they do not train together, they drive each other to new heights of performance as long as they remain sufficiently ambitious. We find more parallels to the hidden champions in sports. The best sportsmen and sports women in one discipline frequently come from one region or even one club. In the 1990s, I visited an athletics meeting in Cologne/Germany, where two new world records were set, one for 800 meters and the other for 3,000 meter hurdles. In the 3,000 meter race, four runners beat the old world record. All of them came from Kenya. Such competitive intensity leads to top performance.

One of my most memorable experiences in this context was in Chicago after a lecture about the hidden champions. A listener came forward and explained that he was from Warsaw, Indiana. As I was unfamiliar with Warsaw, Indiana, nothing came to mind when trying to picture this town. Then he told me that Warsaw, Indiana, is home to the world's three leading companies for orthopedic implants: Zimmer, DePuy, and Biomet. Imagine that a small town with a population of 12,000 in the U.S-Midwest is the home of three hidden champions in a highly demanding technological sphere and is the "Orthopedic Capital of the World." A fourth world-class competitor, Stryker, is also not far away in Kalamazoo, Michigan. In a similar vein, Wichita, Kansas, is called the "Air Capital of the World." It is home to aircraft makers Cessna, Hawker Beechcraft, and Learjet. In addition, Boeing, Airbus, and Aero Systems have manufacturing sites in Wichita.

This local proximity of the strongest competitors is no accident. It occurs frequently among the hidden champions. This is not the classic industry cluster, but competition between individual rivals. The cluster concept, by contrast, has a broader, environment-related framework and is dealt with in Chapter 8.

Fig. 7.10 shows a selection of closely competing hidden champions in regional proximity to each other. The number of examples could be extended to several hundred.

Fig. 7.10: A selection of hidden champions in close competition and geographical proximity

Product	Competitors	Place	Country	Remarks
Shopping carts	Wanzl	Leipheim	Germany	Global No. 1
	Siegel	Jettingen		Strong competitor
Orthopedic implants	Zimmer	Warsaw	Indiana, USA	Global No. 1
	DePuy	Warsaw		All three are leaders
	Biomet	Warsaw		
Private Planes	Cessna	Wichita	Kansas, USA	Cessna global No. 1
	Hawker Beechcraft	Wichita		others leading
	Learjet	Wichita		
Sparkling wine	Freixenet	Sant Sadurni d'Anoia	Spain	Global No. 1
	Codorniu	Sant Sadurni d'Anoia		Global No. 2
				Strong competition
Eyewear	Luxottica	Agordo	Italy	Global No. 1
	Safilo	Padua		Global No. 2
				Very similar strategies
Assembly products	Würth	Künzelsau	Germany	Global No. 1
	Berner	Künzelsau		Global No. 2
Aromas/perfumes	Givaudan	Vervier	Switzerland	Global No. 1
	Firmenich	Geneva		Global No. 2/3
Interface technology	Phoenix Contact	All in the region of	Germany	Global No. 1, all three
	Harting	East Westphalia		global leaders
	Weidmüller			
Golf equipment	Callaway	Carlsbad	California, USA	Both fight for global
	TaylorMade	Carlsbad		market leadership
Wind energy	Vestas	Randers	Denmark	Global No. 1
	Enercon	Aurich	Northern Germany	Global No. 3, techological leader

There is frequently fierce competition between these neighbors. Callaway and TaylorMade in Carlsbad, California, have been fighting for supremacy regarding golf clubs for years. Freixenet and Codorniu in the small Spanish wine village Sant Sadurni d'Anoia are bitterly competitive in the area of sparkling wine. The relationships of these hidden champions in close competition with one another can be anything from friendly to hostile. Sometimes, the new competitor is a former employee of the pioneer, as in the case of Albert Berner, who worked for Würth, the world market leader for assembly products, and then became self-employed. Today, Berner is number two in the world and reports revenues of more than $1 billion.

As we have seen in the discussion on the regional shift of the fiercest competitors, the hidden champions increasingly judge the competition from a global perspective. However, we should not underestimate the importance of a strong competitor in the same region from the point of view of competitive fitness. Would Mercedes, BMW, and Audi be leaders in premium automobiles without the tough, close competition between them? Would the pharmaceutical industry in Basle/Switzerland have risen to world fame without the stiff competition between Roche and Novartis? Would Adidas have achieved the same fame without Puma, also located in the small town of Herzogenaurach? Would Silicon Valley have risen to the same world reputation without the strong competition from the Internet companies? These considerations lead to the apparently absurd conclusion that it can in the long term be better for a company to have strong rather than weak competitors close by. The lone top athlete is unlikely to win the gold medal, the young hopeful who constantly has to battle top competition frequently excels. The top athletes in a discipline often train in the same place because they know this law. Why should the same laws not apply to business? The key factor is that the competition is aimed at performance and innovation. Pure price competition on the other hand often ends in collapse or takeover for one or even both competitors. This has occurred often enough between hidden champions in close competition with each other. The world market leader in industrial chains RUD (Rieger and Dietz) took over the local competitor Erlau after one hundred years of intense competition. Erlau continues to exist as a company and a brand and is itself world market leader in tire protection chains. In a similar way, GKD Kufferath, world market leader in metal fabrics, swallowed its local competitor Dürener Metalltuch (metal cloth). In fragrances, the companies Dragoco and Haarmann & Reimer, both from the same small town, merged to form the new hidden champion Symrise.

Entrepreneurs do not often complain about too little competition. However, for the hidden champions many things are different. The CEO of a very successful mechanical engineering company who increased his world market share to 75% from 40% in recent years[17] told me, "My problem now is that our competitors are too weak and my people are becoming too arrogant. I have consciously increased the price in some recent projects so that the competitors get these orders and my employees learn to be more modest. I would prefer stronger competitors." In another discussion, the CEO of a high-tech company expressed regret that the local competitor was no longer as strong as in the past, meaning that an important source of drive for the employees had been lost. Perhaps sufficiently (but not overly) strong competition is really desirable—even if this makes life a little uncomfortable. In summary, close competition between neighboring hidden champions can contribute considerably to competitive fitness. Even in the age of globalization competitive proximity has not lost its significance.

Excessive Competitive Orientation

Knowing the competitors is important and it can be advantageous to use them as training partners for competitive fitness. Yet this should not result in an obsession for competition. In our book *Manage for Profit, Not for Market Share*, we talk about a "culture of aggression."[18] Some entrepreneurs and managers fight their competitors with a passion that resembles war. This aggressive atmosphere is stimulated by martial book titles such as "Business Warfare,"[19] "Business Wargames,"[20] "Store Wars"[21] or "Guerrilla Marketing."[22] The collection of information about competitors is described as "competitive intelligence," pure military jargon. However, competition is not war. A war ends at some point, competition does not, and there are no customers on a battlefield. Military missions have little in common with everyday business life. In business, the aim is to win and retain customers, not to beat rivals or capture fugitives. An overly strong orientation or excessively aggressive attitude towards competition can be damaging.

This is nothing new. As early as 1958, Lanzilotti detected a negative correlation between excessive competitive orientation and the profitability of companies.[23] A recent survey concludes that competition-oriented targets are damaging if they are overdone.[24] The book *Blue Ocean Strategy: How to Create Uncontested Market Space and Make the Competition Irrelevant* pleads for a strategy that avoids competition as far as possible.[25] This approach resembles the strategy of many hidden champions. Hermut Kormann, CEO of the world market leader Voith, argues decisively against extreme competitive orientation in his book *Long-Term Customer Relationships—Defying the Myth That Only Competition-Oriented Strategies Work* and clearly favors the dominance of customer orientation.[26]

Although we have come across hidden champions obsessed by competition, they tend to remain exceptions. The more successful hidden champions are not fixated on their competitors, but instead focus on their customers and go their own way. Some hidden champions declared that they waive the systematic collection of competitive information because they do not compare themselves with their competitors. One CEO said, "We do not compare ourselves with the competition; the competition keeps an eye on us." Another expressed a similar attitude as follows: "The competition is not our standard. We set our own standards." Kent Murdock, the CEO of O.C. Tanner, world market leader in employee recognition programs, said, "We do not compete. We serve our customers and go our own ways." Such companies define their own benchmarks. Market leadership is not achieved by imitating the competition. A famous management thinker once warned, "Once you fall into the trap of looking to your competitors for solutions to problems and not to your own company, you start to concentrate on imitating existing solutions to problems and will always remain in second place."[27] Following in the footsteps of others means you will never overtake them. Of course, observation of and orientation towards the competition are not the same as imitation. However, excessive orientation towards the competition does not lead to the top. It is better to focus full attention on one's own competencies and on the customers. In this way, the hidden champions have reached the top of their markets and have the best chance of defending their market leadership in the future.

Summary

The hidden champions' competitive strategies do not follow the standard formulas frequently offered in business literature, but are characterized by numerous autonomous features:

- The hidden champions' markets are predominantly oligopolistic. Even on a world scale, there are generally only six relevant competitors. Few hidden champions face global competition from more than 20 competitors.
- The market share of the market leader depends significantly on the number of competitors and has a fairly low elasticity in relation to the number of competitors. This means that the sheer number of competitors does not have a strong impact on the leader's market share.
- Competitive structure and conduct are relatively stable. In the light of Porter's "Five Forces," the situation of most hidden champions appears favorable.

- The intensity of competition between established suppliers is high and relates primarily to performance and innovation, less to price.
- In spite of globalization, new competitors are not very frequent. However, the locations of the most important competitors are shifting. The hidden champions must take account of this and seek out competition with the strongest companies in the world, regardless of where they are located.
- Vendors and substitutes generally do not pose a significant threat to the hidden champions' profitability.
- In sectors with unfavorable "Five Forces," the reasons are due to (1) capacity- and price-driven battles between established suppliers, sometimes of their own making, and (2) the customers' strong market positions. While the latter are very difficult to change, the capacities in such sectors could be more intelligently controlled. An overly strong orientation towards market share instead of profit is frequent in such beleaguered markets.
- The competitive profile of the hidden champions is complex. They typically have several strategic competitive advantages.
- Product quality has retained its outstanding role as a competitive advantage. Every company would be well advised to take this into consideration for its own strategy.
- The hidden champions' competitive position has significantly improved in the parameters of the extended scope of performance. New competitive advantages have been created in advice and systems integration.
- These competitive advantages are difficult to copy and are very sustainable. They raise the entry barriers for competitors. The sustainability of the competitive advantages has increased rather than decreased as a result of these shifts and the massive wave of innovation. It is probably harder to encroach on the hidden champions' markets today than it was ten years ago.
- The hidden champions demonstrate their competitive superiority through numerous high-visibility projects throughout the world. Every company presented with such an opportunity should seize it and communicate the unique message externally and internally.
- Price is the most serious competitive disadvantage of the hidden champions. In principle, this is acceptable in view of their superiority on the performance side. However, the balance between value delivery and value extraction proves delicate.
- For this reason, even the hidden champions should consistently work on their costs and rationalize. Our impression is that the top companies

are very active and effective in this regard. The aim is not to make costs and prices a strategic competitive advantage, but to prevent a company from pricing itself out of the market.

- Many new markets are structured differently with regard to price segments versus the classic markets in highly developed industrial countries. In these cases, new ultra cheap strategies should seriously be taken into consideration. Such strategies involve a holistic approach, including leaner products and processes and the question of the most cost-effective manufacturing method and location.
- In spite of globalization, it probably remains an advantage to have strong competitors in regional proximity, because they fulfill a useful function as training partners for competitive fitness.
- Excessive competitive orientation is dangerous. The greatest attention should be paid to the customers and the competencies, not the competitors. A company wanting to reach the top must set its own standards and not imitate the standards of its competitors.

Competition is a permanent fight for survival. The hidden champions are exposed to the same dangers and fight with the same weapons as other companies. Their arsenal contains no secret weapons or miracle cures. However, they appear to comply with some common sense rules better than others. They supply their customers with superior product and service quality. In recent years they have established top positions in performance attributes such as advice and systems integration, which are increasingly important in the twenty-first century and are difficult to imitate. The customer is prepared to pay a reasonable premium for higher quality and performance. However, there are limits to the willingness to pay, so the costs must always be kept under control. The hidden champions' competitive superiority is not based on one pillar; instead, they do many things a little better. If a company adheres to these simple principles and implements them consistently, it need not fear the competition.

Notes

1 We use the median here to avoid outlier effects.
2 The statistical criteria for this estimate are: R Square = 0.175, t-statistic = 6.59, error probability less than 0.1%. The data for the markets Germany, Europe and world were pooled for the estimate. This is based on the hypothesis that the relation between the number of competitors and the market share of the market leader is the same

across markets. The elasticity estimated for the individual markets and the theoretical considerations support this hypothesis. The individual markets display the following elasticities: world market –0.30, European market –0.25, German market –0.32. The determination coefficient R Square was highest for the pooled estimate.

3 See Michael Porter, *Competitive Advantage: Creating and Sustaining Superior Performance*, New York: The Free Press 1985.

4 See Hermann Simon, Frank Bilstein, Frank Luby, *Manage for Profit, Not for Market Share: A Guide to Greater Profits in Highly Contested Markets*, Boston: Harvard Business School Press 2006.

5 See Michael Porter, *The Competitive Advantage of Nations*, London: Macmillan 1990.

6 See Michael Porter, *The Competitive Advantage of Nations*, London: Macmillan 1990.

7 See Kenichi Ohmae, *The Mind of the Strategist*, New York: McGraw Hill 1982.

8 For this and other principles of the management of strategic competitive advantages, see Hermann Simon, *Strategy for Competition*, New Delhi: Leads Press 2008.

9 See Theodore Levitt, *The Marketing Imagination*, New York: Free Press 1983.

10 See Michael Porter, *Competitive Advantage: Creating and Sustaining Superior Performance*, New York: The Free Press 1985.

11 See *VDI News*, March 30, 2007, p. 19.

12 The Aachen Institute of Technology (RWTH) is one of Germany's elite universities and is considered a globally leading research and education center for mechanical engineering.

13 *VDI News*, March 30, 2007, p. 19.

14 Exchange rate: $1 = 115 Yen.

15 Mahajan, Vijay and Kamini Banga, *The 86% Solution: How to Succeed in the Biggest Market Opportunity of the Twenty-first Century*, Philadelphia: Wharton School 2006.

16 See Michael Porter, *The Competitive Advantage of Nations*, London: Macmillan 1990.

17 This CEO told me that he strictly followed the hidden champion strategy outlined in the 1996 book.

18 See Hermann Simon, Frank Bilstein, Frank Luby, *Manage for Profit, Not for Market Share: A Guide to Greater Profits in Highly Contested Markets*, Boston: Harvard Business School Press 2006.

19 See Quek Swee Lip, *Business Warfare: Management for Market Conquest*, Lewes: Temple House Books 1995.

20 See Barrie G. James, *Business Wargames* , Turnbridge Wells: Kent 1984.

21 See Corstjens, Judith and Corstjens, Marcel, *Store Wars: The Battle for Mindspace and Shelfspace*, Chichester: Wiley 1999.

22 See Jay Conrad Levinson, *Guerilla Marketing*, New York: Houghton Mifflin 2007.

23 See Robert F. Lanzilotti, "Pricing Objectives in Large Corporations," *American Economic Review* 1958, p. 921–940.

24 See J. Scott Armstrong und Kesten C. Green, "Competitor-Oriented Objectives: The Myth of Market Share," *International Journal of Business*, 2007, p. 411–415.

25 See W. Chan Kim and Renée Mauborgne, *Blue Ocean Strategy: How to Create Uncontested Market Space and Make the Competition Irrelevant*, Boston: Harvard Business School Press 2005.

26 Hermut Kormann, *Long-Term Customer Relationships: Defying the Myth that Only Competition-Oriented Strategies Work*, Frankfurt: VDMA 2005.

27 Hans-Jürgen Warnecke, *Die fraktale Fabrik*, Heidelberg-New York: Springer 1992.

Chapter 8
Financing, Organization, and Business Environment

Financing and organization are pillars of corporate strategy. The business environment or context is another important factor of the emergence and the development of the hidden champions. In view of their fast growth, the demands on financing capacity are always high. How do the hidden champions deal with this situation? Do they view their financial capacities as a strength or a weakness in competition? Does financing put constraints on their expansion or is there enough leeway for the realization of the ambitious growth and market leadership goals? How will the role of different financing forms shift in the future? What do they think about going public? We will investigate these questions in the chapter on hand.

The typical hidden champion is a one-product, one-market company with limited organizational complexity. The functional organization is the most natural and frequent form. As we learned in the preceding chapters, numerous hidden champions have broadened their business. How do these companies react to the organizational complexity arising from soft diversification? When and how consistently do they decentralize? Which aspects determine divisionalization? We will see that there are no simple answers to these issues. Finally, we will look at how global, complex organizations with many business units are organized regarding processes. Organization includes the issue of vertical integration. What is the hidden champions' approach? How do they view outsourcing and strategic alliances? We observe a strong preference for solo attempts and do-it-yourself. The deep reserve in R&D is particularly evident. But this coin has two sides. Greater openness when entering new spheres of knowledge appears advisable and is increasingly practiced by some hidden champions.

H. Simon, *Hidden Champions of the Twenty-First Century*,
DOI 10.1007/978-0-387-98147-5_8, © Hermann Simon 2009

If we follow the recent discussion and literature, we could get the impression that industrial clusters are very important for the hidden champions. This impression cannot be confirmed. Our sampling revealed that only one in seven companies considers itself part of a cluster and only 50% of these companies recognize this as an advantage. Instead of typical industrial clusters, local concentrations of hidden champions not belonging to the same industry seem even more important stimulants for young entrepreneurs to set ambitious goals and to strive for international market leadership. It is remarkable that there are numerous locations with the accumulation of several hidden champions from different sectors.

Financing

Financing is often considered a serious constraint for midsize companies. The equity ratio of midsize companies in Germany is estimated to be between 8% and 18% and 16% and 33% in Austria.[1] Midsize companies in the U.K., the US, and Japan reach equity quotas of between 35% and 38%.[2] The average equity ratio of our hidden champions is even higher, namely 41.9%. More than one third of our market leaders (exactly 35.1%) have an equity ratio of 50% or more. Some go even further. Reinhard Zinkann, CEO of Miele, says, "We are completely financed with equity capital." O.C. Tanner, world leader in employee recognition programs from Salt Lake City, says, "We have no debt." Only every 16th company (exactly 6.3%) reports less than 20% equity financing.

In spite of the already high level of equity ratios and the enormous growth rates, equity ratios have continued to rise over the last ten years. Of the hidden champions, 57.9% have higher equity ratios than ten years ago. In view of a growth rate of 8.8% per year, which corresponds to an increase in revenues of 2.3 times over a decade, this is truly astonishing. Only 12.4% report that their equity ratio has dropped. For the remaining 29.7%, it stood unchanged.

First, the hidden champions' very solid financing affects capital costs. The new provisions of Basle II mean that this advantage is becoming more important, because the assessment of credit-worthiness will be more strongly reflected in interest rates than in the past. Hidden champions accordingly have a considerable advantage when it comes to capital costs. However, in view of the growth and the ambitious demands of globalization, this cost advantage may not be the most significant effect. The effects of financing on the strategic leeway of the hidden champions are more important. Do they feel restricted by financing constraints?

In periods of strong growth, financing can easily become a bottleneck. Many—in particular young—entrepreneurs view financing as the resource that limits growth. International expansion, the establishment of a world-wide sales network, research and development, as well as investments in manufacturing facilities, make high demands on the financing capacity. In such situations, financial strength can become a decisive factor of strategy implementation. This involves the question of whether and how market leadership can be established and defended—a key aspect for the hidden champions. The focus of interest in the long-term perspective is not the cost of financing, but rather the strategic leeway of a company. The answer to whether the hidden champions have little or large leeway in this respect is shown in Fig. 8.1.

Fig. 8.1: Financial leeway for strategic investments

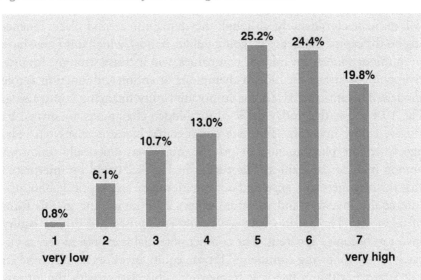

If we add the percentages to the right of the mean in Fig. 8.1 (higher than 4), we get 69.4%. This signifies that 70% of the hidden champions do not regard financing as a constraint on their strategies. The hidden champions clearly stand out positively in this respect when compared with normal companies and the picture of midsize enterprises regularly painted by the press.

Fig. 8.2 shows the answer to the question about the most important past and future financing sources.

Fig. 8.2: Past and future importance of financing sources

	Past	Future
Self-financing	78.6%	77.8%
Traditional bank loans	61.6%	44.0%
Private equity	15.3%	9.7%
Capital market	12.8%	29.6%

Self-financing is by far the most important source of financing and will remain so in the future. In view of the hidden champions' positive profit and cash flow situation and an overall return on capital employed of 13.6%, this is not surprising.[3] The importance of traditional bank loans will decrease considerably, although they remain in second place. Financing on the capital market (e.g., going public, bonds), which until now have been minor sources for midsize companies, will increase strongly. Innovative solutions attract the hidden champions' attention and function as role models. The anticipated decline in private equity financing is surprising. Fig. 10.1 shows that today 8.1% of the hidden champions are owned by private equity investors. This is a considerable increase versus ten years ago when the phenomenon of private equity was practically unknown among midsize companies. The results in Fig. 8.2 could be interpreted that the managers who answered our questionnaire are skeptical about private equity investors and therefore expect a future decline in this form of financing. The tension between family enterprises and private equity investors becomes apparent. The conflict potential is expressed very accurately in the following comment: "Private equity investors usually have an exit strategy within a five-year framework. This clashes with the longer-term horizon of family enterprises. The dynastic view in family enterprises is incompatible with the short-term profit expectations of private equity funds."[4]

Going public remains a controversial subject among the hidden champions, although the situation has changed considerably since the 1990s. Then, only 2.4% of the companies were listed on the stock exchange. Today, this figure stands at 9.5%, a strong increase (see Fig. 10.1). Hidden champions in new sectors such as solar energy have extremely high market capitalizations. The highest market capitalization of Solarworld reached $7.3 billion and that of Q-Cells $11 billion. These figures are a high multiple of the revenues, let alone the profits of these companies.[5] However, there are also numerous disappointments that led investors to back out. Grohe (sanitary fittings), Honsel (light metal processing), Rolf Benz (furniture), Hako (cleaning equipment), and Kiekert (automotive locking systems) are some examples. The ambiguous attitude of the hidden champions toward the stock market is evident from the number of abandoned IPO-plans in recent years.

My discussions have revealed that the hidden champions are mostly skeptical and reserved when it comes to going public. There are two particular reasons for this. First, the reporting and publicity obligations associated with the listing are dreaded. These requirements are diametrically opposed to the preference for discretion described in the first chapter. The following comment by the CEO of a listed hidden champion in the electronics sector expresses the views of many, "When I visit my large customers, our annual report is lying on the table. The first thing I am brought face to face with is our high profitability. This doesn't exactly make it easy to enforce adequate prices." But there are also voices to the contrary. In connection with the IPO of Krones, the world market leader in bottling systems, Hermann Kronseder reports that the IPO has strengthened the position in relation to his customers. Its healthy profitability signals that Krones is not desperate for every order. High profitability also provides future security for the customers.

Second, there are well-founded doubts that a typical hidden champion will achieve adequate market valuation. Most hidden champions do not operate in sectors that are in the spotlight of public's and investors' interest, such as the solar industry. In niche and special sectors, there are limited opportunities to register on analysts' radar screens, so the shares of the hidden champions often languish. In spite of this, we anticipate a higher proportion of hidden champions will go public in the future. The stock exchange will play a bigger role, particularly as an exit option for private equity investors who invest in hidden champions.

In summary, the hidden champions have very solid equity ratios that have even increased for most of them in the last ten years. This situation leads to excellent credit ratings and correspondingly low capital costs. In the process of growth and globalization, financing is not a serious constraint for the further development of the hidden champions. Almost 70% of them see their financial strength as a competitive advantage. Financing hardly limits their leeway for strategic investment. The attitude toward going public is mixed. Hidden champions in new sectors that attract public attention achieve high valuations and are favorites on the stock market. Companies in niche markets tend to achieve only modest market valuations and are hesitant to go public. Publicity requirements are also a deterrent for many hidden champions.

Organization

The right organization is without a doubt a strategic success factor. We have seen in the preceding chapters that the typical hidden champion focuses on one product and one market and is therefore a one-product, one-market company.[6] The hidden champions generate on average 80% of their revenues in their main market. Almost one third realize more than 90% and more than one quarter even earn 100% of their revenues from this main market alone. Examples of such hidden champions are Brasseler (dental drills), Doppelmayr (cable cars), Bruns-Pflanzen-Export (nursery plants), GfK (market research services), LEMO (film-welding equipment), Omicron (tunnel-grid microscopes for nanotechnology), SkySails (towing kite wind propulsion systems for ships), and many, many more. This focus has the great advantage of limiting organizational complexity. Nearly all one-product, one-market hidden champions have a classic functional organization, a form characterized by simplicity and clear allocation of responsibilities.

Several years ago, Hans Peter Stihl, then CEO of Stihl, the world market leader in chainsaws, asked me to investigate the organization of his company. The aim was the reorganization of future responsibilities within the executive board in view of the forthcoming generation handover. The assignment was not too difficult to carry out. After a series of interviews and some analysis, functional organization with five executive board members and the usual functions was recommended and implemented. At Stihl, a relatively large hidden champion with $2.9 billion in revenues and 9,700 employees, the functional division of labor was installed on the top management level. In smaller hidden champions, the division of functions is not always at the top management level, because the top team often consists of only one or two persons. Of the hidden champions, 21.2% have only one person at the C-level. In these companies, the division of labor only begins on the second management level. Clearly, functional organization is the more or less natural form for one-product, one-market companies. The structural simplicity reflects the lean processes, speed, and organizational capabilities of the hidden champions.

Divisional organization

In previous chapters, we have seen that an increasing number of hidden champions engages in soft diversification in adjoining markets. This development and the strong growth create more complex organizational challenges for the hidden champions. How do the hidden champions retain their traditional strengths, particularly their closeness to customers, in view of higher complexity? The answer is decentralization. The hidden champions' consistent and speedy reaction on the organizational level toward the extension of their businesses is truly impressive.

As noted in Chapter 3, the market definitions of the hidden champions are primarily oriented toward applications and target groups. When making the transition from functional to divisional organization, they follow these exact criteria (i.e., the new organizational units are directed primarily toward target groups or applications). Products or technologies play a minor role as organizational criteria. Of course, both aspects frequently come together as different target groups demand modified products. A convincing case of a target group-oriented organization is Westfalia Separator, world market leader in centrifugal and separation technology. Fig. 8.3 shows that Westfalia Separator has a specialized company for each target segment.

Fig. 8.3: Westfalia Separator—divisionalization oriented toward target groups

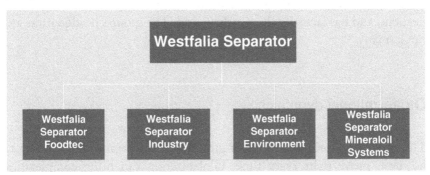

All four divisions of Westfalia are legally independent units with their own management. Organization consistently directed toward target groups can be a great strength. The fact that the divisions are legally independent companies is not only important considering formal responsibilities, but also changes the quality of customer interaction. Heads of divisions bear the official title of CEO of their company. This helps to position them as highly competent partners with decision-making powers in the eyes of their customers. The locations of the Westfalia companies are aligned with the target groups as well. Westfalia Separator Mineraloil Systems mainly deals with the oil and the shipping industry and operates from Hamburg, where the shipping and oil companies are concentrated. Many hidden champions, like Westfalia Separator, have introduced target group-oriented organizations during the past ten years. Examples are Plansee (high-performance materials), Hoerbiger (drive and compressor technology), IBG (welding technology), and many more. Kern-Liebers has also undergone consistent decentralization and is the dominant world market leader with its main product, springs for safety belts. However, Kern-Liebers also holds strong market positions with its other products: for example, printed circuit boards for knitting and hosiery machines with the world's largest product program, or for lancets for medical use. Kern-Liebers has a total of 48 subsidiaries organized in 15 competence centers. This is backed by revenues of "only" $658 million, an average of $44 million per competence center. This rigorous dencentralization signifies that closeness to customer and the integration of market and technology discussed in previous chapters are effectively guaranteed. A further case is the Heitkamp & Thumann Group. Consisting of 25 companies, it has 2,200 employees and reports revenues of $370 million for 2007, which corresponds roughly to the typical hidden champion. On average, every company of the group has revenues of $14 million and 90 employees. Heitkamp & Thumann is the world market leader for battery cans, end covers, and internal coatings. This business is run from Waterbury, Connecticut, and has factories all over the world. The group's headquarters are in Germany.

Organizational dynamics

The application-oriented or target group-oriented organization does not, however, prove right every time. Globalization can bring complexities that require new organizational solutions. Würth, world market leader in assembly products, started introducing target group-oriented divisionalization in the 1980s. In the large countries, separate divisions were established for handicraft businesses in the areas of wood, metal, construction, automotive, and for industrial customers. In doing so, Würth achieved better orientation in line with the customers' needs, a higher degree of competence in the various fields, more specific information materials such as catalogs or brochures, and numerous other advantages. Divisionalization brought Würth an enormous growth impetus and led to a much higher penetration in the individual segments.

However, increasing internationalization also intensified complexity. From the divisionalization point of view, it would have been consistent to leave the worldwide establishment of new business units to the respective divisions themselves. This would, however, have led to several locations or even companies in each country, work duplication and with that cost disadvantages. Würth sensibly founded country companies, having subsidiaries in 86 different countries around the world today. Their CEOs were not only the formal heads but actually coordinated business activities in their respective countries. This gave rise to a matrix organization and the associated, well-known disadvantages such as double reporting, time-consuming consultation processes, and so on. An organizational review that Würth asked us to conduct at the end of the 1990s led to the surprising result that the target groups of craftsmen within one country are traditionally relatively similar but very different across countries. A Spanish carpenter has more in common with a Spanish locksmith than with a German carpenter. It is also difficult for a divisional CEO at the head office to make a sound judgment about problems arising in a faraway country and to find solutions for them. The Würth country head is far closer to these problems, has a better understanding of employees and customers, and can therefore react more effectively at the local level.

These insights drove Würth to change its organization from a divisional to a regional organization in the year 2000. In this system, the divisions primarily have coordinating functions but no direct authorization. Würth's great strength is personal selling, which, by definition, takes place locally. It became clear that, in this case, a regional organization was the better solution. The organizational structure is only a part of the overall organizational reality of a company comprising many business units. At Würth, consultation processes, management meetings, and inter-divisional activities are very important. Top management devotes a lot of time and energy to these processes, which are an integral part of the Würth culture and, in turn, form it. Alongside their responsibility for lines, managers also assume cross-divisional tasks and, in doing so, hold everything together.

However, a reverse transformation can also take place, as the following case shows. ERA, a company that produces small transformers and is today a subsidiary of the US firm Technitrol, supplied customers in the automotive, heating, air conditioning, and appliances sector, and it historically organized its sales force regionally. In other words, one representative visited all the customers in his area, regardless of the sector. The CEO at the time, Erich Aichele, had the feeling that the customers' demands had become more differentiated and demanding, and asked us to review the organization.[7] This led to restructuring the sales force according to sectors, resulting in sales representatives being able to offer a higher level of expertise and competence to their customers. This organizational structure also has its disadvantages, as the distances between customers become greater and traveling times are longer. The representatives' net selling time is reduced. However, we could substantiate that the improved performance more than compensated for the spatial disadvantage.

Early decentralization

Hidden champions implement decentralized, customer-oriented organization forms of a new business or target group at an early stage of development. The following example is representative of many similar cases: Herrenknecht is the world market leader in tunnel-drilling technology. Tunneling usually involves horizontal drilling or if neccessary drilling at slight gradients. Herrenknecht saw an opportunity to transfer its competencies from horizontal to vertical drilling. The largest vertical drilling market is in the oil industry, but strong competitors were already established in this field. A new area is deep drilling for geothermal purposes (i.e., drilling to obtain heat from the earth's depths). These holes are up to 6,000 meters (4 miles) deep, a major technical challenge. This new source of energy appears to have a great future, because—compared with wind and solar energy—it can produce a base-loadable supply. To develop this new business, Herrenknecht founded the company Herrenknecht Vertical in 2005. This new company can concentrate fully on the new business, addressing a different target group and comprising new technological challenges. It is not only a department in the much larger Herrenknecht company, it is its own company. Doppelmayr, world market leader in cable cars, took a similar approach. As reported in Chapter 3, the subsidiaries Doppelmayr Cable Cars and Doppelmayr Transport Technology were founded for the new businesses of inner city transport and company internal transport before realizing its first projects. However, Doppelmayr uses its worldwide sales organization for all three businesses. This is another exemplar of early proactive decentralization.

Hidden champion CEOs often emphasize that new businesses remain orphaned if they are established within the existing larger organization. A new business unit is by definition small at the outset and in a weaker position than the far larger main business unless it is separated from the organization. Closeness to customer is also of central importance in this context. In previous chapters we have seen that the high degree of closeness to customer is one of the great strengths and competitive advantages of the hidden champions. Closeness to customer is generally seen as an aspect closely associated with employees' attitudes. I believe this is a mistake. Closeness to customer is at least just as much—if not more so—a question of organization as it is of behavior. Only small units guarantee optimal closeness to customer and therefore become the foundation of the successful implementation of the hidden champions' strategy. This is why the formation of an independent company is often the first and most important step towards future market leadership, because this new unit can then consistently implement all facets of the hidden champions' strategy outlined in this book.

Hidden champion groups

Numerous midsize hidden champion groups have formed in the course of soft diversification. Examples are the Friedhelm Loh Group, Heraeus, Voith, Schäfer-Werke, Plansee or Körber. The steady expansion of the hidden champions' concept into the organization and strategy of an entire group that retains the typical characteristics of midsize companies is demonstrated in an exemplary way by the Körber Group. Fig. 8.4 shows the (almost) complete organization chart.

Körber has a hidden champion organization on two levels. The divisions Hauni, Körber Paperlink, Körber Schleifring, and Körber Medipak are each directed toward specific markets. The individual companies are on the second level: they either contribute to Körber's value chain or again focus on a submarket. Many of these companies are world market leaders in

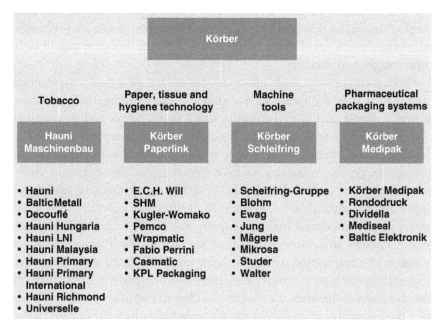

their own right. The decentralized organization and management are pre-conditions for the Körber companies to orientate themselves fully towards their markets in hidden champion fashion and to establish superior market positions there. It is important to note that behind this very decentralized and complex structure, there is only a midsize group with revenues of $2.2 billion and 9,100 employees, not a $10 billion company. On average, the 30 companies listed achieve revenues of $73 million each and are therefore predominantly small companies. Only a few companies follow the hidden champions' strategy of decentralization with the same determination and consistency as the Körber Group. If the markets can be segmented, this is a very effective way of retaining the culture and the strengths of a hidden champion in spite of the overall increasing size. Heraeus was presumably a pioneer in this area. As early as 1985, he founded a strategic management holding company with six very independent subsidiaries: Heraeus Holding. "We were the first family enterprise to take this step," says Chairman Jürgen Heraeus.

Process organization

Until now, we have mainly looked at the organizational structures. But how do the hidden champions function with regard to process organization? How are such midsize and nevertheless complex organizations managed? Generally, we observe a heterogeneous picture in the formalization of processes. Few respondents chose the extremes 1 (very little formalization) or 7 (very high formalization). Two thirds of the answers were in the middle, meaning an average of 3.76 on the 7-point scale. The slight deviation from 4 (the mean) could be interpreted as a tendency toward less formalized procedures. Process organization is of high interest because there is generally a very lean top management level. More than one fifth (exactly 21.2%) of the hidden champions have only one manager on the first level. The lean management concept need not have been newly invented, but could have been copied from the hidden champions. This is illustrated by several examples.

- A consumer goods company has 25 foreign subsidiaries, all of which are supervised by one executive who also performs numerous other tasks.
- The advertising division of a hidden champion with a budget of about $100 million consists of two managers and a few assistants. An advertising agency is considered unnecessary.
- I have visited numerous innovative hidden champions. Sometimes, the R&D department consists of only one person. As shown in Chapter 6, the R&D budgets and the headcount within these departments are extremely small relative to their output in patents and innovations.

The small number of employees means a heavy workload, but it considerably reduces the need for and the complexity of communication. This is easy to understand because the number of bilateral relationships increases with the square of the number of participants.[8] For 4 participants, we get 6 possible communication relationships, for 10 participants the number is 45, and 20 create 190 bilateral relationships. The lean occupancy within the hidden champions simplifies communication significantly.

Nevertheless, divisionalization and internationalization induce sufficient complexity that must dealt with. The following two case studies show how hidden champions employ very modern solutions and new communication technologies. The IBG Group, a world market leader in welding technology,[9] has three divisions: welding technology, components, and chemicals. IBG's revenue increased to $254 million in 2007 from

$88 million in 1995. In the same period, the number of employees rose by 1,000 to 2,200. Today, 70 companies are located in more than 40 countries under the IBG umbrella (eight in China). Acting as an operative management holding, IBG is extremely lean with only 12 employees.

Richard Sattler, the long-standing CEO of IBG, has introduced a network organization that is designed to help manage this global enterprise. The following is a brief description of IBG's network organization:

- The 500 most important employees (roughly a quarter of all employees) are listed in a data bank along with their skills.
- All important decisions are made according to a so-called Generic Decision Process (GDP), which is governed by simple rules.
- The initiator of a decision enters key words, and the software system, with the aid of the skills data bank, recommends the team for the GDP.
- This team must reach a decision by a set deadline.
- A neutral arbitrator supervises the procedure, which is also carefully documented.

To ensure the functionality of this network organization, information technology is crucial. IBG has established advanced video conference studios at 25 locations. Nine of these can be interconnected simultaneously. This allows the decision-making teams to be put together and be able to cooperate efficiently irrespective of location and division. In addition to the worldwide linking of the most competent decision-makers for the respective problem, Richard Sattler considers the objectivity of the GDP-process the greatest advantage. "Decision-making is largely free of politics," he says. For this to work properly, all employees must strongly identify with the company's culture and the strategy. That is why a long preparation period is required to introduce a system as such along with the IT infrastructure. According to Sattler it is sometimes necessary to part with employees that do not cooperate constructively within this kind of a network organization.

DMT Technology, one of the world's leading providers of bi-axial film stretching systems, has a similar modern organization. CEO Wolfgang Pinegger explains, "We call our new project Tower, we manage the company like an airport is controlled from its tower. Put simply, all of our customers are given access to a video system to which all of our subsidiaries are connected. All managers have worldwide access to this tower via Internet with especially equipped PCs. We handle our orders and the entire management of the company through this tower. Once an order has been defined, the individual steps and tasks in the work process are assigned to employees within the company. Any consequential change or innovation is exclusively controlled through the tower and leads to a new definition of tasks. This is how we protect our company from potential negative effects of today's very fast communication technologies. The speed and openness of communication, particularly through e-mails, means that every customer employee can constantly communicate with our employees, and all our employees can continuously correspond among themselves, meaning that it would be easy to lose control of this communication. For this reason, we centralize the entire process in the tower. The general manager of a project has full control and directs all the information and assignments."

Identifying with the company and its goals is crucial for the efficiency of decentralized organizations. The strong employee identification is one of the hidden champions' strengths. We will look into this more deeply in the next two chapters. If people share common values and goals, and thereby function as a team, less organization is required than when values and goals differ. Most hidden champions flourish with very little "organization."

In summary, typical hidden champions are one-product, one-market companies for which an efficient organization is virtually the natural form. More complex hidden champions consistently decentralize at a very early stage. That way, even larger, softly diversified companies manage to retain the strengths of focus, closeness to customer, and entrepreneurship. Some hidden champions practice innovative network organization and employ modern information technology to control their global organizations with very limited resources. Deep employee identification with the company means that hidden champions require comparatively little organization.

Organization of the Value Chain

How do the hidden champions organize their value chain? How strongly are they vertically integrated and what are their preferences for in-house solutions and outsourcing? They do not follow modern management fashions for these issues, but prove to be deeply conservative. However, there have been some shifts when compared to the situation ten years ago.

Fig. 8.5 shows selected key figures on the organization of the value chain.

	Ten years ago	Today
Value added in % of revenues	48%	42%
Vertical integration*	57%	50%
Vertical integration >70%	25%	24%
Vertical integration 40–70%	50%	44%
Vertical integration <40%	25%	32%

*vertical integration = percent of total manufacturing done in-house

The value added measures what a company adds to the value of the materials and services purchased. It thus corresponds to the sum of wages, tax, interest and profit. This key figure is often expressed as a percentage of the revenues. Today, the added value of the hidden champions is 42%, a high figure for modern industrial companies. The average for the German industry is 29.8%.[10] The hidden champions have a far deeper value chain than an average company. This is due to the fact that they outsource less and that their employees are creating high value (i.e., they are extremely productive), not necessarily in terms of sheer volume, but in terms of unique, high-value products as reflected in the competitive advantages (see Chapter 7). The changes over the last ten years are very interesting. The value added has decreased to 42% from 48% in revenues. This decrease is above all attributable to a slight increase in outsourcing. Let's have a closer look at this issue.

Vertical integration and outsourcing

Vertical integration here expresses the share of manufacturing done within the company. Today, the average vertical integration of the hidden champions is positioned at 50%. While this figure is 7 percentage points lower than ten years ago, it nevertheless remains high for modern manufacturing companies. Almost a quarter have a vertical integration of over 70%, which could loosely be described as "they make everything themselves." The proportion of hidden champions with vertical integration of at least 40% has only decreased slightly to 68% from 75%. This decrease is much smaller than I had expected. Resistance to or dislike for outsourcing are confirmed by the answers to the question of whether vertical integration is lower than the competitors'. More than half (exactly 51.6%) vigorously denied this, only 13.4% answered with yes. In addition, 42.4% are decidedly against heavy outsourcing, while only 12.1% strongly favor it. The hidden champions display a distinct preference to do things themselves and are against outsourcing. This is very different from large corporations, where I frequently hear "we outsource as much as possible."

In modern management theory and literature, outsourcing is often praised as the cure for everything. Many companies boast that they hardly produce anything themselves any longer, and have thus largely freed themselves from the shackles of wage costs and union demands on the one hand and fixed costs on the other. Decisions to outsource are usually dominated by cost aspects. The cheapest supplier gets the order. The hidden champions feel very differently about these issues. In Chapter 7, we saw that the product quality is the outstanding competitive advantage of the hidden champions. They are convinced that their elevated standard of quality prohibits the outsourcing of core components. It is almost certain that their uniqueness would be endangered in the process. A further outsourcing risk is the potential loss of expertise. This applies to manufacturing, but even more strongly to R&D. The hidden champions are extremely reserved when it comes to R&D and averse to cooperation and outsourcing. For all of these reasons, the hidden champions very much prefer keeping core activities inhouse, even if this involves certain cost disadvantages. Although these attitudes are a little less extreme than they were ten years ago, the fundamental approach has hardly changed. The relatively small reduction in the percentages of the value added and vertical integration are probably more attributable to the increased outsourcing of noncore competencies. Hidden champions have always been great outsourcers when it comes to noncore competencies. Many of them, for example, don't have a legal or tax department of their own but instead commission outside specialists with these and other noncore tasks.

Several case studies are illustrative of the anti-outsourcing attitudes. The following comment by Wanzl, world market leader in shopping and baggage carts, reflects the typical attitude, "We have a very high vertical integration, we manufacture nearly all parts and components ourselves according to self-defined quality standards. Our products get their unbeatable surface refinement from our own galvanization facilities." Hasenkamp, one of the world market leaders in the shipment of objects of art, does everything on its own. "We don't outsource anything and accept full responsibility. This is the root of our qualitative superiority compared to other shipping companies that transport artwork as a sideline and do a lot of outsourcing," says Hasenkamp CEO Hans Ewald Schneider. We observe a similarly pronounced do-it-yourself philosophy in leading luxury goods companies. In the Richemont Group all core products stem from its own manufacturing, including famous labels such as Cartier, Montblanc and many top watch brands such as Piaget, IWC, Jaeger-Le Coultre, Lange & Söhne, and so forth. When Montblanc, traditionally a manufacturer of pens, entered the watch business, it immediately acquired its own watch making factory.

Kaldewei is the European market leader in steel bathtubs. Kaldewei manufactures its bathtubs using 3.5 mm thick steel sheet instead of the 1.5 mm sheet commonly used by the industry. Every manufacturer that worked with 1.5 mm has meanwhile abandoned the market. The statement "Kaldewei does everything itself" is close enough to the truth, as the company even makes the forms to press the bathtubs as well as the enamel compounds for the coatings. These enamel mixes define the surface and with it the customer's quality perception. Kaldewei's secret lies in its own formulas. It is the only bathtub manufacturer that offers "pearl enamel," a surface to which practically no dirt adheres. When I visited the factory, Franz Kaldewei, owner-CEO, told me, "Of course we could buy the enamel mix for less somewhere else. However, our competitive uniqueness and superiority come from doing these things ourselves. None of our competitors can claim the same." There is no more accurate description for the importance of this insistence on do-it-yourself for competitive uniqueness. Of course, even a market leader like Kaldewei cannot afford to ignore the costs, despite these special features. Higher efficiency and productivity are therefore a second root of the success of this hidden champion.

Enercon, the technology leader among wind turbine manufacturers, has a vertical integration exceeding 75%. Whereas competitors purchase most components and assemble the parts, Enercon does virtually everything itself: towers, rotorblades, even the transportation with its own ships. Enercon's superior quality is essentially attributable to its comprehensive control of all manufacturing steps.

The same applies to the casting house of world market leader Heidelberg Printing Presses. Many experts believe that Heidelberg would do better reducing its vertical integration by outsourcing this part of its value chain. However, despite a serious crisis at the beginning of the century, the company remained faithful to its foundry activities. CEO Bernhard Schreier tells us why. "We are more able to meet the very high customer demands regarding quality and precision in-house. We cannot purchase critical parts for any less from outside suppliers. An important reason being our unique machines."[11] Hans-Joachim Boekstegers, CEO of Multivac, world leader in vacuum packaging systems, joins in, "We manufacture our own machines in large numbers. Therefore it is economical for us to produce most components inhouse instead of purchasing them."[12] Miele, the world's leading producer of premium washing machines and dishwashers, feels very much the same. "We produce as many parts as possible ourselves, preferably within a small region with down-to-earth people." This attitude expressly relates to core competencies. On the other hand, Miele practices intensive outsourcing for noncore activities. Even in the twenty-first century, 95% of the Miele appliances are manufactured in factories that can be reached within a 45-minute drive from the company's headquarters. How can a company like O.C. Tanner, world leader in employee recognition programs, afford to keep a manufacturing base—which in some cases includes batch runs as small as one unit—within the US instead of moving it offshore? The answer lies in its successful control and management of the manufacturing process, including intensive lean management practices and the production of its own tools. Superior flexibility, quality, and speed of delivery are the results of keeping manufacturing inhouse at O.C. Tanner. Braun, world market leader in several areas of small electrical appliances, says, "Braun manufactures almost everything itself, including the special production machines and all the key parts in its shavers. These high-quality standards cannot be fulfilled at any better conditions on the market." Braun, a subsidiary of Gillette and therefore indirectly of Procter & Gamble, is world market leader in three product groups (laminated razors, depilatory equipment, hand mixers). A manager of Bobcat, the American world market leader for so-called skid steer loaders, told me, "Whenever possible, we keep the work inside the company. I find out how much a part costs on the market, I then call on my people to build it for the same cost or cheaper. Usually they succeed. And I know what quality I get in-house. Wherever possible, we avoid outsourcing." Presumably Bobcat's location in Gwinner, North Dakota, has a strong impact on this attitude. The aim is to avoid employee redundancies in a rural environment. Increased outsourcing could result in increased employee dismissals. The attitudes of these hidden champions run contrary to current trends and are thought-provoking.

Internal mechanical engineering and machine building

The hidden champions' preference for doing things themselves often goes further and includes earlier steps in the value chain. As mentioned in Braun's quote, many of these companies have their own mechanical engineering departments. At Hoppe, one of the market leaders for door and window fittings, I was told, "Around 10% of our workforce build our own machinery which we keep very secret. We develop and produce our own machines and we don't sell them to others. These machines encompass our core competencies." O.C. Tanner in Salt Lake City, the world's largest company for employee recognition, produces all awards and emblems on self-designed and self-built machines. "We couldn't find some of the equipment we needed on the open market, so we decided to build and maintain it ourselves," says Mike Collins, the company's vice president for lean enterprise development. At Brita, world market leader for so-called point-of-use water filters, I also found a machinery department, and the CEO commented, "Why should anyone else be better at producing these machines? Brita is world market leader because it has a unique product and this product is manufactured on unique machines." The situation is similar at Gardena, European market leader for gardening equipment. The machinery is built simultaneously while products are being developed, resulting in the side-effect of saved time. Weidmüller, one of the market leaders in electronic interface technology, builds its own tools. CEO Ralf Hoppe says, "We make our own tools. We can only deliver top quality if zero tolerance begins with these tools."[13] Of Weidmüller's 3,000 employees, 200 are engaged in tool construction.

These approaches are common among hidden champions all around the world. Seiichi Hirata, CEO of Brother Industries from Japan, explains the reasons for Brother's success, "In our machine tool department, we build our own tools for our products. This in particular pays off for high-tech equipment, such as our knitting machines. They contain far more technology than a printer. In the future, mechatronics will be the technology behind our machines. We're very strong in mechatronics." The Spanish hidden champion Chupa Chups, world market leader for lollipops, makes a similar statement, "More than 80% of the machinery used by Chupa Chups has been developed internally and is protectively guarded from the competition." Lorenz Bahlsen Snack-World buys its machines from the salty snacks manufacturer, but its own technicians modify these machines and the associated processes and thereby achieve significant improvements. CEO Lorenz Bahlsen considers this a critical driver of their competitive superiority. "This is how we win a temporary margin over the competition and use it to strengthen our brand. Our own development and improvement of the machines create a technological advantage that we transform into a market advantage. The technological advantage will only be temporary; the market advantage arising from it is more permanent."

Leading cookie manufacturer Griesson-de Beukelaer proceeds likewise. According to CEO Andreas Land, the machinery and facilities Griesson buys are the basis for the company's internal further development. The gummi bear world market leader Haribo, the highly innovative confectioner Ferrero from Italy, and many other consumer goods companies that apparently make simple products showed similar attitudes, although we could presume that all of these products could be manufactured on pre-fabricated universal machines. In some cases, new companies or even hidden champions emerge from a company's own mechanical engineering. Boy, one of the market leaders in small injection molding machines, emerged from the mechanical engineering of toothbrush manufacturer M+C Schiffer.

The high degree of vertical integration almost automatically means preventing imitation by competitors. Jürgen Nussbaum, member of the executive board of Sachtler, the world market leader for professional camera tripods, said, "In some countries, competitors try to imitate our products. But they fail because they don't have the same tools. We make our own tools that cannot be purchased on the market. This is our best protection against pirates." In an age where many companies complain about imitators, vertical integration of this kind becomes increasingly important as protection against copycatting. We should think more carefully about hasty outsourcing or terminating a company's own mechanical engineering activities.

One variant of high vertical integration can be found at Lorenz Bahlsen Snack-World. With the Lorenz brand and a prominent premium price position, the company is one of the leading European companies for salty snacks.[14] One explanation for this market success is the excellent quality, which in turn is based on Bahlsen's control of the entire value chain right down to the raw materials. Owner Lorenz Bahlsen explains, "One of our secrets is that we monitor the cultivation, selection of type, seeds and fertilization of the potatoes we use for our chips very closely. We do the same with other raw materials, like peanuts, even on an international scale. The unique quality of our products begins with the unique quality of our raw materials." Everyone who compares Lorenz' products with those of its competitors understands what he is talking about.

Internal research and development

Hidden champions show the strongest desire for self-reliance in research and development. More than four fifths of our respondents said that they aim for a high or very high vertical integration in the R&D sector. Two important reasons for this are specialization and know-how protection. The often extreme specialization and focus mean that simply no one sufficiently specialized can be found who is able to contribute anything of value. It is probably difficult for third parties to be better than Hauni in tobacco processing or Baader in fish processing. With world market shares of 80% and more, these hidden champions have the world's most competent experts in their R&D teams and often have more specialist know-how than all of their competitors put together. In Japan, we also observe a strong preference for solitary R&D. Seiichi Hirata, CEO of Brother Industries, states very clearly, "We develop everything ourselves."

Hidden champions are extremely reserved about R&D cooperation. The CEO of a market leader in the automotive supply industry shared his experiences with me, "We once got involved in R&D cooperation with another company. We hardly learned anything ourselves. However, the others adopted a lot of our expertise. Since then, we have been very reserved about R&D. We consider this the only secure way to protect our superior knowledge." Although this reserve continues to dominate, we see an increasing openness when companies penetrate new fields of knowledge in which their own competencies are insufficient. Otto Bock, whose classic orthopedic products are based on mechanics and electronics, researches new areas along with partners that have their own specific competencies in this field. In the section on strategic alliances, we investigate this kind of cooperation in more detail.

Strategic assessment

A comprehensive assessment of the optimal degree of vertical integration is difficult. Behind the hidden champions' preference for doing things themselves, there is a deeper general truth: Competitive uniqueness and superiority can only be created internally. Everything bought on the open market is also available to others and therefore does not create a unique position. This fact is the explanation why many hidden champions do not confine themselves to the end product stage of the value chain, but go one or even more stages deeper. This is where they create the unique processes, machinery, tools or components that ultimately result in the superiority of the end product. Many CEOs told me that they could never achieve this superiority if they were to confine their activities to producing only the end product. This is the deeper truth hidden within our observations on vertical integration. It seems to run contrary to prevailing modern management thinking.

However, there is a reverse side to this truth that is relevant both to manufacturing and to R&D. In manufacturing, a philosophy of excessive self-reliance can give rise to grave cost disadvantages. This is an argument in favor of objectively investigating the issue of outsourcing, at least where noncore components are concerned. Many hidden champions actually outsource numerous activities that are not part of their core competencies. But the aspect of uniqueness should remain paramount in core competencies. The deciding factor should be qualitative superiority and not only cost advantages.

Research and development form the most important source of a company's uniqueness. Our findings on innovation discussed in Chapter 6 have shown that many hidden champions are highly efficient in R&D and master the corresponding challenges well. As a rule, these skills, coupled with a high degree of specialization and the desired know-how protection, favor going it alone. However, we should also strive for judgment free of ideology. If a company launches into a new sphere and reaches the boundaries of its own competencies, the risk that opportunities may be missed increases strongly. Conversely, if new technologies that a company does not master threaten the existing core business, this further warning signal must be heeded. It is difficult to say whether solitary self-reliance is better than cooperation in situations like these, but they must be dealt with openly when they arise. Ideology and prejudice are out of place here.

We can summarize these considerations as follows: Hidden champions generally display a clear preference for doing things themselves in manufacturing and R&D. They avoid outsourcing core competencies, whereas outsourcing noncore activities is widespread. Reservation is generally very pronounced in the R&D sector. Although these fundamental attitudes have shifted somewhat over the last ten years, there has been no significant change. These principles of the hidden champions are an important foundation of their uniqueness and superiority. The awareness that disadvantages may arise from excessive application of these principles is stronger today than previously. As a result, we observe somewhat more openness toward outsourcing and strategic alliances. However, the hidden champions' positions in this regard remain far from what is propagated in literature and practiced in many large corporations.

Strategic alliances

Siemens has formed strategic alliances with Nokia for telecommunications equipment, with Bosch for household appliances, with the French world market leader Areva for nuclear technology, with Voith for water turbines, and with partners around the world for many other areas.[15] A constellation like this would be hard to imagine for a typical hidden champion, as it prefers to remain solitary and in charge. We have observed this in previous chapters with numerous case studies. For example, 77.1% of hidden champions go it alone when entering foreign markets and only 16.8% commit to alliances for this purpose. These alliances are mostly considered a temporary means of entry. Overall, strategic alliances are rare among the hidden champions, they prefer the motto of the Swiss national hero Wilhelm Tell, "The strong one is most powerful alone."

In spite of this, the significance and frequency of strategic alliances have increased in the last ten years. There are two particular reasons for this development: the new configuration of the supply chain towards hierarchical supply systems and the extension of business activities. The strongest effects of the reconfiguration of the supply chain can be found in the automotive sector. Entire modules or subsystems often exceed the competencies of one single supplier, who is then forced to cooperate with others to remain a first-tier supplier. In Chapter 6 we discussed several strategic alliances by Behr that are based on such motives. HBPO, the international strategic alliance between Hella, Behr, and Plastic Omnium, offers a complete front-end module integrating lighting, cooling, aerodynamics, pedestrian protection, and crash management. None of the three enterprises would have been able to develop such a comprehensive solution alone. A second strategic alliance is Behr-Hella Thermocontrol (BHTC), which now has a leading position in air conditioning.

Plansee, the Austrian world market leader in powder metallurgic high-performance materials, operates two of its three divisions in the form of strategic alliances in which Plansee Holding owns a 50% share respectively. The Ceratizit division was created in 2002 through a merger with the Luxembourg company Cerametal and has a leading market position in hard metals and tools. The PMG division, focusing on the automotive industry, sells sintered moldings and is operated along with Mitsubishi from Japan. These strategic alliances have strengthened Plansee's position as a supplier to automotive and mechanical engineering companies and have provided a strong growth impetus. The group's overall revenues doubled to well over $2 billion in 2007 from $1 billion in 1995. According to Plansee's CEO Michael Schwarzkopf, cooperation with the joint-venture partners is smooth. The focus on powder metallurgy is not threatened, and the business units are consistently directed towards their target sectors.

I consider this important: If strategic alliances retain or—even better—strengthen the strategic principles of the hidden champions, such as focus, high innovation, and globalization, as is definitely the case with Plansee, they can be very useful. However, sharing power is not easy for many hidden champions' CEOs.

In sales we also observe an increase in strategic alliances, mainly in the form of cooperations, and less frequently as joint ventures. The driving force here is soft diversification, addressing new target groups or sales channels. Gelita, world market leader in gelatines, has traditionally been an industrial supplier and consequently has no sales capacity for consumer or pharmaceutical markets. It is therefore logical to sell the new joint protection product "ch-Alpha" in cooperation with an established pharmaceutical sales organization. Otto Bock historically had no access to doctors that treat stroke patients. Therefore, it began a cooperation for a new product for stroke patients with Krauth & Timmermann, a company that specializes in electrical stimulation and that has access to the relevant group of doctors.

When it comes to selling in foreign markets, smaller hidden champions are willing to cooperate with established companies that have the same target group. Brainlab, world market leader for medical positioning software, took this approach. In countries where the company does not have its own subsidiaries, Brainlab cooperates with medical equipment vendors who approach surgeons and whose competencies are similar to Brainlab's own. Brainlab has a considerable number of R&D and marketing partners. Many of them are hidden champions themselves, such as the American companies Biomet, DePuy, and Zimmer in orthopedic implants; Aesculap, world market leader in surgical instruments; Gyrus in invasive technology; and Varian, the world's leading manufacturer of integrated cancer therapy systems. Stefan Vilsmeier, CEO of Brainlab, nevertheless emphasizes that such alliances need constant attention, "as in a marriage."

A major innovative thrust is the integration of different fields of knowledge such as mechanics and electronics (mechatronics), chemistry/physics and nanotechnology or medical technology, pharmacy, and biology/biotechnology. Such networks are a source of opportunities and of risks at the same time. Anyone succeeding in linking previously unconnected areas opens up new markets with great opportunities. Companies that remain confined to their technical competencies can end up on the sidelines. In any case, there are often wide-ranging demands on R&D competencies that a hidden champion cannot always master alone. Therefore, strategic R&D alliances have become more important in recent years and will be even more so in the future. The case of Otto Bock, world market leader in prostheses, is an exemplary example of this development. Other than with classic prostheses, Otto Bock goes "under the skin" with its most recent innovations. This touches upon new areas such as osseointegration and neurostimulation. Hence Otto Bock acquires companies with equivalent competencies (e.g., the Danish company Neurosan), and additionally enters into R&D alliances, such as with Med-El, a firm specializing in the processing of nerve signals. Such cooperations will intensify in the future. One of the core problems is the question of who owns the R&D results or how these results are shared. The simplest solution is a permanent joint enterprise that uses the results itself. Then again, this means that sole control is permanently lost and the fruits gained must be shared with others, which is not to many hidden champions' liking. A second alternative is the use of the R&D results by both partners. This implies that from the outset a competitor with a similar technical starting base emerges. This solution is also not favored by a typical hidden champion striving for market leadership. Complete takeover is often the preferred alternative, but this can be expensive in case of highly valuable research successes. If none of these alternatives proves feasible, a different agreement must be reached.

Difficulties in operating a profitable business alone is one motive frequently underlying strategic alliances of large corporations but is rare among hidden champions. Some of the Siemens examples above fall into this category (e.g., the telecommunications enterprise with Nokia). Our impression is that hidden champions prefer to completely abandon a business they cannot get under control rather than to bring it into a strategic alliance. The reason may be the conscious avoidance of distraction so that their full concentration is on the core business.

In summary, strategic alliances of hidden champions still remain the exception, but are increasing in importance. Integrating systems and crossing the traditional competence boundaries in R&D force these hidden champions to cooperate with other companies. Although strategic alliances harbor conflict potential with the traditional hidden champion strategies, they should be considered more openly. However, for a substantial number of hidden champions such alliances are still not an option for the future due to the personality profiles of the individuals involved.

Business Environment

Entrepreneurs and companies emerge and operate in specific environments that are the result of social value systems, local resources, networks, educational institutions, and various other factors. The environment can encourage or deter the development of a hidden champion. I do not aim at delivering a comprehensive economic or sociological explanation for the regional prevalence of hidden champions. I look at the hidden champions from a business perspective and inquire about the strategic consequences of certain environmental factors. In some cases the answers remain unclear (e.g., we definitely cannot answer the question whether it is better for a hidden champion to be part of an industrial cluster or not). Another observation is that a surprisingly high number of hidden champions are based in rural locations. Does this imply that a rural location is better than an urban one for this type of company? Naturally, this conclusion cannot be drawn from our empirical observations.

Industrial clusters

In recent years, the so-called industrial cluster concept has become fashionable. This wave was triggered by the publication of Michael Porter's book *The Competitive Advantage of Nations*[16] in 1990. Some authors speak of a "new paradigm of business policy."[17] Politicians gladly use the paradigm as a justification to interfere with the economy. Industrial clusters look very modern, but in fact the cluster idea is ancient. Historically, however, clusters were referred to as agglomerations, and economists talked about so-called agglomeration advantages (also agglomeration disadvantages). Agglomeration is described as "geographic concentrations of companies that are either linked vertically along the value chain or belong to the same industry. These location-related groups comprise legally and economically independent companies. Special location factors are usually decisive for the development of such clusters."[18] It should be added that a cluster typically includes schools, research institutes, and specialized service providers. It is obvious and well known that national economies and sectors typically have regional concentration cores. Such phenomena deserve our attention. Regional concentrations are evident in virtually all economic indicators.

What role do industrial clusters play for the hidden champions? Fig. 7.11 showed a selection of hidden champions that are direct competitors located in regional proximity to one another and who supposedly drive each other on. However, direct horizontal competition is only one aspect of the cluster concept. Clusters are much broader. The wave of press coverage of industrial clusters could lead us to believe that most hidden champions are part of them, and that belonging to a cluster is a very important root of their success. In order to verify this presumption, we asked several questions related to the cluster idea. Only one in seven hidden champions, exactly 14.3%, considers itself part of an industrial cluster. The following percentages were obtained regarding the concentration phenomena that determine the respective cluster:

- Competitors   64.7%
- Suppliers   55.6%
- Customers   35.3%
- Research/educational institutions   35.3%

The hidden champions predominantly define industrial clusters by the regional concentration of competitors and suppliers. It cannot be expected that customers of globally active companies such as the hidden champions are concentrated in one region. Research and educational institutions also play a specific role for the definition of clusters. Is belonging to an industrial cluster believed to be a strength or a problem? Only half of the hidden champions that are part of a cluster considered this fact a strength; the other half saw neither a strength nor a weakness. Of the respondents, 7% perceived agglomeration disadvantages, such as scarcity and poaching of qualified employees, a drain of expertise or atmospheric tensions between the close competitors. These results lead me to the conclusion that indus-trial clusters are of limited relevance for the hidden champions. The cluster concept cannot conclusively explain the high number of hidden champi-ons and their successes in the German-speaking countries.

However, this general conclusion does not apply to every individual sec-tor. Industrial clusters appear in a variety of sectors and the hidden cham-pions in these sectors belong to such clusters. This finding does not permit clear inferences for the strategy of individual companies. Belonging to a cluster was the reason for the origin and success of some of the hidden champions. But the cluster concept is irrelevant for the vast majority of hidden champions, as they are not part of one. The cluster concept hype appears exaggerated in the light of these findings. Hidden champions can emerge everywhere; industrial clusters are not a prerequisite. In my opin-ion, politics should keep out of these processes, clusters either form in open competition or they don't.

Entrepreneurial Clusters

Even if sector or industrial clusters have no particular strategic significance for the hidden champions, another peripheral factor might be more impor-tant. Either way, we observe that the hidden champions are distributed very unevenly across regions. On a local level, we found strong concen-trations. Windhagen, a village with 4,332 inhabitants, has three hidden champions: Wirtgen in road-recycling machines, the JK Group with its main brand Ergoline for professional tanning beds, and Geutebrück in monitoring systems. These three companies have no technological or mar-ket points of contact and therefore do not constitute an industrial clus-ter. Neutraubling, a small town with a population of 13,509, is home to the Krones headquarters, world market leader in bottling systems, also to Zippel, a leading manufacturer of mini-breweries and constructor of the largest industrial cleaning installation in the world among other things, and to Micron, a leading company for electronic controls for airbag trig-gers.

There is a high concentration of hidden champions in the small town Künzelsau and its surrounding area. The world's two largest dealers in assembly products, Würth and Berner, are located here, along with other world and European market leaders. These include Ziehl-Abegg for fans; R. Stahl in explosion protection equipment; Mustang, the pioneer jeans manufacturer in Germany; and Veigel, one of the leading international manufacturers of driving school systems and handicapped person equipment in cars. Sigloch, one of Europe's largest bookbinders that offers both bookbinding services and machines, also has its origins in Künzelsau. It has only 15,032 inhabitants, but the spirit of the place is obviously conducive to the creation of hidden champions—an entrepreneurial cluster in its prime sense. There is another massive cluster of hidden champions in Haiger, Hesse. The Friedhelm Loh Group has its headquarters there, having 11,600 employees and generating revenues of nearly $2.7 billion. The town also includes the world market leader for electronic enclosures, Rittal, and other market leaders such as Lampertz (data security) and Ritto (intercom equipment). Haiger is also home to Cloos, one of the world market leaders in welding technology, and Klingspor, a global market leader in sanding equipment. The Joachim Loh Group, also located in Haiger, includes Hailo, a market leader in household ladders and ironing equipment. We can find several world market leaders from different sectors in Oberkochen (population 8,500, Carl Zeiss in optoelectronics, Leitz in wood processing tools), or in Laupheim (19,192 inhabitants, Kässbohrer in PistenBully special vehicles, Uhlmann in pharmaceutical packaging systems).

Entrepreneurial clusters can be found in the most diverse situations. My childhood world was made up of a tiny village with seven farmers' families who produced five successful entrepreneurs in only one generation. Every day the children from this village walked to a town school five kilometers (three miles) away. This probably nurtured two decisive characteristics for entrepreneurs: tenacity and the love of freedom. The oldest of the five entrepreneurs founded a successful cardan shaft factory. This inspired the others to follow his role model, in other sectors such as cooling technology, office machinery, and bicycles. Clearly, an entrepreneurial cluster can emerge in the smallest of villages. In contrast to an industrial cluster, the uniting factor is not the sector but the social network that provides inspiration to follow the example of someone successful and become a hidden champion oneself. Time and again, I have heard of such role models and their effects. Spatial and social proximity strengthens this incentive effect, along the lines of "anything my neighbor can do, I can do also." One hidden champion can thus become an incubator for further future world market leaders. The sector can play a role, but the contagion works across industry boundaries. This effect is strongest with a high local concentration of hidden champions, even if they operate in different sectors. Hidden championship is contagious.

Summary

Financing, organization, and the business environment create conditions for the core processes by which companies deliver value to their customers. The hidden champions display a high degree of autonomy in forming these conditions, and other companies can learn from them.

- In spite of fast growth, financing is sound. This has a positive effect on credit-worthiness and capital costs, and ultimately on profitability.
- Self-financing is and remains the most important source of financing. It requires adequate profitability—yet another reference to the paramount importance of profit. This gives rise to a virtuous financial circle.
- Financing is not a constraint for the future strategy of the hidden champions. The weight of financing is shifting. Traditional bank loans are becoming less important when compared to direct capital market financing. The picture is mixed with regard to going public. An IPO is not envisaged by most hidden champions. We nevertheless anticipate an increase in the number of IPOs. One lesson is that the hidden champions want their financial structure to remain conservative, but that they do not rule out new forms of financing.
- Simple corporate structures permit simple organization. This is an advantage not to be underestimated. Functional organization is appropriate for the one-product, one-market company that remains typical for the hidden champions.
- Hidden champions that extend their business activities are aware that the greater organizational complexity threatens their traditional strengths. Their early and consistent reaction to this threat is decentralization. They avoid matrix structures and mainly direct their divisionalization toward customer groups, which may be defined according to sectors or regions. These hidden champions show that the strength of focus can be retained in spite of more complex business structures provided the willingness to decentralize is given.
- The top management of the hidden champions is very lean. The most modern executives manage their global businesses with the aid of network organizations that make use of the latest information technology to the greatest possible extent. These new forms of process organization can become role models for smaller and larger companies alike.
- The value chain and the vertical integration of the hidden champions have decreased in the last ten years. This tendency shows that the traditional preference for doing things themselves is not based on an ide-

ology, but is gradually being adapted. The value chain and the vertical integration nevertheless remain deeper than in the general industry. Our impression is that the reduction in vertical integration primarily relates to noncore competencies.

- In core competencies, the hidden champions continue to favor high vertical integration and avoid outsourcing. They attribute this to their high-quality standards. They are also convinced that uniqueness in competition cannot be bought on the market but can only be created internally. This is why they frequently build their own machines or produce primary products themselves. These attitudes run contrary to current trends and are thought-provoking.
- In R&D, the hidden champions are very keen on autonomy and high depth. Protection of their know-how and the desire to keep qualified employees in the company are further reasons for the high vertical integration in R&D.
- Hidden champions strongly outsource noncore competencies. They do this for cost reasons, but also because they expect higher quality from specialized suppliers. The noncore competency of one is the core competency of the other.
- The hidden champions have an aversion to strategic alliances. They doubt that others can solve their problems and prefer remaining in charge.
- These traditional attitudes are softening for two reasons. First, the integration of systems can make cooperation between partners necessary. Second, where innovations are concerned, areas of knowledge that one company alone cannot master must be accessed. In such cases, strategic alliances can help. Skeptical attitudes toward strategic alliances should not become an ideological barrier.
- Industrial clusters are far less important for the hidden champions than discussion in literature might lead us to believe. Only one in seven companies belongs to a cluster, and only half of these cluster members consider this an advantage.
- Local concentrations of hidden champions in different sectors are frequently observed. We presume that such entrepreneurial clusters create a stimulating social environment conducive to the formation of other hidden champions.

In summary, the hidden champions tend towards conservative attitudes and are reserved about modern concepts. This applies to financing and to complex organizational forms as well as to outsourcing and strategic alliances. Particularly where core competencies are concerned, the hidden champions are very reserved and prefer self-reliance. Many believe that the strong one is most powerful alone. In other areas, they are surprisingly modern, as in decentralization or in the use of information technology to manage their global groups of companies. In contrast to the current discussion, industrial clusters are of low relevance for most hidden champions, because they do things their own way.

Notes

1 According to one source the equity ratios for German midsize companies is 8%, and for Austrian midsize companies 16%. Ernst & Young quotes 18% for German and 33% for Austrian companies. Dun & Bradstreet specifies equity ratios for midsize companies in Germany of between 10.8% (construction industry) and 28.7% (chemical industry). Schauer et al. quote 19% for Austrian companies. See Andreas Georgi, "Notwendigkeit und Instrumente eines ganzheitlichen Risikomanagements für Mittelständler, Gewerbetreibende und Freiberufler," *Zeitschrift für Betriebswirtschaft*, January 2007, pp. 7–18; Ernst & Young, *Wege zum Wachstum*, Stuttgart 2005, Dun & Bradstreet, *Konkrete Orientierungshilfen für Unternehmen*, Düsseldorf, July 2005; Reinbert Schauer, Norbert Kailer and Birgit Feldbauer-Durstmüller (Eds.), *Mittelständische Unternehmen*, Linz: Trauner Verlag 2005.

2 See Stefan Orthsiefen, "Eigenkapitalbasis deutlich gestärkt," *VDI News*, May 18, 2007, p. 27.

3 Return on capital employed before tax/ROCE), see also Fig. 1.3.

4 BDI Forum Familienunternehmen, "Familienunternehmen im Zeitalter der Globalisierung," Berlin, September 21/22, 2006.

5 Here, we refer to the all-time highs before October 2008.

6 By "one" market, we mean the market defined by content. If a product is sold to the same target group in several countries, this would therefore be considered "one" market.

7 ERA-Elektrotechnik was taken over in 2005 by the American company Technitrol and has since belonged to its Pulse Division, with its global headquarters in San Diego. Part of the former company stayed with Erich Aichele and now carries the name Aichele Group. A company in this group, Era-Contact, is one of the world's leading manufacturers of railroad couplings.

8 The number of bilateral relationships between the parties is calculated by $n(n-1)/2$.

9 IBG is the abbreviation for Industrie-Beteiligungs-Gesellschaft, headquartered in Cologne.

10 *Wertschöpfung am Bruttoproduktionsort 2004*, German Federal Statistics Office.

11 Personal communication, April 2007.

12 *Bayerisch-Schwäbische Wirtschaft*, 1/2008, p. 95.

13 *VDI News*, April 13, 2007, p. 35.

14 The Lorenz brand was introduced after the split-up of the Bahlsen Group. The salty snack business was taken over by Lorenz Bahlsen. The sweet snacks business is run by his brother Werner Bahlsen under the Bahlsen brand. Both companies are today independent of one another. A third part of the former Bahlsen Group continues in the Nordeck Group that likewise operates in snacks and in biotechnology.

15 The strategic alliances specified by name here are all operated in the form of joint ventures, Siemens holding a share of 50% or less (Areva 34%, Voith Siemens 35%).

16 See Michael Porter, *The Competitive Advantage of Nations*, London: Macmillan 1990.

17 See for example B.G. Dybe and Hans Joachim Kujath, *Hoffnungsträger Wirtschaftscluster: Unternehmensnetzwerke und regionale Innovationssysteme*, Berlin: edition sigma 2000.

18 Rainer Kämpf et al., *Industrieparkkonzepte*, Stuttgart: EBZ-Beratungszentrum 2003.

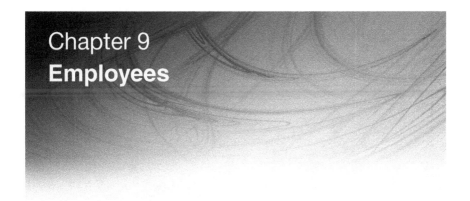

Chapter 9
Employees

It is common knowledge that employees' motivation and sense of identification are key to a company's success. The difference between companies lies in the energy with which these aspects are actually lived out. In this chapter, we look at employees and corporate culture. The growth of the hidden champions means they create numerous new jobs, particularly in foreign markets and for highly qualified employees. How do the hidden champions approach factors such as performance, sickness, employee turnover, and flexibility? We will see that they practice traditional values. Scant human resources and decentralization ensure high productivity and performance transparency. The hidden champions' predominantly rural locations create a special relationship between employers and employees. Recruiting highly qualified employees in a global context presents the hidden champions with new challenges.

Job Creation

The hidden champions' growth generates numerous new jobs. Internationalization is responsible for major shifts in where these jobs are located. Ten years ago, the hidden champions in our sample employed 1,285 people on average. Since then, this number has risen to 2,037. This represents an increase of 58.6% or 753 jobs per company in absolute terms. However, the majority of the new jobs are created not in the home market, but in other countries. Fig. 9.1 provides an overview of the growth of jobs at home and abroad.

H. Simon, *Hidden Champions of the Twenty-First Century*,
DOI 10.1007/978-0-387-98147-5_9, © Hermann Simon 2009

Fig. 9.1: Employees of the German hidden champions, both foreign and domestic

	Home market	Abroad	Total
Ten years ago	810 63%	475 37%	1.285
Today	1.039 51%	998 49%	2.037
Change	+229 +28%	+523 +110%	+752 +59%

Fig. 9.1 shows that many more new jobs have been created abroad than in the companies' home market. Nevertheless, employment at home has also increased 28%, or 229 jobs per company. However, these figures cannot clearly answer the frequently asked question of whether the jobs created abroad are at the cost of jobs at home.[1] This theory is refuted at least as regards the net result. The hidden champions have created a significant number of new jobs both in their home markets and in foreign markets. This indicates that their investments abroad strengthen rather than weaken the home business location.

Ten years ago, almost two thirds (63%) of the hidden champions' employees were employed in the home market, whereas this figure today has fallen to 51%. In the near future, the majority of the hidden champions' employees will work abroad. As the hidden champions become more international in scope, their culture and character will naturally change. As far as the workforce is concerned, they are in fact already changing from domestic to global companies—a process that, as we have seen, has long since taken place regarding revenues. Although about 80% or 90% of revenues do not come from the home market, about half of the workforce is still employed there. Globalization of the personnel and of the value chain usually follows globalization of revenues with a considerable time lag. However, some companies are already much further along than the average in terms of international personnel. Fig. 9.2 lists selected companies that employ at least 70% of their workforce in countries other than

Fig. 9.2: Selected hidden champions with large shares of employees abroad

Company	Main product	Share of foreign employees (in %)
CEAG	Mobile phone chargers	99
Siemens Voith Hydro	Equipment and service for hydraulic power stations	89
Siemens Audiologische Technik	Hearing aids	87
RHI	High temperature systems	86
Klöckner & Co.	Distribution of steel and metals	85
Elektrisola	Thin copper-coated wire	84
GfK	Market research services	81
Böwe Systec	High-performance cutting and enveloping services	75
Gelita	Gelatines	75
ProMinent Dosiertechnik	Chemical fluid handling	75
Webasto	Sunroofs for cars	73
B. Braun Melsungen	Infusion therapy	72
Andritz	Paper/cellulose facilities	>70
Groz-Beckert	Needles	70
Vogt electronic	Customer-specific inductive components and modules	70

the home market. These companies have become global employers. The internationalization of the management is the final step, to be discussed in the next chapter.

The proportion of employees abroad illuminates just one important aspect of the phenomenon of internationalization. This process results in teams of people with very different national and cultural backgrounds. Nokia's design department employs people from 30 nations, at Adidas the employees come from 42 countries, and 15 nationalities are represented in the marketing department at Braun, the electrical appliances manufacturer. Even at a small company like Simon-Kucher & Partners there are 26 nationalities. Such variation did not exist a few decades ago, but in the twenty-first century it is becoming increasingly commonplace. Internationalization is also on the increase in areas such as research and development, traditionally very close to headquarters or located in the home country. Sick, one of the world market leaders in sensor technology, has 13 R&D facilities in six countries. Givaudan, the world market leader for aromas and fragrances, operates 39 Flavor Creation Centers and 23 Fragrance Creation Centers in Paris, Bangalore, New York, Cincinnati, Shanghai, São Paulo, Singapore, South Africa, and other locations.

But what does it mean when a company like CEAG, the world market leader in chargers for cell phones, has more than 18,000 employees in China and only 270 employees in Germany? Can we still call it a German company? Or is John Naisbitt's proposed division of the world economy into domains rather than national states more appropriate?[2] CEAG would accordingly operate in the domain for mobile phones, and the nationality of the employees would no longer be important. One significant challenge for the hidden champions is to retain their traditional strengths during and after their transition from a national to a global entity. The changes that will result from this process cannot currently be anticipated. What is the long-term implication when—as at CEAG—far more employees work for a company in China than in the home country? When companies such as Danfoss, Grundfos or Audi declare China to be their "second home market" and—we take this seriously—this relates to more than just sales figures. Will Danfoss or Grundfos become Danish-Chinese companies and Audi a German-Chinese enterprise?

The hidden champions have created a considerable number of new jobs. This involves massive shifts in the geographical spread of the jobs and the value chain. As the workforce makeup becomes more international, retaining traditional company strengths poses major challenges. Today's workforce structure at most hidden champions can no longer be compared with the situation in the 1990s.

Corporate Culture

In my experience, the real differences between good and bad companies are not found in machinery, installations, processes or the organization, but in the corporate culture. Reinhold Würth once expressed this as follows: "More can be achieved with a highly motivated team working on old machinery in a shack than with an unmotivated group with the latest machinery and premises." Peter Drucker accurately described the challenge to management, "It's about putting people in a position to perform as a group by giving them goals and values, as well as continual learning and development opportunities." Sonova from Switzerland, the market leader in hearing aids, sums up its corporate culture with the slogan, "Nothing is possible without people." Corporate culture encompasses all of a company's goals and values, ideally accepted and embraced by all employees. Directing everyone's efforts toward identifying with shared goals and priorities is the fundamental purpose of corporate culture. I use two questions to ascertain where companies stand in this regard:

- What percentage of your energy do you use to overcome internal resistance within the company?
- How would you manage the company if it belonged to you?

Honest answers to these simple questions reveal the underlying culture of a company. Managers in large corporations frequently answer the first question with percentages of between 50% and 70%. In midsize companies, the answers are usually between 20% and 30%, and at hidden champions 10% and 20%. Presumably, this percentage should not hit zero, because some resistance must always be overcome in order to find the best solutions. However, it is neither desirable nor efficient for a large proportion of management energy to be expended on internal friction— a clear indication that not everyone is pulling in the same direction. Too many companies suffer from a lack of common values and goals. Individual employees and managers make the most of the situation for themselves or their department, but have lost sight of the bigger picture. A greater division of labor increases this danger.

There is a spectacular range of answers to the question "How would you manage the company if it belonged to you?" A branch manager from a large insurance company told me he would manage the same work with half the employees. In a chemicals company, a divisional head reported that he could improve results dramatically, but that this would involve extremely unpopular decisions. The insurance manager did actually take over the branch some time later, and today he generates double the revenues with half the employees. In other words, productivity has quadrupled. The chemicals company eventually sold the division to a private equity investor, who gave the management a share. The former division has been generating profits ever since. Such examples illustrate the disparity between value systems, a lack of mobilization of the skills of management and employees, and serious flaws in corporate cultures.

There is no doubt that the importance of corporate culture has increased and will continue to do so. People are increasingly unwilling to work for money alone. They expect work to provide more meaning, to bring enjoyment, and to satisfy overarching goals and values. In highly developed societies, work motivation must address a higher level of the needs pyramid. This applies to the greatest extent in advanced service providers and intellectual capital companies. The more intellectually demanding the work, the more important the corporate culture. The performance of highly qualified knowledge workers is virtually impossible to directly measure and control, as Peter Drucker pointed out 40 years ago. These experts can ultimately be managed only by motivation and targets rather than conventional control mechanisms. To a certain extent, corporate culture replaces the time clock.

What about corporate culture and performance at the hidden champions? Fig. 9.3 shows the answers to the question about the company's inner strengths, in each case as a percentage of respondents who marked 6 or 7 on the 7-point-scale.

Fig. 9.3: Inner strengths of the hidden champions

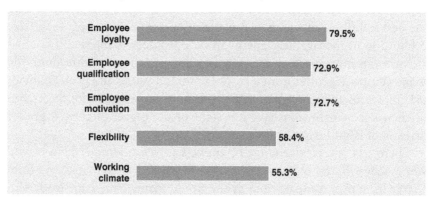

Most hidden champions see the employee-related characteristics as their strengths. This applies in particular to employee loyalty, qualifications, and employee motivation, as evidenced in Fig. 9.3. There can be no doubt that the corporate cultures and the attitudes of the employees are important foundations of the hidden champions' superiority.

Numerous statements were made regarding corporate culture in our discussions and in brochures in connection with independent responsibility, freedom, team spirit (Axel Barten, CEO of Achenbach Buschhütten, says, "We really live the team spirit. It takes precedence over hierarchical thinking"), trust, a welcoming atmosphere, dialogue, openness, enjoyment of the work (according to SMA, the world market leader in electrotechnical transformers for solar installations, enjoyment of work is the "actionable right of every employee"), independent thought by employees (Brainlab CEO Stefan Vilsmeier reports, "I'm not satisfied with clones"), and many other cultural aspects. Frank Straub, head of Blanco, the global market leader in kitchen sinks, sums up these values by saying, "We do not push, we pull." The hidden champions are self-confident about their corporate culture, as Markus Flik, CEO of Behr, the world market leader for engine cooling systems, indicates. "We have a major bonus that makes us stand out from our competitors: the inner strength of our company that allows us to overcome challenges, that ensures we never give up, and that enables us to achieve the apparently impossible." Furthermore, he says, "This inner strength rests in our corporate culture." This may sound very grand, but the words do not ring hollow because the hidden champions do have this inner strength. The real effects of this are shown in specific indicators such as sickness and employee turnover rates.

Sickness and employee turnover

Inner values are not only nice to have but are reflected in hard productivity figures. The average sickness rates at the hidden champions are very low at 3.2%. Every tenth hidden champion even reports sickness rates below 2%. On average over the last ten years, the figure for Germany as a whole was 4.2%. This means that of a workforce of about 2,000 employees, hidden champions have 20 fewer sick employees every day than the average company.

The employee turnover rate is a further indicator. Rapid employee turnover is very disadvantageous if the employees have specific qualifications that are hard to obtain on the labor market. By contrast, it is easier to close gaps left by employees with general skills like bookkeepers. Many of our survey respondents emphasized that the employees of hidden champions have special qualifications at the highest level, so high turnover rates would mean a serious setback. Consequently, these companies do all they can to retain their specialists and are successful in this respect. The hidden champions' long-term turnover rate of 2.7% is extremely low. Some companies have virtually no attrition at all. "Anyone bitten by the coffee bug can never escape," claims Stephan Lange, CEO of Probat, world market leader for coffee roasting facilities with a global market share of 60%. The picture becomes even clearer if we compare the hidden champions' turnover rate with the average rates in German-speaking countries. For illustration purposes, Fig. 9.4 also shows the rate for Daimler, Germany's largest corporation. The 5.3% of Daimler is already low for a large company, but still twice as high as the average hidden champions' rate. We also include the so-called separations rate for the US.[3]

Fig. 9.4: Comparison of employee turnover rates

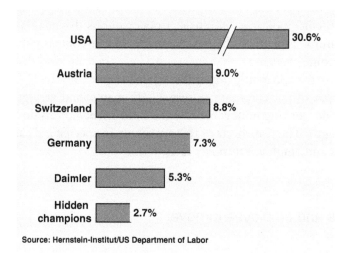

Source: Hernstein-Institut/US Department of Labor

The hidden champions' extremely low turnover rate of 2.7% implies an average length of service of 37 years (100 divided by 2.7). By contrast, at a turnover rate of 8% employees stay for only 12.5 years (i.e., 25 years less). The difference between the hidden champions' rate and the average rates in the German-speaking countries is 5%. What does this mean? First, it means that every year, one employee out of every 20 employees more is lost—along with his or her expertise. Second, a considerably greater number of employees must be found, hired, and trained year after year. In relation to the average number of employees at the hidden champions (2,037), this means that in comparison with an average company of the same size:

- Every year, the skills and knowledge of 100 employees remain in the company/are not lost.
- Every year, the time, effort and expense of hiring and training 100 new employees are saved.
- At an average company, half the workforce has gone after eight years; at the hidden champions, 80% of the original team are still on board after the same period.

The separation rate for the US reveals that the American labor market is extremely different from the labor markets in German-speaking countries. The annual separation rates in the US vary strongly across industries, ranging from 50% for accommodation and food services to 10.3%

for government jobs, but they are generally much higher than in Europe and for the hidden champions in particular. The high attrition points to a serious problem when it comes to highly and specifically qualified employees.

Public awareness focuses on sickness rates and absence from work. However, in my opinion the employee turnover rate is of far greater strategic importance, which is why hidden champions pay so much attention to it. Nothing is more important for building and retaining expertise than a low turnover rate—and nothing more damaging than a high one. All companies operating in high qualification businesses should internalize this crucial aspect.

The average length of service of 37 years appears unrealistically long, and it immediately raises the question of what happens to underperformers. Does it make sense to keep underperformers, shirkers, and incapable employees on board for as long as possible? After all, continuity is not an end in itself, so the entire system of strong employee loyalty and low attrition makes sense only if the right people are retained. Rigorous selection from the outset is therefore vital. Years ago, I won a valuable insight from Heinz Hankammer, founder of the hidden champion Brita. Hankammer first of all stated, "We have practically no turnover." On reflection, however, he said, "But our turnover is high at the beginning." He added that he did not have to ensure that the right people were kept on after their probationary periods; the team did so of its own accord. Like with a sports team, employees are aware that they damage the company and themselves if they put up with unwilling or incapable colleagues in the group. Dietmar Hermle, head of machine tool manufacturer Hermle, shares this view. "If someone doesn't fit in, he or she has to leave." This is precisely the point! More than 100 years ago, Frederick Taylor, the inventor of Taylorism, stated that choosing the right employees is more important than any organizational, procedural or training activities. This perspective is also evident at Globetrotter, Europe's market leader for outdoor equipment. Globetrotter hires only people who make their hobby their profession. They are enthusiastic mountaineers, canoeists or cyclists, and most are previous customers of the company. The same is true at Burton Snowboards in Burlington, Vermont, a market leader for winter sports equipment. Founder and chairman Jake Burton says that, like he himself, practically everyone at the company is passionate about snowboarding and "top management snowboards before our meetings."[4] Such enthusiasm among personnel naturally carries over to the customers.

High continuity, low employee turnover, and rigorous selection at the start are inextricably linked. The hidden champions know this and act accordingly—with their own brand of consistency.

Comebackers

This section is somewhat speculative in nature, because the statements cannot be substantiated by hard or representative data. During visits and discussions with hidden champions, it occurred to me that there were more "comebackers" than in other companies. The following incident illustrates what I mean. The CEO of a very successful hidden champion was explaining his organigram to me. All of the managerial functions were labeled with the names of the people performing them. I remembered that one of these people had left the company about a year before, and remarked on the fact. "He came back," answered the CEO. The fact that this happened in three other cases is striking.

Companies with very distinctive corporate cultures like the hidden champions are well advised to hire young people who grow into these cultures at the start of their careers and feel comfortable with them. There is, however, one problem with this approach. After several years, the Italian proverb "La felicità è sempre sull'altra riva"[5] starts to bite. Employees develop a feeling of uncertainty about whether another company might not be more interesting or whether they should not perhaps venture into another sector. Some, especially ambitious young people with leadership potential, act on this feeling and change direction. They later often find that they have failed to understand the second, implied, part of the proverb, because they are still chasing happiness even after arriving on the other side of the river.

From my own extensive experience, I can report that comebackers become very valuable and loyal employees. Simon-Kucher has a considerable proportion of such comebackers among the partners and the consultants. Some companies categorically exclude this kind of return. This attitude may make it less likely for people to resign, but I am convinced that this is a waste of a valuable resource. What are the advantages of comebackers? They know the company and the company knows them. In comparison with new hires, the familiarization periods, uncertainties, risks of flops and so on are minimized. And these employees are immune to the call of the Italian goddess of fortune, because they have learned that the side of the river they started on can make them happy, too.

Comebackers are above all a valid indicator of a company's attractiveness. My impression is that the number of comebackers at the hidden champions is disproportionately high, although I cannot support this assertion with representative statistics. Having a large number of comebackers conclusively proves the uniqueness of these companies' corporate culture.

High-performance cultures

Most hidden champions have a culture of high performance. "I used to work for one of the world's largest retailers, with several thousand employees at the head office," reports the head of sales at a successful hidden champion. "In the course of the day, you would often see people in the open-plan office reading magazines because they had nothing to do. That didn't seem to worry anyone, but it would be unthinkable in my present company." The CEO of another hidden champion says, "We have 120 employees, and everyone has to be fully committed and get down to work. Nobody can laze around. Shirkers may get by in large corporations, but they are very unlikely to survive here." How do the hidden champions create the conditions for high performance? And what are the reasons for these marked differences between large and smaller companies? I see three fundamental explanations: number of employees, corporate culture, and organization.

My first, oft-made observation relates to the number of employees: hidden champions do not have a large enough workforce. They are lean not only at the top, but on all levels. "We have always had more work than heads to do it, and that's how it should be," states one respondent. "This is not only good for productivity but it actually keeps people happier. If people are not challenged to work hard, they resort to unproductive activities like writing memos, holding meetings and drafting unnecessary guidelines. Most of the intrigue and bureaucratic hassle that plagues large companies is avoidable when there's an abundant amount of work." The effect of a lean workforce on productivity cannot be described more accurately.

The opposite is also true: having too many employees kills productivity and fosters dissatisfaction. Parkinson's law applies only if there are too many people on board.[6] People with surplus work capacity find ways to keep themselves busy. Employees are very creative when it comes to inventing unproductive work, usually involving internal activities that create little or no value. The larger a company is, the greater the risk that this will happen. "More work than people" is probably the most effective driver of productivity. Naturally, the balance between workload and human resources is delicate and must not be overstretched. The principle of having "slightly more work than people" would therefore be more accurate, although "slightly" cannot be exactly quantified.

How is "more work than people" achieved? The simplest way is growth. When a company grows, it almost automatically reaches a situation where employee capacity lags behind the amount of work. This calls for a careful recruiting policy. According to Heraeus, a hidden champion in numerous markets, "We don't hire the second employee until we need the third." The situation is much more difficult to achieve when a company's revenue shrinks. In this case, the only way to avoid having surplus employees is to make workforce cutbacks at an early stage. Increases in productivity even lead to overemployment if sales remain the same. The CEO of a hidden champion in the automotive sector describes this problem as follows: "Our productivity increases by around 5% every year. We want to keep the headcount numbers stable, but this means we have to sell 5% more units every year. If that fails, we automatically have too many employees. To avoid this, we are damned to grow."

The second condition for top performance is having the right corporate culture. As we said about selection during the probationary period, intolerance of underperformance and shirking should be a concern not only of the management but of the entire team. As in a sports team, employees must be aware that underperformance threatens the whole company and therefore their own jobs. In a soccer or football team, a player who is considerably weaker than the team average is naturally not accepted, because it is common knowledge that such players weaken the team and its league position. The same applies to companies. Employees should not put up with situations like the one found at the large retailer mentioned above. People who identify with the company must play their part in avoiding such situations. Most hidden champions have no doubts about this attitude. Companies cannot become world-class unless they have a culture of intolerance regarding bad performance and shirking. There are of course also large corporations with high-performance corporate cultures. The world market leaders Bosch (automotive electronics) and Linde (industrial gases), for example, have always impressed me in this respect, as have many American corporations, such as General Electric, Procter & Gamble, and Microsoft, to name only a few.

The third condition for high performance is of an organizational nature. Given good management, which must always be assumed, high performance is easier to achieve in and with small units. I have often stated that underperformance is much more likely to go unnoticed in large organizations. At visits to large corporations I have frequently wondered how labor can be divided in a manner that makes more or less equal use of each of the thousand employees' working capacity in an organizational unit. My experiences of large Japanese open-plan offices were particularly impressive and illustrative. Hundreds of employees sit in rows and do their work. How can work be allocated under these conditions to ensure that everyone puts in high performance?

Achieving this is relatively easy on an assembly line, and it may also be possible with routine procedures such as handling insurance claims in which performance can easily be measured. However, as soon as knowledge work becomes involved, I consider it impossible to precisely assess the necessary time and effort in advance and allocate it accordingly. It is an illusion that work in large units can be allocated by micromanagement in such a way that all employees achieve high performance. This is far easier in small, decentralized units. It is tempting to counter this argument with the theory that "large" tasks can be performed only by large units. Many sectors have proven that this is not true. The value chains in the automotive and aerospace industries have been completely restructured in recent years. The most important change was to transfer both development and manufacturing tasks from the large organizations of the original equipment manufacturers (OEMs) to suppliers. Unlike work allocation by micromanagement, this involves shifting entire parts of the value chain to independent companies or business units. This is a fundamental difference. Decentralization is definitely a very effective means of achieving high performance.

A further problem is the alienation that increases in line with more pronounced division of labor and a greater distance from the end-result of one's work. Alienation damages motivation and harms performance. Decentralization is very effective for counteracting alienation and its negative consequences. There can be no doubt that employees of hidden champions are closer to the results of their work and identify more strongly with them than is usually the case in large corporations.

As early as ten years ago, many executives at hidden champions expressed to me their fear that company growth could mean sacrificing the strengths of the small enterprise. One such example was Karl Schlecht, founder of Putzmeister, the world market leader in concrete pumps, who decentralized his company to prevent inertia. The American champion Gore, famous for its Gore-Tex brand, undertakes cell division as soon as an organizational unit exceeds the threshold of 150 employees. The founder of the Mormons, Brigham Young, instructed his followers that a "ward" should not have more than 300 souls. In Chapter 8, numerous examples illustrated that the hidden champions are early and almost fanatical decentralizers. IBG, the market leader in welding technology, has 2,200 employees and comprises 70 companies. The Hoerbiger Group, one of the leading names in drive and compressor technology, has 6,300 employees and more than 100 companies. On average, an IBG company has 31 employees and a Hoerbiger company fewer than 63 employees, small companies by any standard. We need not speculate whether this cell division is motivated predominantly by customer orientation or the high-performance culture. Decentralization promotes both goals.

Flexibility

In many markets, one of the greatest management challenges is to reconcile the volatility of market demand with the inflexibility of resources. This inflexibility partially results from the legal framework, including labor protection laws and other regulations restricting a company with regard to employee transfers, assignment to different jobs, and wage adjustments, for example. However, part of the rigidity is based on circumstances for which the company itself is responsible, such as collective wage contracts, bargaining agreements, policy and company culture. My consistent impression is that the hidden champions achieve greater flexibility than the large corporations within the legal and political constraints. It is no surprise that small and midsize companies are generally more flexible than large enterprises. Claas, with a strongly cyclical seasonal business, has weekly working hours of between 24 and 51 hours without supplementary payments. At Wacker Construction, the working week can be up to 48 hours at peak times. Hidden champions were pioneers in introducing flexible worktime agreements, and they make widespread use of this method.

One important aspect of the high-performance culture is the flexibility and availability of employees for work abroad, often including weekends. As a result of globalization, international deployments are becoming increasingly important. Wolfgang Pinegger, CEO of DMT Technology, one of the leading firms in biaxial film-stretching equipment, explains the challenge, "Our people cannot expect to have regular eight-hour workdays. We have to be more flexible and faster. For instance, we often have to travel over the weekend, and people who stay with us aren't rigid about Monday through Friday as the work week. We are very demanding, but we also offer more than just monetary compensation." Even the smallest companies that operate worldwide (such as Klais, the organ builder) constantly rely on being able to send their employees anywhere in the world and keeping them there often for months on end.

The hidden champions also prove highly flexible in their internal reassignment of tasks. During a crisis in the 1990s, Würth managed to move almost 10% of the workforce from internal positions to external sales within a year. A study found that successful companies undertake roughly five times as many transfers between functions as less successful companies.[7] Southwest Airlines, the most profitable airline in the US since 1980, is a pioneer in this respect. Employees take on up to 14 different tasks, from ticket sales to baggage handling. European low-cost carriers such as Germanwings and Ryanair have also adopted this approach, which considerably cuts costs in addition to speeding up procedures. Such multifunctional assignments occur frequently at the hidden champions. Winterhalter, the world market leader in dishwashing systems for hotels and restaurants, requires its employees to be able to perform at least two functions. At hidden champions, shop floor workers often help out when service bottlenecks arise. Compared to large corporations, the division of labor and detailed work allocations are less prevalent and less detailed, the overall understanding is broader, and the deployment capacity of the employees is more flexible.

Rural locations

The worldlywise believe they know where to find the leading experts: at MIT or Harvard University in Boston, at the California Institute of Technology, the University of Tokyo, the Ecole Polytechnique in Paris or Imperial College in London. There are certainly many excellent academics at these places. However, the experts in practice are elsewhere, in places you have never heard of. Experts for artificial joints are congregated in Warsaw, Indiana. The leading authorities for prostheses work in Duderstadt, Lower Saxony. The world-leading wind energy technicians work on their innovations in the remote town of Aurich in northern Germany. The most robust small excavators in the world are called Bobcats and come from the 800-inhabitant village of Gwinner in North Dakota. Harsewinkel, in a remote part of western Germany, is the home of the world's most powerful combine harvesters. No one in the world knows more about high-performance materials than the researchers at Plansee in Reutte, Austria. If you need metals in powder form, you will find the experts in Höganäs, Sweden or Cinnaminson, New Jersey. And when it comes to ski bindings, you should go to Fritschi in Reichenbach, Switzerland, which produces 70% of all ski bindings in the world. The world's most advanced plasma cutting systems are created at Hypertherm in Hanover, New Hampshire, a company that generates revenues of more than $300 million with 1,000 employees.

About two thirds of the hidden champions have their headquarters in rural locations. This fact alone is surprising. People who care deeply about their mission ply their trade in these remote places with the greatest possible concentration and continuity. The hidden champions are shaped by their locations and the locations are shaped by the hidden champions. This interdependence has an important impact on the corporate culture and the relationships between employers and employees. Typically, the hidden champion is the largest (and often the only large) employer in town. Employees have fewer job prospects in small towns than in large cities. On the other hand, the pool of qualified employees is limited in rural areas, so the company depends on its employees and their goodwill. These conditions create mutual dependence: the company needs the employees and the employees need the jobs the company offers. This gives rise to a relationship characterized by a sense of identification and avoidance of confrontation. Employees know that they will be affected if the company fails to do well, and the company leader knows that he or she depends on the motivation of the workforce. Alfons Veer, CEO of the Krone Group in the small town of Emsdetten, says, "Our location is ideal for us. We find enough hard-working, committed employees at affordable costs. We produce in a rural area, which in particular benefits our agricultural technology, and we can manage the worldwide sales network from here without difficulty."[8]

The fact that the owner-manager of a company was often born and raised in the same small town as his or her employees leads to intimate relationships that are difficult to duplicate in large city corporations. In many of these small towns, several generations of a family work or have worked for the company. Mathias Häfner, head of personnel at Neenah Gessner, a leading manufacturer of filter papers in Bruckmühl, Bavaria, reports, "We have some third-generation employees. The people who work here are also our neighbors." Some 90% of Neenah Gessner's workforce come from the immediate vicinity and the company is located in a residential area. The distance between management and employees is very small. On factory rounds with CEOs, I have often observed that they know many of their employees by name. At O.C. Tanner in Salt Lake City, the plant manager knew the names of practically all of the several hundred shop floor workers.

The relationships between the hidden champions and their local communities have a number of distinguishing features. The inhabitants are proud to have a world market leader in town. The company is usually the biggest taxpayer, so the local community has an interest in its wellbeing. "If Zeiss coughs, we get pneumonia," says the mayor of Oberkochen, a town with a population of 8,500 where Zeiss has 4,407 employees. The municipal authorities endeavor to keep their biggest taxpayer happy, and the company in turn shows its appreciation by sponsoring local associations, museums, and cultural activities. The same is true for Wolfertschwenden, home to vacuum packaging market leader Multivac. The mayor Karl Fleschhut says, "We know that Multivac is reciprocating the favors we do them through their social responsibility and commitment."[9] Otto Kirchner, CEO and shareholder of Fränkische Rohrwerke, the world market leader in corrugated pipes based in Königsberg, Bavaria, comments, "My responsibility is not least toward the town, because we are by far its largest employer." Anton Milner, CEO of Q-Cells in Thalheim, Saxony-Anhalt, seconds, "We have a responsibility to our employees and the region. I know we are considered a beacon here, giving hope to many people." RIM, manufacturer of the BlackBerry, has made Waterloo one of the most important technology centers in Canada. To a great extent, this is due to the largest supporter of academic institutions, Mike Lazaridis, inventor of the BlackBerry and founder of RIM. Local proximity ensures a down-to-earth atmosphere. All of these factors help the employees to identify more closely with their company.

A further advantage of the rural location is that there are fewer distractions. Klaus Grohmann of Grohmann Engineering pointed out this advantage to me many years ago and reiterated it even more energetically in a recent discussion. "I am from Düsseldorf, a big city, and my first company was there," he says. "At the time we had a successful worldwide engineering business with customers in the steel industry. But what we are doing for the electronics industry and other sectors today couldn't be done in Düsseldorf because there would be too many distractions for our superior performers. We require deep concentration that can be evoked only in quiet surroundings. I decided to go to the little town of Prüm (population 5,343) in the Eifel, close to the Belgian border, because I wanted to create a permanent bond between employees and the company, and it worked. Our job turnover rate is less than one percent. We don't waste time in traffic jams, we live close to the fields and the forest, and when we go home we can relax. Our employees can afford their own homes, for land is cheap. We have some trouble attracting people from large cities, but it's not too serious a problem." Similarly, piano builder Bechstein built its new factory in Seifhennersdorf, a quiet town in Saxony near the Czech border. "We could have set ourselves up in the big cities of Berlin or Leipzig, but there would have been too much distraction for our employees," explains Bechstein's CEO Klaus Schulze. "If you're looking for quiet recreation and you love peace and tranquility, you will certainly feel at home here," concludes the website of the small town (population 4,700).

Rural locations should not be glorified as a perfect world. Like everything, they have their pros and cons. However, they have strong and significant effects on corporate culture and on employees' sense of identification with their company. The mere fact that so many global market leaders are located in small towns and villages is thought-provoking.

Qualifications and Learning

The key factors in international competition vary across markets. In mass markets, where low costs are decisive, the ability to procure, manufacture, and distribute at the lowest possible cost becomes a core competency. This typically involves resorting to cheap labor or a high degree of automation. But a minimum standard of quality and the capacity to guarantee it are crucial even in markets characterized by fierce price competition. As we have seen, the hidden champions' competitive advantages are typically not low costs and low prices, but superior product quality, advice, service, and systems integration. Qualified, rather than cheap, employees are required to achieve these advantages. In highly developed markets, employees' level of education and capacity to learn are key to retaining market leadership.

Fig. 9.3 showed that employee qualifications are considered a significant company strength by 72.9% of the respondents. Regarding higher education, the situation has changed considerably since ten years ago. Fig. 9.5 illustrates the increase in the percentage of university graduates among the employees of the hidden champions.

Fig. 9.5: Ten-year comparison of the percentage of employees with a university degree

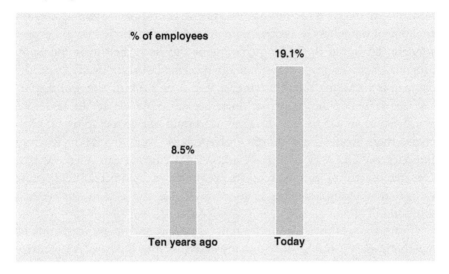

The percentage of hidden champions' employees with a university degree has more than doubled in the last ten years. In combination with the increase in employment, this has had a dramatic effect in absolute terms. Ten years ago, the average hidden champion employed 109 graduates; today, 389 employees have a university degree—almost four times as many. This development does not come as a surprise. The technologically most advanced hidden champions already had a proportion of more than 20% with university degrees (e.g., Hauni 25%, Trumpf 22%) ten years ago, and many others have followed their example since then. Every tenth hidden champion today has a workforce comprising 50% or more university graduates, who are generally highly specialized. At Omicron, the world market leader for tunnel-grid microscopes, 80 of the 200-strong workforce are highly qualified physicists. There is a dense concentration of knowledge and intellectual capacity in such companies.

In addition to university graduates, highly skilled specialists make an equally important contribution to the hidden champions' competencies. The proportion of employees in formal vocational training programs in

Germany is also higher today than it was ten years ago: 5.2% compared to 4.5%. In absolute figures, this means that the average hidden champion had 58 apprentices in the 1990s. Today, this figure has almost doubled to 106. In the German vocational education system, apprentices complete a three to three-and-a-half year program. One or two days a week they attend a vocational school, where they gain a solid theoretical grounding in their trade or industry. The rest of the time they work for a modest salary in the company and get practical instruction by "masters." This unique vocational education system is considered one of the pillars of Germany's continued competitiveness and export strength. However, the hidden champions also need their own education programs because there are often no specialist workers available at the company's location. Kai Büntemeyer, CEO of Kolbus, the world market leader in bookbinding machines, explains, "As we are located in a provincial town, we have no choice but to train our own employees. Otherwise there would be a shortage of specialist workers." Hans-Joachim Boekstegers, CEO of Multivac, adds, "We educate our own experts. Our manufacturing process requires ever better trained personnel because we insource additional parts of the value chain and extend our systems solution."[10]

Givaudan, worldwide number one in aromas and fragrances, runs its own perfumery school. The company describes it as follows: "A legendary institute that creates the world's leading fragrance artists. The Givaudan Perfumery School nurtures and inspires tomorrow's leading fragrance artisans with generations of knowledge, passion, and expertise. Open since 1947, Givaudan is the first fragrance company in the world to have its own school, which is widely considered the crème de la crème of fragrance training for those in the fragrance industry. The Givaudan Perfumery School is located in a brand-new facility near the Givaudan European Creative Center in Argenteuil, France on the picturesque banks of the Seine, where Monet painted some of his early pieces. The school, under the direction of Jean Guichard, has established a new standard of perfumery training—a structured technique that enables perfumers to systematically learn the entire spectrum of the olfactive genealogy and develop an olfactive memory of over 1,200 ingredients."

Many hidden champions apply Germany's dual vocational training system to their foreign subsidiaries. They see this as the only way to educate skilled workers with similar qualification levels as in their home country. Stihl, the global market leader in chainsaws, uses the German approach in the US and Brazil. Kern-Liebers, the world market leader for springs in safety belts, and Fischerwerke, number one in dowels, have together set up a "German Center for Tooling" in Taicang in China, where they train 24 specialist workers every year in line with the German system. In many countries, a shortage of highly qualified and specialized workers is a bottleneck for the development of the hidden champions' businesses. If no adequately skilled workers are available, the hidden champions train them themselves. The situation is similar with regard to continuing education. In previous chapters, we saw that high performance, innovation, and closeness to customer make serious demands on the level of employee training. Eckart Schmitt describes the situation at Zumtobel, world market leader in lighting technology, "We offer our customers complex lighting solutions. To realize them, we need our employees even more than our innovative lighting and control systems. Our employees design every lighting solution in cooperation with the customer, and they need in-depth technical, business and communication competencies to do the job. That's why we have our own academy for the continuing education of our specialists. We offer mandatory as well as voluntary courses, and the graduates are awarded the title of lighting solution advisor. The costs are high, but we benefit twice over: our customers repeatedly confirm in surveys that they consider our employees to be among the best-trained in the sector, and the employees respond very positively to the company's investment in their education because they see that the slogan 'Employees are our most important asset' is not mere lip service, but daily reality."

Training and continuing education of this kind require large investments, and these investments are worthwhile only if the employees stay in the company for long enough after completing their training programs. The training intensity must therefore be assessed in connection with the low employee attrition. Large investments in education in combination with low attrition ensure an uninterrupted supply of specialist workers and a permanently high level of expertise.

In summary, the share of university graduates among the employees of the hidden champions has more than doubled in the last ten years. These companies have made a leap forward in knowledge and their employees' qualification levels. The number of apprentices is also significantly higher than ten years ago. These investments in education, combined with low employee turnover, secure a consistently high level of expertise in the long term. In view of the increasing complexity of the hidden champions' product and service portfolio in the twenty-first century (with technology, advice and systems integration) this aspect is more important than ever before.

Creativity of Employees

Every company must constantly be on the lookout for new ideas to improve productivity and quality, accelerate processes, cut costs, and minimize activities that do not create value. The employees themselves constitute a rich source of such ideas. They best know the work and are in a position to recognize scope for improvement. With sufficient motivation, they will ensure that their ideas become known and changes for the better are made. Every company of course acknowledges these maxims, but it often remains unclear whether and how they are actually put into practice. The Japanese developed the famous kaizen system for making continuous improvements, and have achieved impressive results with it.

In Germany, the German Business Institute (DIB) collects statistics about the number of improvements suggested by workers.[11] In 1993, 16 proposals per 100 employees were submitted in Germany, versus 2,500 per 100 employees in Japan. The differences were thus considerable. In Germany, the number of ideas put forward has since then quadrupled to 64 per 100 workers. For the 324 companies in the DIB survey, this means an absolute figure of 1.29 million proposals, leading to savings totaling $2.18 billion.

Evaluating the DIB figures is difficult. A total of 306 companies and 18 public agencies took part in the most recent survey, presumably organizations that attach particular importance to ideas for improvements. This could explain why the number of improvement suggestions is relatively modest at our hidden champions, at 32 per 100 employees—contrary to all other indicators. This figure is still double the German average 15 years ago, but only half the average in the current DIB survey. In our survey only 45% of the respondents answered the question about the number of suggestions per 100 employees, although the questionnaires were otherwise completely filled out. The most likely explanation is that many hidden champions have no formal ideas management system and therefore do not record the figures. According to a survey in the early 1990s, only 12.8% of the hidden champions had introduced a system of this kind. This may be for a deeper reason. The core question is whether making suggestions for improvements belongs to the normal duties of an employee or whether a separate system with special incentives is appropriate. My perception is that most hidden champions take the former view, and I strongly agree. Of course, this should not exclude the possibility of offering incentives for especially valuable suggestions. But such incentives should not become a rule.

Another reason why the hidden champions do not head the statistics on employee suggestions (the same situation as ten years ago) could be that they are already highly productive and do many things right. A young manager, who had recently joined a large automotive manufacturer, pointed this aspect out to me, "In my current company, the employees submit lots of improvement proposals, and there really is a great deal to improve. I used to work for a hidden champion where far fewer ideas were submitted because we did things so well that there wasn't much to make better." The mere number of improvement proposals should not overly impress us; it may simply indicate that much has been wrong to date. Every company must endeavor to mobilize the creativity of its employees as far as possible. This can be accomplished through a formal ideas management system, but the same effect can be achieved if employees are highly motivated and have a strong sense of identification with the company. These attitudes may actually contribute more effectively to continual improvements in the course of their normal work than any form of special incentive system.

Recruiting

Given that employee qualifications are a key resource of the hidden champions, attracting and keeping the best talent is extremely important. We have seen that retaining employees is obviously not a bottleneck. Employee loyalty is very high. But what about attracting top talent? For various reasons this is a major bottleneck for the hidden champions. First, there is a general shortage of engineers. In the tough competition for technical graduates, the hidden champions' lack of public prominence may well prove to be a competitive disadvantage. In surveys among students, there is always a preference for large, well-known companies, ideally with famous brand names. "Everyone knows what BMW makes," says one respondent. "The automaker ranks high on the list of the most popular employers, whereas the names of the hidden champions don't even appear in these rankings."[12] However, the situation is not as bad as it appears. Fig. 9.6 shows the distribution of answers to the question "How attractive is your company to high potentials?"

The average score on a scale of 1 to 7 (7 being very attractive) is 5.2. Most respondents chose an above-average rating, but only 7.5% chose the highest level. The percentage of those who consider their company unattractive to high potentials is very low. Overall, the hidden champions

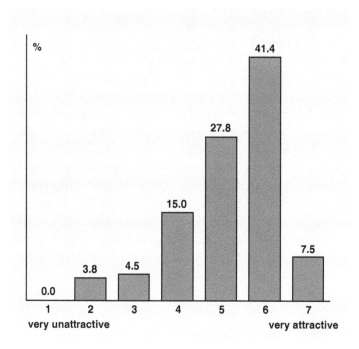

are attractive, but not excessively so. In view of the enormous demand for highly qualified employees and the more intense competition, the hidden champions should be dissatisfied with this situation, as should all other companies that depend on top talent.

Midsize companies generally find it hard to make a national, let alone a global, name for themselves as appealing employers for high potentials. In competing with large corporations, hidden champions have the best chances if they focus their recruiting activities on specific universities. These are usually universities close to the company's headquarters or locations. Hidden champions have to more deliberately display their advantages and position themselves more consciously. In addition to emphasizing their strengths such as world market leadership, technological expertise, and international outlook, they should underline swift career progress and the early delegation of responsibility. These arguments make an employer particularly attractive to entrepreneurial young people. In Chapter 10, we will see that promotion to top positions takes place at a much younger age at hidden champions than in large corporations.

We have already seen that about two thirds of the hidden champions are located in rural areas and that this fosters employees' loyalty and identification with the company. However, rural locations are likely to be a disadvantage for attracting high potentials. Many hidden champions find it difficult or even impossible to attract top graduates to remote regions, although this problem seems more serious among business graduates than among scientists and engineers. The latter are more interested in the work than the location. What can we recommend in this situation? Accepting reality is the first step towards addressing the problem. If non-local talent cannot be motivated to move to a particular region, companies must make the most of the talent they can find in that region. Many hidden champions have been very successful with this approach. In their vicinity, these companies generally have an excellent image as an employer. And young people with leadership potential can be found everywhere. They only have to be identified and introduced to the company through internships, subsidies for tuition, or similar forms of cooperation. After completing their studies elsewhere, many are happy to return to where they grew up. Walter Winkler, founder and CEO of Witron, a leading provider of dynamic logistics systems based in Parkstein, Bavaria, reports, "Most of our 600 employees are local. Many want to return to live and work at home after graduating. Our down-to-earth employees are very committed." Young employees from the region should be sent to foreign countries for a few years early in their careers, to prepare them for leadership tasks in a globalized world. These managers subsequently have both a global outlook and an appreciation of where they were raised, and generally remain loyal to the company in the long term.

When it comes to recruiting managers to a rural location, the needs of their spouses and partners should not be neglected. While the manager's main priorities might be professional challenges and the attractiveness of the company, aspects such as social environment and leisure opportunities in the region are very important to spouses, partners and families. How do the hidden champions deal with this? "We have learned that there is no point in hiring a manager if the family doesn't feel comfortable here," explains Michael Schwarzkopf, CEO of Plansee in Reutte, Austria. "That's why we also invite the spouse or partner to the interviews. We try to get the most complete picture we can, and we only make an offer once we are sure that everyone in the family will be happy in the region."

However, once a manager has been persuaded to move, the rural location can again become an advantage. Christoph Friedrich, executive vice president at Wampfler in Weil, world market leader for mobile energy and data transmission, says, "We have very low management turnover. People who have settled here don't want to go back." At Carl Zeiss in Oberkochen, it is said that, "Once they are here, they never want to leave." This brings us back to the low attrition rates discussed earlier.

Recruiting top talent abroad is even more difficult than at home. Against the backdrop of globalization, we have discovered that management internationalization is one of the biggest challenges and constraints for many hidden champions. Some follow the strategy of filling management positions with people from the country in question. At Phoenix Contact, the world market leader in electronic interfaces, every foreign company is headed by a local manager. IBG, a leader in welding technology, also employs only local managers abroad. Together with swift international expansion, such practices quickly lead to a high demand for foreign employees and managers. There is no miracle cure for this problem. Many hidden champions use their excellent reputation in their respective industries to lure experienced experts away from the competition, or from companies serving other stages in the value chain. Such newcomers dominate appointments for international management positions. Systematic global management development programs (typical of multinational companies) are still in their infancy at most hidden champions, although they are becoming more important as internationalization continues and business activities expand into non-western cultures.

Summary

A company's performance is the employees' performance. Managers only lead. The importance of soft factors such as corporate culture, employees' sense of identification, and motivation can hardly be overestimated. The cultures of the hidden champions are often distinctive and are not subject to the political correctness of our time. Instead, they are characterized by aspects such as long-term loyalty, intolerance of laziness, strict selection during the probation period, and a rural location. Our most important insights are as follows:

- The rapid and continuing growth of the hidden champions makes them significant job creators at home and abroad.
- New jobs are predominantly created outside the home markets; there the number of employees has more than doubled in the last ten years. Today,

about half the workforce is employed abroad. The hidden champions are becoming truly global companies with regard to personnel.

- This growth is coupled with a considerably higher level of employee qualifications. The percentage of university graduates has doubled and their absolute numbers have almost quadrupled. The hidden champions employ personnel who are able to deal with the increasing complexity of their businesses.
- The hidden champions see employee loyalty, training, motivation, and flexibility as pronounced competitive strengths. These factors are the foundation for the external competitive advantages in product quality, service, advice, and systems integration.
- Sickness and turnover rates are low. The hidden champions understand that a low employee turnover rate is strategically even more important than a low sickness rate. Their turnover rate is about one third of the national average. Low attrition retains expertise, cuts recruiting costs, and makes investments in training and continuing education profitable.
- It appears that hidden champions harness the potential of comebackers to the full. Comebackers represent a valuable pool of experienced employees.
- The hidden champions have high-performance cultures and are intolerant of shirkers. The likelihood that underperformance remains undetected is significantly lower than in large corporations. This is primarily a result of self-control at the team level, rather than specific systems or management monitoring.
- Hidden champions ensure that they have more work than people. This condition minimizes unproductive activity and proves to be an extremely effective productivity driver.
- These outcomes are achieved through the formation of small units that make the performance of individual employees transparent. The hidden champions are enthusiastic decentralizers.
- Multifunctional assignments and transfers between functions are more widespread at hidden champions than in large corporations. This flexibility results in better performance at lower cost.
- Hidden champions rely less on formal systems and key figures when it comes to mobilizing employees' creativity.
- About two thirds of the hidden champions have their headquarters in rural locations. This situation gives rise to mutual dependence between employer and employees, and promotes constructive cooperation.

- Attracting highly qualified employees is a serious challenge for the hidden champions. In this regard the rural location is a disadvantage. Recruiting activities should have a local or regional scope.

The hidden champions have distinctive corporate cultures. Their values are based on conservative principles such as hard work, strict selection, intolerance of underperformance, low sickness rates, and high employee loyalty—and most hidden champions are based in smaller towns. This all sounds far from the modern world, yet it is precisely how these companies create so many new jobs for people with a high level of education. Precisely these principles equip the hidden champions best for the twenty-first century.

Notes

1 It may be that without the new jobs abroad, more jobs would have been created at home.

2 John Naisbitt, *Mind Set! Reset Your Thinking and See the Future*, New York: Harper Collins 2006.

3 In the United States separations rates are reported on a monthly basis, see US Department of Labor www.dol.gov, www.bls.gov. Separations are terminations of employment that occur at any time during the course of the month. Over the years, the separations rates are at about 3% per month. We calculated the annual separations rate not by multiplying 3% by 12, but raising $(1.0-0.03)=0.97$ to the twelfth power, yielding an annual rate of 30.6%

4 See *Fortune*, April 2, 2007, p. 19.

5 Happiness is always on the other side of the river.

6 See Cyril Northcote Parkinson, *Parkinson's Law: Or the Pursuit of Progress*, 1957. The law says that work expands to fill the time available for it, or in another version: employees make work for each other to fill the time.

7 See Günter Rommel, Felix Brück, Raimund Diederichs and Rolf-Dieter Kempis, *Simplicity Wins*, Boston: Harvard Business School Press 1995.

8 *VDI News*, March 16, 2007.

9 *Bayerisch-Schwaebische Wirtschaft*, 1/2008, p. 95.

10 *Bayerisch-Schwaebische Wirtschaft*, 1/2008, p. 95.

11 Deutsches Institut für Betriebswirtschaft (DIB), Ideenmanagement/BVW in Deutschland, DIB-Report 2005; Frankfurt, April 2006.

12 *Süddeutsche Zeitung*, April 21, 2007.

Chapter 10
The Leaders

Is there one single explanation for the outstanding and continuing success of the hidden champions? If I had to choose one, it would without a doubt be the personalities at the top. Many of them are founders, but following generations of leaders have often made a lasting impression on me. What characterizes the leaders, their systems, and styles in these companies? Roughly two thirds of the hidden champions are still family-run, but the role of managers who are family members is declining. A particularly notable feature is the leadership continuity, based among other things on the appointment of leaders to top positions at an early age. On average, CEOs of hidden champions remain at the top for 20 years. Female leaders play a significantly greater role than in large public corporations. In contrast to the internationalization of the business itself, the internationalization of top management is still in its infancy, but it is already well advanced in some companies.

What types of personality do the leaders of the hidden champions have? Here we should distinguish between "founding entrepreneurs" and "entrepreneurs of perfection." The former identify 100% with their company, are single-minded, fearless, full of energy, and inspire others. Compared to them, the entrepreneurs of perfection from the later generations have a better education and are generally more sophisticated and urbane.

What leadership styles do we encounter at the hidden champions? The styles are ambivalent: authoritarian when fundamental principles are concerned, and participative when it comes to execution and implementation. And what about leadership succession, the greatest challenge for the hidden champions and an area in which their otherwise excellent performance is not always evident? The strength and long tenure of the leaders sometimes get in the way of handling the succession problem sensibly.

H. Simon, *Hidden Champions of the Twenty-First Century*,
DOI 10.1007/978-0-387-98147-5_10, © Hermann Simon 2009

Structures of Ownership and Leadership

In midsize companies, ownership and leadership structures are closely intertwined. These relationships are in flux and have changed considerably since the 1990s. Fig. 10.1 shows a ten-year comparison of the ownership and management structures.

Fig. 10.1 Ten-year comparison of ownership and management at the hidden champions

Ownership/management	Ten years ago (in %)	Today (in %)
Family with family management	62.3	51.8
Family with non-family management	14.1	14.5
Large corporations	21.1	16.1
Public	2.4	9.5
Private equity	-	8.1

Today, two thirds of the hidden champions (66.3%) are primarily owned by families (i.e., the family holds a majority share and therefore controls the company). Ten years ago, the share of family companies was more than 10% higher. In particular, the percentage of companies run by managers who are family members has fallen. Whereas almost two thirds of the hidden champions were run by family-member managers ten years ago, meaning that ownership and management were in the same hand; today this applies to only just over half (51.8%). Within the family-run companies, outside managers now play a greater role. The percentage of hidden champions listed on the stock exchange or owned by private equity investors has increased significantly, and there has been a clear opening towards capital markets. By contrast, the percentage of companies belonging to larger corporations has dropped. This is primarily the result of such corporations' focus on their core businesses within the last ten years. We can assume that the majority of hidden champions will soon be run by managers who are not family members. However, we should also bear in mind that managers in private equity-owned and publicly listed hidden champions often hold shares in the company, making them co-owners. Overall, we see a decline in the influence of families in ownership and management. Capital-oriented owners and managers play a considerably stronger role than they did ten years ago. Our findings regarding growth, market position, and profitability show that these changes seem to have benefited the hidden champions. The phenomenon and the success of the hidden champions are primarily a question of strategy and leadership rather than of family ownership.

The educational background of the hidden champions' leaders breaks down as follows: 55.7% received a business education, 53.4% a technical education, and 10.7% an education in a different field. These percentages add up to 119.8, so we can conclude that almost 20% of the company CEOs have double degrees, usually a combination of technology and business administration. Generally, hidden champion CEOs have both in-depth business and technical knowledge. This is due both to their education and to the low division of labor at the top of the company. More than one fifth lead their company alone and therefore bear sole responsibility for all functions. Compared to ten years ago, the level of education of CEOs has increased sharply.

Many members of the post-war founder generation were at the helm of the hidden champions until the 1990s. These founders often received no higher education. Examples are Reinhold Würth, Hermann Kronseder of Krones, Reinhard Wirtgen of the world market leader for street-recycling machines of the same name, and Heinz Hankammer of filter manufacturer Brita. They are typical of the post-war generation in this respect. Alois Kober founded AL-KO, the world market leader for mobile home chassis, in 1931. After World War II, his three sons Herbert, Kurt, and Wilhelm completed mechanical engineering apprenticeships in their father's firm and together managed the company in the following decades. Kurt Kober is still the CEO today. The managers of the subsequent generation all have university degrees and have also often studied abroad. Most founders of the last 20 years are university graduates, many with PhDs. Dr. Norbert Stein, founder of Vitronic, one of the market leaders in industrial image processing, studied electrical engineering, as did Dr. Aloys Wobben, who founded Enercon in 1984. Norbert Nold, founder of the tunnel-grid microscope manufacturer Omicron, studied economics. Prior to founding EOS, the world market leader in laser sintering, Dr. Hans J. Langer worked as a scientist for the Max Planck Institute for Plasma Physics. Stephan Wrage, founder of SkySails, the world market leader for towing kite wind propulsion systems for ships, studied industrial engineering. We will look at the various profiles of yesterday's and today's leaders of the hidden champions in more detail below.

The hidden champions prefer to promote their leaders from within. In total, 53% of the respondents strongly agreed with this statement (6 or 7 on a 7-point-scale) and only 9.8% disagreed (1 or 2 on the 7-point-scale).

However, integrating external managers is regarded as a problem by only 14.0%, while almost 40% take the view that this integration does not pose serious difficulties. Compared with the situation ten years ago, promotion from within the company ranks has lost some of its significance, and the appointment of managers from outside is on the increase. Some hidden champions have explicit guidelines about this, as do many large corporations (stipulating, for example, two thirds of management appointments from within and one third from outside). Plansee, the world market leader in high-performance powder metallurgic materials, aims to appoint eight out of ten managers internally. Only 20% of its future managers are supposed to be externally appointed. Andritz, a leader in paper and cellulose technology, states in its strategy principles, "Most of the managers come from the company's own ranks."

I have mixed impressions on this subject. The distinctive corporate culture of the hidden champions makes it difficult to integrate externally appointed leaders. There are several reasons for this, and the manager's close personal relationship with the CEO or owner is doubtlessly the most important. Two thirds of the hidden champions are still family-owned and run by one person or a small handful of people. If the external manager gets along well with these key people, the foundation for long-term cooperation is laid. But if friction occurs, the manager's departure is generally swift. In this respect, managers coming from the outside are also subject to the pattern for employees discussed in the previous chapter: high attrition at the outset of employment, very low attrition thereafter. Managers who have previously worked in similar companies find entry easier than those who come from large corporations. This is not surprising, because the leadership processes and structures in hidden champions, which are more heavily influenced by individuals, are very different from those in a more formally run large company.

A further barrier to attracting and integrating externally appointed managers can be the rural setting, as described in more detail in the previous chapter. If the manager's family is unwilling or unable to settle in, he or she faces constant tension. The place of residence can also be a difficult issue. Some managers prefer to live in a large city and commute to work, often staying away from home from Monday to Friday. This decision often leads to instability, however, because it is an obstacle to integration beyond the workplace. On the whole, the hidden champions and similar companies are well advised to ensure that enough young managers are promoted from within their own ranks. In spite of this, fresh blood from outside is also valuable. Plansee's 80:20 rule would appear to be a sensible target, taking into consideration the idiosyncratic corporate cultures of the hidden champions.

In the last ten years, there has been an interesting shift in the assessment of leadership strengths. Ten years ago, 73.9% of respondents said that the personality of the leader at the helm was a major strength of their company, and 79.8% considered continuity to be a significant advantage. In my recent study, "only" 50.8% consider the leader's personality to be a strength, whereas more than seven out of ten (73.3%) still specify continuity as such. This clearly reflects the transition from the charismatic founder personalities to a new generation of leaders who tend to be team players rather than lone fighters. The sustained importance of continuity is noteworthy. The hidden champions usually ensure a high degree of continuity by appointing managers at a young age. This even applies to CEOs, as we will see in more detail below.

How Crucial Is Leadership?

The employees, professionalism of the management, leadership, and other factors are key to the success of a company. But which of these factors is most important and how do they relate to one another? My own subjective view from many years of researching hidden champions is that leadership and entrepreneurship are the most important aspects of all. To investigate this subject, we carried out an analysis, using satisfaction with the profit situation as an indicator of company success. Fig. 10.2 shows the results.

Entrepreneurship/leadership clearly has the greatest influence on success. The other two factors are weighted more or less equally and are considerably less important than leadership. People at the top should of course combine entrepreneurship and professional management, but entrepreneurship/leadership is definitely the most important driver of the hidden champions' success.

Leadership Continuity

So far we have repeatedly encountered the subjects of stability, continuity, and long-term orientation. These aspects influence growth and market leadership goals, and are reflected in the hidden champions' low employee turnover, rare restructurings, and constant values. Continuity of a com-

Fig. 10.2 Importance of three factors for company success

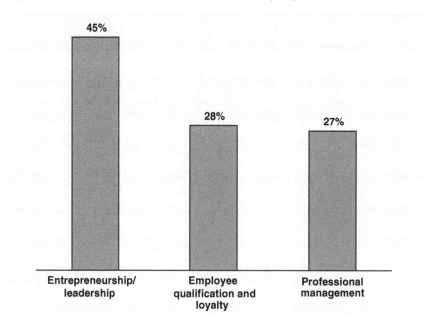

pany is rooted in continuity at the top. Hermut Kormann, CEO of Voith, comments on family-run companies, "The long-term nature of the strategy automatically follows from the continuity of the leaders and their long tenures."[1] Continuity in itself is neither good nor bad. A long tenure of a weak CEO is obviously a disadvantage, whereas a good leader who stays at the helm for a long time is a blessing. Surprisingly, continuity is seldom addressed in management literature. One of the exceptions is the book *Built to Last* by Collins and Porras, who compare the tenure of CEOs of successful, "visionary" companies with those of a control group of less successful firms.[2] In the "visionary" companies, referred to by the authors as the "best of the best," the CEOs achieve an average tenure of 17.4 years, while those in the control group remained in charge for only 11.7 years. All of the companies in this study were founded before 1945 and were therefore at least 50 years old when the study was conducted. Current tenures of CEOs of large public corporations are much shorter. According to a 2008 study by Booz & Company the average CEO tenures are 6.6 years in the USA, 5.1 years in Germany, and 9.4 years in Japan.[3]

The CEOs of hidden champions live in a very different world, their average tenure is 20.0 years. If we consider only those hidden champions founded before 1945 to enable a more direct comparison with the findings of Collins and Porras, the average tenure for CEOs is even 23.7 years. Interestingly, our figures have not changed significantly in the last ten years (20.0 for all hidden champions versus 20.6 and 23.7 versus 24.5 for the ones founded before 1945). By contrast, I am sure that the tenure at the "visionary" companies chosen by Collins and Porras have fallen drastically during the last ten years. The "visionary" category included companies such as 3M, Boeing, Ford, HP, Motorola, and Sony that have since then undergone several CEO changes, sometimes in response to serious crises. This categorization once again proves how ephemeral and fleeting such classifications of companies can be. The successful companies listed in the bestseller *In Search of Excellence*,[4] published in 1982, experienced a similar fate. Among these "excellent companies" were Amdahl, Digital Equipment, Western Electric, Kodak, Delta Airlines, Data General, and K-Mart, companies that no longer exist today or face serious difficulties. The hidden champions' continuity and capacity for survival appear far better.

It is revealing to examine a selection of older companies and their leaders from the point of view of continuity. Fig. 10.3 contains the data for hidden champions with at least two generations of leadership.

Fig. 10.3 Average tenure of hidden champions with two or more generations of leadership

Company	Founded in	Main product	Age of company	Number of CEOs	Average tenure per CEO
Schenck RoTec	1881	Balancing machines	126	3	42
August Friedberg	1884	Special screws	123	3	41
Witzenmann	1854	Flexible metallic elements	153	4	38
SEW-Eurodrive	1931	Drive technology	76	2	38
Ekato	1933	Industrial mixing machines	74	2	37
Carl Jäger	1897	Joss sticks, joss candles	110	3	37
Glasbau Hahn	1836	Showcases for museums	171	5	34
Erich Netzsch	1873	Pump/grinding technology	134	4	34
Dorma	1908	Doorlock systems	99	3	33
Bruns	1876	Tree nursery plants	131	4	32
Huf Haus	1912	Design timber-framed houses	95	3	31
Gerriets	1946	Stage curtains	61	2	31
Scherdel	1889	Valve and piston springs	118	4	29
McIlhenny	1868	Tabasco sauce	140	5	28
Robbe & Berking	1874	Silver cutlery	133	5	27
Wacker	1848	Construction equipment	159	6	27
ARKU	1928	Coil systems	80	3	27
Alberdingk Boley	1828	Coatings	180	7	26

Fig. 10.3 shows that average CEO tenures exceeding 25 years are no exception at the hidden champions. Some individuals have been at the helm for even more spectacular periods of time. Hans Riegel has man-

aged Haribo, world market leader in gummi bears, for 63 years, and Horst Brandstätter has headed Playmobil for 54 years. Long tenures of CEOs are of course not the only reason for a company's success, and extremely long periods of leadership can become a problem with regard to the office-holder's age and succession. A CEO's refusal to hand over to the next generation in good time can threaten the company's existence. Does a company enjoy long-term success because the same person runs it for many years? Or does a person remain at the helm for so long because the company is successful? Either of these causalities can apply, although leadership continuity as cause and success as the result is doubtless more important than success continuity as cause and leadership continuity as the result.

Continuity is not confined to the CEO. Kent Murdock who has served O.C. Tanner, world market leader in employee recognition programs in Salt Lake City, as CEO since 1997, joined the company as president in 1991. The current president, Dave Petersen, joined O.C. Tanner in 1983, but he's still not the longest tenured senior manager. Tim Treu, executive vice president of sales, originally joined the company in 1981, and Clark Campbell, senior vice president, has been onboard since 1979. Kaye Jorgensen, the senior vice president of human resources, began as a personnel clerk at O.C. Tanner in 1974. The management group—with an average tenure at O.C. Tanner over more than 20 years—does not sequester itself in king-sized offices on the top floor of some anonymous high-rise, but works from the low-rise buildings that constitute the O.C. Tanner campus, reflecting the company's de facto flat hierarchy and the motto "bureaucracy be damned."

Continuity should be considered in connection with the long-term goals discussed in Chapter 2. If the CEO of a young, small company aims to become the global market leader, he or she must think in terms of generations, because this goal cannot be achieved in a few years or even decades. There may be markets (related, for example to the Internet or new technologies, known as "born global markets") in which worldwide market penetration is possible in just a few years. But it takes two or three generations to build up a global presence in more conventional businesses. As we have seen, the bottleneck is typically not financial or technological, but people-related. Continuity is therefore the most essential aspect for long-term success. Accompanied by perseverance, it paves the way to global market leadership. By contrast, discontinuity is the surest way not to become a world market leader. If directions and priorities are changed frequently and if the people at the top change every few years, a company is highly unlikely to achieve the level of performance and the market position of a hidden champion. This is a big difference to the business units of large corporations, where management positions are frequently only stages *en route* to higher appointments and the current officeholders feel uneasy if their career progression is too slow and they stay in one place for too long.

Young to the Top

A long tenure and high continuity are possible only if CEOs are appointed to management positions at a comparatively young age. The possibility of a CEO being appointed at an advanced age and staying there to an even older age will not be discussed here. Early appointment to positions of leadership is intriguing from the aspect of hidden champions' continuity and long-term outlook, but it also relates to entrepreneurial energy and dynamism. Most founders of hidden champions set up their companies at a young age, especially the post-war generation. Reinhold Würth was 19 when his father died and he had to take over the firm, which had just one employee at the time; today, it has 65,000. Reinhard Wirtgen started his own company at the age of 18; Lothar Bopp was the same age when he founded Lobo Elektronik, now the market leader for laser shows. We still see fundamentally the same situation today, with the difference that many of the new founders have studied at university, so typically set up their companies in their 20s or early 30s. Stefan Vilsmeier founded Brainlab at the age of 22. Frank Asbeck was the same age when he launched his own engineering firm, which later gave rise to Solarworld. Ralf Dommermuth started United Internet at 25; Aloys Wobben founded Enercon at the age of 34. Mark Zuckerberg was 19 when he launched Facebook. Founder entrepreneurs are typically young, and this also applies to the founders of today's large corporations. Steve Jobs of Apple, Bill Gates of Microsoft, and Michael Dell of Dell were all very young when they set up their companies. Sergey Brin and Larry Page were in their mid-20s when they launched Google in 1998. William Hewlett and David Packard were just 26 when they formed Hewlett Packard. Most company founders are between 20 and 35 years old. This does not appear to have changed recently.

More surprising is the fact that hidden champions appoint later generations of CEOs at young ages as well, especially when compared to large corporations. Whereas managers in large corporations often only reach top management positions — especially the position of CEO — after the age of 50, the CEOs of the hidden champions sometimes take over the helm in their 20s, often in their 30s, and at the latest in their early 40s.

In family-run companies, the early appointment of a family member as the CEO may not be surprising, because their situation cannot be compared to that of large public corporations. Yet hidden champions also appoint young CEOs who do not belong to the family. Hartmut Jenner became CEO of Kärcher, the world market leader in high-pressure cleaning equipment, at the age of 34. Kay Fischer was 36 when he was named CEO of the leading jam manufacturer Schwartau. Robert Friedman was 38 when he took over control of Würth, a company that now posts revenues of $12 billion. I could list many other examples like these.

As with continuity, the starting age of the CEO has a double-edged nature. Young managers are dynamic, energetic, and have a long-term outlook, but they are also less experienced, may be overburdened by the complexity of their job, and may become agitated more easily. The great strengths of older managers lie in their long-standing experience, confident leadership, and mature personalities. These advantages and disadvantages should not be overgeneralized because each individual has his or her own traits. However, I take the view that top managers in large corporations are often too old when they reach the CEO position and that the hidden champions on balance reap considerable advantages from appointing their leaders at a young age. In view of growth and globalization, the energy emanating from these young managers is very important. The risk of not appointing the right person may be greater, but the advantages for the long-term development of the company will probably prevail overall. The managers mentioned here, and many others I have met, confirm this tenet.

Powerful Women

The subject of equal opportunities for women is a hotly debated one. Today, very few large corporations have female managers at the top level.[5] In some countries such as France and the USA, we see a higher proportion of women in the management echelons than in Germany or Japan. At the hidden champions, the leaders are often women, both in the operational management of the companies and in corporate governance. There are three typical roles in which women decisively influence and direct hidden champions:

- Assumption of leadership after the death of their husbands
- Supervisory board or advisory board membership
- Operational management as CEOs

I am not aware of many cases in which a woman alone founded one of today's hidden champions. However, women often play an important role as co-founders together with their husbands.

There are numerous cases in which a wife assumed the management of a company after the death of her husband. Maria-Elisabeth Schaeffler has owned and managed INA-Schaeffler, the world's second largest manufacturer of ball and roller bearings, since the death of her husband Georg in 1996. At that time, the company generated revenues of $2.1 billion; by 2007, revenues had increased to $12.2 billion. In 2008, INA-Schaeffler took over the automotive supplier Continental in a spectacular fashion. With 152,000 employees and revenues of $22.8 billion in 2007, Continental is twice as large as INA. The forces behind this are Maria-Elisabeth Schaeffler, her son Georg F.W. Schaeffler, a New York lawyer, and the non-family CEO Jürgen Geissinger. Another case in point: following the death of her husband Konrad in 1967, Ursula Wiegand took over the operational management of WIKA, today the world market leader in pressure and temperature measurement technology. WIKA's revenues in 1967 stood at $14 million. The first woman to be named entrepreneur of the year, Ursula Wiegand managed the company until her death in 1996 and during these 30 years increased the revenues 20 times to more than $280 million. Irene Kärcher assumed the leadership of Kärcher after her husband's death. In 1972, she appointed Roland Kamm, who was then 30 years old, as CEO and started out on a vigorous growth course. In 1974, Kärcher generated revenues of about $26 million, and by 2007, they had risen to $1.9 billion, 73 times as high. Following the death of Wilhelm Harting in 1962, his widow Marie Harting took over the management of the company founded by her husband until her son Dietmar, at the time 28, joined her in 1967. He still manages this market leader for industrial plug connections today. When Peter Pilz died in a plane crash in 1975, his wife Renate decided to raise their two children first. She formed an advisory board of which she became chairwoman, but initially left the management to externally appointed managers. Two years later, she joined the operational business and turned the family company into a leading worldwide provider of safety technology for automation. Within just a few years, the number of employees rose to 1,000 from 400 and the number of branches abroad to 23 from 7. Today, Renate Pilz and her children, Susanne Kunschert and Thomas Pilz, form the management team. Erwin Sick, the founder of sensor manufacturer Sick, died in 1988. His widow Gisela managed the company as the majority shareholder and is today honorary chairwoman of the advisory board. Sick has also had a female CEO, Anne-Kathrin Deutrich, from 2002 until her retirement in September 2006. After Reinhard Wirtgen died in an accident in Hungary in 1997, his widow Gisela took on the company management together with her sons Jürgen and Stefan, then aged 31 and 26. They developed Wirtgen from a company with revenues of about $550 million into today's Wirtgen Group with revenues of about $2 billion. Martina Hoerbiger also had a significant long-term effect on her company. After the death of her husband in 1945, she oversaw the development of Hoerbiger over several decades to become a worldwide leading provider of compressor, automation, and drive technology. With 5,300 employees, Hoerbiger posted revenues of about $1.3 billion in 2007. In many of these cases, the woman at the top made at least as valuable a contribution to the development of the hidden champion as the husband who died early. In some cases, globalization only began after the widow assumed the leadership. These achievements are just as important as those of the founders.

The supervisory and the executive functions are not always clearly divided in family-owned companies. Chairwomen or female members of advisory boards at the hidden champions often assumed these tasks at a relatively young age and exercise strong influence on the company. After five years on the Würth Group's management team, Bettina Würth assumed the top position on the board from her father in 2006 at the age of 44. Cathrina Claas joined the shareholders' committee of Claas in her mid-20s in 2001 and leaves us in no doubt as to her influence on the direction of the company today. In 2006, Heinz Dürr appointed his 43-year-old daughter Alexandra to the board of the world market leader for automotive paint shops. The mother of two has Ph.Ds in medicine and human genetics and heads the neurogenetic clinic at the Hôpital de la Salpêtèrie in Paris.

Few hidden champions were founded by a woman. One example is Eva Maria Roer, who founded DT&Shop in 1978. Within just a few years, her company had become the European market leader in dental laboratory supplies. Roer has not only created jobs for more than 200 employees, but is also chairwoman of the executive board of Total E-Quality, an organization dedicated to promoting equal opportunities for women at work. Several of the famous toy manufacturers were founded or co-founded by women. Margarethe Steiff (1847–1909) began producing soft toys in 1879. The "teddy bear" was introduced in 1902 and became immensely popular in the US due to President "Teddy" Roosevelt. A total of 974,000 teddy bears were sold in 1907. Steiff Knopf im Ohr[6] is still a strong brand today. Rosa and Max Zapf founded Zapf Creation, Europe's market leader for play and functional dolls, in 1932. Aenne Burda was also a founder in the wider sense of the word. In 1949, she took over a small publishing house and turned it into a worldwide business. By 1961, Burda Moden had become the biggest fashion magazine in the world; today, it is published in 16 languages and sold in 89 countries.

Numerous hidden champions have female CEOs. The management of Trumpf, world market leader in laser cutting machines, has been in the hands of Nicola Leibinger-Kammüller since 2005. Sybill Storz, daughter of founder Karl Storz, has been responsible for double-digit growth at her father's company every year since 1996 as the sole managing director of the market leader in endoscopic devices. Dorothee Stein-Gehring, granddaughter of the founder of Gehring, the world market leader in honing technology, represents the third generation of her family to manage the company. She was 44 years old when she took over the helm. In 2000, Horst Brandstätter, sole owner of the Playmobil manufacturer Geobra Brandstätter, appointed 41-year-old Andrea Schauer to manage the company instead of his sons. As the CEO of SKW Metallurgie, Ines Kolmsee runs the world market leader for industrial cored wire used in the steel industry. At clothing manufacturer Ahlers, Stella Ahlers has headed the executive board since 2005. In 2002, Kristina Strenger took over the family company with the same name, Europe's largest manufacturer of locking bars, from her father. Friedberg, founded in 1884 by August Friedberg, is today run by his granddaughter Ingrid Brand-Friedberg. The company produces connecting systems for the wind energy sector (including Enercon) and is the global market leader in this field. Eva Mayr-Stihl played a key role in the development of the world market leader in chainsaws. Although she was CFO and her brother Hans Peter Stihl CEO, she was always the *éminence grise* at this hidden champion. Katharina Geutebrück was appointed co-managing director by her father Thomas when she was 22. He then gradually withdrew and handed over the operational management of this leading company for video surveillance and motion sensors to his daughter. When the founder of Erhardt + Leimer died in 1972, his daughter Hannelore Leimer became CEO of this leading worldwide provider of web guiding, tension measurement, and control technology. As president of the local chamber of commerce and industry, Leimer is also the only woman in Germany to date to hold the highest office in a chamber of commerce and industry for two terms.

These numerous cases show that women play key roles as leaders of hidden champions. The majority of the female leaders are family members, with occasional externally appointed managers such as Andrea Schauer and Ines Kolmsee. These leaders prove that women can be high achievers in global companies. Women clearly have a better chance of advancing to top management in hidden champions than in large corporations. Significant potential is lost in many countries because of the failure to promote women to top management positions.

Internationalization of Management

The management teams of large multinational groups are becoming increasingly international. In Germany in 2004–2006, 40% of newly appointed executive board members of DAX[7] companies were non-German nationals. In 2007, 24% of all DAX executive board members were not German, and some large corporations have even more internationalized top management teams. Adidas has four executive board members from three countries. Fresenius Medical Care's seven executive board members are from five countries. Switzerland-based Nestlé is the largest food manufacturer in the world, and the ten members of its top management body represent nine nations. As we have seen in previous chapters, the hidden champions often generate 80%–90% of their revenues outside their home markets. On average, they employ about half their personnel abroad. They are very international in terms of where they generate revenues and where their workforce comes from. We also observe strong internationalization in middle management. I have attended numerous management conferences of hidden champions, where the typical attendance figures are between 50 and 100. In relation to the average number of employees (2,037), this represents approximately 2.5%–5.0% of the workforce. These extended management teams are likewise very international, often comprising members from more than 20 countries. Many hidden champions pursue a policy of appointing local heads for their operations abroad. Andritz, the market leader in paper and cellulose systems, includes this subject in its strategy principles: "The Andritz Group relies upon a divisional organization with local management. The nationalities of the business area managers and managing directors of Andritz affiliates reflect the geographical distribution of the companies and their employees. Whenever a company is acquired, great attention is paid to integrating the local management." International development of managers is becoming increasingly important. English is almost always the conference language, generally without simultaneous interpreting. It is assumed that all participants speak and understand English.

Some hidden champions have an exceptionally international scope. One example is Hillebrand, the world market leader in the shipping of wine and alcoholic beverages, which is headquartered in Mainz, Germany. The six-strong executive board has two French, one Dutch, one British, one American, and one South African member—but no Germans. Hidden champions from Switzerland are the most progressive when it comes to the internationalization of top management. The eight members of Logitech's management board come from six countries. At Givaudan, the global market leader for aromas and fragrances, the six-strong management team comprises two French, one Swiss, one Mexican, one Indian, and one American member. We find seven nationalities in the 12-strong management board of Richemont, the worldwide number two in luxury goods with headquarters in Geneva. Executive Chairman Johan Rupert is South African and CEO Norbert Platt is German. Patrick de Maeseneire, CEO of the market leader for industrial chocolate, Barry Callebaut, comes from Belgium; Valentin Chapero, CEO of Sonova, number one in hearing aids, is Spanish; and Calvin Grieder, CEO of Bühler, world market leader in grinding technology, is a dual citizen of Switzerland and the USA.

Generally, however, such an international makeup of top management is the exception rather than the rule at the hidden champions. Foreigners are less frequently found in the top echelons of the hidden champions than of large corporations. Compared to the 1990s, there have been no radical changes. There are various reasons for this. As we have seen, the top managers of roughly half the hidden champions are members of the founding family. In addition, top management teams are usually very small, typically comprising two or three, or at the most five people, so there are fewer top positions available than in large corporations. These small management teams work closely together and their cooperation is frequently built on shared cultural foundations. The rural location of many hidden champions mentioned earlier also makes it more difficult for foreigners and their families to settle in and integrate. No swift changes are expected in this regard. Although the global nature of the businesses may result in a call for top management to become more international more quickly, there are—as always—two sides to the coin. The advantages of a small management team with a shared culture and values should not be underestimated. In contrast to some of the cases discussed above, Groz-Beckert, world market leader for needles, prefers to fill management positions abroad with people who have a long track record of work in the German headquarters. As CEO Thomas Lindner explains, "You need a 'Stallgeruch.'[8] For us it's critical that our company philosophy is observed in every location. It takes 15 years for an adult to internalize our corporate culture."[9]

The business activities, the employees, and the management typically do not become internationalized at the same time and speed. First, revenues are internationalized, followed by the employees, then the extended management group. Finally, the top management positions are filled with people from different countries and cultures, but not until up to two generations later. The hidden champions are far advanced in the first three phases. Completion of the fourth phase is hard to forecast and will differ from company to company.

Personalities

Who are the people who lead the hidden champions? What types of personalities are involved in founding and expanding these companies? Why are they so successful? What differences are evident between the founders and the subsequent generations of managers? Would you recognize these leaders if you met them in the street? My wide-ranging experience is that CEOs of hidden champions cannot be pigeonholed. They are ordinary people like you and me, ranging from extroverts who personify the stereotype of the dynamic entrepreneur to extreme introverts. Some are gifted communicators, while others hate public speaking and are men or women of few words. When I visited them, some were always surrounded by their entourage while others hid in the privacy of their offices.

I will confine my following characterization to specific common traits I have observed among these leaders. I distinguish between two groups, "founding entrepreneurs" and "entrepreneurs of perfection." Founding entrepreneurs are generally founders, but can also be members of the second or third management generation who have taken an existing company from a modest basis to the position of a global player. Entrepreneurs of perfection inherit a sound international network, which they then expand and bring to perfection. This second part of the internationalization process can extend over several management generations. The personalities of the leaders in the perfecting phase are very different from those of the founding entrepreneurs. Another, less pronounced, distinction is that the more recent founders differ from the founders of the post-World War II years.

Founding entrepreneurs

Founding entrepreneurs tend to have five traits in common:

- Unity of person and purpose
- Single-mindedness
- Fearlessness
- Stamina and perseverance
- Inspiration to others

We will now briefly discuss each of these characteristics and their effects on company management.

Unity of person and purpose

CEOs such as Hans Riegel, Reinhold Würth, Kurt Kober, Heinz-Horst Deichmann, and Günther Fielmann form an entity with their companies. The person and the company are indivisible. It is said about Hans Riegel of Haribo, world market leader in gummi bears, that "his person and his company have always been an entity." Heinz-Horst Deichmann, whose father had a shoemaker's workshop from which the European market leader for shoes emerged, says, "I savored the smell of leather from my infancy. I love people and I love shoes." Such close connections remind us of the relationship between artists and their work. "For many creative people the life is the work. Some creative people integrate rather than separate their personal life and their work."[10] Jake Burton, the founder of Burton Snowboards from Vermont, advises, "Live your work."[11] This could be said to apply to most founding entrepreneurs. As genuine people who totally identify with their companies, they have persuasive power. Unlike many managers in large corporations, they do not just perform a function but live what they are and what they want to be.

This attitude toward work implies that money is not their primary driving force. Motivation is the result, first, of these leaders' identification and satisfaction with their work. Economic success follows in second place.

Robert Bosch, founder of Bosch, today's world market leader in automotive electronics, once said, "I would rather lose money than trust. It has always been unbearable for me to think that someone could say on examining my products that I produce something of inferior quality." Henry Ford held the same view, "When one of my cars breaks down I am to blame." Their absolute commitment and responsibility gives such leaders tremendous credibility among employees and customers. They have no reservations about their work and assume full responsibility. True leadership can never be play-acted; it must reside in the leader's core of beliefs and values.

Single-mindedness

Peter Drucker[12] wrote about two scientists he knew personally who made history, physicist Buckminster Fuller and communication expert Marshall McLuhan, "They exemplify to me the importance of being single-minded. The single-minded ones, the monomaniacs, are the only true achievers. The rest, the ones like me, may have more fun, but they fritter themselves away. The Fullers and the McLuhans carry out a 'mission'; the rest of us have interests. Whenever anything is being accomplished, it is being done by a monomaniac with a mission."[13] This hits the nail on the head for many leaders of hidden champions: they are monomaniacs with a mission. One may rephrase this a little more mildly as "targeted ambition," a phenomenon I will briefly outline with the case of a late friend. Gerhard Neumann, also known as "Herman the German", influenced the development of jet engines like no other.[14] He was born in Frankfurt (Oder), Germany, in 1917 and educated at a German engineering school. He spent the war years in China as a mechanic with the Flying Tigers and, for a time, as a CIA agent. After World War II, he became a U.S. citizen under a law passed specially for him. In 1948, he accepted a job at General Electric Aircraft Engines today, the world market leader for jet engines rose within just a few years to become CEO, and retained this position until his retirement in 1980. Under his leadership, both the best-selling civilian and military jet engines were developed. I first met Neumann in the 1980s and until his death in 1997 saw him often, both in the United States and in Germany. He was a "jet engine" himself, the true personification of dedication to his task. At four o'clock in the morning, he would wander through the plants of General Electric with his German shepherd dog. Whenever we met he animatedly turned the conversation to jet engines. As a reserve officer of the German Air Force and from my time with the 33rd Bomber Wing I am familiar with one of his creations, the GE J79 engine, which powered our Lockheed F-104G Starfighters, and I always enjoyed his stories.[15] He was obsessed by jet engines and the challenge of making them better and safer. And he did it.

Characters like Neumann are frequently found among the leaders of the hidden champions. These monomaniacs are everywhere within these companies. Beware of them as competitors! I have met them. If you wake them up at two o'clock in the morning and ask them what they are thinking about, they are sure to answer the same thing: their product, how to make it better, and how to sell it more effectively. The hidden champions' founding leaders may be no smarter than you or I, but they are more obsessed by their ideas, and their absolute commitment to their mission makes them unbeatable.

Fearlessness

Courage is a trait that is often ascribed to entrepreneurs. Berthold Leibinger, who led Trumpf to world market leadership in laser equipment, regards "courage to take a risk" as the most important entrepreneurial quality of all. However, I would prefer to call the hidden champions' founding entrepreneurs fearless rather than courageous. They appear to have understood and embraced the Chinese proverb "ignorance of your freedom is your captivity," and they do not have the same inhibitions and fears as other people so they can deploy their skills more effectively. It is very impressive to see how many of these leaders have conquered the world's markets without higher education or language skills.

Stamina and perseverance

Managers of hidden champions appear to possess inexhaustible energy, stamina, and perseverance. Presumably, the source of this energy is that they identify 100% with the task in hand. One American manager expressed it this way, "Nothing energizes an individual or a company more than clear goals and a grand purpose."[16] The fire burns in the founders of the hidden champions, often until retirement age and even beyond (which may be a problem in itself). Many are still actively involved in their companies beyond the age of 70. As I entered the office of many a hidden champion leader, I had an almost physical sense of the energy that emanated from the person. Is there a secret source of energy known to just a few?

Artists may acquire world fame as individuals, but in an economic enterprise nobody can single-handedly create a world market leader. He or she always needs cooperation with and support from others. Therefore, the fire that burns in a leader alone is insufficient; he or she must ignite it in others, usually in many others. According to leadership researcher Warren Bennis, we still don't know why people follow certain leaders and don't follow others.[17] A key capacity among the founding leaders of the hidden champions is to inspire others with enthusiasm for the task and encourage them to deliver the best performance they can. I can only say that they are very effective and successful in this respect. This cannot be attributed to superficial attributes such as manner or communication because many of them are not great communicators in the usual sense. I believe that the qualities discussed above—unity of person and purpose, single-mindedness, stamina, and perseverance—play a crucial role in the ability to ignite the fire in others.

Entrepreneurs of perfection

The management generation that has taken control at existing hidden champions in the last ten years is very different from the founding entrepreneurs. New CEOs often take over companies whose progress with internationalization is already far advanced. These younger leaders are now concerned with filling in the white spaces on the global map and driving further growth. The most obvious difference between the members of this generation and their predecessors is their better education. Practically all the younger CEOs have a university degree. Many of them have studied in foreign countries, especially in the USA or the UK, and have an excellent command of English. In addition, most have worked in several countries, either within their own company or in other enterprises. Typical founding entrepreneurs lacked such experience.

These experiences lead to a cosmopolitan outlook and a well-versed urbanity among young managers. The new CEOs move with great self-confidence and ease around the international business stage, and have known their company only as a global player. I consider this the most important addition to the profile of the founding entrepreneurs. Of course, strengths such as identification with the company and single-mindedness remain crucial for the younger CEOs. The entrepreneurial energy of the founders is supplemented by the management professionalism of the new leaders. My impression is that the younger generation of managers is acutely aware of the need to preserve the strengths of the hidden champions. Aspects such as ambitious goals, market leadership, focus, and global presence continue to top the list of priorities for the entrepreneurs of perfection. They combine these with the sophistication and international experience expected of an entrepreneur in a globalized business.

Leadership Styles

It is not easy to describe the leadership styles of the hidden champions' CEOs. Leadership always oscillates between the two poles of the leader's authority and the implementer's own responsibility. If the leadership style tends too strongly toward the leader's authority, we speak of "authoritarian leadership" and a commanding attitude. If the leader is too relaxed and fails to provide clear goals, the whole enterprise suffers from a lack of coordination and can descend into chaos. Overbearingly authoritarian leadership results in demotivation, working to rule or the resignation of employees who dislike this style. In this book, we have seen that the hidden champions are high-performance organizations. For this reason, we could presume that one particular style of leadership dominates, ensuring clear goal orientation on the one hand and high motivation on the other. How do the leaders of the hidden champions reconcile this apparent contradiction?

The answer is that the leadership styles are ambivalent, combining an authoritarian and a participative approach. Berthold Leibinger of Trumpf calls this leadership style "enlightened patriarchy." Employees referred to Dietmar Hopp, co-founder and the first CEO of SAP, world market leader in business standard software, as "a strict but caring patriarch." One hidden champion CEO, who wishes to remain anonymous, states that his leadership is both group-oriented and authoritarian. The style is authoritarian where the principles, values, and goals of the company are concerned; there is no discussion about core aspects, and those are decided and dictated from the top down. There is, however, a great deal of leeway in the participation of individuals and groups in deciding how these principles should be put into practice. Hidden champions' employees are usually faced with far fewer rules and regulations in carrying out details than their counterparts in larger, more bureaucratic organizations. This dual leadership style, both authoritarian and participatory, is typical of the hidden champions.

The decentralization discussed in Chapter 8 fits into this context. There, we saw that the companies that choose "soft" diversification follow a deliberate policy of decentralization. They give the new business units considerable latitude, but this works only if the freedom is accompanied by equally clear responsibility for the outcome. "The greater the success, the greater the degree of freedom," explains Reinhold Würth. Tom Peters refers to "decentralization and accountability" as two sides of the same coin. This duality characterizes the leadership styles of the hidden champions.

So who monitors the results? Lenin's maxim was, "Trust is good; control is better." Control can be exercised from the top and/or by a group. At the hidden champions, social control by the group and individual control rooted in the common value system play a more important role than in more anonymous large corporations. In this book, we have seen that group control affects many areas, such as selection during probationary periods, high-performance cultures, and employee loyalty. Social and individual control are integral parts of hidden champions' leadership.

The ambivalent nature of the hidden champions' leadership styles is reflected in the views of employees. I frequently observed somewhat divided attitudes towards the leaders. On the one hand there were complaints about the authoritarian style of the CEO. Yet, on the other hand, the same employees also expressed their admiration for the person at the top and had no desire to work anywhere else. This contrast reminds me of a student's attitude toward a strict, demanding teacher. The student may not like the teacher very much, but at the same time knows that he or she learns more than with a less demanding one. Effective leadership must unite both of these elements, and this is the polarity we find in many hidden champions.

Management Succession

Management succession is one of the greatest challenges facing the hidden champions. It is valid to say that the stronger the personality of the current leader, the more difficult it is for him or her to hand over power to the next management generation. "The story of strong company leaders often unfortunately ends with unsuccessful succession," reports Michael Stoschek, himself CEO of world market leader Brose for 34 years. This problem is particularly pronounced in the case of company founders. The dilemma between management continuity and the necessity of yielding power to the next generation becomes very evident here. I will mention three cases in point. The founder of a successful service provider is 67 years old. When I asked him about succession, he answered, "I feel very fit. I think I can play an active part in the management for another ten years. We have several people in middle management who would be able to take over the helm when I retire." Almost ten years earlier, I had asked him exactly the same question and received the same answer. The tone was similar in another conversation with the CEO of a hidden champion with revenues of more than $1.4 billion. He had just turned 72 and explained that the matter of succession had been taken in hand, but that he would be forced to continue until a suitable, tried-and-tested successor became available. In a third case, I threw in the towel after several meetings and said to the CEO in question, who was approaching 80, "We should stop talking about succession. You can't relinquish power. That's a fact. We'll just have to wait until you can't go on." He answered: "You're probably right," and has happily continued managing his company ever since.

Leadership succession at the top is decisive for the future direction of every company. This issue is particularly serious in family-run companies that wish to keep management in the family. According to one study, more than 90% of all family entrepreneurs want the company and its management to stay within the family. However, only a small minority of less than 10% makes it to the fourth generation. One third fails after one generation; two thirds of the remaining companies fail at the second change of generation.[18] As we saw in Fig. 10.1, the percentage of family-managed hidden champions has declined to 51.8% from 62.3% over a ten-year period. In these cases, there were no suitable successors in the family; potential successors did not wish to assume control, or the succession was disputed. Conflicts of interest between the older and younger generations or disputes among the heirs occur frequently. The older generation, particularly the founding members, typically want to keep the company and its management within the family. This attitude is understandable, but problematic for two reasons. First, it should not be assumed that sons or daughters automatically have, or have inherited, the ability to run a business. The fact that many hidden champions have become midsize, global, complex companies aggravates this situation. Managing such organizations requires a combination of skills that is seldom found. If the children are capable, so much the better, but otherwise the family should be prepared to pass the baton to a non-family person or team. The data show that this is increasingly the case, but we do not know whether this is attributable to necessity or choice.

A second aspect relates to the children's own life planning. In traditional societies, it was natural for the oldest son to take over the farm or trade of his father. There was no choice or freedom in this respect for the firstborn. The family tradition had to be continued, and this view of the world is still held by a number of entrepreneurs. Yet this often leads to conflict with the children, who want to make their own choice of profession and lifestyle.

Many founder-leaders underestimate how long it takes to develop a successor. The ideal retirement age depends on each CEO's constitution. My conversations with CEOs in their 50s typically reveal that they believe they still have many years in which to solve the succession problem. I think that by their mid-to late 50s, leaders should know who they want to succeed them. In our study, 79.6% of respondents answered that they had considered the issue of succession. Slightly more than half (52.2%) said succession had already been arranged, and 57.5% considered the last succession to have been successful. Is the figure of 57.5% high or low? Actually, it's close to the middle, so things may not be as bleak as individual succession failures might lead us to believe.

Yielding power is a second serious problem. Many leaders consider themselves irreplaceable and, perhaps subconsciously, do everything they can to make themselves so. Under these circumstances, the desire for continuity causes a succession crisis. And even if power is formally handed over to a successor, the retiring CEO often does not really withdraw, but keeps intervening. I have often observed a "retired" CEO continuing to come to the office every day or working from an office that is close enough to enable him or her to keep a watchful eye on things. The successor's frequent reaction is to resign—which from the point of view of the retiring CEO provides the ultimate proof that he or she is irreplaceable.

One interesting option increasingly used in recent years is to give the successor a share in the company, even if he or she is not a family member. In this way, the manager becomes a genuine co-owner and entrepreneur and has a stronger position than a mere employee, internally and externally. This approach has been successfully taken by Heinz Gries, founder of Griesson-de Beukelaer, a leading European cookie manufacturer. He gave his successor Andreas Land a share in the company and this liaison has proved successful for more than ten years. Klaus Fassin, founder-leader of the confectionery manufacturer Katjes, also gave his successor, Tobias Bachmüller, a 10% share in the company. In my discussions, I have observed a greater willingness to take this route. However, this tends to apply to younger family-owned companies rather than those that are several generations old. In longstanding family companies, the willingness to grant non-family managers a share remains limited. There are also several cases in the history of the hidden champions in which managers gradually took over the company for which they worked. Berthold Leibinger started out as an employee at Trumpf. Today, his family owns the company. Dietrich Fricke of Tente Rollen, the world market leader in hospital bed casters, worked as a manager at Tente and acquired the company when the second generation of the founding family did not wish to continue running the business. If the family values the company's continued independence and does not want it to be sold to a corporation, these are interesting ways of solving the succession problem. Some founders place their company in a trust or foundation. Cases in point are O.C. Tanner in Salt Lake City or Kjellberg Finsterwalde, the main competitor of Hypertherm. The founder of Hypertherm, Richard Couch, the world market leader in plasma cutting systems based in Hanover, New Hampshire, chose a different alternative. He transferred the ownership of the company, founded in 1968, to the employees.

A sale to private equity investors can also help to solve the problem of succession. As shown in Fig. 10.2, 8.1% or every 12th hidden champion is today in the hands of private equity investors. They usually give top management a share in the company, thereby making the business more attractive to high potentials and offering incentives consistent with the goals of the investors. I consider such models and the management solution associated with them to be a decisive success factor of private equity investors.[19] This approach naturally leaves the ultimate fate of the company open, because private equity investors generally want to exit after a few years. Whether or not the company then retains its independence depends on the type of exit.

In the past, many hidden champions were sold to larger corporations because the family could not solve the succession problem. Managing an increasingly complex company became too much for them, or the young generation simply lost interest. The fate of hidden champions acquired by larger corporations is mixed. If the corporation gives the company sufficient leeway, the hidden champion can flourish and experience rapid growth with the more plentiful resources available. Mannesmann was exemplary in this respect.[20] But more often the integration into a large corporation hampers the hidden champion, so that it withers over time. An executive board member of a corporation said to me, "We are always acquiring small companies with the hope of retaining their strengths and avoiding our weaknesses. But too often, in about three years' time, we find that we have imposed our weaknesses on them and destroyed their strengths." It may be possible to solve the succession problem by selling out to a large corporation, because it has a larger pool of young talented managers. Whether this is a guarantee for the long-term survival of a hidden champion is, however, a question that goes much deeper.

When it comes to developing future leaders, many hidden champions face the problem that they have fewer "training opportunities" for general managers than large corporations. The typical hidden champion is a one-product, one-market company with only a small number of general management positions. Managing a foreign affiliate is an excellent learning opportunity, but many subsidiaries are confined to sales and service and do not offer sufficient breadth. Managing them therefore involves narrower responsibilities than managing a division of a large corporation that covers every stage of the value chain. Hidden champions that have undergone soft diversification hold a stronger position in this respect. Their policy of decentralization provides ideal training positions for future general managers in the form of independent companies. This fosters not only new businesses, but also the development of future leaders.

Summary

The leaders are the source of the hidden champions' success. The fire that burns within them has enabled their companies to climb to the top in their markets. Regarding leadership, our conclusions are as follows:

- Two thirds of hidden champions are still family-owned, although the share of family-member managers has fallen considerably. Conversely, capital-oriented owners are playing an increasingly important role.
- Who owns the company is not key to its success. Leadership personalities are far more important.
- Globalization and greater complexity call for more professional management. The top managers of the hidden champions are today far better educated than their predecessors.
- Leadership continuity is extremely important. Hidden champion CEOs stay at the top for a very long time. This is one of the most striking differences between hidden champions and large public corporations.

- Many hidden champion CEOs come into office at a young age. This applies not only to family members, but also to externally appointed managers. In weighing up the energy of youth and the experience of age, large corporations might want to consider appointing younger top managers, as this could have a positive impact on continuity and dynamism.
- Female managers influence the development of many hidden champions decisively. In the vast majority of cases, these top managers belong to the family. They demonstrate the potential that remains unfulfilled in other companies, where so few women are appointed to top positions.
- Top management becomes internationalized long after other parts of business do. Only a few hidden champions already have a multinational management board.
- The balance between a set of shared cultural values and multinationalism is very delicate in view of the small size of the management teams. There is no reason for overly hasty internationalization.
- The "founding entrepreneurs" display very marked personality traits, including unity of person and purpose, single-mindedness, fearlessness, inexhaustible energy, and the capacity to inspire others.
- The subsequent generation of leaders, which we call "entrepreneurs of perfection," continues the course of globalization. These leaders are urbane, cosmopolitan, and well prepared for the challenges of the twenty-first century.
- Perhaps leadership styles ought to be ambivalent. This is definitely the style that we find among the hidden champions. Their leaders are authoritarian when it comes to basic values, but participative on how to put these values into practice. Management is "both-and" rather than "either-or." Leadership requires balancing apparently irreconcilable poles.
- This is the point at which decentralization and responsibility meet. The hidden champions that pursue soft diversification are deliberate decentralizers, but they also require their managers to be fully accountable for the results. The two principles of decentralization and responsibility are inextricably linked.
- Management succession is a serious problem for every company, but for family firms it is "the" problem. Handling succession is often the greatest weakness of strong leaders because they find it difficult to relinquish power. It is essential to address this issue early and to find a solution. Family firms are well advised not to assume that management should remain in family hands. New models such as private equity or shares held by managers should be considered.

The lessons from this chapter on leadership are quite varied. We have seen that the leaders are the ultimate reason for the success of the hidden champions. But it also becomes clear that they are all too human. The hidden champions' managers are neither superhuman nor magicians, but they do share certain traits that can lead to impressive results. In this respect, they are role models for others. They demonstrate that leadership should have two sides: the leader is responsible for the fundamental direction and values of a company, whereas the details of execution are left to the employees. Continuity is crucial for the long-term success of a company, and it requires that the leaders reach top positions at a young age. Finally, every leader should remember that life does not go on forever, so it is vital to arrange succession early.

Notes

1 Hermut Kormann, "Gibt es so etwas wie typisch mittelständische Strategien?," Discussion Paper No. 54, University of Leipzig, Economics Faculty, November 2006.

2 See James C. Collins and Jerry I. Porras, *Built to Last: Successful Habits of Visionary Companies*, New York: Harper Collins 1994.

3 *Focus Money*, 37/2008, p. 10.

4 See Thomas J. Peters and Robert H. Waterman, Jr., *In Search of Excellence*, New York: Harper & Row 1982.

5 In 2009, only one of the 30 German DAX companies, Siemens, had a woman as an executive board member, and there was only one woman executive board member in the 100 largest companies. Of the American Fortune 500 in 2008, 15, or 3%, had female CEOs, *Fortune*, May 18, 2009.

6 "Steiff button in the ear."

7 DAX (Deutscher Aktien-Index), index of 30 largest public corporations in Germany, similar to the Dow Jones Index in the US.

8 "Stallgeruch" (stable smell) is a quality ascribed to someone you recognize as coming from the same stable. There is no real English equivalent.

9 *Süddeutsche Zeitung*, April 21, 2007.

10 D. B. Wallace and H. E. Gruber (eds.), *Creative People at Work: Twelve Cognitive Case Studies*, New York: Oxford University Press 1989, p. 35.

11 See *Fortune*, April 2, 2007, p. 19.

12 My late friend Peter Drucker, the most famous management thinker of our era, was enthusiastic about the hidden champions. I often discussed my ideas, findings and conclusions with him. From his early years in Austria and Germany he was well familiar with the environment and the history of the hidden champions. He truly

understood these world market leaders and was always interested in their development. But we missed the last opportunity to share my ideas for the present book. We had made an appointment for November 12, 2005 at his home in Claremont, California. When I called to confirm the evening before, I was informed by Doris Drucker, his wife for nearly 70 years, that he had passed away that morning. I owe Peter Drucker many ideas and helpful suggestions for this book.

13 Peter F. Drucker, *Adventures of a Bystander*, New York: Harper Collins 1978, p. 255.

14 See Gerhard Neumann, *Herman the German: Just Lucky I Guess*, New York: Author House 2004. A biography of Gerhard Neumann is available on Wikipedia.

15 The Lockheed F-104 Starfighter was a single-engined, high-performance, supersonic aircraft. A total of 2,578 F-104s were built, 914 of which were F-104G models for the German Air Force. The Starfighter was powered by the General Electric J79 engine, a creation of Gerhard Neumann. For their part in designing the J79, Gerhard Neumann and GE Aircraft Engines were jointly awarded the highly prestigious Collier Trophy. Clarence Johnson also received the Collier Trophy for designing the Starfighter.

16 Lee Smith, "Stamina: Who has it. Why you need it. How you get it.," *Fortune*, November 28, 1994, p. 71.

17 Warren Bennis, *Why Leaders Can't Lead*, San Francisco: Jossey-Bass 1989.

18 Deutsche Bank (Ed.), *Geschäfte mit Geschwistern*, Frankfurt, June 2006.

19 I often discussed this topic with Dr. Dieter Vogel, former chairman of the executive board of ThyssenKrupp, who is now a private equity investor. He considers the participation of top management to be a key factor in the success of private equity investors.

20 Mannesmann was one of the largest industrial corporations in Germany. It probably gave rise to the biggest number of hidden champions in history. In the 1990s Mannesmann began to diversify very successfully into mobile telecommunications. After a heated battle it was taken over by the British telecom giant Vodafone in 2000—to date the largest corporate merger ever, with a value of $172 billion at current rates. Mannesmann was subsequently broken up and all manufacturing-related operations were sold off. Many current hidden champions emerged from this spinoff.

Chapter 11
Hidden Champions: Audit and Strategy Development

How can a strategy be developed that turns a company into a hidden champion? Where is the best place to start? What results does strategy development achieve? What is the role of consultants in this process? We will address these and similar questions in this chapter. There are naturally no standard answers. The lessons of the hidden champions are not a checklist to be worked through, automatically resulting in a strategy for success. There is not even a standard procedure for strategy development. The right approach, taking either the market or the company's competencies as a starting point, must be determined for each case individually. Despite this warning against one-size-fits-all approach, the strategy development process usually encompasses the following stages:

- Analyzing the current position: Where do we stand? In modern management this is referred to as a strategy audit.
- Setting strategic goals: Where do we want to go?
- Defining the business/market: What is our business? In which market do we want to do business?
- Analyzing internal competencies: What are we capable of? What skills do we have? Innovativeness, financial resources, and personnel are examined here.
- Analyzing the market/customers: How large is our market? How quickly is it growing? Who are the customers? What do they expect from us? How much are they willing to pay?
- Analyzing the competition: Who are our current and potential competitors? What are our competitive advantages and disadvantages? This aspect includes the issue of costs.
- Establishing plan of action: Who will do what, and when?
- Anticipating outcome analysis/forecast: What outcomes do we expect?

H. Simon, *Hidden Champions of the Twenty-First Century*,
DOI 10.1007/978-0-387-98147-5_11, © Hermann Simon 2009

We could extend and refine this list. In recent decades, numerous methods and tools have been designed and proven valuable for strategy development. In this chapter, we will explore a number of issues and methods and describe how hidden champions have addressed and applied them. To do this, we will refer to "modules" that can be combined to create a comprehensive concept for a hidden champion strategy.

What Is Strategy?

Strategy is the art and science of developing and employing a company's resources to secure profitable, long-term survival. As strategy itself always implies creating something original and different, strategy development cannot be a pure science. The French philosopher Henri Bergson pointed out in 1907 that science must deal with repeatable phenomena if new laws are to be discovered. Strategy, on the other hand, cannot be repeated or imitated. The great error of many strategists is that they are continuously looking for the laws of strategy. They study the success stories of yesterday in order to imitate them. This is the wrong course, even if it involves following the lead of the hidden champions.[1] Superior strategies result only from creativity, originality, and lateral thinking. An American proverb states, "Find out what everybody else is doing, then do it differently." The only problem is that no one tells us what "differently" means. We have to find this out for ourselves.

Strategy is all-encompassing. It is neither long term versus short term nor large scale versus small scale. It is neither central nor decentral. Carl von Clausewitz, the father of military strategy, accurately outlined the purpose of strategy, "Strategy must go with the army to the field in order to arrange particulars on the spot, and to make the modifications in the general plan which incessantly become necessary. Strategy can therefore never take its hand from the work for a moment."[2] Strategy requires intelligence and intuition, reason and emotion, will and analysis—and people to turn ideas into action. These remarks are intended to forestall naive beliefs about strategy tools and methods.

Hidden Champion Strategy: For Whom?

Since the concept of the hidden champions first emerged around 20 years ago, I have, in my role as a consultant, used their lessons for the strategy development of companies of different sizes and industries. The strategies based on these principles usually lead to a noticeably stronger market position and to sustained profitable growth. Here are five examples:

- A textile machinery manufacturer applied the hidden champions' strategy with vigor and increased its world market share to more than 70% from 40% in five years.
- A manager who had previously headed a global market leader for chemical plants took over an ailing competitor, implemented a hidden champion strategy, and edged out his former company to become the number one on the world market within six years.
- A service provider focused on a narrow market niche from the time of its foundation. It began the internationalization process very early and achieved world market leadership within 15 years.
- A raw materials supplier decentralized its business divisions according to customer groups. The divisions adhere to the principles of the hidden champions and have experienced tremendous improvements in their market positions.
- A mechatronics company was already the world market leader in the premium segment, but an insignificant player in the low-price segment. An analysis of its internal competencies revealed that it would have been virtually impossible for the company alone to develop the capacities necessary to improve its standing there. The company therefore took over a leading provider in the low-price segment, thereby achieving market leadership in both segments. Both units are managed decentrally. The firm has quadrupled its revenues in the last ten years and increased its profitability eight times over.

These cases show that the hidden champion strategy can be applied to companies of varying sizes and starting positions.

Hidden Champions – Audits

Developing or modifying a strategy should always start with an analysis of the point of departure. Only if the current status is fully understood can the right course for the future be set. There are two distinct approaches to assessing strategic positions. The first is based on objective, quantitative data such as financial indicators (including return on equity and equity ratio), market data (such as market share and the number of competitors), and internal indicators (R&D intensity, sickness rates, and so forth). Although this approach captures relevant aspects of strategy, it is naturally limited in scope. One disadvantage is that the data necessarily relates to the past. The second approach relies on more qualitative data based on assessments from the company's customers, employees or other experts. This data is subjective in nature. While usually recorded using quantitative scales, the findings cannot be objectified. Aspects that fall into this category include closeness to customer, employee motivation, and quality of management.

For each approach, we will now examine a module that can be used for a strategy audit. These two modules complement one another.

Module 1: Hidden Champion-Benchmarking

A situation cannot be classified as good or bad unless it is compared to another. Even apparently absolute judgments are implicitly based on comparisons. A statement such as "a 10% return on investment is too low" implies a comparison in the sense that a satisfactory return on equity would have to be higher than 10%. A simple, obvious form of comparison is to use performance indicators from other companies as benchmarks. Alternative comparisons can be made with indicators originating from the company itself (such as from various business units) or from outside sources (such as capital markets, banks, and industry associations).

The first question for benchmarking concerns which peer group to use as a basis for comparison, as this decision affects the outcome. The following situation illustrates the problem. A hidden champion that builds plants for the food industry is dissatisfied with its growth performance, although its profitability appears acceptable. It conducts a benchmarking study against its direct competitors and performs quite well; in most indicators it is above average. When the scope of the benchmarking study is extended to include the plant construction sector as a whole, the company's results look much poorer. Comparison with the hidden champions leads to even more disadvantageous results. In this situation, there is no objective truth. On the one hand, it is important not to select weak peer groups as a basis for benchmarking. On the other, it may not make sense to compare an engineering company or a retailer with a pharmaceutical manufacturer. It does no harm to apply benchmarks with different backgrounds. This can only contribute to gaining deeper insights.

The information in our hidden champions database enables very detailed benchmarking processes. We can illustrate this using various key performance indicators (KPIs). Fig. 11.1 shows the distribution of the hidden champions' pretax return on investment (ROI).[34] The figures at the bottom are the mean, the median, and the boundaries between the first and second quartiles (Q12) and the third and fourth quartiles (Q34). Exactly half of all companies lie between Q12 and Q34. One quarter lies below Q12 and one quarter is above Q34.

Fig. 11.1: Distribution of the hidden champions' pretax ROI

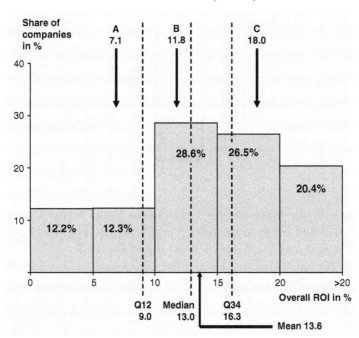

Every company can see from this distribution how it fits in vis-à-vis the hidden champions. The peer group can of course be redefined for benchmarking purposes (companies in the same industry, of a similar size, and so forth). At the top of Fig. 11.1 we show the ROI for three companies, A, B and C, all from the same sector. Company A's return on investment is 7.1%, thus in the lowest quartile Q1. Company B's 11.8% falls into quartile Q2, and C has an ROI of 18.0%, falling into quartile Q4.

The R&D ratio (R&D expenditures divided by revenue) provides a second illustration.[5] The bottom of Fig. 11.2 shows the distribution of this

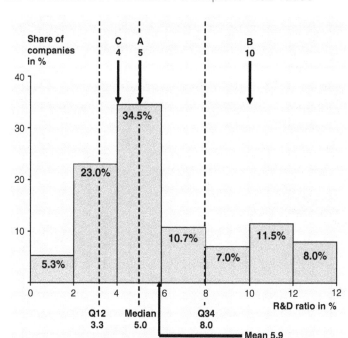

Fig. 11.2: Distribution of the hidden champions' R&D ratios

indicator with the mean and median, and the limits between quartiles 1 and 2 (Q12) and between quartiles 3 and 4 (Q34). The R&D ratios for companies A, B and C are shown at the top of Fig. 11.2.

The R&D ratios lead to a more differentiated assessment than the sole consideration of ROI as shown in Fig. 11.1. Company C, which was in the top quartile in ROI, only ranks in quartile Q2 as regards its R&D ratio and has the lowest R&D ratio of the three companies. Conversely, company B, which only reached the second quartile in ROI, has a very high R&D ratio. Company A also has a far better R&D ratio (in quartile Q3) than it has in ROI, where it only reaches the lowest quartile. These observations lead to important strategic insights, in this instance, for example, regarding short-term versus long-term orientation. Company C should, for example, try to significantly increase its R&D ratio at the expense of its short-term ROI.

Our database of hidden champions contains many key performance indicators that can be used for benchmarking purposes. Fig. 11.3 shows benchmarking results for two hidden champions employing 32 performance indicators. We do not explicitly specify the distribution of these indicators here; instead we use a rougher classification into quartiles. Some

	Q1	Q2	Q3	Q4
Overall ROI				A,B
Growth rate - revenues			A	B
Equity ratio				A,B
R&D ratio				A,B
Absolute world market share		A	B	
Absolute European market share		A	B	
Absolute German market share		B		A
Relative world market share	A		B	
Relative European market share	A		B	
Relative German market share		B		A
Change in market share			A	B
Number of competitors worldwide		B		A
Number of foreign companies		A,B		
Export share		A	B	
Revenue share Europe (w/o Eastern Europe)			A,B	
Revenue share Eastern Europe	B			A
Revenue share USA		A,B		
Revenue share Asia		A	B	
Service/spare parts revenues		B	A	
Age of company	B	A		
Employee growth rate			A	B
.... in home market			A	B
.... abroad		A		B
Sickness rate	A	B		
Employee turnover			B	A
Average CEO tenure		A,B		
Ratio of university graduates			A	B
Ratio of trainees	B		A	
Percentage of value added	A			B
Vertical integration level		A	B	
Travel budget ratio		B	A	
Improvement proposals per 100 employees	B		A	

indicators in Fig. 11.3 are "directed" or "directional" in the sense that one direction means "better". All else being equal, a higher ROI or a lower sickness rate, for example, is always better. Other indicators do not have such a "directionality." Examples are the service/spare parts revenues, the travel budget ratio, and the age of the company. If we choose to add up the assessments to create an overall performance index, all characteristics would have to be "directed," or we could take only "directed" indicators into consideration. Quartile 4 would then always be best, and a higher total would mean a better performance. However, the most interesting insights are gained from comparing the various key performance indicators individually. Where and how does the company in question diverge from the hidden champions overall or from its peer group? What is the reason for this divergence? Is it deliberate or unwarranted? If it is unwarranted, how can it be corrected? These questions resulting from the benchmarking process form the point of departure for strategy development and adjustment. The relevance of the benchmarks depends on the indicators, the industry and the peer group selected. It makes little sense to compare the R&D ratios of a service provider and an electronics company. By contrast, cross-sector comparisons regarding continuity of leadership, employee turnover or internationalization can produce valuable insights.

In Fig. 11.3 we show the quartile positions for two companies, A and B, in the 32 key performance indicators. A and B are very innovative, research-intensive hidden champions from the high-tech sector. They are positioned in the top two quartiles for indicators such as return on investment, revenue growth rate, equity ratio and R&D ratio. By contrast, they differ widely in other KPIs. A has a significantly lower market share in Europe and in the world than B. A remains strongly dependent on Germany. Although B is a younger company, its internationalization is much further advanced. However, this does not apply to Eastern Europe, for which B's revenue share is in the lowest quartile. Although both companies have lower sickness rates than the median figure for the hidden champions, the reverse is true for employee turnover. Both companies would be well advised to tackle this weak spot. B is in the lowest quartile in improvement proposals, so this area too requires attention. A is in the lowest quartile for percentage of value added and in quartile 2 for vertical integration—very different from B and the hidden champions in general. We should note that such benchmarking is not a strategy generator. But our brief discussion points to the areas in which action must be taken.

Module 2: Qualitative Hidden Champion-Audit

In this book, we have encountered numerous strategic principles and patterns of conduct of the hidden champions and distilled many lessons from them. It makes sense to assess a company's strategic position and approach in the light of these lessons. As the lessons contain complex constructs, they can only be subjectively assessed, usually with the aid of a quantitative scale. Here, as throughout our study, we use a scale from 1 to 7. Other scoring systems (such as rankings) can also be used for such an assessment. The involvement of people who can make well-founded judgments of the relevant facts and circumstances is more important than the intricacies of the measurement methodology. Such assessments are usually obtained during interviews and workshops. My experience from numerous projects of this kind clearly shows that the discussion and understanding is often as important as—or even more important than—the actual outcome.

The first step is to draw up the list of strategic attributes or lessons. This list can be general or detailed. Our database contains dozens of variables that can be used for purposes of comparison. In the second step, each attribute is assessed in terms of the need for strategic action (i.e., the pressure or the importance of the problem). The need for action differs depending on the sector or company, so individual assessments are necessary. In the third step, the company's performance in each attribute is rated. This three-step method has been thoroughly tried and tested in hundreds of projects. We will illustrate the qualitative hidden champion audit for two companies.

Fig. 11.4 shows the strategic attributes and scales for the company performance and the strategic need for action. In this example, we will restrict ourselves to the most important lessons learned from the hidden champions. These attributes can be further subdivided as necessary.

Fig. 11.4: Questionnaire for a qualitative strategy audit

Strategy characteristic	Strategic need for action 1=low, 7=high	Company performance 1=low, 7=high
1. Ambitious targets	1 2 3 4 5 6 7	1 2 3 4 5 6 7
2. Focus	1 2 3 4 5 6 7	1 2 3 4 5 6 7
3. Soft diversification	1 2 3 4 5 6 7	1 2 3 4 5 6 7
4. Globalization	1 2 3 4 5 6 7	1 2 3 4 5 6 7
5. Closeness to customer	1 2 3 4 5 6 7	1 2 3 4 5 6 7
6. Service portfolio	1 2 3 4 5 6 7	1 2 3 4 5 6 7
7. Innovation	1 2 3 4 5 6 7	1 2 3 4 5 6 7
8. Competitive advantages	1 2 3 4 5 6 7	1 2 3 4 5 6 7
9. Value chain	1 2 3 4 5 6 7	1 2 3 4 5 6 7
10. Decentralization	1 2 3 4 5 6 7	1 2 3 4 5 6 7
11. Employee motivation	1 2 3 4 5 6 7	1 2 3 4 5 6 7
12. Leadership	1 2 3 4 5 6 7	1 2 3 4 5 6 7

In order to relate the need for strategic action to performance and to determine the extent to which a company follows the lessons of the hidden champions, we recommend a two-dimensional matrix, as used in Chapter 7, to illustrate competitive advantages. The need for action is shown on the vertical axis, performance on the horizontal axis. Fig. 11.5 illustrates matri-

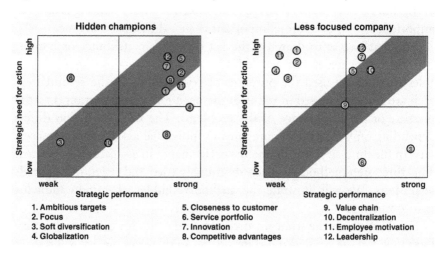

1. Ambitious targets	5. Closeness to customer	9. Value chain
2. Focus	6. Service portfolio	10. Decentralization
3. Soft diversification	7. Innovation	11. Employee motivation
4. Globalization	8. Competitive advantages	12. Leadership

ces for two companies. Ideally, the need for action and performance should be on the diagonal running from top right to bottom left. The matrix on the left applies to a hidden champion that implements the lessons relatively well. The matrix on the right shows the situation of a less focused company where the need for strategic action and performance are not well aligned.

Comparing the profiles of the two companies' need for action is interesting in itself. There are clear differences regarding decentralization, ambitious targets, and service portfolio, for example. These discrepancies can be explained by the marked differences in the companies' starting situations. At the hidden champion in the left matrix, we observe a high degree of consistency between the need for action and the strategic performance. The most urgent issue (number 6) appears to be expanding the service portfolio to strengthen advice and systems solutions. There is only medium pressure to act on competitive advantages (number 8) and globalization (number 4) because the company's performance in both attributes is good. The situation is very different for the less focused company. Several hidden champion principles are being neglected here. More ambitious goals (number 1), more decisive globalization (number 4), and stronger employee motivation (number 11) are required to attain the position of a hidden champion. Likewise, the company needs to work on its focus (number 2) and competitive advantages (number 8). The extension of the service portfolio and soft diversification should be scaled back, and the resources saved there should be diverted to improve the performance in the other attributes. By contrast, the company on the right is consistently positioned with regard to innovation, closeness to customer, and decentralization. The company plans to pursue a hidden champion strategy. It will take a long time to achieve a consistent profile like that shown in the left matrix. I would like to emphasize that Fig. 11.5 provides only a diagnosis. The audit reveals strengths and weaknesses in the strategy profile and indicates what should be done, but it does not stipulate how to get from A to B. This requires further-reaching and original thinking.

Strategy Development

Strategy development has two aspects: content and process. Content encompasses the formulation of goals, business/market definition, competitive analysis, and so on. We will illustrate this content aspect by selected cases without striving for completeness. Strategy development is also— or even primarily—a process. Arie de Geus, a former strategy planner at Shell, considers the learning in the course of this process to be even more important than the actual outcome.[6] Employees of different levels must be involved in strategy development to achieve company-wide strategic learning. Is this compatible with the strong leadership of the hidden champions? In Chapter 10, we saw that leadership is double-sided: authoritarian on principles, participative in the details of execution. This dual nature should also be applied to strategy development, by including both top-down and bottom-up elements. Content and process cannot be strictly divided from one another.

Strategy Development as a Process

Fig. 11.6 shows a strategy development process of a hidden champion. The company is an industrial service provider with approximately 500 employees and 17 foreign subsidiaries.

The process began in July when the executive board set the direction for the targets and the overall strategy. Based on these stipulations, the teams responsible for segments and countries drew up more detailed strategies and relayed them back to the board. Once assessed and revised, the targets and plans were passed back to the middle management level for dis-

Fig. 11.6: Top-down, bottom-up strategy development

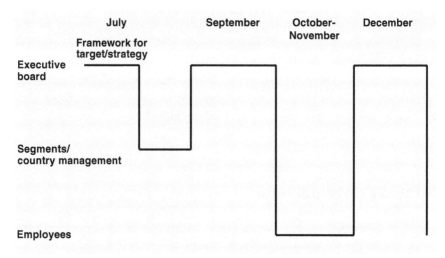

cussion with the employees. This route was intended more to enlist the employees' buy-in than to elicit further suggestions, although the latter were not expressly ruled out. Further minor corrections were made, and the new strategy was approved by the executive board at the start of December and publicized at various events. The process involved numerous workshops, interviews, and analyses that were overseen by a consultant. Such a process sensibly combines top-down and bottom-up elements, in line with the double-sided leadership style that is widespread among the hidden champions. The involvement of as many employees as possible in the process is helpful for the idea of "strategic learning" propagated by de Geus.

Module 3: Target-setting

In the case described above, defining the company's business and market was not really a problem. The company was clearly positioned and knew what it wanted. However, setting goals for the next ten years proved a real challenge in view of the firm's strong growth in the past. Ten years previously, the company had set the strategic target of doubling its revenues every three years, corresponding to an annual compound growth rate of approximately 25%. The burst of the Internet bubble in 2001 exerted serious pressure, but a compound annual growth rate of 21% was nevertheless achieved for the decade 1998–2007. In these ten years, the company's revenues rose to more than $110 million from about $14 million and the number of employees increased to about 400 from 60. The CEO was known for demanding ambitious growth targets and pursuing a course of rapid globalization. On the other hand, it was generally accepted that the high degree of specialization required the company to develop its own specialists from within, and that personnel remained a bottleneck. The board set the following targets to the division and country managers for the new ten-year strategy:

- Double revenues every three to five years, corresponding to an annual growth rate of between 15% and 25%.
- Internationalize more rapidly.
- Strengthen the market position while retaining focus. The strong fragmentation of the market made it impossible to estimate absolute market shares, but the company estimated that its relative market share was double that of its strongest competitor.

Once the process shown in Fig. 11.6 had been completed, and following some heated debates, these goals were formulated for 2017:

- Revenues: $515 million, corresponding to an annual growth rate of 16.7%
- Employees: 1,200, corresponding to an annual growth rate of 14.8%
- Growth rates for the divisions between 15.2% and 23.4%

The very fast overall growth, involving an almost fivefold increase in revenues and a fourfold increase in the number of employees within ten years, forces this hidden champion to continue focusing on personnel development in the coming decade. The bottleneck of recruiting qualified employees does not permit faster expansion, especially if newcomers are to be prepared for and deployed to faraway countries and cultures. The greatest challenge is gaining access to the Asian markets. My earlier statement that globalization takes two to three generations definitely applies to this company. Today, we can say that involving as many employees as possible in setting strategic goals resulted in a healthy balance between growth ambition and growth realism. An additional result is that the company's growth targets were sensibly quantified, although a reliable quantification was not possible for absolute and relative market shares. The board was confident that it could defend its market leadership if the ambitious goals were realized.

Module 4: Integrated Strategy, Business/Market Definition

Integrating market and technology is a particular strength of the hidden champions. Two thirds of our survey respondents said that they balance these two aspects well, while only 19% of large corporations achieve such a balance. Strategy must always endeavor to be both externally (market) and internally (resource) oriented and to avoid one-sidedness. The challenge is to give both sides the same weighting. We refer to this balance as integrated strategy. Fig. 11.7 illustrates the concept.

Fig. 11.7: The concept of integrated strategy

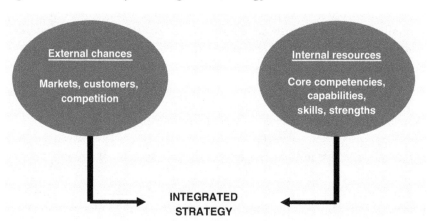

This integrated approach makes the strategy development considerably more complex, because both sides must be considered simultaneously.

In assessing the strategic situation, we recommend analyzing external competitive advantages and internal competencies in a similar way. Quantitative assessments are required for both aspects. Externally, customer judgments should be used. Internal competencies can be assessed during workshops with managers and employees who know their own company and the competition well. Benchmarking or questioning independent external experts can likewise be useful. Both internal and external findings can be incorporated into the strategy development. This approach takes into consideration competitive aspects and includes fundamental issues of business and market definition. Strategy development usually starts not from scratch, but from a point of departure that excludes certain strategy options.

This was the case with a hidden champion that manufactures propulsion technology. Before the fall of the Iron Curtain, this company was heavily involved in the defense sector and specialized in non-price-sensitive high-performance propulsion units. It was regarded as the technological leader and the world market leader in this segment. However, the market started to shrink after the Iron Curtain fell and national defense budgets were cut, whereas the volume market, which was more price-sensitive and less demanding with regard to performance, grew rapidly. Both market segments were still considered attractive, because new segments opened up outside the defense sector. Where should strategy development begin in such a situation? With the market or the company's own competencies? It is often better to start with the question "What can we do?" or "What do we do better than our competitors?" That's how we started in this case. Fig. 11.8 shows the matrix of internal competencies for the company's special market and the volume market, with competencies measured in relation to the strongest competitor. The information for the internal matrices was collected during numerous workshops with managers and well-informed employees. Additional, more detailed matrices were drawn up for individual product groups/segments (military, police, coastguard, high-speed ferries, yachts, and so on).

Fig. 11.8: Internal competencies in the special and in the volume market

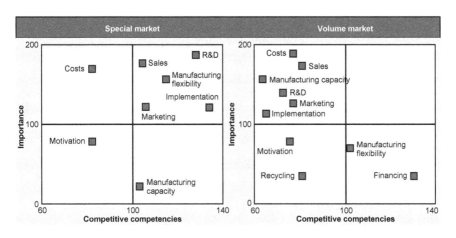

Not surprisingly, it transpired that the company performed extremely well in the special market. By contrast, its position was weak in the volume market, where business had previously only been done opportunistically. In all important competencies the competition was stronger.

Manufacturing flexibility and financing were the only advantages, both of lesser importance.

The picture was similar with regard to the company's external market position. Fig. 11.9 shows how the customers perceived the company's performance attributes in relation to those of the strongest competitor. A position to the right of 100 signifies performance leadership, and to the left of 100 it means that a competitor is stronger.

Fig. 11.9: External competitive advantages in the special and in the volume market

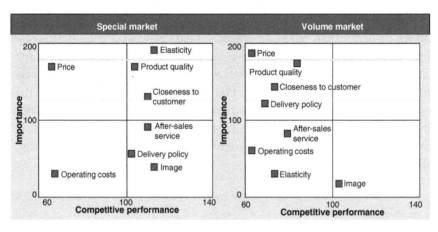

In the special market, customers see the company as the clear performance leader. It has very pronounced competitive advantages in the elasticity of the propulsion units, product quality, and closeness to customer. The company fails to beat the competition in price and operating costs only. However, this is not a serious problem in view of the company's superior performance in several important attributes and the relative unimportance of operating costs.

As we have seen, both markets were very attractive to the company, which did not want and could not afford to abandon the special market despite the cuts in defense budgets. What strategic options did the company have?

1. Continue to serve the special market and defend its position there. This basically represents the continuation of the previously successful hidden champion strategy. The risk is considerable that the market remains small or even shrinks. Cost disadvantages could get worse as a result. In

addition, some customers in the special market may in the future buy more standard products that were originally intended for the volume market.

2. Develop the competitive competencies required for success in the volume market. Most importantly, this means developing simpler, less sophisticated propulsion units and manufacturing them at cheaper locations. This option was discussed at length, but it ultimately proved to be too time-consuming and risky. The management was unsure whether these competencies could successfully be developed within an acceptable timeframe.

3. Acquire a company that is strong in the volume market but weak in the special market.

Option 3 was chosen. Three candidates were considered in depth, and the most suitable one was taken over in stages. The company has since multiplied in size many times over and its revenues increased to $3.9 billion in 2007 from approximately $250 million in the early 1990s. In 2007, the company was very successfully floated on the stock exchange. By summer 2008, its market capitalization had reached $2.8 billion. This case study illustrates the importance of pursuing an integrated strategy for choosing businesses and markets.

The strategy development described here typifies the soft diversification confronting many hidden champions. Choosing the integrated strategy approach is vital in such cases. In our experience, the greatest risk is being too strongly influenced by the attractiveness of a market and underestimating the importance of internal competencies. As Fig. 11.8 shows, internal competencies must be interpreted widely and not only in the sense of technical skills or financial criteria. One frequently underestimated capacity is sales competency, either from a content point of view or with regard to access to sales channels. The case of a company that defines its business as producing cleaning machinery for buildings and equipment illustrates this problem. This company is technically in a position to efficiently manufacture a wide range of high-quality machines. However, its target groups and sales channels are unusually broad: DIY stores, specialist retailers and wholesalers, cleaning companies, industry, car repair shops, and consumers. One of the most critical questions for this company's strategic development is therefore whether it has the resources and competencies to attain a sufficiently strong position in all of these channels and target groups. The challenge is compounded by the need to be global, and it is far greater than the challenge of designing and manufacturing a new machine.

The situation is different for a manufacturer of cleaning machines that serves only the professional cleaning segment and consequently needs only one or very few sales channels.

These cases and considerations show that business/market definition, market attractiveness, focus, soft diversification and competencies are inextricably linked to one another and must each be integrated into strategy development.

Module 5: Competitive Strategy

Competitive strategy consists of two aspects. The first and obvious task is to analyze the competitive situation and change it for the benefit of the company. This essentially relates to the issue of competitive advantages. The matrix of competitive advantages shown in Fig. 11.9 has proved extremely useful in practice. By condensing and visualizing all of the relevant information, it helps companies to identify the need for action and is therefore highly recommended. However, existing and would-be hidden champions should look beyond this initial step, because it mainly means accepting the rules of the existing competitive framework. This passive attitude does not match the hidden champions' claim to market leadership. Hidden champions aspire to set the rules themselves, or at least influence them. At the same time, they endeavor to define their markets in such a way that they achieve a leading market position and sidestep ruinous competition (i.e., they prefer what is known as the "blue ocean" strategy[7]).

A full overview and a deep understanding of the competition landscape are necessary to achieve these goals. This is the only way to determine where a company's greatest strengths lie, where (and where not) to fight for market share, where (and where not) to retaliate if attacked, and how competition can be steered to the company's own advantage. We have developed what we call a competition map to address such questions.[8] This map shows the segments in which a competitor "deserves" the leading position in the market by offering the greatest customer value in this segment. We call these areas the "natural spaces" of a company. The benefit to the customer may be superior product quality, service, delivery policy or other performance attributes. A map like this is especially helpful in complex markets where competitors offer differentiated products to diverse target groups. The map is constructed in three steps:

- Step 1: Create a matrix showing the product segments on one axis and either customer segments or applications on the other.
- Step 2: Determine how attractive each cell in this matrix is for the company. The usual methods of assessment (market data, expert judgment, scoring models, and so on) can be used here.
- Step 3: Divide up the market. Who is the best in each cell? In other words, which company offers the greatest customer value? Hidden champions may well be the best in every segment. In such cases, we advise basing this assessment on comparative advantages.[9]

In order to sort the competitors within the matrix, their market aims must be assessed. This involves answering questions such as the following:

- What does customer behavior tell us about how well the competitors perform?
- What public statements have the competitors made recently regarding their future strategy?
- What resources do the competitors have (value proposition, financial backing, capacity, sales force, and so forth) to follow through on their goals?
- Has a competitor recently opened a new facility whose output would allow it to serve certain customers?

We will illustrate the application of the competition map with a case study of all-terrain vehicles (ATVs) used noncommercially, semi-professionally, and professionally for purposes such as leisure, gardening, and snow removal. There are three relevant providers in the market: Konrad (K), Rextar (R), and Aspen (A) (names changed by the author). The market is subdivided into four product segments and four customer segments, giving the competition map 16 cells in all. Fig. 11.10 summarizes the results of the assessment. The letter in each cell shows which company offers the greatest value to customers and is therefore typically the market leader.

Traditionally, all three competitors aimed to cover as much of the market as possible, being active in every segment and selling the maximum number of units in order to take advantage of economies of scale. This strategy was not particularly successful, because each company had limited resources (for R&D, distribution channels, service, and so on) and one competitor might simply offer greater customer value in a particular cell. Market shares were fiercely contested, which in turn ruined margins. The competitors therefore started to focus. If we look at the situation shown in

Customer segments	Product segments			
	Large motor	Small motor	Full equipment	Turbo/high performance
Professionals	A	A	R	K
Semi-Professionals	R	R	R	K
Private individuals	K ⚡	R ⚡	K ⚡	K
Brand-oriented	A	A	K ⚡	R

Market attractiveness: ☐ high ▨ medium ▧ low

⚡ = Ruinous competition/price war

Fig. 11.10, we see that the overall market leader Aspen, a genuine hidden champion, is no longer present in the two right columns of the competition map. Several years ago, Aspen, which is primarily renowned for the quality of its engines but otherwise delivers few frills, withdrew from the full-equipment and turbo/high-performance product segments. The company now concentrates on its four "natural spaces" (each shown with an A) in the two left columns, namely large and small engines for professionals and brand-oriented customers. All of its resources, from R&D to marketing and advertising, are channeled into these segments. The segments of semi-professionals and private customers are of secondary importance, unless these customers are extremely brand-oriented with a correspondingly high willingness to pay. In contrast to Aspen, Rextar and Konrad are less clearly positioned. These companies waste considerable resources on fighting for the cells in the two right-hand columns, which Aspen no longer actively pursues. Konrad is stuck in several less attractive segments and attacks Rextar in the cell of small engines for private customers, apparently to gain leadership in the entire noncommercial segment. Rextar hits back in several cells, repeatedly resulting in price wars and other forms of ruinous competition. So while Rextar and Konrad are fighting price wars in several segments, Aspen keeps its distance. Each company must respect the "natural spaces" of the others. Konrad and Rextar refrain from attacking Aspen's natural space, while Aspen controls the competition and does not become a pawn in their game. This is the role for which a genuine hidden champion should strive. All too frequently, a company's own influence on competitors' conduct is not accurately predicted. For example, the CEO of a consumer goods hidden champion told me, "We had a great product. The market segment was attractive. We only made one mistake: we overlooked the fact that Procter & Gamble considers this segment its own stomping ground, so we ended up with a bloody nose." The competition map often provides illuminating insights in this respect. In this case, it could have helped the hidden champion to remain unscathed.

Strategies for Value Propositions and Pricing

Hidden champions typically offer their customers superior value and can therefore enforce higher prices. However, pressure is growing from competitors who are improving their performance or producing more cost effectively. The value proposition, the cost situation, and the pricing policy are therefore of great and recurrent importance for many hidden champions. The next two modules deal with these issues. First, we will consider the two sides of the value coin shown in Fig. 11.11. The supply side is called "value delivery," the other side "value extraction."

Fig. 11.11: Value delivery and value extraction

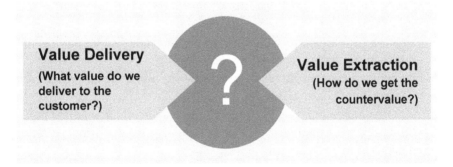

Value delivery concerns the value or benefit offered to the customer, and value extraction refers to the countervalue that should be obtained from the customer in return. The price and the terms and conditions form the core of value extraction. On the value delivery side, the challenge is gaining indepth knowledge of customer demands and being able to meet them with regard to performance and costs. In view of the customers' high-performance expectations, hidden champions cannot afford weaknesses in this respect. But they must also avoid expensive overengineering. Hidden champions sometimes offer too much, generating excessive costs in doing so, and thereby endanger their own price competitiveness. Most hidden champions, however, are strong on the delivery side. Value extraction presents more of a problem for many of them. We repeatedly face the question of whether hidden champions exploit their pricing latitude or leave money on the table. Although they generally have satisfactory margins, we observe great uncertainty in this field. Considerable potential for improvement is almost always identified when pricing projects are conducted. A broader view of both value delivery and value extraction is often necessary, incorporating not just the product and the price in the narrow sense, but the entire value proposition and the conditions.

Module 6: Value Delivery

In the context of strategy, we think not of a gradual but rather a fundamental revision of the entire value proposition, based on a quantitative evaluation. This can involve various standard methods that we will not examine in detail here but are referred to in specialist literature:[10]

- Scoring models in which various attributes regarding importance and level of performance are assessed on a scale.
- Conjoint measurement, a method of simultaneously quantifying the value to customer and the willingness to pay.
- Economic assessment in which cost and value aspects (e.g., savings) are recorded in monetary terms.

Ultimately, such methods result in a type of price-performance ratio, often depicted in a visual form.

We will now look at how one hidden champion, the world market leader in a building technology segment, strategically repositioned its value delivery. The company had a dominant position with a global market share of 53%, but had for a number of years faced growing pressure from Chinese suppliers, particularly in the American market. This situation forced the management to closely examine what the company offered in terms of performance, costs and price competitiveness. Fig. 11.12 shows the situation in simplified form.

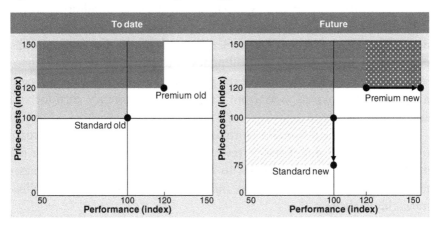

To date, the company offered a premium and a standard product, shown in the left diagram as "premium old" and "standard old." The standard offer is in line with the market average with regard to performance and price (index = 100) and the premium offer is positioned at 120. Both offers fall within the price-performance diagonals. Accordingly, all customers in the light or dark shaded areas are potential buyers of these products. For the standard product (the light shaded area), this includes all customers who do not demand more than 100 on performance and are willing to pay at least 100, but not more than 120. For the premium product (the dark shaded area), it includes all customers who do not require more than 120 on performance and are willing to pay more than 120. The left part of the diagram shows the situation to date.

Future ambitions extend beyond the existing performance, price and cost limits. The company aims to improve its position in both the premium segment and in the standard segment by offering the same performance in the standard segment at 25% lower costs, and a 25% higher performance in the premium segment for the same costs and price. The new situation is shown in the right part of Fig. 11.12. The new standard product delivers the same performance as the old standard version but 25% more cheaply, and some or all of the savings can be passed on to the customer. Potential buyers are now all customers who do not demand performance that exceeds 100 and who are prepared to pay more than 75, but not more than 120 (in addition to the light shaded area on the left, the hatched area on the right diagram). The new premium product offers a higher performance level of 150 at no added cost. It attracts all buyers that demand performance of at least 150 and are willing to pay 120 or more (i.e., the dotted area on the right half of the diagram in addition to the dark shaded area). The expansion of the potential customer base is enormous. The actual number of customers depends on the distribution of the performance demands and the willingnesses to pay. This strategic expansion may well change the rules of the game, because the hidden champion in question has moved away from its previous consistency corridor and established a new one.

The issue of the optimal performance level is frequently raised. Proactively pursuing a value delivery strategy at an early stage is crucial for the market leaders. They should aim to find a performance level that maximizes the difference between costs and value to customer. Fig. 11.13 illustrates this challenge.

Fig. 11.13: Optimization of value delivery and performance

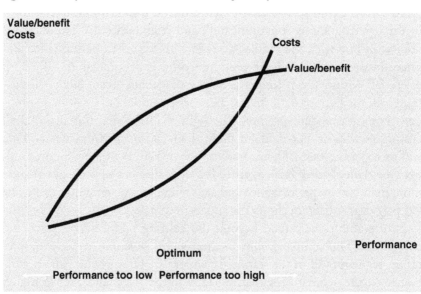

Costly overengineering is always a risk for perfectionists like the hidden champions. Target costing and target pricing alone are not sufficient; they must be based on sound target valuing. Two examples illustrate this problem:

- Plans called for the Transrapid maglev train between Hamburg and Berlin to depart every ten minutes.[11] An analysis of the value to customer revealed that 20-minute intervals offered the same benefit in the customers' perception. It was then decided to configure the system for 20-minute intervals, which would save an estimated $1.4 billion.

- A manufacturer of medical equipment considered reducing its guaranteed service time from eight hours to four or even two. An analysis revealed that the value to customer increased greatly through the reduction from eight to four hours, but that a further reduction to two hours brought only a minimal additional increase in value. The obvious decision was therefore to cut the guaranteed service time to four hours and not to two.

Optimized value delivery is the key to success. This subject therefore deserves close attention in an age in which performance demands and price pressures are constantly increasing.

Module 7: Value Extraction

The flipside of value delivery is value extraction: How does a company obtain the countervalue from its customers that delivers an adequate margin? The key tool here is price in its various facets, including all terms and conditions. As most hidden champions operate in business-to-business markets, value extraction is highly complex. It is therefore critical to understand this issue, like pricing in the narrower sense, not as a decision but rather as a process. Fig. 11.14 illustrates the process of value extraction or pricing in a highly condensed form.

Fig. 11.14: Value extraction/pricing as a process

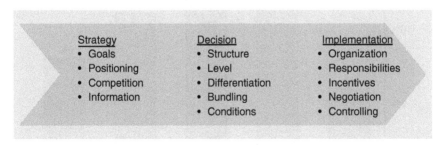

The three stages are strategy, decision-making, and implementation. In each phase, there are several factors to consider. In the strategy part, for example, the company in question needs to decide how to behave towards competitors. Hidden champions frequently claim price leadership, a very sensible goal for a market leader. How do they respond to aggressive behavior? How do they proceed in a new market? Aggressively or peacefully? How is signaling used? Although hidden champions tend towards discretion, in relation to price it is often better to state intentions publicly at an early stage. Other questions arise in the decision-making phase: What is the right price structure? Linear, nonlinear or multidimensional? To what extent should the company differentiate prices? Within the product line or country by country? How can frictions between distribution channels be avoided? Should products and services be bundled or sold separately? How should the conditions be structured? The importance of price implementation is often seriously underestimated. Who is responsible for what? What are the incentives for the people who negotiate prices? Do we know and apply the right strategies for negotiations and auctions?

Fig. 11.15 shows the enormous margin differences realized by 76 selected hidden champions in different business units or business types.

Fig. 11.15: Margins posted in different business units and business types

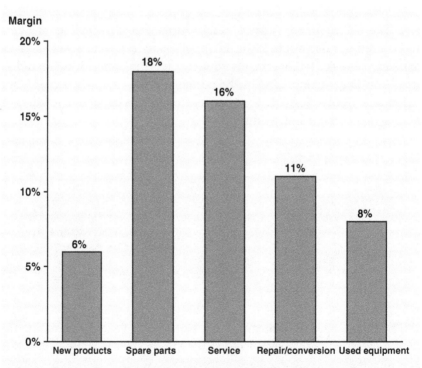

Source: Study by Simon-Kucher & Partners of 76 mechanical engineering companies

It is evident that maximum effectiveness in value delivery and value extraction is crucial in view of such enormous differences in margins. If a company can, for example, invoice services, components and guarantees separately, it can achieve a far higher overall margin.

Fig. 11.16 shows the large differences that can result from the negotiation process, taking the example of 56 firms in the automotive sector. These companies faced price reduction demands from the manufacturers of between 4.7% and 5.1%.

Fig. 11.16: Demanded and actual price cuts of automotive suppliers

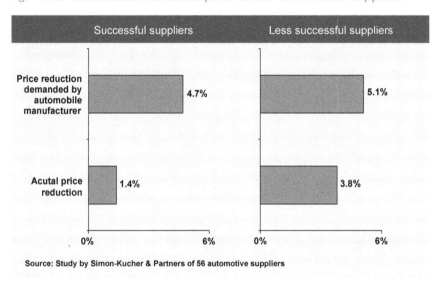

Source: Study by Simon-Kucher & Partners of 56 automotive suppliers

Among the suppliers that were successful in enforcing prices, the actual reductions were far lower than those demanded, namely 1.4%. Most of these successful suppliers were hidden champions. The less successful suppliers, however, had to accept average price cuts of 3.8%. The difference of 2.4 percentage points was higher than the margins of most suppliers in the year under review. It is very interesting to examine the attitudes and priorities behind the pricing process of the successful and the less successful suppliers. Some 83% of the successful companies paid the greatest attention to price implementation, but only 25% of the less successful suppliers had the same priority. By contrast, the less successful suppliers attached the highest weight to cost-cutting. If we combine both factors in the sense of maximizing margins (keeping apart costs and price), the successful suppliers have a "value extraction" indicator of 75 as opposed to a "value extraction" indicator of 50 for the less successful suppliers. In other words, the successful suppliers put 50% more energy into improving margins than their less successful counterparts. Above all, these findings tell us that it is worth investing acumen and energy into value extraction. This lesson from the hidden champions contains valuable advice for all kinds of companies.

But our experience also shows that even the hidden champions have considerable room for improvement in value extraction. They are less professional in value extraction than in value delivery. Reorganizing the value extraction process normally raises the margin 200 basis points[12] (2 percentage points or more) (i.e., to 7% from 5% or to 12% from 10%. "All of the processes we have approached systematically have led to large improvements in earnings," reports Bernd Hoffmann, the CEO of the hidden champion Cargobull. "Our pricing process must be organized as systematically as any other process." Friedhelm Loh from the Loh Group agrees, "There is enormous profit potential in improving pricing processes." Interestingly, margin improvements are not only possible at companies with low profitability. In fact, they are often easier to achieve at companies that already earn good returns. This is presumably because the top performance creates pricing latitude that will be fully exploited only if full information on value to customer plus the necessary courage are in place.

Organization and Implementation

According to the Harvard Business School's maxim "structure follows strategy," a company must first know what it wants before it can organize its structure accordingly.[13] In reality, the reverse can also occur—and rightly so. Once a particular organization is in place, its internal competencies shape the strategy. Implementation is the final stage of strategy development. Many experts consider this phase to be the most important and the most difficult of all. We will now turn to the final two modules of strategy development: namely, organization and implementation.

Module 8: Organizational Development

The traditional one-product, one-market hidden champion faces no serious organizational problems. It is naturally organized along functional lines. However, the internationalization process and a growing number of subsidiaries can force these companies to create intermediate levels such as regional headquarters. The subject of a more fundamental reorganization is regularly raised in the context of the soft diversification route taken by an increasing number of hidden champions, as discussed in Chapters 3 and 8. The hidden champions pursue a course of early decentralization. I can only encourage companies to follow this course decisively, even if it proves difficult to surrender power and control to the business units. The key factor for success is having "entrepreneurs" who can manage these units with as much autonomy as possible.

However, opting for a decentralized organization leaves many tricky questions unanswered, each of which needs diligence and consideration:

- How will the decentral units be arranged? By product groups and/or customer groups? Or perhaps by region? The latter seems to be an exception, but it is sometimes the best option, as shown in the case of Würth in Chapter 8.
- Decentral units should ideally control as many stages of the value chain as possible. However, this often runs counter to utilizing economies of scale in R&D, procurement, production, sales or service. How can the units be organized taking these trade-offs into consideration? This is a very tricky question.
- How can the company retain the traditional hidden champions' strengths such as simplicity, lean processes and low overheads in spite of the increasing complexity?
- Which functions should a company perform itself and what should be outsourced? And how should the outsourcing be organized? Bühler, the world market leader in milling technology, delegates important tasks to suppliers, but also encourages them to occupy premises on the Bühler site.

Organizational development is often based on trust in theoretical concepts, but the hidden champions demonstrate that the most important factor is in fact common sense. Organization is a means to an end. The aims are to increase the value to customer and/or to strengthen competitive advantages (such as lower costs, greater closeness, to customer and faster processes). The organization should be efficient, simple, logical, transparent, fast and adaptable. The underlying principles are obvious:

- Unity of responsibility and control of resources
- Minimization of internal costs
- Knowledge-sharing across organizational boundaries

The hidden champions have observed these principles in their traditional one-product, one-market organizations. They should endeavor to remain true to them when their businesses and organizations become more complex. There is no general pattern for how to tackle organizational development. In each case, it is advisable to give reasonable, well-balanced consideration to internal and external aspects, including different levels and functions. It is risky to develop an organization in the "ivory tower," (i.e., detached from practice). The involvement of consultants may help an organization to benefit from the experiences of other companies or sectors.

Module 9: Implementation

According to Alfred Brittain, the former CEO of Bankers Trust, "You can come up with the best strategy, the implementation is 90% of it." Every strategy must include a plan of action: who will do what, and when? Implementation is one of the hidden champions' outstanding strengths. This is the result of strong leadership on the one hand and a broadly accepted corporate culture on the other. Strategy always involves change, which is why the capacity for change is a key success factor. The hidden champions are exposed to varying influences concerning their capacity for change:

- As companies that have been highly successful in the past, they must be wary of the saying, "Past success is the greatest enemy of change." Rather than resting on their laurels, they should continue to question their winning formulae of the past.
- As explained in Chapter 10, leadership continuity is a great strength, but it also harbors the risk of petrification and failure to adapt.
- Strong focus is one of the pillars of the hidden champions' superiority, but it can also contribute to a narrow view that fails to recognize threats from the outside in time or to take them seriously.
- Hidden champions' manageable size makes implementation easier. What the CEO orders is carried out—but only until the company reaches a certain size. Beyond this, change is increasingly difficult to dictate from the top; instead, managers and employees must be persuaded and won over.

Increasing size and complexity mean that the hidden champions face challenges in the implementation of their new strategies. It is therefore a good idea to support strategy implementation with broad-based activities such as workshops, group work, and accompanying events. Most hidden champions have now reached a size and complexity that make such exercises, normally typical of large corporations, advisable. Change becomes a constant challenge for the hidden champions, because even market leaders do not enjoy a divine right of superiority. Walter Wriston, the former chairman of Citicorporation, addressed this danger as follows: "The philosophy of the divine right of kings died hundreds of years ago, but not, it seems, the divine right of inherited markets. Some people still believe there's a divine dispensation that their markets are theirs—and no one else's—now and forever. It is an old dream that dies hard, yet no businessman in a free society can control a market when the customers decide to go somewhere else. All the king's horses and all the king's men are helpless in the face of a better product. Our commercial history is filled with examples of companies that failed to change in a changing world, and became tombstones in the corporate graveyard."[14] This warning applies to the hidden champions of the twenty-first century as well as to every other company.

Hidden Champions and Consultants

There is no general answer to the question of whether consultants should be involved in the development of a hidden champion strategy or whether in-house expertise is sufficient. You might expect a consultant like myself to argue in favor of the former. However, the issue is not that simple. I would first like to correct some widespread misconceptions. Midsize companies in general and hidden champions in particular are said to be wary of consultants. This is a twofold fallacy because these companies actually work very closely with tax and legal advisors, who are also frequently consulted about strategic issues. The reason for this is not so much the advisors' expertise in these areas, but rather the strong relationship of trust that exists. Trust is absolutely crucial for the cooperation between the leaders of midsize companies and consultants. In this context, many hidden champions do indeed have reservations about working with the giants in the consulting industry.

With regard to engaging consultants, hidden champions can be divided into two groups. One group is keen to employ strategy consultants, typically for several sequential projects. This group is growing and includes many of the larger hidden champions. The second group is more hesitant, because it lacks confidence in external consultants or prefers to solve its problems alone. This reservation is especially pronounced in relation to large, well-known consultancies. Rightly or wrongly, many hidden champion CEOs believe that the methods and experiences of large corporations, for which most of the big consultancies work, are mostly irrelevant to them. The high fees charged by the large consultancies naturally also constitute a serious barrier for hidden champions. Arrogance and overbearing self-assurance are likewise unhelpful in relation to the hidden champions.

However, most hidden champions are becoming increasingly aware of the need to call on outside experience. Careful handling and a high degree of sensitivity are nevertheless required of consultants. It is not easy to tell a company what to do when it is as highly specialized and successful as a typical hidden champion. Abstract principles and "ivory tower" generalizations are soon rejected. Hidden champion managers are people rooted in reality who know exactly what they are talking about.

Given this reserve and the trust barrier, it is a challenge for consultants to get a foot in the door at hidden champions. However, once the first projects have proved successful and the trust has been created, a long-term business relationship often develops. This depends, of course, on individuals, because hidden champion entrepreneurs have a strong preference for having just one contact person. They expect the same continuity with the consultant that they practice in their own management. Changing consultants is therefore difficult. Consultancies that advise hidden champions need a long-term perspective and high continuity of personnel.

Summary

In this chapter, we have presented nine modules for auditing and developing a hidden champion strategy. These modules apply to current and would-be hidden champions alike. Fig. 11.17 provides an overview of the nine strategy modules.

The modules of organization and implementation run alongside the other modules. In a strategy project not all modules will necessarily be addressed. It may, for example, be advisable to carry out a hidden champion audit as a first step (modules 1 and 2). These audit modules reveal the need for action in other areas (such as value delivery and value extraction), which can then be dealt with in a second phase. Alternatively, a project can be confined to organizational development and implementation, because the existing strategy is sound. Conversely, the nine modules explained here

Fig. 11.17: Modules for hidden champions audit and strategy development

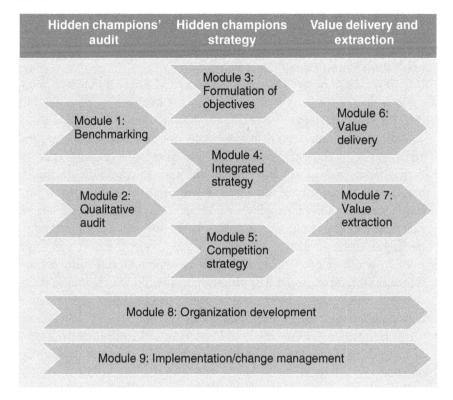

Hidden champions' audit	Hidden champions strategy	Value delivery and extraction

Module 3: Formulation of objectives

Module 1: Benchmarking

Module 6: Value delivery

Module 4: Integrated strategy

Module 2: Qualitative audit

Module 7: Value extraction

Module 5: Competition strategy

Module 8: Organization development

Module 9: Implementation/change management

do not cover every strategic problem. Strategy considerations can also focus on areas such as internationalization, innovation, supply chain, and human resources, which are dealt with in additional modules.

We summarize as follows:

- Many companies can draw on the strategic principles of the hidden champions to develop their own strategy.
- One obvious method of assessing a company's own position is to conduct benchmarking against the hidden champions using the existing database. This procedure reveals where and to what extent a company differs from the hidden champions. The peer group for the benchmarking can be defined in different ways.
- A qualitative hidden champion audit examines the extent to which a company adheres to the strategic lessons of the hidden champions, thereby pointing to need for action.

- Strategy development is not a one-off decision but involves a top-down and bottom-up process. Each company should review its strategy at reasonable intervals (typically every three to five years, depending on the dynamics of the sector).
- A strong will is required to set targets, but the precise formulation also needs solid workmanship.
- It is advisable to observe internal resources and external market opportunities in equal measure when defining the business/market. We call this integrated strategy.
- The competition map can help a company not only to behave appropriately within the rules of the game, but also to redefine the rules itself.
- Performance and value delivery call for astute, conscious decisions, because the superiority of the hidden champions is based on better performance and value. Changing or adding to the rules of the game of value delivery is a promising approach here. But cost-driving overengineering must be avoided at all costs.
- Even in times of good profits, margin management and value extraction should receive the greatest attention in the hidden champion strategy. Value extraction/pricing must be understood as a process that offers considerable unexploited profit potential.
- Organizational development should observe tried and tested principles of the hidden champions, in particular simplicity, efficiency, and transparency.
- Hidden champions have natural advantages in effective implementation. But there are also risks because past success breeds inertia. There are no divine rights, even for market leaders. Hidden champions—as other companies—must remain aware of the need for constant change in order to survive.

The hidden champions provide us with valuable insights and tools for strategy development. Every entrepreneur or manager should bear these lessons in mind for his or her own company. The hidden champions are excellent strategic role models. However, we should not fall into the trap of believing that their successes can be replicated by simple imitation. Individual creativity and energy are always necessary for achieving outstanding success.

Notes

1 See the instructive book by Phil Rosenzweig, *The Halo Effect . . . and the Eight Other Business Delusions That Deceive Managers*, New York: Free Press 2007.

2 Carl von Clausewitz, *On War*, York: Oxford University Press 2007 (German original published in 1832)

3 ROI = return on investment. Alternatively, ROCE = return on capital employed, defined as profit before tax divided by total assets.

4 The question was "Please state the average ROI (i.e., total return on investment before tax, for the last ten years in percent)."

5 The question was "What percentage of revenues do you spend as a long-term average on research and development?"

6 See Arie de Geus, "Planning as Learning", *Harvard Business Review*, March-April 1988, p. 70–75.

7 See W. Chan Kim/Renée Mauborgne, *Blue Ocean Strategy: How to Create Uncontested Market Space and Make the Competition Irrelevant*, Boston: Harvard Business School Press 2005.

8 For a more detailed description of the competition map, see Hermann Simon, Frank Bilstein and Frank Luby, *Manage for Profit, Not for Market Share*, Boston: Harvard Business School Press 2006, p. 33–38.

9 To explain the difference between absolute and comparative advantage, we use the relative market share (company's own market share divided by market share of the strongest competitor). Let us assume that a company is the market leader in all segments. Then it has an absolute advantage everywhere and its relative market share is always larger than 1. There can nevertheless be large differences between the relative market shares. In segment A, it may be 2.5; in segment B only 1.1. In this case, the company obviously has a "comparative advantage" in segment A when compared to segment B. If the company had to choose one segment and all other things were equal, the decision would be in favor of A.

10 Reference is made to specialist literature, e.g., Hermann Simon, Frank Bilstein and Frank Luby, *Manage for Profit, Not for Market Share*, Boston: Harvard Business School Press 2006 or Hermann Simon and Robert J. Dolan, *Power Pricing*, New York: The Free Press 1996.

11 The Transrapid is a magnetically levitated (maglev) train that has no wheels but is propelled by magnetic forces and reaches speeds of up to 280 miles (450 kilometers) per hour. The Hamburg-Berlin route was not built due to opposition from the Green Party. The first Transrapid line opened in Shanghai on December 31, 2002 and has been operating smoothly since then. The maximum speed of the Shanghai Transrapid is 432 kilometers per hour (268 miles per hour).

12 A basis point is 1/100 of 1%, so 200 basis points equal 2 percentage points.

13 "Structure follows strategy" was coined in 1962 by the late Alfred Chandler, then professor of business history at the Harvard Business School. Chandler showed in four case studies (DuPont, General Motors, Standard Oil and Sears Roebuck) that the need to restructure emerged from strategy shifts driven by new technologies and market changes.

14 Hermann Simon, *Strategy for Competition*, New Delhi: Leads Press 2008.

Chapter 12
The Lessons of the Hidden Champions

What do the hidden champions teach us? According to modern management literature, we mainly—or only—learn from large successful corporations. In this book we have changed this perspective radically. We have discovered that many of the most consistently successful, longest-surviving, most competitive companies operate behind a veil of discretion and remain unknown—even to business experts. Consequently, their strategies and leadership methods are not finding their way into the textbooks, business magazines, and heads of the management community. However, the case studies of the hidden champions teach us extraordinary and valuable lessons that often differ from the patterns of large corporations and the management fads of the day.

Leadership and Goals

Ambitious goals are the foundation of outstanding success. Extraordinary success is never based on pure luck or coincidence. In the beginning there is always a vision of what the person wants to achieve, or at least there is a state of preparedness. Luck and windfall incidents may contribute, although luck is but a "by-product of the desire for perfection."[1] Most human beings follow more or less well-trodden paths and many have no particular ambitions at all. And there are few with a goal, a mission—the monomaniacs, as Peter Drucker called them. The founders and managers of the hidden champions belong to this second category. They know what they want and they have the willpower and the energy, sometimes even the obsession, to realize their goals. The issue of will hardly ever comes up in management literature, but it is of fundamental importance for the development of companies.[2] We need not consider here whether willpower and ambition can be learned or whether these characteristics are hereditary. In any case, we encounter the core of the personality here.

However, one individual's willpower and ambition are insufficient to create a company, let alone a world market leader. This may work for an artist, but it takes a lot of peers to develop a world market leader—people from all over the world. The entrepreneur must ignite the fire that burns inside him in many others of different nationalities and cultures. That's leadership. Willpower and leadership combined ensure that everyone's energy is directed toward becoming and remaining the best. This is the true goal that must be pursued consistently. If this is achieved, world market leadership results practically as a side effect.

Lesson 1. *Willpower and goals always come first. For hidden champions, leadership means inspiring employees from all over the world to be the best, to become a world market leader.*

High-Performance Employees

High performance can only be accomplished with a team that is highly motivated and strongly identifies with the company. The selection of the right employees is the foundation. Hidden champions select their employees very rigorously. This choice is accomplished primarily through social control, less through top-down intervention. Intolerance toward poor performance and shirking is a necessary part of a performance-oriented culture. It is helpful to have more work than people. This does not lead to employee discontent, on the contrary. The hidden champions create—and profit from—conditions that lead to an extremely low employee turnover. In addition, comebackers are frequent and an indicator for attractive corporate cultures. Low attrition retains expertise and makes investments in education profitable. It is impressive that the hidden champions successfully globalize these demanding values.

Lesson 2. *High performance requires intolerance against shirking and swift dismissal of employees who do not pull their weight. The low employee turnover proves that the remaining employees appreciate the hidden champions' corporate cultures and reciprocate with due commitment and high performance.*

Depth

A striking difference between the hidden champions and normal companies is the depth of the value chain and the high vertical integration. Time and again I was amazed to observe that the best enterprises do far more themselves than average companies. "We do everything ourselves," is the frequent statement made by many of the best. Conversely, I heard average companies say "we don't do that ourselves," "we outsource that," "we leave that to others," and so forth. I believe the word "depth" describes this attitude and phenomenon precisely. The greatest ones have an incredible depth in their value chain, a very high vertical integration in manufacturing, and even stronger in R&D. They are very reserved when it comes to outsourcing and strategic alliances, especially where their core competencies are concerned. Is that old-fashioned? Or is this the core of their superiority? There is no straightforward answer.

Lesson 3. *Uniqueness can only come from within and cannot be bought on the market. It therefore requires depth and a certain reserve toward outsourcing.*

Decentralization

In view of the strong leadership personalities, we could have expected centralists practicing authoritarian leadership styles at the hidden champions. Leadership is in fact authoritarian when it comes to the principles. Yet, as we have discovered, the hidden champions are also fervent decentralizers and leave more freedom for execution and implementation than large corporations do. Some of these companies are confronted with growth restraints because their markets are narrow and their market shares are high. The reinvestment opportunities in their traditional business segments are therefore limited. They choose the route of soft diversification, fully aware that this could threaten their traditional strengths. Their answer is rigorous decentralization, usually up to the point of legally independent business units. New, smaller hidden champions thus emerge from older businesses. The importance of decentralization as a means of mobilizing entrepreneurial energies can hardly be overestimated.[3] Decentralization must naturally be accompanied by responsibility and accountability.

Lesson 4. *Decentralization is the most effective way to retain the strengths of the hidden champions, even in larger and more complex structures. Decentralization should be put into practice wherever possible.*

Focus

There may be those who are top performers in different fields. There are even a few who have won two Nobel prizes.[4] However, such people are extremely rare exceptions and hardly suitable as role models for the average entrepreneur or manager. More normal people and companies wanting to achieve something are well advised to concentrate on one area. "We only do one thing, but we do it right," as the hidden champion Uhlmann says. Such focus is realistically the only way to attain world class. The hidden champions exemplify that it can be done. They are generally not geniuses, but they focus their limited resources better than others and stick with the direction they have chosen until they reach the top position. Focus also includes knowing what you do not want to do. This is just as important as knowing what you do want to do. It's the only way to avoid the ineffective use of scarce resources. Likewise, the hidden champions teach us that the definition of the "playing field" is critical. Markets, target groups, and applications are not predefined by nature; an astute market definition often forms the foundation for superiority. The business and the market selection must take into consideration the external opportunities and the company's internal competencies. It is advisable—at least at the outset—to avoid stiff competition and confrontation.[5]

Lesson 5. *Ambitious goals can only be achieved by focusing one's resources. The definition of the playing field itself is an essential means of getting the focus right.*

Globalization

Nothing in our era and in the decades to come will change our world more than globalization. Extraordinary growth opportunities present themselves to companies that take advantage of this secular trend. Global markets are many times larger than national markets. In global dimensions even niche markets reach sizes making adequate economies of scale possible. The Internet and modern transportation make the world market accessible for companies large and small. Yet the establishment of world-wide sales and manufacturing networks typically takes several generations and requires never-ending perseverance. Revenues are the first to internationalize, followed by personnel and eventually management. Most hidden champions are in the middle of this process. However, there will still be sectors and companies in the future that continue to operate only locally. The decision between local or international business must be well considered.

Lesson 6. *Globalization opens up unprecedented growth opportunities, even for small companies. In order to use these opportunities, leaders and employees must put aside their national and cultural boundaries. Incessant stamina and perseverance are required to survive the multigenerational globalization process. The greatest challenge is the internationalization of the people.*

Innovation

The massive increase of the hidden champions' relative market shares is primarily attributable to their innovativeness in recent years.[6] Whatever may have triggered this wave, the hidden champions are currently in a phase of significant innovative activities. They integrate market and technology as equal driving forces. Few large corporations achieve this balance. For hidden champions, innovation is less a question of budget than of heads. They can obtain a patent in approximately one fifth of the expenditure required by large corporations. And they have five times more patents per employee. Continuous improvements are more typical than breakthrough innovations. Customers are closely involved in the innovation activities.

Lesson 7. *Innovation is the only effective long-term means of succeeding in competition. Innovation is primarily a question of creativity and quality, less so a matter of money.*

Closeness to Customer

The hidden champions teach us that customer orientation is more important than competitive orientation.[7] They consider the long-standing relationships with their customers their greatest strength, even ahead of their technical competencies. Closeness to customer is most effectively achieved with small units. Closeness to customer is more important than marketing professionalism, although the latter also grows with the increasing size of the company. High performance for the customer automatically leads to competitive advantages. Top customers, and likewise top competitors, should be considered performance drivers and consciously used as such. Multiple complex competitive advantages rooted in inner values and competencies create customer commitment and raise the barriers to entry.

Lesson 8. *Closeness to customer almost automatically creates competitive advantages. Top customers, like top competitors, should be employed systematically as drivers of performance.*

Three Circles and Eight Lessons

In Fig. 12.1 we present the eight lessons that distill the most important insights from this book in three circles. This makes the lessons easier to memorize.

Fig. 12.1: Three circles and eight lessons

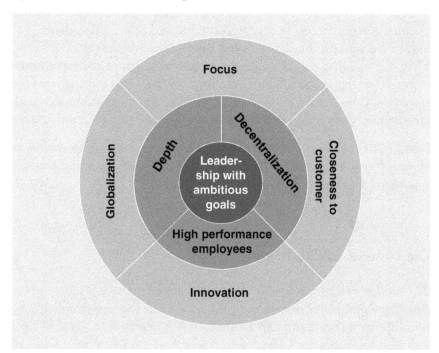

The core is strong leadership expressed in ambitious goals that mobilize and align the employees' energies. The middle circle encompasses the inner competencies. Depth is required because competitive superiority can only be created internally. Decentralization means freedom for entrepreneurial behavior and a high degree of autonomy for the "executors." All of this is implemented by employees who are willing and able to produce high performance. These inner strengths are projected to the outer circle. The hidden champions focus on a business that they define autonomously. Even hidden champions that pursue soft diversification maintain their focus on the individual businesses. Continuous innovation guarantees the retention of competitive superiority. Closeness to customer warrants that technology and customer needs do not drift apart. All this takes place on a global scale that leaves room for growth and sufficient size.

While these eight lessons result directly from the chapters of this book, the hidden champions' experience encompasses further paramount lessons for specific target groups such as strategy planners, companies of different sizes, investors, countries, and job candidates. In the second part of this chapter, we summarize the most important insights gained from the hidden champions.

Lessons for Strategy Planners

Strategists and strategy planners are always looking for fundamental truths and formulae for success. However, all kinds of rules on leadership and management have situative rather than general value. There is no universally valid wisdom on corporate strategy. The philosopher's stone of strategy has not been found and will not be found. We nevertheless attempt to distill insights and lessons that have been tried and tested at the hidden champions.

Long-term orientation and survival

Hermut Kormann, CEO of the multiple world market leader Voith, raised a number of issues during a discussion with me. "Voith is more than 100 years old. We want to survive the next 100 years. How can this be achieved? What do we have to do right now? How have companies that are 200 years or older managed to survive?" The mere fact that these questions are being posed by a hidden champion top manager is remarkable. I cannot remember ever having been confronted with questions like these in large public corporations. Dave Petersen, president of O.C. Tanner, summed it up in one sentence, "We can't think short-term." Fig. 1.5 showed that almost 40% of the hidden champions are older than 100 years. The oldest company in our study, Achenbach Buschhütten, was founded in 1452. Prym, world market leader in snap fasteners, dates back to 1530, and Zwilling Henckels, the global number one in high-quality knives and scissors, started business in 1731. The roots of today's world market leader for bookbinding machines, Kolbus, reach back to 1772, and Europe's leading private bank, Sal. Oppenheim, was founded in 1789, the year of the French Revolution.

By contrast, normal companies tend to be short-lived. They are definitely not masters of survival. More than half of all companies listed on the stock exchange go under or are sold within one generation. This applies both to the US and to Germany. In Germany, 37% of the largest listed industrial companies disappeared or were taken over by other companies since the 1990s alone.[8] If we accept survival as the primary goal of a company, we are confronted with a great challenge. Profit is not the main goal in this sense, but rather a means to ensure survival. Or as Peter Drucker put it, "Profit is the cost of survival." How do the hidden champions manage to survive for so long? This subject would be enough to fill a book of its own. Here, we will just briefly list the points that effectively contribute to survival from our point of view.

- Thinking in generations instead of over a short period of time, (e.g., three, five, or ten years as is common in strategic planning);
- Maintaining high continuity in top management;
- Promoting conservative financing that does not endanger the company even in difficult times, which includes rejecting the fastest possible growth and short-term profit maximization;
- Resisting management fads, and observing timeless maxims instead;[9]
- Maintaining stamina in trying situations, not least commitment to the respective market in good and bad times;
- Fostering the loyalty of the employees and the entrepreneur's reciprocally high responsibility; and finally, in my opinion, deciding whether focus or diversification of the portfolio fosters the capacity for survival. For family companies, one useful side effect of diversification and the

split into separate companies is the possibility of dividing the business into fair parts that are then distributed to the heirs.

Here I deliberately leave open whether and how strategists in modern companies can include such goals and insights into their planning. Is the question of how a company will survive the next 100 years relevant for what is planned and done today? Even if this is the case, it is by no means clear what needs be done today to ensure a company's existence in 100 years' time. These difficult questions are definitely worth contemplation, and the hidden champions are presumably a fruitful source for deeper insights.

Avoiding serious mistakes

Here too, I draw on Hermut Kormann's ideas. He assumes that mid-size entrepreneurs are not capable of higher strategic insights than other entrepreneurs, nor are they more intelligent. It might be sufficient to be less stupid and to avoid hazardous mistakes others make, or to correct errors sooner.[10] Kormann summarizes his theory as follows: "In order to be successful, you don't have to be clever, it is sufficient to not be stupid."[11] What sort of high-risk failures do the hidden champions avoid? Here we list some frequent mistakes:

- Short-term profit maximization, for example cutting R&D expenditure;
- Frequent change of direction in the strategic course of the company;
- Diversifications that result in a drift away from the core business;
- Risky financial activities and excessive leveraging;
- Overhasty or oversized acquisitions;
- Unreflected outsourcing;
- Disproportionate reliance on external managers;
- Distraction by activities that do not benefit the business.

This list could be continued. The errors avoided are mirror images of the typical strengths of the hidden champions. Also, the hidden champions probably correct their mistakes more quickly and decisively than other companies do. Perhaps mistakes cannot be avoided, but they can be corrected—and fast.

Lessons in Polarity Management

In Western culture, we tend to distinguish right from wrong, true from false, black from white. By contrast, Eastern cultures consider the world as flowing, without strictly defined boundaries. What people from the West see as contradiction, people from the East see as complementarity. Edward de Bono speaks of a Western stone culture and an Eastern water culture in this context. A classic that addresses such contradictions in relation to centralization and decentralization in organizations is the book by Lawrence and Lorsch entitled *Organization and Environment: Managing Differentiation and Integration.*[12] Addressing broad management issues, the physician Barry Johnson dealt with similar problems in his book *Polarity Management.*[13] Hidden champion Gore, world market leader in Teflon-based products, has included specific polarities in its company philosophy. The principle of "freedom" applies in so far as each employee has the freedom to do what he or she considers right. The freedom is, however, restricted by the "waterline" principle. As soon as a decision could hit the corporate ship below the waterline, a colleague must be consulted to share the responsibility for the decision. While the freedom principle encourages all employees to make use of their full potential, the waterline principle is intended to guarantee that the company does not suffer any serious damage.

Contradictions or polarities are typical of the hidden champions and arise in many forms. There is simply no (mathematical) optimization in relation to polarities like centralization versus decentralization or customer orientation versus technology orientation. Instead, it is better to permit flowing relationships or "gray areas" between these polarities and to allow for different courses of action, depending on the situation. Fig. 12.2 describes aspects in which the hidden champions practice such "both - and" courses of action.

The strategy and leadership of the hidden champions could be interpreted as contradictory in many aspects, as shown in Fig. 12.2. Yet these contradictions and the capacity to handle them precisely conform to Johnson's proposals for the solution of "unsolvable problems" in his book, *Polarity Management.* The main result of the study conducted by Lawrence and Lorsch pointed to the same direction. The most successful organizations were those that displayed a high level of integration (centralization) as well as a high level of differentiation (decentralization).

Aspect	both . . .	. . . and
Market definition	Narrow: product/technology	Broad: regional/world
Strategy	Internal Competencies	External opportunities
Driving force for innovation	Market	Technology
Leadership	Authoritarian in fundamental values	Participative in details
Value chain	Internal for core competencies	External for non-core competencies
Time horizon	Short-term (efficiency)	Long-term (effectiveness)
Organization	Functional one-product, one-market case	Divisional/decentral for soft diversification cases
Competitive advantage	Product: quality, systems integration	Service: Advice/customer service
Employee turnover	High in initial phase	Low: permanent staff
Workforce	Global: employees	National: top-management

This is not a culture of black and white or a stone culture, but rather a water culture according to Edward de Bono—and therefore perhaps a leadership role model for our globalized world of the twenty-first century.

Lessons for Small Companies

Not every company can become a world market leader, nor should it try to do so. Even in the globalized world of the future, there will be businesses with a local radius. The local café will continue to exist alongside Starbucks and the general practitioner will not be replaced by a faraway diagnosis specialist in Bangalore, India, or Guangchou, China—at least not completely. However, these examples of typical local businesses also indicate that every company and self-employed person must think about how globalization affects its/his/her business. American healthcare providers are outsourcing complex radiological diagnoses to India. Naturally, the opening of a Starbucks does not leave the local café business untouched. Tailor Jim, who has 70 employees in Bangkok, regularly visits companies in Europe, takes measurements, and three weeks later delivers tailor-made suits to the employees by DHL. Almost no small enterprise remains untouched by globalization. On the other hand, globalization creates untold opportunities for companies of all sizes. Lingua-Video.com, a company with seven employees that offers audiovisual media for educational purposes, in various original languages has access to customers throughout the world via the Internet and delivers its films to all five continents either physically or through the

Internet. A one-man business selling Asian herbal teas has acquired customers from all over the world through its homepage. Such scopes of small businesses would have been unthinkable only a few years ago.

Small and very small-scale companies that offer internationally marketable products or services can learn a lot from the lessons of the hidden champions. Ambitious goals, narrow market focus, globalization, closeness to customer, innovation—all these fit perfectly. Some of these firms have the chance to become hidden champions themselves. Even for companies with a local business, the lessons of the hidden champions can be useful. There is a champion in every local market, be it the best restaurant, the leading clothes shop or the deli with the freshest products. The ambition to be the best in one's market and to strive for market leadership through better performance and innovation appears just as worthwhile and motivating a goal on the local as well as on the global level. All the other lessons like closeness to customer, competitive advantages, low employee turnover or avoidance of excessive outsourcing can equally be applied to local businesses.

If a company has risen to become the local market leader with this strategy and sees only limited growth potential there, how should it continue? The hidden champions have a clear answer to this question: rather expand regionally than embark on new, unknown businesses! Locally oriented business people tend to stay in one place and diversify in such cases. However, even in the local market the "jack of all trades and master of none" loses out to the focused specialist. The likelihood of succeeding in a new and unknown business is therefore low. It is better to remain in a narrow market with proven competencies and to extend the business through regional expansion. This is nothing more than the application of the hidden champions' strategy on a regional scale. Once small companies have made the first steps toward regional expansion and have been successful in doing so, they may well become genuine hidden champions.

Lessons for Midsize Companies

Not every midsize company is already active internationally. Many midsize companies continue to generate the lion's share of their revenues in their home market, although they would be strong enough to succeed in foreign markets. This restraint to internationalize is particularly prevalent in the United States. I have visited many an American company that in my assessment could have succeeded in foreign markets but never seriously undertook venturing abroad. Usually the entrepreneurs contend that the U.S. market is so large that they don't see the need to internationalize. In Japan, I occasionally found similar attitudes with midsize companies. In China, this seems to be very different. Every Chinese entrepreneur I talked to was eager to take on the world market. What can midsize companies learn from the hidden champions? In my opinion, the first and most important lesson in choosing the hidden champions as role models is in regards to deriving the same courage that they use in becoming more internationally active themselves. The intent to go international typically requires a narrower market definition and the formulation of more ambitious goals. An *out of the blue* decision to export or found a sales subsidiary in a neighboring country is definitely not the way to succeed. If a company chooses the internationalization route, the ensuing actions must be prepared professionally and the resources must be deployed in a targeted way, because in a new and foreign market the likelihood of errors is far greater than in the familiar home market. The decision to internationalize requires honing one's strategy. This honing starts with a sober assessment of the current position and ends with the decisive implementation. It makes sense to follow the methods that led the hidden champions to international success. Practically all elements of the hidden champions' strategy contain valuable lessons for midsize companies wanting to internationalize—lessons that have been tried and tested in practice and are far more useful than the academic recommendations often found in textbooks on international management.

Lessons for Large Corporations

What lessons do the hidden champions' successes comprise for large corporations? As I have repeatedly said, large corporations are considered the custodians of management wisdom. They have often invented new management concepts or applied them for the first time, such as Procter & Gamble with product management and later category management, Motorola with Six Sigma, or General Electric with the number one/number two Strategy. We should beware of naïvely transferring the experiences of small companies to the situation of large corporations and vice versa. There is a difference between a CEO who manages a company with several hundred employees, all of whom he may know personally, and a CEO who has to steer a supertanker with several hundred thousand employees. However, large corporations can nevertheless learn a lot from the lessons of the hidden champions, as they tend to be weak in areas where these midsize companies are top. For the purpose of our further discussion, it makes sense to distinguish between two types: the focused large corporation (referred here as big champion) and the diversified large conglomerate, comprising business units that operate in separate markets.

Lessons for big champions

A big champion is basically a hidden champion that has grown very large. In Chapter 2, we illustrated the emergence of big from hidden champions with the case studies of Fresenius Medical Care, SAP, and Würth. It is evident that the big champions follow a similar strategy as the hidden champions, but on a larger scale. In this respect, the situation has changed radically since the 1990s. The massive restructuring of companies in the last ten years was mainly a metamorphosis from diversified conglomerates to focused large corporations. Prior to the 1990s, focused large corporations were the exception, and diversified conglomerates the rule. In most cases, the process of focusing was accompanied by strengthening the global market position, often through acquisitions from the new focus market. It is no exaggeration to say that the large corporations that are focused today essentially followed the hidden champions' strategy in their transformations.

This transformation is evidenced by numerous case studies. A typical case is Linde, currently the world market leader in industrial gases. For decades, Linde was a conglomerate with four businesses that hardly bore any relation to each other: industrial gases, forklift trucks, refrigeration, and plant engineering. Linde even thought to establish establish a fifth pillar and diversify even more strongly. Under the leadership of Wolfgang Reitzle, Linde has transformed itself into a big champion solely focused on the industrial gas business. The acquisition of the British company BOC enabled Linde to achieve clear world market leadership. A further champion has emerged from the forklift division that was sold to a consortium of Goldman Sachs and KKR and today operates under the name of Kion. Kion is market leader in Europe and number two in the world behind Toyota. By 2015, Kion wants to be the global number one. Linde's refrigeration division was sold to the American world market leader Carrier.

What is the difference between the old Linde on the one hand and the new Linde and Kion on the other? In the 1980s and 1990s, I got to know Linde from the inside. Linde's managers were excellent in every respect and always impressed me with their special competencies and their deep knowledge. However, we often sat down with the same managers for gas, forklift, and refrigeration projects, although there were also specialists from the respective divisions involved. Managers from headquarters had to deal with gases today, forklift trucks tomorrow, and refrigeration the day after. To a certain degree this is unavoidable in a diversified conglomerate. This has changed completely in the new Linde and in Kion. The managers of the new Linde deal with industrial gases. Kion managers concentrate on forklift trucks. Carrier people are continuously thinking about the refrigeration business. This is the hidden champions' strategy in its purest form: focus on one market in global dimensions. Given equal mental capacity and intelligence, it should be clear who fares better.

There are only two possible arguments against this type of focus. The first counterargument is that dealing with different businesses brings so much more knowledge that the disadvantage of lack of focus is overcompensated. Diversified conglomerates like to employ this argument, which was also a favorite of Jack Welch at General Electric. There may be cases in which learning across divisions has such a high value. I am convinced, however, that these are exceptional cases. The second argument against focus is risk diversification. This argument, of course, is justified. In the context of the current lessons, diversification for reasons of risk can well make sense, but this in no way implies that the diversified businesses are centrally managed. We will look at this issue in the next subsection.

Linde's development from a diversified conglomerate to a focused big champion is illustrative of the most important corporate trend in the last ten years. Eon (which emanated from the groups VIAG and VEBA that were even more broadly diversified than Linde) has focused decisively on energy. The same applies to RWE, Daimler, BASF (world market leader in chemicals), as well as Novartis and Roche in Switzerland. In the US, we have seen numerous spin-offs and split-ups. The split-up of the conglomerate Tyco into three independent companies for industry, electronics, and healthcare is a typical case. In the course of this development, large corporations that were strongly diversified, such as Hoechst, ITT or MG Technologies have completely disappeared. The fact that capital markets largely reacted positively to these movements toward focus is evidence that the investors consider the advantages of concentration to outweigh the benefits of risk diversification. According to a study by spin-off advisors from Chicago, two thirds of all enterprises spun off have beaten the respective index, and fared better than the remaining original group.[14] However, there are also counter-examples such as TUI, the world's largest tour operator, or the semiconductor company Infineon, where the stock price remained low in spite of focus. If a market does not grant adequate margins, for whatever reason, even focus cannot act as a panacea. It is essential that focus concentrates on the right market to remain competitive with regard to both performance and costs.

Without succumbing to overestimation of the importance of the hidden champions or wishing to attribute such developments to the influence of the hidden champions' concept, it is clear that the strategies of large focused corporations have become more similar to those of the hidden champions in recent years. In this sense large corporations actually have learned from the far smaller but more successful hidden champions. To ensure profitable growth, both pillars of the hidden champions' strategy are necessary: confinement to a narrowly defined market (focus) must be accompanied by the regional expansion of the market (globalization). Both pillars together determine the hidden champions' route to success and will do so for the big champions in the future.

Lessons for diversified conglomerates

Ten years ago, diversified conglomerates were widespread. Today, they have become the exception. However, the diversified conglomerate retains its justification and can be very successful. General Electric is an example of a conglomerate that has been in the top echelon for decades in relation to performance criteria such as return on investment, market capitalization or capacity for survival. In other countries, there are still numerous diversified conglomerates. In Germany, Siemens springs to mind: Siemens constantly extends its portfolio by buying up hidden champions (in recent years, for example, Flender/clutches, Kühnle, Kopp & Kausch/turbo machines, US Filter, units of Bayer as well as Dade Behring in the diagnostics sphere or GSD/clinical information systems). However, Siemens has also divested itself of numerous businesses in recent years (cell phones, semiconductors, personal computers, dental technology, and so forth.). Today, genuine diversification is more widespread among very large family enterprises, especially in emerging countries. Koc and Sabanci, the largest companies in Turkey, are, for example, extremely diversified.

What lessons do the hidden champions hold for diversified conglomerates? The answer is obvious: the art of managing such conglomerates suggests giving the individual business units the freedom to develop like hidden champions. Soft diversification should logically be followed by decentralization, coupled with clear accountability. Many traditional large corporations have great difficulty in yielding power to the decentral units. They are too strongly centralized, interfere with the individual businesses, prevent full concentration on the business, and thereby paralyze entrepreneurial initiative at the business unit level. In large corporations, I have often heard complaints from the heads of such business units that they spend too much time reporting to headquarters, that reports are constantly being demanded, and that there is too much interference with the business. However, the leaders of the business units do not always match the picture we have painted of hidden champion entrepreneurs. Leading a hidden champion requires a form of self-control and decentralization that is not easily found in large corporations. Yet here also, there are exceptions. General Electric is one of them. Bosch is also clearly able to run its units like hidden champions, (e.g., world market leaders Bosch Rexroth in hydraulics, Bosch Power Tools in electric power tools, Buderus/Junkers in heating technology). In fact, one would have to do an extensive search on the homepages of heating specialists Buderus and Junkers to find even a trace of Bosch.

One prerequisite for the success of the hidden champions' strategy is control of the full value chain in the respective unit. As we have seen, the success of the hidden champions is essentially based on not doing one major thing much better but doing many different things a little better than their competitors. This means that the competencies for the core activities must be in the hidden champion unit and are not spread over several business units. This is what we call "depth." Both market-related and internal functions should be in the business units. The separation of product and market is always a problem because it endangers closeness to customer. This condition is often harmed for dubious reasons of efficiency. Business units that lose their core functions have lower chances of becoming or remaining a champion. Nevertheless, I have to concede that in industries with a strong integration of development and manufacturing (e.g., chemicals or electronics) it can be difficult or even impossible to realize the model of full delegation of the core functions to a champion unit.

The art of finding the optimal middle between the two poles of centralization and decentralization will decisively influence the future success of large corporations. I visualize the diversified conglomerate of the future using very few common key resources (e.g., finance, management development, brand), but otherwise letting the units operate like independent hidden champions—with ambitious goals, focus, global orientation, a high degree of closeness to customer, and so forth. Small, autonomous units are more likely to achieve the specialization, the integration of market and technology, and the employee motivation that have made the hidden champions so successful. One probable constraint could be the entrepreneurial leaders required to manage such units. Leadership personalities who are competent in both technology and marketing, and who devote themselves wholly to their business, and do not consider it merely a station to pass through on the way to higher echelons, are a rare species in large corporations. For this reason, the development of entrepreneurs is the greatest challenge to a diversified conglomerate en route to becoming a group of hidden champions. The transition from a strongly centralized to a decentralized hidden champions group requires not only an organizational but above all a cultural and behavioral transformation. I am convinced that the employees have the capacity and the will for this transformation. Many managers and employees prefer to work in smaller, more manageable units rather than in big centralized structures. A manager in a large conglomerate described the difference well. For three years, he had worked in a subsidiary that was a hidden champion and received a high degree of autonomy from headquarters due to the unit's success. After his return to the parent company, he told me, "I was three times as effective in the small unit as I am in the large organization. There, I could use three quarters of my energy for the business. Here, I need the same percentage for internal skirmishes and friction." This statement says it all.

A lesson on the dynamics of companies

One of the most important insights in my investigations for this book is the following: The more successful a hidden champion strategy is, the faster it reaches its own limits. Globalization has a delaying effect, possibly even for one or two generations, but it does not fundamentally solve the problem—unless a company chooses not to grow. Consistent application of the strategy means that the hidden champion will achieve a high market share in its focus market. A further increase of this market share is confronted with increasingly stiffer resistance from competitors. Even if this obstacle is overcome and a company has obtained a monopolistic position (see the examples in Fig. 3.5), there will be limits to growth and reinvestment. The cash flows from the market in which the company has a high market share can no longer be profitably reinvested in this market. If further growth is nevertheless desired (most want further growth, with the exception of the few who choose not to grow), the step into soft diversification becomes almost inevitable. As a consequence of this process and over time, a diversified company emerges. Initially, the diversification will be soft, not hard, but the businesses will develop centrifugal forces as time goes by. Growth gives rise to a larger structure with a complexity that makes management increasingly difficult. At some point in this process, the question must be asked whether this structure should be split into independent companies. This would be the third phase of the dynamics of corporate development. Smaller, independent companies emerge that can in turn continue to apply the hidden champions' strategy. Today, such ideas are largely accepted. When I expressed similar thoughts more than ten years ago, voluntary splitting of company units or the division of entire companies was considered akin to heresy. Fig. 12.3 illustrates the possible dynamics of a hidden champion.

I am convinced that this cycle can be one of the most efficient methods of keeping companies dynamic and alive over centuries. It is based on

Fig. 12.3: Possible dynamics of the hidden champions in three phases

Classic hidden champion	Soft diversification	Independence/separation
• One-product, one-market company • "Focus"	• Group of hidden champions • "Multifocus" • Decentralization	• Independent companies emerge from the group and start over at phase 1

Phase 1   Phase 2   Phase 3   Time

mother nature's cell division principle and requires the voluntary handover of power from the leaders of these companies. New, independent companies arise in this way. Business units of large corporations are given their independence and can develop new growth dynamism. Recent developments, favored not least by the capital markets and private equity investors, give cause for optimism. Spin-offs of corporate units have made a significant contribution to growth in recent years. We only have to think of the industrial part of Mannesmann, from which very dynamic, independent companies (e.g., Demag Cranes, Mannesmann Plastics Machinery, Stabilus) have emerged. The electronics group Philips has spun off the semiconductor manufacturer NXP; Motorola has done the same with Freescale Semiconductors. Such spin-offs have been particularly popular in the US. Agilent was separated from Hewlett Packard. Teradata, a spin-off of NCR, and the split-up of Tyco are examples. Such processes lead to a noticeable, authentic decentralization of business. The side-effect is that large corporations themselves become leaner and more focused. The release or independence of numerous units has done many a large corporation a lot of good. Where family companies are concerned, splitting them up and dividing the parts among heirs lead to a similar decentralization and often to new dynamism for the "liberated" units.

Lessons for Investors

In view of their excellent long-term performance, the hidden champions are very interesting targets for investors. Focus, world market leadership, and continuity are characteristics highly valued by investors. Investors also love uncomplicated, focused companies and shy away from conglomerates with intransparent structures and responsibilities. For our discussion, we distinguish between private investors who can only invest in publicly listed hidden champions and private equity investors who are able to invest directly in, or take over, hidden champions even if they are not publicly listed.[15]

Lessons for private investors

Today, 9.5% of the hidden champions are traded on stock exchanges and are thus accessible to private investors. This is a strong increase compared with the situation ten years ago, when only 2.4% of the hidden champions were listed. Further IPOs of hidden champions can be expected (see Fig. 8.2, which points to an increased importance of capital markets).

In any case, the listed hidden champions deserve consideration as investment targets. Their long-term value appreciation promises attractive returns on investment. However, in the short term these shares can be relatively volatile, because they are closely linked to the development of the respective focus markets. Strong export orientation means that fluctuations in exchange rates have a strong influence on the results. In spite of the fundamentally positive assessment, euphoria would be inappropriate. Many of the companies are genuinely "hidden" and therefore unknown to the public and do not appear on the radar screens of analysts and fund managers. Due to their extreme specialization they may not even surface in the sector schemes of analysts. There are simply no analysts who are sufficiently specialized to follow watch drives, shopping carts or stage microphones. For larger funds, the narrow nature of the respective markets is a limiting factor. All of these factors restrict the market and the demand for such specialized shares. A share price is the result of supply and demand. The fact that the fundamental data are right is not sufficient in its own to help the share price and the market evaluation. Enough investors must be aware of the hidden champions and buy their shares. These circumstances have led to some disappointments for issuers and investors. Some hidden champions have been taken private, almost always with the argument that the value is not adequately reflected by the market. Strict stock exchange regulations have also contributed to the reasons for withdrawals.

Conversely, there are sectors in which hidden champions' shares have developed spectacularly. SAP, the world market leader in business standard software, was a case in point. More recently, Internet or solar shares have multiplied their value many times over. This may indicate that the investors are gradually gaining a better understanding of the hidden champions' true values, which are then better reflected in the share prices. Funds specialized in small caps play an important role. Some of them have done significantly better than blue chips in recent years. Hidden champions can become an attractive asset class for private investors with a long-term horizon.

Lessons for private equity investors

Hidden champions are dream targets for private equity investors. They fulfill virtually all requirements of professional investors: strong market position, good returns on investment, growth, focus, competitive advantages, innovation—and above all unrealized value potential. The ideal strategy profile of a hidden champion comes very close to a private equity investor's catalog of requirements. Private equity firms therefore line up wherever there is an opportunity to invest in or take over a hidden champion.

However, there is a frequent catch: some owners or founders of hidden champions do not like private equity investors. Various reasons lead to this attitude. Understandably, founders do not want to lose control of their company. They prefer to remain master of their own destiny, even at the expense of faster growth. Reservations may also arise because the investor comes from a different culture. Image aspects are often very important in this context. If the old owner is intended to remain as a shareholder or CEO, the chemistry between the parties and their willingness to cooperate are key success factors.

These considerations show that dealing with the existing owners and the founders is of crucial importance for private equity investors wishing to invest in hidden champions. The founder's heart and soul must be won. Investments in such companies transcend financial aspects. For this reason, investors with a low profile similar to that of the hidden champions are frequently preferred over better-known and more aggressive private equity companies. The investor's discretion suits the hidden champions well.

After the takeover, the investor faces new challenges. How can the hidden champion's strengths be maintained and the investment targets achieved at the same time? In this respect, private equity investors often display more intelligence than some large corporations that force the acquired company into their group structure, thereby destroying its strengths. Private equity investors often leave existing top management in place and give them a share in the company (not just in the company's results). In this way they make the managers real co-owners who are not only interested in short-term profits, but also in the appreciation of the value, in which they will participate upon exit. This is doubtlessly an astute move and a decisive reason for the success of private equity investors. Some family companies would be well advised to apply this method when they employ managers who are not family members. Private equity investors mostly stay out of the operative business. They control the company by setting goals and observing results, not through micromanagement. We are often asked how these very lean investment companies can manage so many investments. The answer is that they do not manage them but have them managed. The investors engage extensive consulting services to support the acquired companies in the realignment of their strategy. This amounts to an outsourcing of management tasks. A new growth spurt is often initiated after the takeover. Many hidden champions have benefited from new investors.

However, there are also counterexamples in which the companies taken over have been burdened with enormous debts. Investments in fixed assets and in R&D usually suffer most under such financing burdens. It is generally difficult to determine from the outside what ultimately initiates a crisis. Some hidden champions that initially appear to be well positioned have inner weaknesses that become apparent in such situations. From the investor's point of view, it does not seem rational to drag an operationally successful company into difficulties by excessive debt burdens. After all, the private equity investor normally plans to exit at some point and can only expect an attractive price when the company is doing well. It is certainly not an intelligent strategy to hope for a naïve buyer that is willing to pay a higher price than the true value of the company. We can therefore assume that many of these problem cases are simply attributable to management failure from, either the acquired company's or the investor's fault.

Lessons for Politics, Regions, and Countries

The hidden champions' successes contain important lessons for individual regions and countries. The importance of midsize companies for the development of national economies is generally underestimated. Throughout the world, there is admiration for the large corporations of the day, and the dream even from smaller countries is to have their own corporations appear with such giants on the Fortune Global 500 or similar international rankings. There are 247 autonomous countries in the world, but the Fortune Global 500 list only contains companies from 35 countries, almost half of which have three or fewer entries.[16] In 2007, almost two thirds (exactly 65.4%) of the Fortune Global 500 originated from five countries (US 153, Japan 64, France 39, Germany 37, UK 34); 86% of all countries do not appear on this list (i.e. have no large company of global significance and depend on midsize firms for their economic development. The hidden champions are far more relevant role models for these countries than the large multinationals. Although the hidden champions are hardly known, they belong to the best-managed and most successful companies in the world. Their performance outshines most large corporations that attract far greater attention from the press, the general public and politics. Hidden champions deserve more attention and public awareness.

What role does politics play for the creation of hidden champions? Not one of my numerous contacts said that his company had attained world market leadership through government incentives. There are sectors such as wind or solar energy in which state incentives created conditions that made the establishment possible in the first place, but such cases are exceptions. Politics cannot claim to be responsible for the success of the hidden champions. Instead, hidden champions are becoming increasingly immune to the influence of national politics due to their global presence. One CEO told me, "We generate 85% of our revenues outside our home market. The majority of our employees work in other countries. Most of our value added is generated in these countries. National politics are no longer relevant for us." We can only hope that politicians in the various countries are aware that they have to court these internationally mobile companies. If the conditions at one location are not right, the hidden champions are not tied to this location.

Lessons for highly developed industrial countries

Hidden champions play very different roles in highly developed industrial countries. If we look at the situation in Europe, we find that there is a similar density of hidden champions in Scandinavia, the Benelux countries, and Northern Italy versus those found in the German-speaking countries. By contrast, the rest of Europe has far fewer midsize market leaders of this kind. This company segment is little developed particularly in France and the Iberian Peninsula.[17] In these countries, we observe a preference for and admiration of large corporations and the so-called "national champions." Yet in these countries also, there are individual examples of model hidden champions. The Portuguese company Amorim, for instance, is world market leader in cork products and cork flooring. Amorim has more than 50 locations in 30 countries. Hidden champions from Spain such as Freixenet (the world's number one in cava sparkling wine) or Chupa Chups (world market leader in lollipops) can lead the way for midsize companies from these and other south-European countries. In the US, we find many midsize companies with excellent competencies, who consider their home market so large that they have not seen the necessity for internationalization. This attitude not only misses opportunities on the global market, but also harbors serious risks. Exclusive presence in the U.S. market makes such companies vulnerable when leading international hidden champions enter this market. Japanese hidden champions often operate as suppliers for the large Japanese multinationals in the electronics and automotive sector. These hidden champions primarily sell through the large corporations, but usually have not established their own global sales organization. Many midsize Japanese companies with excellent products therefore fail to make full use of the potential for globalization.

In some countries and with quite a few politicians the idea of "national champions" has become popular. This idea, which originated in France, also has numerous followers in other countries. As this book shows, I believe in the champions' idea. I have great respect for companies that succeed in open competition and achieve world market leadership. These companies have proven their exceptional performance and have left their competitors behind. But what should we think about national champions that have achieved this position "through the grace of the state" (i.e., through government influence and intervention with open competition). Or whose survival—against the competition—is ensured by the state? Should France be a role model in this respect? Should other countries imitate France in its endeavors to create or protect national champions?

I consider the role of the state a major distraction to the true course of hidden champions. There is no evidence that states can create long-term successful companies, let alone manage them. The former Japanese MITI (Ministry of Trade and Industry, today METI), admired for decades, eventually turned out to be one big bureaucracy. French *planification* led to a series of failures, which included the supersonic Concorde and the computer company Bull. When I argue against national champions, my arguments are often countered in Europe by the example of Airbus. Is Airbus not a success, exemplary of a champion not only at the national but also at a global level? Yes, I consider Airbus a success. However, we should note that Airbus operates in a business largely dictated by political and in particular defense policy aspects, not solely by market forces. Today and in the future, the aerospace industry is and will remain more than just a game of open competition. This was especially true in the early days. Jet engines were initially developed for military jets. The Boeing 707, the first mass-produced jet in civil aviation, was derived from the tanker KC 135. The Boeing Jumbo was a parallel development to the military transporter Lockheed Galaxy. Business only functions with government support in this environment. Airbus does not provide overall proof that the state should play a more general role in the creation of national champions.

The hidden champions themselves tell us that the state should not get involved and should leave the creation of market leaders to their own strengths and to the competition. In the long term, this leads to the best results for everyone. We can do without national champions fostered and maintained by the grace of the state.

Lessons for emerging countries

As we said at the beginning of this section, there are few corporations of global dimensions in emerging countries. This even applies to the largest countries in the world. The Fortune Global 500 list for 2007 contains only 29 companies from China, 7 from India, and 5 each from Russia and Brazil. If we look at smaller emerging countries, really large corporations will long remain an illusion. In contrast, multinationals are greatly admired in these countries. Both governments and entrepreneurs consequently strive for grand scale and favor larger companies. Instead, emerging and, in particular, smaller emerging countries would be better advised to pin their hopes on internationally competitive midsize companies. Hidden champions can be strategic role models for this group of countries. I am astonished to find over and over again that there are individual companies in these countries that already pursue the hidden champions' strategy and are successful in doing so. Fig. 12.4 lists examples of hidden champions from emerging countries.

These examples show that companies from emerging countries can rise to leading positions in the world in their respective markets. In my experience, the hidden champion concept generates the greatest interest in China. Thousands of people have attended my hidden champion lectures in that country. Chinese entrepreneurs are fascinated by the idea of becoming the world's number one. Today, there are probably already more than 25 Chinese hidden champions.

The hidden champions offer a further important lesson for entrepreneurs in emerging countries. Many of these entrepreneurs that are successful in their core business tend to diversify and embark on numerous other business ventures. This pattern applies right up to the highest size category, so that extremely broad-based conglomerates are typical (such as Koc and Sabanci in Turkey or Samsung and Hyundai in Korea). The Chinese company Haier, with its core business in household appliances, now produces virtually everything concerning electrical engineering and

Company	Country	Main product	Market position
HSM	Argentina	Top-management conferences	World market leader
Cutrale	Brazil	Citrus fruits	Largest manufacturer worldwide
Embraer	Brazil	Regional aircraft	World market leader
Fischer	Brazil	Fruit concentrates	World market leader
China International Marine Containers	China	Containers	World market leader
Galanz	China	Microwave ovens	World market leader
Pearl Clock	China	Quarz watches	World market leader
Pearl River Piano	China	Pianos	Largest manufacturer worldwide
Essel Propack	India	Toothpaste tubes	World market leader
Reliance	India	Polyester	World market leader
Uralkali	Russia	Potash and titanium salts	World market leader
VSMPO-AVISMA	Russia	Titanium	World market leader
Sappi	South Africa	Soluble cellulose	World market leader
Hon Hai Precision	Taiwan	Entertainment electronics	One of the world market leaders
Herend	Hungary	Porcelain	One of the world market leaders
Akrapovic	Slovenia	Entertainment electronics	World market leader
Nakhla Tobacco	Egypt	Tobacco for water pipes	One of the world market leaders

electronics. The reasons for this broad diversification lie in opportunities found everywhere in the fast-growing home market, reservations regarding internationalization and an overestimation of the entrepreneur's capacity. In any case, this is not the route to world class. These companies would be better advised to focus on their core business and to build up leading global market positions in this field (i.e., to follow the hidden champions' strategy).

Lessons for job candidates

Large corporations always head the rankings of the most popular employers. This is true regardless of country and the subjects studied by graduates. Generally, large corporations with well-known names are more popular with applicants than hidden champions. There are various reasons for the hidden companies' low attractiveness. The most important is the low degree of public awareness of the hidden champions. The fact that such companies frequently have rural locations contributes to making them less known and less attractive outside their own region. Many graduates do not know that numerous large corporations have dismissed employees in recent years whereas most hidden champions have expanded strongly. As is with the purchase of shares, growth of a company is highly important for one's career. The argument of wanting to work for a market leader and therefore a large company is only valid on the surface. As we have seen, the hidden champions are market leaders with world market shares of which large corporations can only dream.

The strategies and successes of the hidden champions described in this book show that these companies can offer very interesting career opportunities. When I graduated in the early 1970s, many top graduates joined the famous corporations of the day, of which IBM was the most popular. Most of them achieved relatively modest careers at IBM for two reasons. First, IBM had too many good people, and second, IBM's development had already peaked. Later, when IBM found itself in a crisis, half of the employees were dismissed. Good performers who joined the software company SAP, which was then totally unknown (and not even yet a hidden champion), did far better financially and in career terms. Growing midsize companies such as the hidden champions offer excellent career perspectives for young, ambitious candidates whose motivations include varied work, the swift assumption of responsibility, and the opportunity to work internationally. Hidden champions meet these criteria well. Compared to large corporations, they offer opportunities to look beyond the boundaries of narrowly defined tasks right from the outset and assume responsibility at an early stage. One's own contribution to the company's success thus becomes more visible. In addition, commitment to the company and identification with the employer are often deeper than at more bureaucratic large corporations. The hidden champions are typically headed by charismatic people who motivate and enthuse as role models. Anyone wanting to achieve a lot right from the start of the career, and displaying independent initiative and entrepreneurial spirit, will find highly attractive career prospects at the hidden champions.

Summary of the Lessons

The hidden champions provide us with many valuable insights and lessons. They mainly refer to common sense: delivering real value to the customer, establishing long-term relationships, innovating continuously, fulfilling one's tasks with utter commitment, and being better than the competition in relevant attributes. However, the hidden champions also teach us that many of the modern management concepts like outsourcing, strategic alliances, fashionable leadership styles, and so forth are either short-lived fads or one-sided exaggerations of specific aspects. Sound and successful leadership changes remarkably little over time. Instead of slavishly going along with every new management fad, entrepreneurs would be well advised to consistently follow the principles of the hidden champions.

Hidden champions teach us that instead of managing only one great thing brilliantly good management means doing many small things better than the competitors. I repeatedly heard from hidden champion CEOs that they do not have a grand magic formula to beat their competitors. The sum of many small advantages ultimately leads to success. One facet is that the mere avoidance of serious errors and of stupid moves can make a significant contribution to long-term success. These facts mean that normal people and companies can become hidden champions. Genius is not required. To become a hidden champion, we must do many small things a little better in a targeted and consistent way and with stamina. Focus is a condition *sine qua non*. No one is a master of all trades. For this reason, it is important to concentrate on the field where championship is possible. This finding particularly applies to companies with limited resources. The one with focused ambition beats the generalist.

Simplicity is another important lesson. It is closely connected to decentralization. Simplicity relates to organizational structures and processes. Hidden champions are lean. Their classical one-product, one-market situation permits simple organizational structures. If the business becomes more complex, they decentralize. The condition "more work than people" also favors simplicity. It keeps employees from inventing unnecessary complexity. Parkinson's law that employees invent the work which keeps them busy doesn't stand a chance. Simplicity requires the capacity to get to the core of things and avoid distractions. Given the increasing complexity of the world, it is becoming more crucial to see the wood for the trees without succumbing to naïve simplification. Hidden champion managers excel at this.

The hidden champions go their own way with greater determination and more success than ever before. In the last ten years, they have further honed their strategies and implemented them with even greater determination. They do not follow the management fads of the day, but instead are guided by tried and tested timeless principles—and by common sense. They are ready to face up to the challenges of the twenty-first century and are prepared to master them better than ever.

Notes

1 This sentence originates from Richard von Coudenhove-Kalergi (1894-1972), the founder of the Pan-Europe Movement.

2 I can only think of two management books spontaneously with titles featuring the word will. Marvin Bower, *The Will to Lead*, Boston: Harvard Business School Press 1997, and the same author, *The Will to Manage*, New York: McGraw-Hill 1966. Marvin Bower (1903-2003) was one of the founders of McKinsey and decisively shaped the firm after the early death of James McKinsey (for more detail, see: Elizabeth Haas Edersheim: McKinsey's Marvin Bower, *Vision, Leadership, and the Creation of Management Consulting*, Hoboken, NJ: John Wiley & Sons 2004). If we enter the words "will" and "management" at amazon.com/de, no books appear that cover what we mean here.

3 See also John Naisbitt, *Mind Set!*, New York: Harper Collins 2005.

4 Double Nobel prize winners are Marie Curie (1867-1934; Nobel prizes in Physics in 1903 and Nobel prize in Chemistry in 1911) and Linus Pauling (1901-1994; Nobel prizes in Chemistry in 1954 and Nobel Peace Prize in 1962).

5 This is the message of the book: W. Chan Kim and Renée Mauborgne, *Blue Ocean Strategy*, Boston: Harvard Business School Press 2005.

6 As a reminder: The relative market share is the company's own market share divided by that of the strongest competitor. In 1995, it averaged 1.56, in 2005 it was 2.34 for the hidden champions.

7 This aspect is clearly pointed out by Hermut Kormann, CEO of Voith. See Hermut Kormann, *Long-Term Customer Relationships: Defying the Myth that Only Competition-Oriented Strategies Work*, Frankfurt: VDMA 2005.

8 See Hermut Kormann, "Gibt es so etwas wie typisch mittelständische Strategien," Discussion Paper No. 54, University of Leipzig, Faculty of Economics & Business, November 2006.

9 Helmut Maucher, *Management-Brevier: Ein Leitfaden für unternehmerischen Erfolg*, Frankfurt: Campus-Verlag 2007. This book contains a wealth of timeless maxims that are fundamentally common sense but are frequently neglected in management practice. Helmut Maucher was CEO of Nestlé from 1981 to 1997.

10 I tend toward a slightly different view. Even if midsize entrepreneurs are not more intelligent than others, the difference may be that they are more committed to their mission (or "obsessed", as we said in Chapter 10).

11 Hermut Kormann, Gibt es so etwas wie typisch mittelständische Strategien, Discussion Paper No. 54, University of Leipzig, Faculty of Economics & Business, November 2006, p. 1.

12 See Paul R. Lawrence and Jay W. Lorsch, *Organization and Environment: Managing Differentiation and Integration*, Homewood (Ill.): Richard D. Irwin 1977, Revised Edition published by Harvard Business School Press 1986.

13 See Barry Johnson, *Polarity Management: Identifying and Managing Unsolvable Problems*, Amherst, Mass.: HRD Press 1992.

14 See *Frankfurter Allgemeine Zeitung*, March 6, 2007, p. 20.

15 Private investors can acquire shares in a company directly. However, this method has little practical relevance for most private investors, so we do not discuss this any further here.

16 See *Fortune*, July 21, 2008, figures are for the financial year 2007.

17 On the situation in France, see: "Pourquoi les PME francaises ont du mal à grandir," *Le Monde*, March 6, 2007, Business, p. 2-3.

About the author

Hermann Simon is chairman of Simon–Kucher & Partners, Strategy & Marketing Consultants, with offices in Europe, Asia, and the United States. He is an expert in strategy, marketing and pricing, advising clients and speaking to business organizations worldwide. Prior to taking on consulting full-time, he was a professor of business administration and marketing at the Universities of Mainz and Bielefeld, and has served as a visiting professor at many universities, including Harvard Business School, London Business School, INSEAD, Keio University, Stanford, and MIT. Named one of Europe's most influential management thinkers, he has served on the boards of numerous journals, including the *International Journal of Research in Marketing*, *Management Science*, and *European Management Journal*, and has published over 30 books, including the worldwide bestseller, *Hidden Champions* (1996), *Power Pricing* (1997), and *Manage for Profit, Not for Market Share* (2006), and *Beat the Crisis: 33 Quick Solutions for Your Company* (2009)

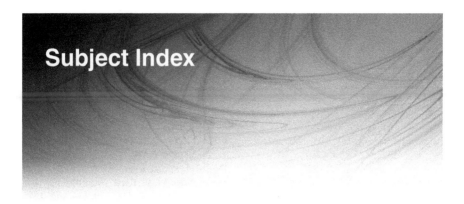

Subject Index

Note: page references with f and n notation refer to a figure or note number on that page.

Name Index

Note: page references with *n* notation refer to a note on that page.

Company Name Index

Note: page references with *f* and *n* notation refer to a figure or note number on that page.

CPSIA information can be obtained
at www.ICGtesting.com
Printed in the USA
LVHW011659041118
595906LV00003B/38/P